A Romantic's Guide to Italy

A ROMANTIC'S GUIDE TO

Italy

INTIMATE TRAVEL, HONEYMOONS, WEDDINGS,
AND OTHER SPECIAL OCCASIONS ABROAD

Gina Podesta

Ten Speed Press
Berkeley | Toronto

For David, who continues to inspire the romantic in me.

A KIRSTY MELVILLE BOOK

Ten Speed Press
P.O. Box 7123
Berkeley, California 94707
www.tenspeed.com

Distributed in Australia by Simon and Schuster Australia, in Canada by Ten Speed Press Canada, in New Zealand by Southern Publishers Group, in South Africa by Real Books, and in the United Kingdom and Europe by Airlift Book Company.

Cover photograph by Hidemi Kanezuka/Photonica
Cover design by Toni Tajima and Nancy Austin
Text Design by Nancy Austin
Typesetting by Tasha Hall

Library of Congress Cataloging-in-Publication Data on file with the publisher. 1-58008-469-9

Printed in Canada
First printing, 2004

1 2 3 4 5 6 7 8 9 10 - 09 08 07 06 05 04

CONTENTS

UMBRIA

Bucolic Country Farms and Monasteries, 229

LAZIO

Palatial Rome, 275

SOUTHERN ITALY AND THE ISLANDS

Secluded Escapes, 307

INTRODUCTION

Open my heart and you will see,
Graved inside of it, "Italy."

—Robert Browning (1812–1889)

Italy has always inspired the romantics among us. For centuries, it has been a mecca for artists, poets, and dreamers, inspiring great love affairs, masterworks, and symphonies.

Italy has always been a place of romance for me as well, and this book was born out of my own romantic travels. When I was growing up, my grandparents told me intriguing stories about my great-grandparents who had immigrated to California from Liguria. Prized family recipes, a polenta pot, and my great grandmother's original mortar and pestle (for making pesto) were all objects from the "old country" that drew my imagination to Italy. Before starting college, I spent a year with a wonderful family in Piedmont in northern Italy, going to school, soaking up culture, and discovering a magical place where a passion for living and eating seemed to guide every part of daily life. I became completely enamored with Italy—and in the summer of 2000 my husband and I were married on the grounds of a tenth-century Tuscan castle.

For me, the romance of Italy is steeped in its history and traditions, from chasing the "shadows" in Venetian wine bars, to holding a wedding under the stars in a Tuscan castle courtyard. Part of the charm of traveling in Italy is waking up under the frescoed ceiling of a baroque palace or sipping a cappuccino in the cloister of a converted Benedictine monastery.

For this book I searched throughout Italy to find quintessential locations that embody romance through their setting, architecture, and history. In each chapter you will find places where you can enjoy a romantic stay, hold a wedding, or spend an evening dining with someone you love. You can amble through an enchanting contessa's garden, sleep in a medieval hamlet where Dante once found refuge, or celebrate an evening with friends in the wisteria-filled courtyard of an ancient olive mill in Puglia.

While searching for romantic ideas and excursions in Italy, I unearthed ancient festivals commemorating contests for pretty maidens and marriages between noble families. In northern Italy's Marostica, you can watch a human chess match played with costumed game pieces, which originated with a medieval duel between two knights over the hand of a nobleman's daughter. In Liguria, the village of Lavagna still bakes a thirty-foot-high wedding cake each year, a replica of a cake prepared in 1230 for the wedding between Opizzo Fiesco and Bianca dei Bianchi.

For modern-day romantic excursions, you can attend outdoor cinema on Rome's Tiber island, ride a 1920s railway to Savoy fortresses, and relax in Etruscan spas.

Whether you are planning an Italian wedding, a second honeymoon, or a romantic getaway, I hope this hand-picked collection will inspire the romantic in you.

HOW TO USE THIS GUIDE

This book offers a personal collection of romantic accommodations, restaurants, places to get married, and ideas for activities.

A special section at the end of the book (A Practical Guide to Planning a Wedding in Italy, page 377) includes resources for couples planning a wedding in Italy. There is information on how to make your Italian wedding legal in the United States and what steps to take if you are planning a Catholic ceremony in Italy. A directory, organized by region, includes a variety of wedding resources such as caterers, photographers, and wedding planners.

In the following pages, you will also find resources for accommodations in Italy. As an alternative to staying in a hotel, you might consider a holiday on a farm, renting a villa in the country, or renting an apartment in a city center. You will also find resources for associations of historic homes and restaurants in Italy.

Accommodations

The accommodations listed in this book include a range of historic properties, ranging from privately owned villas and farms to luxury hotels. Each was selected for its unique setting, architecture, and hospitality. With very few exceptions, the properties are not chain hotels and many offer just a few carefully furnished rooms to guests.

The price ranges quoted reflect the lowest-priced rooms during low season, followed by the highest-priced room during high season for double rooms and/or suites, depending on the property. As rates are subject to change, please check directly with each individual hotel for up-to-date pricing.

Price ranges in euros for a double room or suite with bathroom, including service and taxes:

E: up to E150   EE: E150 to E299   EEE: E300 to E399
EEEE: E400 to E499   EEEEE: over E500

Restaurants

The restaurants in this book were selected based on two key criteria: first, they must offer excellent, authentic, Italian cuisine; second, there must be an element of romance to the restaurant, whether it is situated in a historic building, offers a pretty view, or has a particular atmosphere.

Most of the restaurants included in this guide change their menus according to the season. Therefore, the dishes mentioned in the descriptions are intended as an indication of the cuisine offered and the chef's approach to cooking rather than as a reproduction of exact menu items.

Restaurants in Italy usually close one day each week, and they will often close for religious holidays and vacation periods. In my own travels I have discovered that "published" closing dates are often subject to change, so in order to avoid any confusion it is always a good idea to call ahead.

Lunch service in Italy traditionally begins from 12:30 P.M. to 1:00 P.M. and can last, depending on the region and the restaurant, until 2:00 P.M. The peak time for dinner is between 8:00 P.M. and 9:00 P.M., although during the summer this can be later.

Reservations are always a good idea, especially if you want to reserve a "romantic" table for two.

Price ranges for a three-course meal for one, excluding wine:

E: under E35   EE: E35 to E45   EEE: E46 to E65   EEEE: E66 to E85
EEEEE: over E85

Wedding and Reception Locations

Costs for wedding locations in Italy vary greatly depending on the time of the year, day of the week, and number of guests. High season for weddings begins in May and ends in October. To give some idea of how the locations compare, the cost range is based on the rental of the venue plus an estimated per-guest catering cost. The estimates are based on planning a wedding with fifty to one hundred guests, depending on the capacity of the location. For the most part, the estimated costs include reception chairs, tables, flatware, glassware, linens, china, food, and wine. Basic rental fees for the locations in this guide ranged from zero to US$6,000 or more, while catering can range from US$50 per guest and up, depending on the number of courses, the menu, and the type of wines you choose. Some locations do not charge a site rental fee; instead, they include those costs in the catering estimate. This is intended as a guide only, and as every wedding is individual, please contact any venue you are interested in for an individually prepared estimate.

E: From E50 to E100 per guest   EE: From E101 to E150 per guest
EEE: Over E150 per guest

CITY HALLS (UFFICI STATO CIVILE)

Many historic city halls in Italy are interesting locations for civil wedding ceremonies. If you would like to inquire about a ceremony in a city that is not listed, you will usually be able to find the contact information by searching on the Internet using the city name and *comune* to find that city's official website. The most popular locations have sliding fee scales based on residency, day of the week, and times, while smaller locations may charge only administrative fees. If neither of you speaks Italian, a translator must be present. Civil ceremonies are conducted with the presence of at least two witnesses. Most city halls only have room for a small number of additional guests; please check directly with them for policies. Please refer to the section on civil ceremonies for more information on how to make your civil wedding legal.

E: From E0 to E250   EE: From E250 to E750   EEE: Over E750

Agriturismi Holidays on Italian Farm Estates

Hospitality in the countryside has a long history in Italy, beginning with shelter provided for religious pilgrims traveling to Rome and continuing through the Renaissance, when noble families built *foresterie* (guesthouses) to accommodate guests from all parts of the country. Today, this same practice continues in Italy's country *agriturismi.* An *agriturismo* is an agricultural estate, usually a working farm, where guest accommodations are offered. In 1985, legislation was passed in Italy creating an official program for agricultural tourism. The intent of the government-sponsored program was to promote and preserve Italy's rural heritage by encouraging farm owners to offer holiday stay facilities to travelers. By bringing tourism out of the cities and into the countryside, they could offer travelers to Italy an experience of the traditions and culture, as well as the indigenous products of each region. Staying in an *agriturismo* gives you access to an authentic Italian experience and a glimpse of everyday living in Italy.

In this guide I have suggested some of my favorite agriturismi. For accommodations in other regions, both *Agriturismo.it* and *AgriItalia.it* offer directories of agriturismi across all of Italy's regions. Their websites will give you lots of ideas for alternative accommodations, whether you are looking for a southern Italian *masseria,* a Tuscan farmhouse, or an alpine chalet. Both their websites put you in direct contact with the property owners.

Contact www.Agriturismo.it and www.agriitalia.it.

Historic Hotel and Restaurant Associations

Formed in 1995, ABITARE LA STORIA is an association of independent hospitality operators of historic properties throughout Italy. All the properties in the association are located in buildings of considerable architectural importance and have been well preserved by their owners. www.abitarelastoria.it

LOCALI STORICI—Historical Sites of Italy is a directory of hotels, bars, restaurants, pastry shops, and cafes of cultural or historical importance in Italy. The nonprofit association publishes a directory in English on their website, searchable by region. www.localistorici.it

DIMORE STORICHE provides resources for companies planning meetings and conferences at historical sites in Italy, but their website also includes hotels and interesting historic itineraries for leisure travelers. www.dimorestoriche.com.

One of my favorite ways to travel through Italy is to follow the path of the BUON RICORDI. Since 1964, the Unione Ristoranti del Buon Ricordo (Union of Restaurants of the "Good Souvenir") has been committed to preserving Italy's regional gastronomic traditions. Restaurants belonging to the association offer a signature dish, which is commemorated with a hand-painted ceramic plate from Vietri. Diners who order the culinary specialty receive the plate as a ricordo (souvenir) of their experience. A directory of restaurants is available on the Buon Ricordo website along with photos of each establishment's commemorative plate. Unione Ristoranti del Buon Ricordo—Viale Libertà, 4/D, 27100 Pavia, tel. +39 0382 25180, fax +39 0382 302611, email info@buonricordo.com, www.buonricordo.it.

Additional Resources—Villa and Apartment Rentals

If you are planning on spending at least a week in a location, renting an apartment or villa can be an economical and fun way to spend your holiday. Most rental properties are offered for weekly periods, with a few making provisions for shorter time periods. Cleaning, heat, extra towels, and meals are usually added as a separate cost. Many historic properties are well suited for groups as they were often built as ancestral homes and designed to house multigenerational families.

CAFFELLETTO specializes in finding luxury bed-and-breakfast accommodations in ancestral homes throughout Italy. Their hand-selected locations include rooms with a view over the Piazza della Signoria in Florence, a nineteenth-century winemaking estate in Piedmont, and baroque villas on the Amalfi coast. Caffelletto, Via Procaccini 7, 20154 Milano, tel. +39 02 331 1814, fax +39 02 331 3009, email info@caffelletto.it, www.caffelletto.it.

ITALIAN VILLA RENTALS offers properties like a beaux arts villa on Lago Maggiore with seven bedrooms, a room for two in a secluded Sicilian winery, a medieval farmhouse in the Umbrian hills for six, a renovated Tuscan monastery with loggia and a pool, or a modern townhouse on a hillside above the Cinque Terre. Italian Villa Rentals—Internet Villas, Inc., 8 Knight Street, Suite 205, Norwalk, CT 06851, tel. 800-700-9549, www.italianvillas.com.

HOME IN ITALY represents an elegant collection of private villas, country cottages, and city apartment rentals in Tuscany, Umbria, The Marches, Lazio, and Campania. Their properties range from a pied-à-terre apartment in Rome's Piazza di Spagna to a frescoed Tuscan villa that can sleep up to fourteen guests. Home in Italy, Via Adelaide 50/C, 06128 Perugia, tel. +39 075 505 7865, fax +39 075 500 6127, email info@HomeInItaly.Com, www.homeinitaly.com.

BED & BREAKFAST ITALIA specializes in apartment rentals in private homes and residences. They represent properties in Rome, Emilia Romagna, Venice, Umbria, Tuscany, and the Cinque Terre. Bed & Breakfast Italia, tel. +39 06 596 06395, fax +39 06 540 8877, www.bbitalia.com.

VENICE RENTALS has an exclusive collection of apartments in Gothic palazzos, some available for stays as brief as three days. If you decide to stay longer, note that they also act as agents for those looking to buy an apartment in Venice. Venetian Rentals, email info@venice-rentals.com, www.venice-rentals.com.

AMALFI LIFE offers an insider's collection of villas and apartments for rental along the Amalfi Coast. Amalfi Life, email laurie@amalfilife.com, www.amalfilife.com.

CHAPTER 1

LIGURIA

Enchanted Seaside Hideaways

*I*n the Ligurian Riviera, roads twist past spectacular rock formations, enchanting beaches, and hidden coves. For those who appreciate wisteria and sunshine, villas awash with the scent of flowers and surrounded by sun-warmed terraces offer idyllic spots to get away from it all or to celebrate a seaside wedding.

In 1528, an alliance between Andrea Doria—admiral of Genoa's famous fleet—and the Spanish Empire, then ruled by Charles V, began an extraordinary period in Genoa's history. Genoa became one of the most prestigious cities in Europe, and its bankers were charged with managing the finances of the wealthiest houses of Europe. The surging economy created a phenomenon in Genoa that came to be known as *vivere in villa* (villa living). Looking for new places to invest their wealth, Genovese families began building summer palaces along the Italian Riviera. Unlike the city, where building sizes were constrained by available space, the seaside offered a wide-open setting for lavish residences, surrounded by rambling parks and botanical gardens. Many noble residences remain today as architectural gems that recall the ancient splendors of a rich and cultivated society, and many have been transformed into comfortable hotels or venues for wedding receptions.

For romantic outings, the Riviera offers a rich variety of interesting excursions. You can follow the pilgrim's trail between the ancient sanctuaries above the coastline or dive in the crystalline waters of the Riviera's hidden coves. The region has a rich history, which it preserves through festivals and celebrations like Lavagna's "wedding cake" festival, celebrated each August.

A mild climate, ample sunlight, and ocean breezes make Liguria a comfortable year-round destination. The regional cuisine, based on delightful combinations of aromatic herbs and fresh fish, is Mediterranean cooking at its simplest, offering the possibility of sharing a feast that takes advantage of all the sea has to offer. Basil, marjoram, pine nuts, and walnuts figure heavily in sauces for pastas and are also used to accompany the bountiful catches of the local fisherman. The Ligurians are credited with inventing ravioli, which they fill with an ever-changing mixture of wild field greens they call *preboggion*. The vines that cling to the terraces of Liguria's rocky hillsides produce wines that are a harmonious accompaniment to the cuisine—try the sweet Sciacchetrà, the crisp Lumassina, and the fragrant Vermentino.

Accommodations at the Seaside

PORTOFINO

Portofino Kulm

Near the summit of the mountain that rises behind Portofino's aquamarine harbor, Portofino Vetta (Portofino's summit) rises thirteen hundred feet above the sea. In 1905, the Portofino Kulm first opened its doors, quickly becoming a favorite holiday spot for royalty, Russian noble families, and artists and writers from all over Europe. The hotel was built at the height of the Belle Epoque in the spirit of early-twentieth-century grand hotels. Its architectural style reflects all the elements of the "Liberty" style (Italian art nouveau). The hotel's salmon-hued facade is decorated with lacy white art nouveau balconies, with bouquets of flowers incorporated into the ironwork. Bougainvillea cascades over the lyrical faces of nymphs frescoed and sculpted in relief into the transoms of the doorways. The hotel is surrounded by the Portofino park preserve and stands at the crossroads of the hiking trails that lead to San Fruttuoso, Camogli, and Portofino. Totally renovated in the year 2000, the hotel has been returned to its original grandeur as modern amenities were added. The rooms are spacious, with furnishings that follow the period style; you can select a view of either the garden or the sea. On the premises are an indoor swimming pool and dining areas with views over the gulf. The Portofino Kulm is partnered with the Cenobio dei Dogi (see page 5) in nearby Camogli, which makes its shuttle service and beach facilities available to guests.

HOTEL PORTOFINO KULM, Viale Bernardo Gaggini 23, Portofino Vetta, 16030 Ruta di Camogli (GE), tel. +39 0185 736 1, fax +39 0185 776 622, email reception@cenobio.it, www.portofinokulm.it. Driving directions: from highway A12 take the Recco exit. Follow indications for Camogli, then connect to the SS1 in the direction of Santa Margherita Ligure. Follow the signs for Portofino Vetta. Sixty-seven rooms; doubles from E to EE.

Splendido and Splendido Mare

The aptly named Splendido is one of the Riviera's most romantic hotels, with a long tradition of hosting famous couples: the Duke and Duchess of Windsor were among the hotel's first guests, and other romantic pairs to enjoy the hotel's hospitality over the years have included Lauren Bacall and Humphrey Bogart, and Elizabeth Taylor and Richard Burton. The rooms all have balconies or terraces, some have windows with a view of the sea, and many overlook Portofino's beautiful harbor. This site was once the home of a Benedictine monastery, but with the arrival of the Barbarossa pirates, the monks were forced to flee to safer ground. After periods of abandon, an Italian baron purchased the land and its buildings in the 1800s and turned it into his summer residence. The hotel has been owned since 1985 by the prestigious Orient Express group, which has turned it into a world-class luxury hotel with the highest emphasis on service and comfort. The entire complex is surrounded by lush gardens with paths that wind down into Portofino. If you didn't bring your own yacht, the hotel launch is at your disposal for tours of the coastline. The hotel's restaurant, La Terrazza, has an elegant dining room with a splendid outdoor terrace perched above the yacht-filled harbor.

Down the hill, the smaller Splendido Mare sits directly on Portofino's tiny piazza and shares all the luxury amenities with its sister hotel up the hill. Rooms at the Splendido Mare have views directly onto the harbor and up to Castello di Giorgio.

HOTEL SPLENDIDO AND SPLENDIDO MARE, Salita Baratta 16, 16034 Portofino (GE), tel. +39 0185 267 801, fax +39 0185 267 806, email reservations@ splendido.net, www.hotelsplendido.com. Driving directions: from highway A12 exit at Rapallo. Follow indications for Santa Margherita Ligure and then to Portofino. Sixty-six rooms at the Splendido, and sixteen at the Splendido Mare, doubles from EEEE to EEEEE.

CAMOGLI

Cenobio dei Dogi

Camogli is a lively fishing village on the western side of the Portofino promontory. Its name derives from *case delle mogli* or "houses of the wives," a reference to the long waits of brides for their fisherman husbands to return from the sea. The village is filled with pink-, ochre-, and sienna-hued houses, distinctively painted so fishermen can recognize their houses as they return from sea.

At one end of Camogli's bay, the palatial Hotel Cenobio dei Dogi was once a summer residence for Genovese doges, beginning its life as the Villa Franca del Castellaro. The hotel still houses the original chapel that the doges built to welcome visiting cardinals and other religious dignitaries who traveled here from Rome. While the hotel preserves its historic roots, it has been completely renovated to offer all the services and amenities expected by modern travelers.

Cenobio dei Dogi is one of the few hotels on the Riviera that sits directly on the sea. Relaxing here in the summer months, you can enjoy the hotel's saltwater pool directly in front of the hotel or you can wander down to the private pebbled beach. From either spot, there are sweeping views of Camogli's crystalline bay. Rooms have period style furnishings, and you can choose between sea and garden views. The hotel's Doge's restaurant serves authentic Ligurian dishes and enjoys panoramic views on three sides.

HOTEL CENOBIO DEI DOGI, Via N.Cuneo 34, 16032 Camogli (GE), tel. +39 0185 724 1, fax +39 0185 772 796, email reception@cenobio.it, www.cenobio.com. Driving directions from Genova: take highway A12 and exit at Recco. Follow the indications for Camogli. One hundred seven rooms; doubles from EE to EEEE.

RAPALLO

Grand Hotel Bristol

The Grand Hotel Bristol, with its characteristic pink facade and green shutters, sits in an elevated position at the end of Rapallo. The building, which dates back to 1908, is surrounded by beautiful gardens, and its rooms have balconies that overlook the Gulf of Tigullio. You can also enjoy the view from the roof garden restaurant, with its superb open terrace and elegant Ligurian cuisine. The hotel also features a seawater swimming pool surrounded by a wide sun terrace. At this writing, the hotel is undergoing renovations by the Framon Hotel Group and is projected to reopen in early 2004.

GRAND HOTEL BRISTOL, Via Aurelia Orientale 369, 16035 Rapallo (GE), tel. +39 0185 273 313, fax +39 0185 558 00, email reservation.bri@ framonhotels.it, www.framonhotels.com. Driving directions from Genova: take highway A12 and exit at Rapallo. Ninety-one rooms; doubles from EE to EEE.

SANTA MARGHERITA LIGURE

Grand Hotel Miramare

Open since the beginning of the twentieth century, this "Liberty" style hotel was one of the most popular destinations for the *dolce vita* crowd in the fifties. Laurence Olivier and Vivian Leigh honeymooned here in 1947. Rooms with balconies have sea views and terraces with pretty iron tables where you can enjoy breakfast in the morning sun. The furnishings are simple and feminine, with scrolled iron bed frames, plush velvet chairs, and dainty glass chandeliers. For relaxing by the water, you can enjoy the heated seawater swimming pool or the hotel's private beach, the Bagni Miramare. There are two bars and the hotel's Terrasse restaurant is an elegant spot to watch the sunset over the gulf.

GRAND HOTEL MIRAMARE, Lungomare Milite Ignoto 30, 16038 Santa Margherita Ligure (GE), tel. +39 0185 287 013, fax +39 0185 284 651, email miramare@miramare.it, www.grandhotelmiramare.it. Driving directions: from highway A12 exit at Rapallo. Follow indications for Santa Margherita Ligure. Seventy-five rooms; doubles from EEE to EEEEE.

Imperiale Palace Hotel

The Imperiale Palace is an old-style grand hotel that sits up on a hill above Santa Margherita Ligure. Built as a private mainland residence for the Corsican Costa family, its heavily decorated interiors still have a patrician air. The hotel holds a place in history as the site where delegates signed the Treaty of Rapallo at the end of World War I; you can ask to take a peek at the preserved *Sala di Trattato* (Treaty Hall). Surrounded by a graceful palm-filled park that extends to the water, the asymmetrical pool is a quiet alternative to the slate terrace at the water's edge. The Imperial suites, as well as the Tigullio suite, with their frescoed ceilings and grand chandeliers will have you feeling like Italian aristocracy. The hotel's Ristorante Novecento has beautiful inlaid terrazzo floors with floral motifs, elaborately frescoed ceilings, and a grand fireplace. During the summer months, the Terrazza Paraggi, directly in front of the hotel, is open; here you can dine in the open air, enjoying traditional Ligurian fare and a spectacular view of the gulf. The terrace is illuminated with candlelight, and there is music for dancing under the stars.

IMPERIALE PALACE HOTEL, Via Pagana 19, 16038 Santa Margherita Ligure (GE), tel. +39 0185 288 991, fax +39 0185 284 223, email info@hotelimperiale.com, www.hotelimperiale.com. Driving directions: from highway A12, exit at Rapallo. Follow indications for Santa Margherita Ligure. Ninety-two rooms; doubles from EE to EEEEE.

Villa Gnocchi

Villa Gnocchi is a cliffside villa-inn perched on the hillside above Santa Margherita Ligure. The owners have lovingly restored their family's two stone houses to create a bed-and-breakfast with a warm, homey feeling. The rooms are decorated with family antiques and heirlooms, and have panoramic views that sweep down to the gulf. A path from the villa leads down to the center of Santa Margherita and takes about fifteen minutes to walk.

VILLA GNOCCHI, Via Romana 53, 16038 Santa Margherita Ligure (GE), tel. and fax +39 0185 283 431. Driving directions: from highway A12 exit at Rapallo. Follow indications for Santa Margherita Ligure. Nine rooms; doubles from E.

SESTRI LEVANTE

Grand Hotel dei Castelli

The Grand Hotel dei Castelli is a complex of three castles built atop the ruins of a thirteenth-century fortress. The castles we see today were built in the 1920s, by two esteemed architects whose otherworldly vision for a castle-villa produced one of the most unique properties on the Riviera. Each castle was built with local stone and a combination of rescued archeological finds from southern Italy and beyond. In its eclectic rooms you'll see Roman capitals inset near Romanesque transoms and gothic flourishes near Egyptian elements. Interiors are filled with antiques and guest rooms are spacious; some even have deep sunken bathtubs.

The hotel is set in a park, which covers most of the Sestri Levante peninsula, with long paths where you can appreciate the Mediterranean flora and fauna. In the park, you will find the hotel's swimming pool, carved into a rocky cliff, and the large natural stage used for summer concerts. Amidst the brambles you might also find the vine-covered tower where Marconi performed his first radio transmission experiments.

Two separate elevators connect the hotel with the sea and with street level in Sestri Levante. The adjoining restaurant (see page 17) has a stupendous terrace with a view of Portofino—an ideal spot for a romantic dinner for two. Its dining room has vaulted ceilings supported by marble columns and a large fireplace for hearthside dinners in colder weather. The restaurant is also available for special events and wedding receptions.

GRAND HOTEL DEI CASTELLI, Via Penisola 26, 16039 Sestri Levante (GE), tel. +39 0185 487 220, fax +39 0185 447 67, email info@ hoteldeicastelli.com, www.hoteldeicastelli.com Driving directions: from highway A12 exit at Sestri Levante. Thirty rooms; doubles from EE to EEE.

Villa Balbi

The splendid Pompeian red facade of the Grand Hotel Villa Balbi, adorned by trompe l'oeil cornices and pediments, stands out among the other buildings along the Viale Rimembranza. Built in 1648 by the Brignole, a Genovese family of doges, it later passed to a cardinal whose presence is still felt in the villa today. Over the centuries, many noble guests have stayed under the villa's roof, including Elizabeth Farnese, who stayed here on her way to wed Prince Philip V of Spain in 1714.

The reception desk is in an enormous entrance hall with leather club chairs, ceilings delicately painted in gold and azure, sweeping chandeliers, and a huge carved fireplace flanked by winged beasts and inlaid with majolica tiles. Other common areas have colonnades with frescoed, vaulted ceilings, and you can still play cards in the villa's original billiards room. For a taste of the aristocratic life, you might like to request room 818, once the cardinal's private apartment with a requisite adjoining throne room. Rooms in the old wing have retained more characteristics of the villa's original style, with parquet floors and high ceilings. The newer wings, added in 1947, feel more modern.

The villa has an enclosed Mediterranean garden with a secluded swimming pool. In the summer, the hotel serves dinners on the outdoor terrace shaded by giant magnolia trees.

GRAND HOTEL VILLA BALBI, Viale Rimembranza 1, 16039 Sestri Levante (GE), tel. +39 0185 429 41, fax +39 0185 482 459, email villabalbi@ villabalbi.it, www.villabalbi.it. Driving directions: from highway A12 exit at Sestri Levante. Ninety-nine rooms; doubles from EE to EEE.

MONTEROSSO AL MARE

Porta Roca

Of the five villages that make up the Cinque Terre (Five Lands), Monterosso is the largest and has the most comfortable stretch of beachfront. Like all the "five lands," it can be quite crowded, which is why a room high above the scene at the Porta Roca is ideal. The Porta Roca hotel has its own rocky perch above Monterosso, reached by a very narrow winding road along the cliffs. The views from the hotel are spectacular, so be sure to request one of the seaside rooms whose terraces open over the Gulf. The decor's slight sixties, French Riviera feeling adds to the total charm of the place. There are wonderful outdoor spaces to sit and relax in the shade, and the hotel's restaurant offers Ligurian seafood with a view of Monterosso. There's also a section of Monterosso's beach exclusively reserved for Porta Roca guests.

PORTA ROCA, Via Corone 1, 19016 Monterosso al Mare (SP), tel. +39 0187 817 502, fax +39 0187 817 692, email portoroca@cinqueterre.it, www. portoroca.it. Driving directions: from highway A12 exit at Carrodano. Connect to S566 in the direction of Levanto and Monterosso. Open March through November. Forty-three rooms; doubles from EE.

NERVI

Villa Pagoda

The Villa Pagoda was built by a Genovese merchant who in his travels to the Orient fell madly in love with a young Chinese girl. Marriage was out of the question, so he settled for building a pagoda-style shrine to her, surrounded by gardens. Perched on a hillside not far from the sea, the villa's interiors show traces of the wealth and tastes of the 1800s merchant class with antique furniture, precious fabrics, Murano chandeliers, and original Carrara marble floors. The rooms are cheerily decorated, and the tower rooms' views stretch to the Portofino promontory.

Nervi is one of the first of the villages that dot the coastline from Genova to La Spezia. It has a beautiful cliffside promenade and twenty-four acres of parkland; here are the Villa Luxoro decorative arts museum (see page 42) and the Villa Grimaldi Fassio, which houses the Frugone collections of paintings and sculpture.

VILLA PAGODA, Via Capoluogo 15, 16167 Genova Nervi (GE), tel. +39 010 372 6161, fax +39 010 321 218, email info@villapagoda.it, www.villa pagoda.it. Driving directions: from highway A12 exit at Nervi. Seventeen rooms; doubles from E to EEEEE.

Tables for Two

CAMOGLI

do Spadin

Punta Chiappa is a secluded seaside hamlet named after a rocky point that juts out into the sea. There is no way for cars to arrive here, so visitors make their way either on the boats from Camogli or via the nine hundred steps that descend from Portofino Vetta. In an old building once used as a fish preserving plant is a small restaurant known for its excellent fish dishes. Fresh, locally caught shellfish such as mussels, prawns, and clams are usually on the menu. Dishes include fresh taglierini pasta with conger eel, fish and seafood stews, and fried anchovies and *totani* (flying squid).

TRATTORIA DO SPADIN, Via San Nicolò 55, Frazione Punta Chiappa— Camogli (GE), tel. +39 0185 770 624, email dospadin@libero.it. Closed on Mondays and for holidays from November through Easter. Forty seats. Cost: EE.

Rosa

Rosa, set in a "Liberty" style (Italian art nouveau) villa, enjoys a spectacular view from its hillside setting. As you dine on the sun-drenched terrace of this classic restaurant, at your feet are the brightly painted houses and the boat-filled harbor of Camogli. The menu offers freshly prepared regional dishes like *trofiette al pesto* (fresh handmade pasta with pesto), *tonno fresco in salsa agrodolce* (fresh tuna in sweet and sour sauce), and *taglierini in sugo di triglie* (fresh pasta with mullet).

RISTORANTE ROSA, Largo F.Casabona 11, 16032 Camogli (GE), tel. +39 0185 773 411 and +39 0185 771 088. Driving directions from Genova: Take highway A12 and exit at Recco. Follow the indications for Camogli. Closed on Tuesdays and the last two weeks of November and January. Ninety seats. Cost: EE.

da Giovanni

It's a delight to make a lunchtime outing to this tiny restaurant in the small cove dominated by the Abbazia di San Fruttuoso. To arrive, you will need to either catch the boat from Camogli or hike down the trails from Portofino. This casual restaurant is a good place to enjoy simple pasta dishes prepared with fresh seafood. As you eat, take in the scene in this lively fishing village. Afterward take a tour of the Abbey, now historically protected by the Fondo per l'Ambiente Italiana (FAI). For more information about the abbey, see page 38.

RISTORANTE DA GIOVANNI, San Fruttuoso di Camogli, tel. +39 0185 770 047. Cost: E.

ABBAZIA DI SAN FRUTTUOSO, tel. and fax +39 0185 772 703, email fai.san fruttuoso@fondoambiente.it, www.fondoambiente.it. Hours: March to May, open every day from 10 A.M. to 4 P.M. Boats to San Fruttuoso depart from Camogli, Portofino, Santa Margherita, Rapallo. See www. traghettiportofino.it for schedules. Footpaths: from Portofino Vetta (ninety minutes) or Portofino Mare (ninety minutes).

La Rocca

The little village of San Rocco di Camogli lies at the edge of the Portofino park preserve. From here many paths depart to Punta Chiappa, San Fruttuoso, Portofino Vetta, or Portofino Mare. La Rocca's two dining rooms, at 885 feet above the sea, have a breathtaking view of Camogli's charming harbor. The cooking, managed by chef Enrica Arado, is typically Ligurian, with an emphasis on seafood and fish. In addition to classic Ligurian dishes such as *pansoti* (ravioli filled with greens and served with walnut sauce) or *cappon magro* (fresh fish and vegetables), there are creative dishes like lemon tagliolini with scampi, and fresh squid-ink pasta with prawns and zucchini. Fish come straight from the market, and the daily catch is offered steamed, grilled, or baked.

RISTORANTE LA ROCCA, Via Molfino 164, 16032 San Rocco di Camogli (GE), tel. +39 0185 772 813, email info@laroccaristorante.com, www.larocca ristorante.com. Driving directions from Genova: Take highway A12 and exit at Recco. Follow the indications for Camogli. Cost: EE.

PORTOFINO

Da Puny

Da Puny is housed in a characteristic ochre-stained building; its tables spill onto the square facing Portofino's harbor. You can sit under the vine-covered pergola in front and take in the lively scene. Good dishes to start with are seafood salads, curried risotto with fresh prawns, and *spaghetti ai moscardini* (with tiny octopus). For main courses, either the fish of the day or the classic *fritto misto* won't disappoint. Da Puny is very popular with locals and tourists; reportedly even Prime Minister Berlusconi was turned away when he arrived without a reservation.

DA PUNY, Piazza Martiri dell'Olivetta 5, 16034 Portofino (GE), tel. +39 0185 269 037. Driving directions: From highway A12 exit at Rapallo. Follow indications for Santa Margherita Ligure and then to Portofino. Closed on Thursdays and for holidays from December 15 to February 20. Sixty seats; reservations essential. No credit cards. Cost: EEE.

Lo Stella

Founded in 1850, Lo Stella is one of the oldest establishments in Portofino. Over the years this portside restaurant has hosted kings, dukes, and princesses. From an outdoor table you can watch the comings and goings of the busy harbor. At night, tables are romantically candlelit. Starters include mussels, fish marinated in laurel, and classic Ligurian *insalata di pesce* (seafood salad). Pasta dishes include fish ravioli with prawn sauce, and regional favorites like *trofie al pesto* (fresh pasta with pesto). For a main course, choose from the day's catch for grilled fish specials or order a *fritto misto* (mixed fry). As this is always a popular spot with the yachting crowd, it's wise to reserve ahead.

RISTORANTE LO STELLA, Molo Umberto I 3, 16034 Portofino (GE), tel. +39 0185 269 007, fax +39 0185 269 098, email info@ristorantelostella.com, www.ristorantelostella.com. Driving directions: From highway A12 exit at Rapallo. Follow indications for Santa Margherita Ligure and then to Portofino. Cost: EEE.

RAPALLO

u Giancu

This quirky spot in the hills above Rapallo is known as the *ristorante dei fumetti. Fumetti* are comic strips, and every square inch of this family-run trattoria is covered with framed comic art. The energetic proprietor manages special events, such as musical performances, wine tastings, and cooking classes, and he has even created a children's playground in the garden filled with cartoonesque swings, a carousel, and slides. Situated in the countryside two miles from Rapallo, u Giancu is surrounded by olive trees and a garden that make for pleasurable outdoor dining in the summer months. This is a great place to try local cheeses made by nearby farms and the classic Ligurian mixture of greens, *preboggion*. Enjoy authentic dishes like fresh homemade ravioli filled with asparagus and parmigiano, and braised rabbit and lamb. The wine list has many local favorites like *sciacchetrà* as well as homemade liquors infused with lemon, oranges, and pomegranate to finish your meal.

TRATTORIA U GIANCU, San Massimo Km. 4, 16035 Rapallo (GE), tel. +39 0185 260 505, email ugiancu@ugiancu.it, www.ugiancu.it. Driving directions: take the A12 highway and exit at Rapallo. Weekdays, open for dinner only. Ninety seats, reservations recommended. Cost: E.

SANTA MARGHERITA LIGURE

La Stalla dei Frati

In an old villa high in the hills overlooking the Gulf of Tigullio, La Stalla dei Frati has a warm, welcoming atmosphere and an elegant, refined menu. Try fresh pasta with sea urchins, trenette and trofie with pesto, and freshly caught fish baked with potatoes, olives, and pine nuts, or prepared in *guazzetto* (with white wine, garlic, and tomato). Meat lovers will appreciate excellent dishes like osso buco with fresh peas. The ample wine list has a great selection of international wines, with many available in half bottles.

> La Stalla dei Frati, Via G. Pino 27, 16038 Frazione Nozarego, S. Margherita Ligure (GE), tel. +39 0185 289 447. Driving directions: Take the A12 highway and exit at S. Margherita Ligure. From S. Margherita Ligure, take the road from the port and follow the indications for Nozarego for just over one half mile. Closed on Mondays and for holidays in November. Sixty seats; reservations recommended. Cost: EEE.

SESTRI LEVANTE

Asseü

Along the original rail line between Riva Trigoso and Moneglia is a restored signal station that now houses the restaurant Asseü. Asseü takes its name from the large rock that juts out of the surf directly in front of its tiny strip of beach. The restaurant's large outdoor terrace is naturally sheltered by the shape of the cove; from it you can watch boats entering the harbor. Starters include the house's mixed antipasto plate, a sampling of typical Ligurian starters such as octopus and potatoes, stuffed mussels and anchovies, and fried scampi. For a main course, you can try dishes like sea bass ravioli in crab sauce, fish cooked *al forno* with potatoes and mushrooms, or seasonal mixed grills.

> Asseü, Via G.B. da Ponzerone 2, 16038 Riva Trigoso—Sestri Levante (GE), tel. +39 0185 423 42, email asseu@tiscalinet.it, www.asseu.com. Driving directions from highway A12: Exit at Sestri Levante and follow the indica-

tions for Moneglia. After the first tunnel on the right you will see the restaurant; parking is on the left. Closed on Wednesdays and for holidays in November. Cost: EE.

ai Castelli

Ristorante ai Castelli, part of the magical castle complex that makes up the Grand Hotel dei Castelli (page 8), is managed by the same able team that manages the ever-popular Polpo Mario in Sestri Levante. The restaurant, like the castle-hotel, was built in the 1920s in castle revival style. The dining room has vaulted ceilings, marble columns, and a grand hearth that warms the room in the cooler months. In the summer, the terrace, with its uninterrupted view of Portofino, is used for dining. The cuisine is almost exclusively seafood, offering fish that was caught that very morning. To accompany your meal, the restaurant's sommelier has built a wine list from the best Ligurian labels, as well as national and international wines. The outdoor terrace is often used for wedding receptions and can accommodate four hundred guests.

RISTORANTE GRAND HOTEL DEI CASTELLI, Via alla Penisola 26, 16039 Sestri Levante (GE), tel. +39 0185 456 087 or +39 0185 455 354, www.ristorante aicastelli.it. Driving directions: take the A12 highway and exit at Sestri Levante. Closed from November through the end of March. Cost: EE.

Fiammenghilla Fieschi

Fiammenghilla Fieschi is housed in the historic summer villa that once belonged to the famous Fieschi family. Surrounded by a beautiful garden, the villa has an elegant, intimate dining room decorated with period lamps and mirrors. The menu offers a modern interpretation of classic Ligurian dishes, with bread and pesto made fresh on the premises each day. Recommended dishes include *fiori di zucca ripieni di crostacei* (zucchini blossoms filled with shellfish) and *pappardelle alla Fieschi* (with pesto, zucchini, local prescinseua cheese, saffron threads, and prawns). The well-furnished wine cellar stocks more than five hundred labels from all over the world.

FIAMMENGHILLA FIESCHI, Via Pestella 6, 16037 Riva Trigoso—Sestri Levante (GE), tel. +39 0185 481 041. Driving directions: take the A12 highway and exit at Sestri Levante. Open on Mondays for dinner only; closed for holidays from January 27 to February 10 and November 1 to 10. Thirty-six seats; reservations essential. Cost: EEE.

Polpo Mario

Polpo Mario is a characteristic local, where *polpo* (octopus) is the specialty. It's set in one of Sestri Levante's tiniest streets and carved out of part of Palazzo Federici (1500), another Fieschi family summer palace. The owner, Rudy Ciuffardi, has even written a book on *135 Modi per Cucinare un Polpo (135 Ways to Cook an Octopus)*. It's best to reserve a table in advance for this ever-popular restaurant. At night you'll be sitting shoulder to shoulder with other diners in a convivial atmosphere. The food is consistent: typical offerings are *ravioli di branzino in salsa granchio* (pasta filled with sea bass in crab sauce) and *misto all'antica* (scampi, cuttlefish, catch of the day, potatoes, and artichokes braised in the oven with pine nuts and olives). Next door, the Cantina del Polpo wine bar is a great spot to enjoy an aperitif before dinner; choose from five hundred wines from local and international producers.

POLPO MARIO, Via XXV Aprile 163, 16039 Sestri Levante (GE), tel. +39 0185 480 203 and +39 0185 487 240, www.polpomario.it. Driving directions: take the A12 highway and exit at Sestri Levante. Closed on Mondays. Ninety seats; reservations essential. Cost: E.

RIOMAGGIORE

Ca' de Cian

Ca' de Cian sits 1,150 feet above sea level next to an ancient monastery surrounded by vineyards and pine forests. The views over Riomaggiore and the gulf are spectacular. Tables are set outside in the Ligurian sunshine or inside the monastery's restored refectory. A set menu of simple and traditional dishes is created each day from whatever is freshest and in season.

The monastery, built in 1335, is one of five ancient sanctuaries that line the cliff sides above the Cinque Terre (see "Hiking the paths," page 28). At one time they were linked by a mule path that was the only route between La Spezia and the Cinque Terre. Ca' de Cian also offers small *rustici* (rustic cottages) for rental. This rustic oasis can be reached either via hiking path Number 3, by a short hike from the main road above Riomaggiore, or by the funicular that operates during the grape harvest.

CA' DE CIAN, Santuario di Montenero, 19017 Riomaggiore (SP), tel. and fax +39 0187 920 992. Closed on Mondays, Tuesdays, and Wednesdays, and from the end of October to end of March. No credit cards. Cost: E.

Cappun Magru

Groppo sits high above Riomaggiore and Manarola amid the terraced vines on the hillside. To get to this restaurant you'll need a good local map—as Groppo isn't included in many national maps—or you can try following the road that leads from Manarola to Volastra. In Italy, this is one of Liguria's most cited restaurants because of the quality and authenticity of its food. The menu's offerings are crafted from seasonal ingredients procured locally. Dishes include creamy *stoccafissa* (salt cod) with artichokes and balsamic, lasagna with fresh scampi and fava bean puree, and quail with sun-dried tomatoes and pistachio pesto. The wine list includes great wines from the area, as well as from Tuscany and Piedmont.

CAPPUN MAGRU, Via Volastra 19, Località Groppo, 19017 Riomaggiore (SP), tel. & fax +39 0187 920 563. Driving directions: Take the A12 highway and exit at Borghetto di Vara. Continue along the coastal highway S1 to Riomaggiore. Once in Riomaggiore, follow indications for Groppo. Open for dinner every day and for lunch and dinner on Sunday. Closed on Mondays and Tuesdays and the months of December and January. No credit cards. Twenty seats; reservations suggested. Cost: EEE.

La Lanterna

La Lanterna is perched just above Riomaggiore's tiny marina. The ancient building that houses the restaurant was here during the age of the Barbarossa pirates and later used as a *salatoria di acciughe* (anchovy curing house). The restaurant's straightforward marine fare is popular with locals and tourists alike. The fish is local and fresh, and the desserts are all made on the premises. There is a tiny outdoor terrace and a small inside dining room with just sixteen tables, so reservations are a must.

TRATTORIA LA LANTERNA, Via San Giacomo 10, 19017 Riomaggiore (SP), tel. +39 0187 920 589, fax +39 0187 245 81. Driving directions: Take the A12 highway and exit at Borghetto di Vara. Continue along the coastal highway S1 to Riomaggiore. Closed on Tuesdays (winter only) and the month of November. Forty seats. Cost: EE.

VERNAZZA

Gambero Rosso

Gambero Rosso has earned a reputation of being the best restaurant in Vernazza. In warm weather you'll want to book a table outside on the piazzetta with its view of the tiny port. The menu includes seafood salads, *pansoti* (Ligurian ravioli), and *pesce spada alle erbe* (swordfish with herbs). Other well-prepared Ligurian specialties include perfectly fried anchovies, *ravioli di pesce* filled with the best of the local catch, and the ultra-Ligurian *trofie con il pesto* (a local elongated gnocchi, always made by hand). Main courses include succulent stuffed mussels, anchovies baked with potatoes, and simply prepared catch of the day. All dishes are best accompanied by one of the local wines. A tasting menu and daily prix fixe menus are also available.

GAMBERO ROSSO, Piazza Marconi 7, 19018 Vernazza (SP), tel. +39 0187 812 265. Driving directions: Take the A12 highway and exit at Borghetto di Vara. Continue along the coastal highway S1 to Vernazza. Closed on Mondays. Fifty seats. Cost: EE.

Gianni Franzi

The Gianni Franzi in Piazza Marconi also offers overnight guest accommodations. It's been open for almost a century, coming under the management of its current owners in the sixties. The cooking is faithful to the spirit of authentic Ligurian cuisine; specialties include *acciughe ripiene* (stuffed anchovies), *ravioli di pesce*, *muscoli ripieni* (filled mussels), and fresh local fish served either grilled or *al forno*. In warm weather, outdoor tables are set in the central piazza facing the old Roman harbor; you can also sit inside in the rustic stone dining room.

GIANNI FRANZI, Piazza Marconi 5, 19018 Vernazza (SP), tel. +39 0187 821 003, fax +39 0187 812 228, email info@giannifranzi.it, www.giannifranzi.it. Driving directions: take the A12 highway and exit at Borghetto di Vara. Continue along the coastal highway S1 to Vernazza. Closed on Wednesdays and from January to early March. Cost: E.

PORTOVENERE

Taverna del Corsaro

At the farthest reaches of the village's rocky promontory, this old *taverna* (tavern) is carved from the rocks of a thirteenth-century battlement. From its dining room there are views of the two little islands across the bay. Seafood specialties reign, with warm seafood salads, fresh anchovies, and locally caught fish offered in simple regional preparations. Excellent dishes to try are the *muscoli ripieni* (stuffed mussels) or *tagliolini agli scampi* (fresh noodles with langoustines). Desserts include the *torta del Corsaro*, a cake flavored with sweet Sciacchetrà. The restaurant offers tasting menus, and many wines from its rich wine list are offered by the glass. Note: If you go to Portovenere, don't miss the tiny church at the edge of the promontory (see page 43).

TAVERNA DEL CORSARO, Calata Doria 102, 19025 Portovenere (SP), tel. +39 0187 790 622, www.portovenere.it/sponsor/corsaro. Driving directions: take the A12 highway and exit at La Spezia-Porto Est. Follow the indications toward Portovenere. Closed on Tuesdays and for holidays the month of November. Seventy seats. Cost: EE.

Watching the Sunset

Riomaggiore, Vernazza

There is no shortage of spectacular spots from which to watch the sunset along the coast. Grab a table along the harbor in Vernazza an hour before the sun goes down and watch the show or plan to be in Riomaggiore for the bewitching hour.

If you visit Riomaggiore on the full moon, you might understand why an old legend suggests that at one time the inhabitants became convinced that they could build a staircase to the moon. After much discussion, they decided to build a staircase out of empty wine casks, stacked one atop the other. When they had almost reached the moon, they realized only one last barrel was needed before they could reach up and grab the moon.

Having already used up all the barrels in the village, they pulled one out from the bottom of the stack, and the whole lot came tumbling down.

Places to Propose

Punta Chiappa—The Altar of Stella Maris

The village of Punta Chiappa—or "La Punta," as it is often called—perches on a rocky point at the base of Monte di Portofino, forming the eastern side of the Golfo Paradiso. It's a tiny paradise, where the water is clear and sparkling for swimming, diving, and snorkeling. You can reach Punta Chiappa from San Rocco, an outlying village of Camogli, by descending nine hundred stairs down the hillside along a wooded path with a breathtaking panorama. To avoid the stairs, you can take one of the boats that depart hourly between Punta Chiappa and Camogli. At the farthest edge of the rock point is a tiny altar with a beautiful mosaic dedicated to the Stella Maris (sea star). Stella Maris is the sailor's Virgin; her image was placed here to offer protection from rough seas. Each year, on the first Sunday in August, a procession of decorated boats arrives at this very spot to celebrate a traditional mass (see "Festa della Stella Maris," page 24).

If you decide to brave the path from San Rocco to Punta Chiappa, you will pass a small thirteenth-century gem, the San Nicolò di Capodimonte church. It was built by monks from San Rufo together with the nuns of a nearby convent; the small bell tower was added in the 1800s.

Romantic Lore and Local Festivals

Sagra del Pesce—Camogli

In May, Camogli honors Saint Fortunatus, the fishermen's patron saint, by preparing the largest fish fry in the world. For the occasion, a gigantic frying pan was built with a thirteen-foot diameter and a twenty-foot handle to keep the fryers out of harm's way. Each year the municipality prepares three tons of fried anchovies, sardines, and white fish, distributing over thirty thousand portions to locals and tourists alike.

A fireworks show on Saturday night begins the festivities; on Sunday, the main event is accompanied by traditional folklore displays and live local music for dancing. The Sagra del Pesce is held each year on the second Sunday in May; information in Italian can be found at www.sagradelpesce.it or contact Camogli's tourist information office at tel. +39 0185 771 066.

Torta dei Fieschi—Lavagna

The festival of the Torta dei Fieschi (Fieschi cake) commemorates one of the most celebrated Italian weddings of the medieval era. In 1230, Opizzo Fiesco, a powerful count of Lavagna, married the Sienese noblewoman Bianca dei Bianchi. The wedding, blessed by the pope, was a momentous joining of two Guelph families and was widely celebrated from Liguria to Tuscany and beyond. At the time, the counts of Fieschi owned most of the coastal territory in Liguria; the wedding celebration in Lavagna would certainly have been one of the largest. Many legends surround the enormous wedding cake, a replica of which is still baked each August 14 in Lavagna. According to one, the bride and groom wished to make a gesture to the people of Lavagna in the form of a thirty-foot cake topped by the Fieschi crown. Another says that the cake was actually a gift from the bride's father, in a size commensurate with his love for her. Today the cake resembles a large white cone; it is topped with an electric crown of twinkling lights. During the festival, spectators hoping to enjoy some cake are invited to play a game in the square. Each person is issued a ticket—blue for boys, pink for girls. To receive a slice of the cake, each person must find their *anima gemella* (soul mate) in the crowd, who will hold a ticket with the same number but the opposite color. Once they find one another, they are awarded two slices of cake. For information and schedules of the events see www.tortadeifieschi.com.

Festa della Stella Maris—Camogli

On the first Sunday night in August, thousands of lit candles are set to float on the waves to pay homage to the Madonna. The feast of Stella Maris (Sea Star) was initiated in 1924 by the rector of the church of San Nicolò di Capodimonte; it is celebrated each year as a sign of devotion and invocation to the Madonna as a protector of sailors. The procession of decorated boats, manned by local fishermen and devotees, sails from the port and to the far edge of Punta Chiappa reef. There, on the point, is a four-hundred-year-old altar dedicated to the Madonna, called the Stella di Mare or Stella Maris. Accompanying the flotilla are firemen's boats with choreographed water bursts and the traditional *u Dragun,* a wooden ship equipped with sails and oars, which transports the parish priest. The floating candles fill the gulf with colored light. For information, contact Camogli's tourist office at tel. +39 0185 771 066.

Picnic Spots

Palmaria Island

Portovenere, the last village along the Riviera Levante before you reach La Spezia, is a charming fishing town with tall painted houses, a tiny port, and a beautiful gothic church set on a rocky promontory. The quietude of its tiny harbor is enhanced by Palmaria, a mysterious island just four hundred yards across the water. It one of three islands in front of Portovenere that enclose the Gulf of La Spezia. It's a wonderfully wild spot that few tourists know about, and with its combination of natural and historic monuments, beaches, and vistas, it's a great place to picnic along the Ligurian coast.

Ferries connect the island with Portovenere, departing almost hourly from the small pier. After a short ride, passengers arrive across the bay at Palmaria's main drag, Terrizzo, where there is a small restaurant-hotel and a public beach. The ring trail around the island is just over four miles long and relatively easy to walk. Along the route you can see three old fortresses (one was used to jail Umberto I), the quarries where the Romans excavated marble, and a lighthouse with some of the best views over neighboring Tino Island. The sea-facing side of the island is honeycombed with rocky caves and grottoes, some of which are best seen from the water. The largest, the Grotta Azzurra, is large enough to enter by boat. On the southern edge of the island in Pozzale is a rocky beach with another seafood restaurant and views of La Spezia. A leisurely walk around the island will take approximately three and a half hours. If you decide to stay overnight, note that the Locanda Lorena also rents rooms.

Palmaria Island—Addresses and Practical Information

Waterbus service to PALMARIA (*Navigazione Golfo dei Poeti*): Waterbus schedules and information are available at www.navigazionegolfo deipoeti.it.

Inns, Restaurants, and Bars

LOCANDA RISTORANTE LORENA, Via Cavour, 4, tel. +39 0187 792 370 fax +39 0187 766 077. On the north end of the island, in Terrizzo. Closed Wednesdays and in January and February. The Locanda has a romantic atmosphere at the water's edge, with a view toward Portovenere. The restaurant serves traditional Ligurian seafood. During high season a small boat ferries diners from Portovenere's pier. There are rooms to rent above the trattoria.

RISTORANTE DEL POZZALE, Via Pozzale 22 on the southern edge of the island in Pozzale; tel. +39 0187 791 103. Open April to December.

SPIAGGIA GABBIANO, public beach with a bar and an area to moor small boats, located in Punta Secco near Terrizzo. tel. +39 0187 792 710, email spiaggiagabbiano@tiscalinet.it, http://web.tiscali.it/spiaggiagabbiano/.

Picnic Provisions

Provisions on the island are limited, so you may want to stock up before you depart from Portovenere.

BAJEICO—LA BOTTEGA DEL PESTO (Via Capellini 70, Portovenere. tel. +39 0187 791 054, www.rosticceriamassa.cjb.net) has great savory tortas, various focaccias, cheeses, and wines. For dessert, try their specialty, the *marregiata di Portovenere,* a sweet focaccia-style bread with pine nuts and raisins.

Strada dell'Amore and Riomaggiore's Castle

Another picnic spot with a view lies above Riomaggiore on the grounds of the village's thirteenth-century castle. The best way to arrive is on foot from Manarola, walking along the *Strada dell'Amore* (Lovers' Path). The path between these two picturesque villages has always been associated with couples in love, and many have inscribed their names along the way. The origins of the name are unknown, but because it's the only section of path linking any of the Cinque Terre that's wide enough for two people to walk holding hands, it seems fitting.

Once you arrive in Riomaggiore, you can climb to the castle either along the road that passes S. Giovanni Battista church or from the railway station by taking the Telemaco Signorini path, then climbing a steep staircase.

The castle rises on a cliff that separates the narrow valleys of the Rio Maggiore and the Rio Finale, in an elevated position above the village's old historical center. The construction of the castle's first defensive walls began in 1260 by the Marquis Turcotti, a nobleman of Ripalta and feudal owner of this part of the coast. Later, the castle became part of the defense of the Republic of Genova, which added to its fortifications. Constructed on a quadrilateral base, with low surrounding walls, the castle still has two massive circular defensive towers used to watch for invaders arriving by sea.

From its perch above the village you can enjoy a sunny picnic with a view of the village, the terraced hillsides, and the sea.

Strada dell'Amore and Riomaggiore's Castle—Addresses and Practical Information

Picnic Provisions

There are small *alimentare* (grocery) stores in Manarola near the railway station. Pizzeria La Cambusa, in Via R. Birolli 114, Manarola (SP) tel. + 39 0187 921 029, sells oven-baked focaccia and chickpea farinata. In Vernazza, the Cooperativa Agricola, Via Roma 13, tel. +39 0187 920 435, is a wine cooperative where you can buy a bottle of Cinque Terre white wine or sweet Sciacchetrà.

The Alimentare Dellara Franca, Via C. Colombo 253, Riomaggiore (SP), tel. +39 0187 920 929, is a gourmet shop with many packaged local specialties and wines.

In Groppo, above Riomaggiore, you can buy Cinqueterre, Sciacchetrà, and other Ligurian wines at the Cooperative Agricoltura Cinque Terre, tel. +39 0187 920 435.

Walter de Battè's Sciacchetrà is regarded as one of the best in the region. By appointment, you can arrange a cellar visit. Walter De Battè: Via Pecunia 168, Riomaggiore (SP), tel. +39 0187 920 127.

Romantic Excursions

Hiking the Paths

High above the fishing villages along Liguria's coastline, hiking paths were once the only land route linking each village. The paths pass through terraced vineyards, cypress, pinewoods, and scented Mediterranean scrub. At some points the trails reach altitudes of 2,664 feet and they often provide breathtaking views over the azure waters below. The Club Alpinismo Italiano (CAI) maintains the hiking trails and has established colored or numbered markers identifying each route. Difficulty varies greatly from path to path. The easiest stretch, from Riomaggiore to Manarola, takes twenty minutes to walk with very little change in elevation. The most challenging path, the high trail of the Alta Via, is twenty-two miles long with elevations ranging from sea level to 2,600 feet. The APT and IAT tourist offices are good sources of maps, directions, and information to get you started (see pages 45 and 46 for addresses).

La Via dei Santuari (The Path to the Sanctuaries)

Each village in the Cinque Terre has its own sanctuary, to which the local inhabitants are deeply devoted. Tracing the ancient route that links them leads you along paths first traced by religious pilgrims over a thousand years ago. These spiritual journeys above the seascape combine secluded paths, sweeping vistas, and historic sites that might be missed on typical tourist itineraries.

The inhabitants of the Cinque Terre continue their processional traditions, with special celebrations held on each sanctuary's patron saint's day. The elements of each celebration vary, but they always include a special mass held in the ancient churches.

The path between the ancient sanctuaries follows portions of other routes and passes through some of the territory's most beautiful landscapes. The sanctuaries can also be reached by vehicular roads, with the exception of Our Lady of Montenero above Riomaggiore, which can be reached via a seasonal railway that runs through the vineyards and the wild Mediterranean scrub.

Riomaggiore—Santuario di Nostra Signora di Montenero

The first stop on the pilgrim's trail is the Sanctuary of the Our Lady of Montenero, above Riomaggiore. The Sanctuary sits far above the village at 1,116 feet above sea level, along the coast road that joins the Cinque Terre with La Spezia. The oldest document mentioning this sanctuary dates to 1335, but locals believe it was originally founded by Greek refugees in the eighth century.

It takes about an hour to walk the route—just over two miles—to the Sanctuary of Nostra Signora di Montenero. The path begins near Riomaggiore's parking area and runs parallel to Riomaggiore's channel for a long stretch. Eventually the path climbs through terraced vineyards and finally reaches the bleached white sanctuary, surrounded by a meadow and pine trees. At the top is a broad esplanade and benches where you can rest in the sunshine and enjoy a view of the entire Cinque Terre coast.

Feast Day: Monday after Pentecost

Manarola—Santuario di Nostra Signora della Salute

The path to the Church of Nostra Signora della Salute (Our Lady of Health) passes through some of the Cinque Terre's most productive vineyards. The Sanctuary is actually located in Volastra, a small village on the hill above Manarola. Volastra is known as the "village of olives"; its origins date to Roman times, when the village was used as a station for changing horses. The sanctuary has a simple Romanesque structure with Gothic details on its façade. Inside is an interesting triptych representing St. Domenic, St. Laurence, and St. John the Baptist.

The path begins near Manarola's parking area and follows an old mule track that climbs 880 feet above sea level to CAI path number 6d. Walking time is about an hour. Once you reach Volastra, follow the road to the left to reach the sanctuary.

Feast day: August 5

Corniglia—Santuario di Nostra Signora delle Grazie e San Bernardino

Continuing the walk, you reach the third stop along the Via dei Santuari: the Sanctuary of Santa Maria delle Grazie (Our Lady of Graces), nestled in the terraced vineyards. Corniglia's sanctuary was built in the early

1800s, replacing an ancient chapel founded by Saint Bernardo of Siena. St. Bernardino reportedly spent many hours of prayer and reflection atop this hillside on his pilgrimage from Siena to Genova. The dedication to Saint Mary of the Graces comes from the church's ancient icon, which illustrates the Madonna with St. Bernardo, to whom miraculous events were credited.

Corniglia's sanctuary actually lies on a hillside above the village of Prevo; the walking time from Corniglia is more than an hour. The route begins along the path that stretches from Corniglia to Prevo, which eventually continues to Vernazza. When you reach Prevo, the path climbs to the sanctuary.

Feast day: September 8

Vernazza—Santuario di Nostra Signora di Reggio

The Sanctuary of Nostra Signora di Reggio (Our Lady of Reggio), located in the hills above Vernazza, is the fourth destination on the pilgrimage of the Cinque Terre sanctuaries. It was built in the eleventh century, but its subterranean crypt suggests even older foundations. The Sanctuary has endured many renovations over the years, which changed its original three-nave plan to a Latin cross. The church's interior is filled with paintings and stuccos. A shady square in front of the Sanctuary offers a pleasant place to rest after the climb.

To reach the Sanctuary of Nostra Signora di Reggio, take CAI path number 8 for just under a mile. Walking time is about forty-five minutes. The path departs from Vernazza's railway station, heading toward the cemetery. The route climbs the ridge trail east to the paved route Way of the Cross (Via della Croce). The mule path climbs through vineyards and olive groves to the sanctuary square.

Feast day: first Sunday in August

Monterosso—Santuario di Nostra Signora di Soviore

The Sanctuary of Nostra Signora di Soviore (Our Lady of Sorrows) above Monterosso is the oldest of the Ligurian sanctuaries dedicated to the Virgin Mary. Inside the church a tablet indicates that the sanctuary was a meeting point for pilgrims on their way to Rome for the first jubilee at the turn of the first millennium. The complex includes a church, a bell tower, and a guesthouse, which were restored in 2000. From the Sanctuary's piazza, the view over Monterosso is exceptional.

To reach the sanctuary, follow CAI path number 9 for one and a half miles. Walking time is an hour and a half. The route begins at the end of Via Roma, where a mule path climbs through olive groves and vineyards, then continues through the woods until it reaches the coast road. Along the mule path you can also see chapels along the Via della Croce dedicated to Mary Magdalene.

Feast days: July 7 and August 15

HIKING THE PATHS—ADDRESSES AND PRACTICAL INFORMATION
The CAI hiking club's La Spezia branch is in Viale Amendola 196, tel.+39 0187 228 73, fax +39 0187 296 85.

For regional park information, contact the PARCO NAZIONALE CINQUE TERRE, Via Signorini, Riomaggiore, tel. +39 0187 920 113, email info@parconazionale5 terre.it.

Riding the Genova Casella Railway to the Fortresses of the Savoys
A charming electric railway line runs between Piazza Manin in Genova and the village of Casella in the Apennine mountains. The little train, the oldest working electric locomotive in Italy (established in 1924), winds its way through spectacular passes just north of Genova. Its brightly painted rail cars have been restored, their original pine and brass interiors shined and polished. For refreshments along the way, the train features a delightful bar car with its original porcelain beer tap and brass coffee samovar. Locals ride the train to celebrate birthdays and anniversaries; some couples have even hosted their wedding receptions aboard the little train.

Along the route are four fortresses built in the late 1700s as a ring of defense against the Austrians. To visit them, hikers leave the train at the Campi station and continue on foot through the countryside. The hiking route, well marked by the CAI, takes two to three hours to hike through the hills back to Genoa.

To reach it, take the road uphill from Campi station and continue for thirty minutes until you reach Forte Diamante. This first fort, constructed in 1756, has star-shaped bastions. It was instrumental in defending Genova from an Austrian attack in 1800. From Forte Diamante, the route leads past two other forts, Forte Fratello Maggior and Forte Fratello Minore (1747) atop the summit of Monte Spino; both have views over the Polcevera valley. The last fort on the tour, and one of the best preserved, is the Forte Puin, built in 1828.

Other interesting stops along the rail route include the Sardorella station, which can only be reached by this train and is a good place to stop for a picnic in the woods. At the Sant'Olcese Chiesa station you can visit the Salumificio Parodi (tours by reservation, tel. +39 010 709 827, fax +39 010 709 945, www.parodisantolcese.com), where for over one hundred years the typical cured *salame di Sant'Olcese* has been produced using an ancient regional recipe.

At the end of the line in Casella, discounted bicycle rentals are offered to ticket holders who want to tour the high country above Genova.

FERROVIA GENOVA-CASELLA S.R.L., Via alla Stazione per Casella 15, 16122 Genova, tel. +39 010 837 321, fax +39 010 837 3248, email fgc@ferrovia genovacasella.it, www.ferroviagenovacasella.it.

Diving Hidden Coves

The coastline along Portofino features interesting underwater coves and indigenous wildlife, which make diving here a unique experience. The Portofino Park authority protects over nine hundred acres of undersea park area and has set designated dive sites within the confines of the park. There are also wrecks along the coast from both world wars that offer interesting diving among sunken warships, steamboats, merchant ships, and naval tugs. Off the shore of the tiny fishing village of San Fruttuoso, the giant submerged Christ statue, *Cristo degli Abissi,* entrusted with protecting divers and fisherman, is another popular dive spot.

Many dive clubs and dive centers offer organized group and individual excursions: information about some of them follows.

Another option for exploring the coast is to rent your own boat. No special licenses are required to rent boats in Italy, and a private boat can allow you to reach secluded coves for snorkeling. For chartering information, see the addresses below.

Diving Hidden Coves—Addresses and Practical Information

Portofino Park Management—Consorzio di Gestione Area Marina Protetta del Promontorio di Portofino, Villa Carmagnola, Viale Rainusso 14, 16038 Santa Margherita Ligure (GE), tel. +39 0185 289 649, fax +39 0185 293 002, email amp.portofino@libero.it.

Scuba Diving Equipment Rental and Guided Dives

Abyss Diving Centre, Corso Colombo 26/I, 16035 Rapallo (GE), tel. +39 0185 658 62, email staff@abyss-diving.it, www.abyssdiving.it. Guided dives along the Portofino coast and SSI instruction.

D&WS, Via J. Ruffini 2A, 16038 Santa Margherita Ligure (GE), tel. +39 0185 282 578, fax +39 0185 292 482, email info@dws-scubaservice.com, www.dws-scubaservice.com. D&WS offers dives at varied technical levels along the Portofino coast and NAUI instruction.

European Diving Centre, Località La Valletta, Via Amm. Canevaro 2, 16038 Santa Margherita Ligure (GE), tel. +39 0185 293 017, fax +39 0185 292 466, email staff@europeandc.com, www.europeandc.com. European Diving Centre organizes dives to Cristo degli Abissi, L'Altare, La Punta del Buco, Relitti del Tigullio, and Secca Isuela, and also offers PADI instruction.

Portofino Divers, Via Jacopo Ruffini 47, 16038 Santa Margherita Ligure (GE), tel. +39 0185 280 791, fax +39 0185 291 161, email info@portofino divers.com, www.portofinodivers.com. Portofino Divers offers recreational and technical dives, from the protected marine area of Portofino to Levanto, for single divers, couples, and groups.

Primasporting Club—MASSUB, Via S. Francesco 28A, 16043 Chiavari (GE), tel. and fax +39 0185 301 248, www.massub.it. The Primasporting Club organizes Portofino coast and wreck dives as well as offering SSI and PADI instruction.

Boats for Hire

LIGURIAN MOTOR BOATING, Via Dante 6, Rapallo (GE), tel. and fax +39 0185 231 017, email info@motonauticaligure.it, www.motonauticaligure.it. Small four- to six-passenger boats cost E80 to E250, larger eight passenger boats cost up to E570. No license is required.

GIORGIO MUSSINI, Calata Marconi 38, Portofino (GE), tel. +39 0185 269 327, email info@giorgiomussini.com, www.giorgiomussini.com. Six-, seven-, and eight-passenger boats are available to rent by the hour, day, or weekend.

NISSIM YACHTS, Via Roma 12/e, Santa Margherita Ligure (GE), tel. +39 0185 286 057, fax +39 0185 288 832, email info@nissimyachts.com, www.nissim yachts.com. Nissim Yachts has large boats and yachts available for charter.

SAN FRUTTUOSO S.N.C., Via Favale 11, Santa Margherita Ligure (GE), tel. and fax +39 0185 280 862, email s.fruttuosodc@libero.it, www. sanfruttuoso.it. San Fruttuoso mans captained dive boats for up to fifteen passengers.

Weddings in Liguria

CEREMONY AND RECEPTION LOCATIONS

Villa Durazzo Centurione

In the delightful seaside village of Santa Margherita Ligure, the spirit of the baroque lives within the walls and gardens of Villa Durazzo. Circled by a marvelous park with Mediterranean palms and fragrant plants, the villa sits high on a hill, its feminine rose-pink and green façade facing the Bay of Tigullio. The villa began as a commission by the marquis of Durazzo in the late 1600s, but he did not live to see his jewel box completed. The villa passed through a succession of some of the most illustrious Genovese noble families, from the Durazzo to the Centurione, before ending up as a grand hotel in the early 1900s, the winter residence for the deposed prince of Wied. Since 1973, it has been managed by the city of Santa Margherita Ligure; it is now a city museum that can be rented for civil wedding ceremonies and receptions.

The marquis, and the villa's subsequent owners, hired armies of painters, pavers, glassblowers, sculptors, and cabinet makers to appoint this refined villa. Every aspect of the villa's design expresses passion for gardens and floral motifs; even the multicolored terrazzo floors incorporate scrolls of floral patterns.

Ceremonies are held in the second-floor Sala degli Stucchi (Stucco Hall), where the door frames are decorated with white shell-shaped stucco cornices and lunettes. The room, which is filled with red velvet-cushioned chairs for ceremonies, can accommodate one hundred seated guests. Huge leaded-glass doors open into the adjoining Sala del Belvedere, where large outer doors open to a balcony with an expansive sea view. Decorated in the late 1800s by Giovanni Franceschetti, the room is a lavish swirl of baroque trompe l'oeil medallions, festoons, and Renaissance motifs that culminate in a fantastical ceiling painted with an allegory of the Four Seasons. After the ceremony, guests can wander through the Sala di Murano, whose ceiling bears delicate paintings of exotic fauna, and the Salotto Impero, with its paintings of reclining divinities, before they head downstairs for the cocktail hour.

Downstairs, the halls are full of precious antiques and paintings that belong to the museum collections. Receptions can be held in the appointed downstairs halls or on the wide terrace that opens alongside the villa. The doors to the terrace open from the Sala Verde—which takes its name from the soft sage-green walls framed with white stuccowork and crowned with an Empire-style crystal chandelier—and from the adjoining original dining room, the Sala da Pranzo.

On the terrace, which seats up to 180 guests, diners are surrounded by the fragrance of night-blooming garden flowers and the soft sound of the waves below. Guests will want to wander through the garden's spaces, where statuary satyrs play lutes and tambourines, a large balustrade lined with muses overlooks the sea, and palms are framed by the garden's hedges.

Behind the villa, the wishing well, centered in an elaborate *esplanade* paved in a floral chiaroscuro of tiny stones, makes a perfect place to cut the cake at the end of the evening.

Catholic ceremonies can be held next door at the church of San Giacomo di Corte. The city also rents out the smaller villa next door, a great space for small ceremonies up to ninety guests, with all the benefits of the villa's botanical gardens and views.

VILLA DURAZZO CENTURIONE, Via San Francesco d'Assisi 3, 16038 Santa Margherita Ligure (GE), tel. +39 0185 205 449, fax +39 0185 205 471, email villadurazzo@comunesml.org, www.comune.santa-margherita-ligure.ge.it. Driving directions: take the A12 highway and exit at Rapallo. Continue toward Santa Margherita Ligure. From the central piazza (near the statue of Columbus), signs lead to the entrance of the villa. Cost: EE to EEE

La Cervara

Bathed in the scent of jasmine, wisteria, and pine, the alluring La Cervara waits silently atop its hillside perch. Reached by the winding cliffside road that passes from Santa Margherita Ligure to Portofino, today this former abbey hosts weddings and receptions in its spectacular gardens and halls. Surrounded by sweeping Mediterranean views, its name, *cervara,* means "a wild and wooded place." The monks who founded the abbey in 1364 set about taming its wildness by terracing the hill in front of the monastery and filling its gardens with aromatic plants, medicinal herbs, and citrus trees. The abbey had remained empty and forgotten for many years before its current owner, Gianenrico Mapelli, rescued and carefully restored it. His passion for the place is evident in its every detail.

Wedding guests arrive by shuttle and are greeted by the quiet façade of the restored abbey church. Two massive doors lead to the church's resplendent interior, painstakingly restored by Professor Pinin Brambilla, whose former projects have included the rescue of Leonardo da Vinci's *Last Supper.* Inside, striped pilasters hold up the cross vaults of the ceiling; leaded-glass windows bathe the space in natural light. Because the abbey is privately owned, the church can be requested for a wide variety of religious ceremonies, not just Catholic ones.

After the ceremony, guests can go through a large portal into the cool, quiet space of the cloister, a welcome respite from the coastal sunshine. The airy cloister space is framed by two levels of arched loggias, which surround a central fountain; here the cake can be cut at the end of the evening as guests watch from the balconies above.

Cocktails are served in the gardens, which face the spectacular panorama of the Gulf of Tigullio. The garden spaces create a varied patchwork of spots for dinners, ceremonies, and cocktails. Diamond-shaped box hedges, topiary spirals, and lush green lawns fill a central Italian parterre. The shady space created by the fragrant five-hundred-year-old wisteria provides a perfect spot for small dinner parties; larger dinners are held on the sweeping terrace at the garden's edge, always with that unforgettable view.

The interior rooms, with their clean white spaces punctuated by archways and cool marble, offer an alternative setting if the weather doesn't permit outdoor dining. One of the best parts of hosting a wedding at La Cervara is the room reserved for the bride to dress in before the ceremony. Huge arched windows reveal a sparkling sea view in all three adjoining rooms provided for the bride and her attendants. The space and its panorama guarantee a relaxed, serene state of mind as you prepare to say "I do."

Signore Mapelli and his professional staff specialize in organizing all facets of wedding events and delight in planning individualized menus.

LA CERVARA, Lungomare Rossetti, Via Cervara 10, 16038 Santa Margherita Ligure (GE), tel. +39 0185 293 139, fax +39 0185 291 270, email abbazia@cervara.it, www.cervara.it. Driving directions: take the A12 highway and exit at Rapallo. Follow the signs to Santa Margherita Ligure. After Santa Margherita Ligure, continue on the seaside road toward Portofino. The abbey is atop a hill two and one half miles from Santa Margherita Ligure. It is available for guided visits by appointment. Cost: EEE.

Abbazia di San Fruttuoso

The Abbey of San Fruttuoso is reached one of two ways: either by boat or by the spectacular footpath that passes over the hill from the Portofino promontory. This secluded cove was chosen in the eighth century by Bishop Prospero of Tarragona to shelter the relics of the martyr Fruttuoso. The oldest sections of the abbey date to the tenth century and represent one of Liguria's most important architectural treasures.

Today, a church, two cloisters, and a three-story abbey stand next to the tiny yet lively fishing village of San Fruttuoso. Catholic ceremonies are celebrated in the abbey's church, where other Christian faiths are also welcome. After the ceremony, as the sun sets over the aquamarine waters of this quiet cove, cocktails are served under the arcade along the beach. As evening falls, Roman torches illuminate the abbey archways and the small beach, creating a magical atmosphere. Guests may wander through the abbey's garden or through the lovely colonnaded cloisters, which are

also impressive backdrops for wedding photos. Your wedding dinner can be held in the serene interior, where thirteenth-century trefoil windows frame sparkling sea views. While you dine on local delicacies, the airy cloister can be filled with music by a classical string quartet.

The abbey opens to the public during the day, but after six, when the last tourist boat leaves, the entire complex will be at the disposition of the wedding party. Guests usually arrive from Camogli on a boat reserved especially for them, followed by the bride, who makes a grand entrance in her own boat, greeted by the guests and the groom who await her arrival on the beach. As sea conditions are so important to the success of events here, weddings may be celebrated only during the months of April, May, June, September, and October.

Taking a short walk from the abbey, along the path that leads to the village, you can also visit the watchtower added by Admiral Andrea Doria. The tower was built to ward off attack by Barbarossa's pirates, who liked to hide their treasure in remote spots along the coastline.

The Ristorante Albergo da Giovanni, just next to the abbey, serves delicious combinations of locally caught seafood and rents seven spartan guest rooms. Boats leave at regular intervals from Camogli, Portofino, Santa Margherita Ligure, and Rapallo. If you are adventurous enough to hike into San Fruttuoso, note that the hiking route from either Portofino Vetta or Portofino Mare takes about ninety minutes.

ABBAZIA DI SAN FRUTTUOSO, Località San Fruttuoso, 16032 Camogli (GE), tel. +39 0185 772 703, fax +39 02 481 93631, email omniaservice@libero.it, www.fondoambiente.it. Driving directions: take the A12 highway and exit at Recco. Continue toward Camogli. The abbey is reached by boat, with regular daily departures from Camogli, Portofino, Santa Margherita, and Rapallo. You can also hike to the abbey from Portofino Vetta or from Portofino Mare; both paths are ninety-minute hikes. The abbey is open to the public for visits year-round. Reception capacity ranges from fifty to one hundred guests. Weddings at the abbey are organized by Omni Service, a firm that can offer a broad range of services including catering, boat rentals, flowers, photographic services, and hotel reservations. Cost: EEE.

CIVIL CEREMONIES

The cities of Genoa and Santa Margherita Ligure hold civil ceremonies in four historic city-managed properties once owned by Liguria's most illustrious noble families. Civil ceremonies are held at the regal Palazzo Tursi in the city of Genoa and just outside the city at two patrician mansions: the Villa Luxoro in Nervi and the Villa Pallavicini in Pegli. And at the Villa Durazzo, overlooking Santa Margherita Ligure, you can hold both a civil ceremony and a reception within the same historic building (see page 42).

For civil ceremonies at Palazzo Tursi, Villa Luxoro, or Villa Pallavicini, contact the marriage office: Ufficio Matrimoni, Corso Torino 11, 16124 Genova, tel. +39 010 557 6866, fax +39 010 541 720, email redazione@ comune.genova.it, www.comune.genova.it.

Palazzo Tursi

Genoa's municipal offices are housed in the grand old Palazzo Tursi on Via Garibaldi, a beautiful street closed to car traffic and home to the most famous of Genoa's sixteenth- and seventeenth-century mansions. A great shield and decorative masked faces over the portico invite you into a central courtyard with two levels of arched loggias held up by twenty-four columns of Carrara marble. A dramatic columned marble staircase with vaulted ceilings leads to the upper floors, where the halls are richly decorated with relief stuccos and frescos from the nineteenth century. In the palace museum are three signed letters and other relics of Christopher Columbus, Genoa's most renowned citizen. Weddings are held in the palace's Sala di Rappresentanza on Saturday and Sunday mornings and the second and fourth Saturday afternoons of each month. Behind the palace is a large open garden with fountains, statuary, and indigenous trees, where you can pose for photos after the ceremony.

PALAZZO TURSI, Salone di Rappresentanza, Via Garibaldi 9, 16124 Genova (GE), tel. +39 010 557 6866, fax +39 010 541 720, email redazione@ comune.genova.it, www.comune.genova.it. Walking directions from Piazza de Ferrari: take Via Venticinque Aprile to Piazza Fontane Marose. Follow the signs indicating the way to Via Garibaldi. Cost: E.

Villa Luxoro

Nervi is the first in the spectacular procession of seaside villages along the Riviera Levante from Genoa. Just inside the mile-long promenade that runs along the cliffs, twenty-four acres of Mediterranean parks ramble through the cityscape. The palms and pines were planted by Nervi's patrician families to shade their summer villas, which today are museums filled with seventeenth-century decorative objects. Surrounded by green gardens and facing the sea, Villa Luxoro was one of the later arrivals to the Nervi scene in 1903. The Luxoros were passionate collectors of seventeenth-century Genovese baroque art, and their villa was built following a splendid original plan from that era. Today, Villa Luxoro is a wonderful museum, where civil wedding ceremonies are held in a large hall, surrounded by antiques fashioned by local artisans. The surrounding Mediterranean-style park, with its palms, pines, statuary, and sweeping view toward Portofino, is a scenic spot for photos.

VILLA LUXORO, Via Aurelia 29, 16167 Genova-Nervi (GE), tel. +39 010 322 673, fax +39 010 322 396, email museicivici@comune.genova.it, www.comune. genova.it. Driving directions from Genoa: take the A12 highway and exit at Genova-Nervi. From the town center, follow signs for the Museo Luxoro. Cost: EEE.

Villa Durazzo Pallavicini

The fantastical garden of the Villa Pallavicini meanders through twenty-four acres of parkland just west of Genoa, in Pegli. In 1840, the Marchese Pallavicini inherited the villa and the small botanical garden that had been planted by his aunt, the Marchesa Durazzo. He hired Michele Canzio, the architect and set designer for the Carlo Fenice Theater in Genova, to surround his aunt's garden with an eclectic drama of monuments. Although wedding ceremonies are held in an oval baroque hall inside the villa, you'll want to spend all your time wandering the villa's gardens with a photographer in tow. The themed plantings begin with a Gothic Lane surrounded by hollies and lead to an Alpine Chalet set in its own pine forest. There is a medieval castle, a pink baroque Tempio di Flora covered with relief stuccos, an otherworldly lake with a Chinese pagoda reached by a romantic bridge, and an island with a luminous marble Temple of Diana. A path winds past eighteen hundred exotic plant species, many of which were the first of their kind to reach Italy.

VILLA DURAZZO PALLAVICINI DI PEGLI, Via Pallavicini 13, 16156 Pegli (GE), tel. +39 010 698 2776. Driving directions: take the A10 (Genova-Ventimiglia) highway and exit at Genova-Pegli. From the town center, follow the signs indicating Villa Durazzo Pallavicini. Cost: EEE.

CATHOLIC CEREMONIES

San Pietro di Portovenere

The tiny Gothic church of San Pietro sits high atop a rocky promontory at the farthest tip of the Portovenere peninsula, above the ruins of an ancient Roman temple that once stood guard over the Gulf of La Spezia. Dramatic sheer rock cliffs descend on three sides of the tiny church's perch, and views extend northward toward the Cinque Terre, west toward the island of Palmaria, and south to the Bay of La Spezia. The small gulf between the church and the island was named the Poet's Gulf to

commemorate Lord Byron's two-mile swim across the bay to Lerici. The original temple that stood here was dedicated to Venus, the goddess of love, making this a particularly auspicious spot to wed. Constructed in Gothic Genovese style, the interior and exterior are built of contrasting black and white marble. The illumination inside the church comes from the candlelight of the votive offerings and from two doors opening to the expansive surrounding sea views. Outside the church, a small covered terrace has three Gothic mullioned windows that frame the seascape. A narrow stairway reaches the top of the church, another dramatic spot for photos after the ceremony.

SAN PIETRO DI PORTOVENERE, 19025 Portovenere (SP). Contact the San Lorenzo parish: tel. +39 0187 790 684. Driving directions: take the A12 highway and exit at La Spezia-Porto Est. Follow the indications toward Portovenere. The church is at the farthest end of the promontory. Ceremony capacity: forty.

Santuario di Nostra Signora di Montallegro

The Nostra Signora di Montallegro sanctuary is a dazzling pearl set on a hillside high above Rapallo. Reached by a railcar, the sanctuary was built in 1558 on the spot where two years prior the Madonna had appeared to a farmer in a vision. Mary asked to be venerated on the mountaintop and, to help convince the townspeople, she left behind proof of her visit in the form of a precious Byzantine icon. Despite the difficulties of transporting materials up the mountain, the sanctuary was finished within two years. The new temple, with its singular nave, was inscribed with *Adoramibus in loco ubi steterunt pedes Ejus* (in veneration of where She once stood), above the door. Long visited by pilgrims, the halls of the sanctuary are lined with votive offerings that depict the divine interventions of the Blessed Virgin, who is credited with saving locals from famines, plagues, and imminent invasions. Wedding ceremonies are blessed in front of the church's seventeenth-century marble altar where the famous Byzantine icon is enshrined behind an elaborate frame. Each year in early July the town commemorates the Virgin's visit with feasts and a fireworks display.

Santuario di Nostra Signora di Montallegro, 16035 Rapallo (GE), tel. +39 0185 239 000. Driving directions: take the A12 highway and exit at Rapallo. Ceremony capacity: one hundred.

Practical Information—Liguria

GETTING THERE

By air: Genova's airport is Cristoforo Colombo (airport code GOA), four miles from the city center.

By car: From Torino, take highway A6 and connect to highway A10. From Milano, take highway A7. From Firenze, take highway A11 and connect to highway A12.

By train: Genova has two railway stations, Porta Principe and Brignole.

WHEN TO GO

The climate in Liguria remains mild all year long. Winter temperatures range from the 40s to 50s and summer highs reach well into the 80s. High season begins in May and continues through September. The Cinque Terre are best visited from March through May, when the hills begin to flower and the mild temperatures make for pleasant hiking and sightseeing. The summer months have become increasingly crowded along the coast.

HELPFUL ADDRESSES

Official Tourist Information Offices and Websites

APT—Azienda di Promozione Turistica (Tourist Promotion Agency)

IAT—Ufficio Informazione e di Accoglienza Turistica (Tourist Information and Hospitality Office)

APT Tigullio: www.apttigullio.liguria.it. Available in English. Information on events, beaches, hotels, and restaurants for the communities between Genova and Moneglia.

APT Cinque Terre: www.aptcinqueterre.sp.it. Available in English. Cinque Terre itineraries, beach information, and events.

Portofino: I.A.T. Via Roma 35, tel. and fax +39 0185 269 024.

Rapallo: I.A.T. Lungomare Vittorio Veneto 7, tel. +39 0185 230 346, fax +39 0185 630 51.

Santa Margherita Ligure: I.A.T. Via XXV Aprile 2/B, tel. +39 0185 287 485, fax +39 0185 283 034.

Sestri Levante: I.A.T. Piazza S. Antonio 10, tel. +39 0185 457 011, fax +39 0185 459 575.

Municipal Websites

Comune di Rapallo: www.comune.rapallo.ge.it. In Italian, with many photos of Rapallo's historic sites.

Comune di Santa Margherita Ligure: www.comunesml.org. In Italian, with many photos of the most interesting sites in Santa Margherita Ligure.

Comune di Portofino: www.comune.portofino.genova.it. In English, with information on Portofino's history, monuments, and events.

Tourism Websites

Liguria Turismo: www.turismo.liguriainrete.it. Available in English. History and traditions, tourist information, sights, accommodations.

Parco Naturale Regionale di Portofino: Available in English. www.parks.it/parco.portofino. Portofino regional park information.

Consorzio Turistico Cinque Terre: www.cinqueterre.it. Lots of information about events, hiking trails, and regional cuisine.

Parco Nazionale delle Cinque Terre: www.parks.it/parco.nazionale. cinque.terre/. Available in English. Cinque Terre National Park maps and park information.

CHAPTER 2

LAGHI DI COMO E DI GARDA
Lakeside Retreats

immed by a crown of snow-capped mountains, Italy's northern
lakes have left their mark on travelers since Roman times. Pliny
the Younger, a Roman orator and statesman, built not one, but
two villas on Lake Como.

Leonardo da Vinci recorded his impressions of his voyage to Lake
Como in his painting *Virgin of the Rocks* (1508) and in the mysterious
vista behind the *Mona Lisa*. To the east, Lake Garda was a popular spot
for English writers and statesmen. D. H. Lawrence lived and wrote in
Gargnano, on the western shore, in the early 1900s, and Winston
Churchill often came to the lake to paint what he reportedly described as
its "Madonna blue" waters.

Along the lakeshores, luxuriant gardens thrive in the mild climate. On
Lake Como, two of Italy's most famous gardens are found at Villa Melzi
and Villa Carlotta. On Lake Garda, the vestiges of a once-thriving lemon
industry punctuate the landscape. In the lake gardens, you will find fountains decorated with water-themed allegorical statuary, terraces that offer
multiple perspectives to enjoy the view, and a profuse use of flowering
plants, especially rhododendrons and azaleas.

A multicultural palate influences the cuisine around the lakes, in
which you will find a unique combination of flavors born of mountain

and lake. The abundant freshwater fish that inhabit the lakes' waters (such as eel, pike, perch, and shad) figure heavily in local cooking. One specialty you may encounter is *missoltini,* a shad-like fish preserved in laurel leaves and used to flavor many dishes. Hearty fare from the Alps also plays a part. Buckwheat flour is often used as a base for pastas and crepes, and during the winter polenta is served with game meats and alpine cheeses.

For romantic outings, you can stroll along Varenna's "Lovers' Walk" at sunset, hike through wildflower-filled mountain pastures, or follow the wine route from Bardolino to Valpolicella.

Accommodations in Lakeside Retreats

BELLAGIO

Villa Serbelloni

If Bellagio can be called the "pearl on the lake," it must be due in part to the lustrous yellow-and-white Villa Serbelloni at the tip of its peninsula. In ancient times, Pliny the Younger built one of his lakeside villas on this site. He, like so many visitors to Bellagio, was drawn to the mild climate and clean mountain air.

Since its inauguration in 1873, the Grand Hotel Serbelloni, which shares this park-like setting with the famed villa of the same name, has been Bellagio's most prestigious hotel. The hotel was originally built as a summer home for a wealthy Milanese. The interiors are filled with frescoes and festoons, mythological scenes, and dramatic stuccoed ceilings. Outside, the hotel is surrounded with formal Italian gardens where camellias, lemon trees, bougainvillea, and flowering vines have grown dense and lush. The complex occupies the entire promontory of Bellagio; its privileged position offers some of the most spectacular views along the lake.

The hotel's interiors still have a patrician air, with period furnishings, richly painted thirty-foot ceilings, and grand windows that frame vistas of the lake and gardens. At the hotel's elegant restaurant, The Terrazza, you

can enjoy a dinner under the stars with the lakeshore villages' lights twinkling in the distance (note: jackets are required). The Royal Hall is an enormous and elegant dining room with coffered ceilings, inset mirrors, and parquet floors. There is also a simpler dining hall where breakfast is served under crystal chandeliers. If you're in the mood to act like a visiting dignitary, request the presidential suite with its marble columns, piano, and gilded ceilings. Otherwise, you'll find that many of the hotel's other rooms and suites continue to reflect the original layout of the aristocratic summer villa, with spacious, elegantly decorated rooms. Hotel amenities include a private lakeside beach, a health spa with European spa treatments, and a health club.

The gardens are open to the public for visits from April to October, from 11 A.M. to 4 P.M. Tickets for guided tours are available at the tourist office in Bellagio's Piazza della Chiesa.

GRAND HOTEL VILLA SERBELLONI, Via Roma 1, 22021 Bellagio (CO), tel. +39 031 950 216, fax +39 031 951 529, email inforequest@villaserbelloni.it, www.villaserbelloni.com. Driving directions from Milan: take the P5 highway to Monza, then continue north on highway S36 to Civate. Transfer to highway S639 for Malgrate, then to S583 to Bellagio. Open from April to November. Eighty-five rooms, doubles from EEE to EEEEE.

La Pergola

In the eighteenth century, the tiny hamlet of Pescalo was known all over Europe for its famed herbalist. Kings and dukes from as far away as Austria and Tuscany came to this tiny village on the lake to seek his cures. When herbal curatives went out of fashion, the house in which he practiced his trade became a nunnery. Today, the same spot is home to the charming hotel and restaurant La Pergola.

The building has changed very little and the idyllic fishing village of Pescalo still retains certain aspects of those ancient times. The flavor of the old convent is felt in the inn's architecture, with heavy stone staircases that lead to the upper floors and whitewashed, cross-vaulted ceilings overhead. The terrace restaurant is appropriately named, as its vine-covered pergola spans the lakeside, offering a shady spot to enjoy lunch or a romantic evening for two. In the winter months, the dining room, housed in the old chemist's laboratory with its beamed ceiling and tiled floors, is warm and cozy. The menu highlights local ingredients such as prized Tremezzo olive oil (cultivated just across the lake), wild mushrooms collected in the shady woods of the pre-Alps, cheeses from local farms, and, of course, that alpine-Italian staple, polenta. Guest rooms are tastefully furnished with antique bed frames and armoires; most have a view out over the lake. The center of Bellagio is just a ten-minute walk from the hotel.

LA PERGOLA, Piazza del Porto 4, 22021 Bellagio (CO), tel. +39 031 950 263, fax +39 031 950 253, email info@lapergolabellagio.it, www.lapergolabellagio.it. Driving directions from Milan: take the P5 highway to Monza, then continue north on highway S36 to Civate. Transfer to highway S639 for Malgrate, then to S583 to Bellagio. Eleven rooms; doubles from L.

CERNOBBIO

Villa d'Este

"The precise location of heaven on earth has never been established but it may very well be right here."

This declaration, by the late *San Francisco Chronicle* columnist Herb Caen, refers to one of the most luxurious hotels in the world, the Villa d'Este. This marvelous monument to the aristocratic taste of once upon a time began as a cardinal's summer estate in 1568. Even during the sixteenth century, the complex, then known as Villa Garrovo, was famed worldwide for its gardens and its architecture, inspiring a visit by the Sultan of Morocco (accompanied by his royal entourage), who came to glean decorating ideas for his own palaces. In 1815, Caroline of Brunswick, the Princess of Wales, purchased the property and renamed it "New Villa d'Este" (not to be confused with the villa of the same name at Tivoli). The princess completed many restorations and added Canova's famous sculpture, Eros and Psyche, to her private apartments. (The statue is now conserved in the hotel's Flora Room.) The terraced gardens were planted over many years; part is a Renaissance garden, part is a Victorian-style English garden. Since 1873, Villa d'Este has been an exclusive hotel, hosting such honeymooners as Frank Sinatra and Ava Gardner, Elizabeth Taylor and Nick Hilton, and the Duke and Duchess of Windsor. Although completely renovated and updated, the villa retains the authenticity of a seventeenth-century patrician estate. All the furnishings fit so perfectly you won't know what's original and what has been added over time. As you might expect, close attention is paid to every detail of a guest's stay at the Villa d'Este. A honeymoon spent here can be filled with leisurely walks through the gardens, a tour on the lake in one of the villa's wooden speedboats, and long sumptuous meals at the hotel's famed restaurant (see page 57). Three swimming pools, sailboats, canoes, waterskiing, and a spa are all at the guests' disposal. The villa also offers wedding services and can accommodate large receptions in the villa's gardens or in one of its many elegant halls.

VILLA D'ESTE, Via Regina 40, 22012 Cernobbio (CO), tel. +39 031 3481, fax +39 031 348 844, www.villadeste.it. Driving directions from Milan: take highway A8 and connect to highway A9, exit at Cernobbio. One hundred sixty-one rooms; doubles from EEEEE.

MANDELLO DEL LARIO

Villa delle Rose

If cavernous grand hotels are not your style and you are seeking some respite from the crowds, try Relais Villa delle Rose, a small, charming villa-inn on the Lago di Lecco (the southeastern fork of Lake Como). Over the years, the villa has served as a summer home for aristocratic families in the area; it was only recently transformed into an elegant inn, which also offers its grounds and halls for parties and wedding receptions. There are just six guest rooms in this intimate spot, decorated with period antiques, and each is named after a rose you will find in the villa's lakeside garden.

For wedding parties, tables can be set on the wide terrace directly in front of the villa with views over the lake. If you are honeymooning at the villa, the same spot is a great place to watch the sunset before dinner. Inside the villa, an ample hall on the main floor is large enough that one long "royal" table could be set for a party of forty guests, with the bride at one end, the groom at the other. The villa also has a rustic subterranean stone tavern, now used to host wine tastings in front of a massive stone fireplace. The gardens that span the lakeside are lined with stone columns entwined with flowering vines, which frame the view as you walk along the paths. In the south garden is a quiet gazebo where you can read in the shade and listen to the lake lapping against the shore below.

Whether you plan to stay or hold a wedding at the villa, you can enjoy the delicious local cuisine offered by the villa's restaurant along with wines from the family's private cellar.

Relais Villa delle Rose, Via Statale 125/127, 23826 Mandello del Lario (LC), tel. +39 0341 731 304, fax +39 0341 731 304, email villadellerose@ villadellerose.com, www.villadellerose.com. Driving directions from Milan: take the P5 highway to Monza, then continue north on highway S36 toward Civate, exit at Lierna. Six rooms; doubles from E to EEE.

GARDA

Locanda San Vigilio

Transparent waters, a mild climate, and a secluded setting make this spot on Garda's eastern shore one of the most romantic lakeside retreats. Lawrence Olivier and Vivian Leigh often sojourned here, and Winston Churchill and John Singer Sargent came here to paint the landscape. The Locanda San Vigilio has been receiving guests here since the 1500s.

The inn shares the point with the Baia delle Sirene ("Siren's Bay"), a small beach with ample areas for picnicking, and the historic Villa Guarenti. The villa was commissioned in the 1500s by a Veronese noble, Augostino Brenzoni. Signore Brenzoni was quite a romantic, and the villa's gardens are full of statuary bearing poems and inscriptions dedicated to his *amore*.

The Locanda itself is quiet and secluded. Each of the hotel's seven rooms is unique, and all but one have lake views. One room has a view over the "Stella" cliff, which locals claim is named after a lake nymph who was turned to stone after she rejected a Sicilian satyr's affections.

The inn's restaurant overlooks the lake, and in the summer months umbrella tables are set next to the arbor adjacent to the tiny harbor. After dinner, watch the sunset from the tiny rocky perch at the water's edge, or take a walk through the walled garden, whose lemon and orange trees are particularly fragrant in the spring months. Once you arrive, sightseeing may disappear from your agenda, but conveniently, Verona is just a forty-minute drive away.

Locanda San Vigilio, Punta San Vigilio, 37016 Garda (VR), tel. +39 045 725 6688, fax +39 045 627 8182, email info@punta-sanvigilio.it, www. punta-sanvigilio.it. Driving directions from Verona: take highway A22 and exit at Garda. Continue west on the lakeshore highway S249 to Punta San Vigilio. Fourteen rooms; doubles from EE to EEEEE.

GARDONE RIVIERA

Villa del Sogno

In the 1800s, Gardone Riviera, on the western side of Lake Garda, was one of the lake's most popular destinations, attracting heads of state and intellectuals to its resorts. The poet and hero Gabriele D'Annunzio chose this spot to build his strange and eccentric Vittoriale (Victory) monument and home, where he spent the last years of his life.

Near D'Annunzio's monument and gardens, set on a gentle hillside, you will find the Villa del Sogno. The mild climate and gentle breezes on this side of the lake provide the perfect atmosphere for the rare trees that fill Gardone's gardens; in their midst, this Liberty-style villa receives guests in the spirit of the old Riviera. The villa was built as a lake residence by an Austrian silk magnate in 1904 and still retains much of its original charm and style. The spacious guest rooms have hardwood floors and art nouveau furnishings. Stairs lead to the villa's own *piazzetta* where breakfast is served around a quaint well framed by wisteria. Surrounded by greenery, the villa also has a broad terrace with a swimming pool from which there's an unobstructed view over the lake.

VILLA DEL SOGNO, Via Zanardelli 107, 25083 Gardone Riviera (BS), tel. +39 0365 290 181, fax +39 0365 290 230, email info@villadelsogno.it, www.villadelsogno.it. Driving directions from Brescia or Verona: from highway A4, exit at Desenzano Garda. Continue north on highway S572 to Salò, connect to highway S45 north and exit at Gardone. Thirty-two rooms; doubles from EE to EEEE.

Villa Fiordaliso

At the end of the second world war, Claretta Petacci, Mussolini's young lover, stayed on the third floor of this villa on Lake Garda. Reportedly, she and Benito would meet in the moonlight at the nearby Torre di San Marco, one of the monuments built by Gabrielle D'Annunzio as part of his Citadel. Today, the tower has been appropriated for an American-style bar with an outdoor terrace, and the most romantic room in this inn by the lake is Claretta's suite, with its elegant antique furniture and spacious bathroom with alabaster fixtures.

The historic nineteenth-century villa is part of the Relais & Chateaux hotel group and an enchanting spot to spend a holiday. The hotel and its flower-filled gardens are nestled in a wooded park along the lakefront. Despite its Tuscan Renaissance appearance, the villa was built during Gardone's heyday, and many of its interior frescos weren't added until the 1920s. The six other lovely rooms are each named after a different flower; all enjoy views of the lake and gardens. All around the villa there are shady flower-filled gardens and lakeside paths from which to enjoy the view.

The hotel's restaurant offers seasonal cuisine in the villa's original dining room, which charms with its leaded glass windows and romantic candlelit tables. During warm weather, the restaurant also serves meals on the villa's terrace or in the garden.

VILLA FIORDALISO, Corso Zanardelli 132, 25083 Gardone Riviera (BS), tel. +39 0365 201 58, fax +39 0365 290 011, email fiordaliso@relaischateaux. com, www.villafiordaliso.it. Driving directions from Brescia or Verona: from highway A4, exit at Desenzano Garda. Continue north on highway S572 to Salò, connect to highway S45 north, and exit at Gardone. Closed from November 20 to February 10. Seven rooms; doubles from EE to EEEEE.

Tables for Two

BELLAGIO

da Silvio

Silvio is located in the peaceful fishing hamlet of Loppia, on a little hill with a view over Villa Melzi's blue domed chapel to the lake. Although the interior dining room is stark and modern, for summer dining there are two outdoor terraces, one covered with dense grapevines, the other an open terrace in front with a lake view. The restaurant and inn have been managed for four generations by the same family, who care for the property and the menus with passion and enthusiasm. Each day the owner's son Cristian goes out on the lake to procure fresh fish for the daily menu. In the kitchen, fresh seasonal ingredients from the surrounding farms are turned into a simple and flavorful menu of dishes for guests. A specialty of the house is the *gioie dello Chef* (joys of the chef)—freshly made crepes filled with seasonal cheeses, then baked in the oven and served with a simple tomato sauce. Silvio also has twenty-one modestly furnished guest rooms, some with lake views and balconies. After lunch you can tour the gardens at Villa Melzi, which are filled with giant azaleas, house-sized rhododendrons, Japanese maples, and take the tree-lined walk along the lake's edge (see page 74).

ALBERGO RISTORANTE SILVIO VIA CARCANO 12, Località Loppia, 22021 Bellagio (CO), tel. +39 031 950 322, fax +39 031 950 912, email info@ bellagiosilvio.com, www.bellagiosilvio.com. Driving directions from Milan: take the P5 highway to Monza, then continue north on highway S36 to Civate. Transfer to highway S639 for Malgrate, then to S583 to Bellagio. Closed from December 1 to February 15. One hundred fifty seats. Cost: E. Twenty-one rooms; doubles from L.

La Terrazza

La Terrazza at the Villa Serbelloni hotel is one of the lake's most highly rated restaurants. Its sunlit veranda facing the lake is an ideal setting for summer dinners. The restaurant's cuisine is influenced by the French style of cooking as well as the traditional and regional dishes of the area, and the service is impeccable. First courses are decidedly French in style and include dishes based on foie gras, quail's eggs, and caviar. For a first course, pastas are made in house each day and served in preparations like tagliolini tossed with smoked trout and broccoli, or *spaghetti al torchio* (from the press) with lake shrimp. The excellent main courses include pike served with a vegetable caponata in a basil emulsion or slow-cooked lamb loin in aromatic herbs and *lardo* (aged pork fatback). Chocolate lovers will want to save room for the "fantasy"— a lake of white chocolate soup with a floating chocolate fondant island, two types of chocolate mousse, and chocolates flavored with mint and Fernet. The ample wine list offers labels from Italy's best growing regions.

LA TERRAZZA (Grand Hotel Villa Serbelloni), 22021 Bellagio (CO), tel. +39 031 950 216, fax +39 031 951 529, www.villaserbelloni.it. Driving directions from Milan: take the P5 highway to Monza, then continue north on highway S36 to Civate. Transfer to highway S639 for Malgrate, then to S583 to Bellagio. Open for dinner only. Closed from November 15 to March 26. One hundred forty seats; reservations recommended. Please note that for gentlemen dining here, jackets are required. Cost: EEEEE.

CERNOBBIO

La Veranda

The glassed-in Veranda restaurant at the Villa d'Este is one of the most beautiful dining rooms in Europe. An enormous expanse of glass is all that separates the room from its spectacular view of the lake and the gardens below. In the summer, the glass is removed, letting in warm breezes into the elegant dining room. Royal blue and yellow striped cushions cover the restaurant's elegant gilt chairs, and the tables are set with crystal and fresh flowers. The dining room is usually filled with patrons who've come here to celebrate a special occasion in the romantic and refined ambience. The staff fawn over you without being intrusive, offering your choice of tasting and à la carte menus drawing on regional ingredients and lake fish. The restaurant's executive chef, Luciano Parolari, has been supervising Villa d'Este's kitchen for over twenty years and creates elegantly prepared haute Italian dishes.

LA VERANDA (Hotel Villa d'Este) 22012 Cernobbio (CO), tel. +39 031 348 1, fax +39 031 348 844, www.villadeste.it. Driving directions from Milan: take highway A8 and connect to highway A9, exit at Cernobbio. Closed from November to February. One hundred eighty seats, reservations recommended. Note: Men must wear jacket and tie for dinner. Cost: EEEEE.

COMO

Crotto del Lupo

Crotto del Lupo is set in a woodland park along the Swiss border. The restaurant's dishes are fashioned according to old mountain traditions and recipes. Traditional first courses include *pizzoccheri,* a dish made with layers of fresh buckwheat tagliatelle, cabbage, and potatoes, and *panzarotti,* the local version of ravioli. Oven-braised veal in white wine with sautéed mushrooms and the classic *stinco di vitella* (veal shank) are excellent main dishes to try here. When in season, the restaurant offers game meats served with polenta and locally made goat's milk cheese. Desserts include a classic chestnut mousse and an apple tart served with green apple sorbet. The wine list is dedicated to regional wines.

CROTTO DEL LUPO, Via Pisani Dossi 17, 22100 Como - Località Cardina (CO), tel. +39 031 570 881, www.crottodellupo.it. Driving directions: from Como, take highway S35 and exit at Via Bellinzona. Closed on Mondays and for the month of August. Reservations recommended. Cost: E.

Locanda dell'Oca Bianca

The Oca Bianca (White Goose) restaurant is set in a seventeenth-century farmhouse just a few kilometers from Como in Trecallo. The menu features a great selection of French and alpine cheeses as well as excellent *salumi* (cured meats) from the area. This is a good place to taste one of the staples of Lombard salumerie, *bresaola*—an air-dried salted beef filet aged for at least one month—and *caprino,* a fresh local goat cheese. Among the fresh pasta dishes, you can try one served with *missoltini,* a preserved fish that is first dried, then reconstituted in vinegar and dressed with olive oil. Among other dishes, the *strudel di verdura con fonduta di caprino* (vegetable strudel with goat-cheese fondue) may seem more Swiss than Italian; remember, you are only steps away from the border. For two to share, the kitchen will prepare roasted lamb and for dessert you can try the *bonet piemontese,* a chocolate-amaretto-flavored pudding from nearby Piedmont. The wine list has over 150 labels.

LOCANDA DELL'OCA BIANCA, Via Canturina 251, Località Trecallo, 22100 Como (CO), tel. +39 031 525 605, www. ocabianca.it. Driving directions: from Como, take highway S35 south and exit at Via Canturinia. Open for dinner only. Closed on Mondays. Fifty seats. Cost: EE.

Navedano

This restaurant's namesake, Navedan, was an officer who fought in the war for Italy's independence in 1859. When he retired from service, he chose this old mill in Camnago Volta as his peacetime home. In later years it became an osteria. As such, it has been managed by the Casartelli family for over one hundred years. The proprietors describe Navedano as a "restaurant within a greenhouse," and the dining rooms are always filled with fresh-cut flowers and flowering plants. There is also a pretty veranda planted with lemon trees, open in the summer for outdoor dining.

Chef-owner Mariella Casartelli prepares elegant, creative dishes inspired by the region's cuisine. Dinner might begin with *code di gamberi al fegato d'oca* (prawns with goose liver) or a terrine of local rabbit from the Orsi valley. The wines are well chosen, and there is a nice selection of grappas as well.

NAVEDANO, Via Pannilani, 22030 Camnago Volta (CO), tel. +39 031 308 080, fax +39 031 331 9016, www.ristorantenavedano.it. Driving directions: from the A9, exit at Como Sud. Closed on Tuesdays, from January 2 to 25, and from August 5 to 21. One hundred seats; reservations recommended. Cost: EEE.

MANDELLO DEL LARIO

Ricciolo

At Ricciolo, a small, family-managed restaurant, you can enjoy eating regional specialties along the lakeshore. There are two pretty dining rooms, and the wine list includes prestigious wines from all over the Italian peninsula. The *menu del lago,* which can be prepared for the entire table, takes diners on a tour through the best of the lake's fish. The menu begins with *siluro in agrodolce,* a concoction of Wels catfish in a sweet-sour sauce. Next, fresh tagliatelle are tossed with *salmerino* (Arctic char), black olives, and tomato. The next dish on the menu is the indispensable *lavarello,* (Pollan whitefish) prepared in white wine, and to finish the tour, *luccioperca* (pike) is served with lentils and coriander. For two, the chef will prepare his *padelada del lago*—his own unique interpretation of the classic paella of Valencia, with a combination of lake fish and golden rice.

Delicate desserts include pears in zabaione cream, a light gelatin of oranges in mandarin sauce, and, for chocolate lovers, crepes filled with a chocolate "surprise."

RICCIOLO, Via Provinciale 165 to Olcio, 23826 Mandello del Lario (LC), tel. +39 0341 732 546. Driving directions from Milan: take the P5 highway to Monza, then continue north on highway S36 toward Civate, exit at Lierna. Closed on Sunday evenings and Mondays, from December 26 to January 15, and from September 1 to 15. Thirty seats; reservations recommended. Cost: EE.

VARENNA

Vecchia Varenna

The Vecchia Varenna is a charming spot in the heart of Varenna, a wonderful medieval town on Lake Como's eastern shore. Owners Luca and Maurizio Castiglioni, together with their chef Giulio Molteni, prepare monthly menus based on the specialties of the territory. There is a warm dining room with bright blue and yellow tablecloths and a covered terrace that looks over the water. For a first course, begin with a warm lake fish salad or a smoked duck breast paired with Trevignano radicchio and walnut oil. For two, the chef will prepare a risotto *all'ubriaca,* a "drunken rice" dish with beans, bay leaves, and Inferno Mazer wine. Entrees include a stew of lake fish and tomato called *cacciucco,* or *salmerino* (Arctic char) in white wine and black-olive tapenade. There's a great selection of regional cheeses from local farms. For dessert, *latte in piedi* is a *panna cotta* (cooked cream) flavored with vanilla and served with berries from the woods.

VECCHIA VARENNA, Contrada Scoscesa 10, 23829 Varenna (LC), tel. +39 0341 830 793, www.vecchiavarenna.it. Driving directions from Milan: take the P5 highway to Monza, then continue north on highway S36 toward Civate, then continue north to Varenna. Closed on Mondays and for the month of January. Twenty-four seats; reservations recommended. Cost: EE.

DESENZANO DEL GARDA

Cavallino

Cavallino is one of the most prestigious restaurants on the Garda Riviera. Opened in 1983, it quickly became famous for its creative menus and world-class cuisine. In the summer you can reserve a table in the hydrangea-filled garden; at other times of the year, dine in the restaurant's pretty dining room adorned with antiques and oriental carpets. Three tasting menus can help you to decide among the creative dishes offered by the chef. First courses include a terrine of lake fish wrapped in savoy cabbage leaves with mint, or garbanzo bean soup with hand-cut noodles and prawns roasted in grappa. Other handmade pasta dishes include *agnolotti* filled with fennel and anise served with a ricotta chive sauce, gnocchi *di pesce di lago* (gnocchi with lake fish), or risotto with pike in a *gardesana* sauce (tomato, chili, garlic, parsley, and marjoram). The wine list includes over four hundred labels, with particular attention to wines from the region.

CAVALLINO, Via Gherla 30 (at Via Murachette), 25015 Desenzano del Garda (BS), tel. +39 030 912 0217, fax +39 030 991 2751, email info@ ristorantecavallino.it, www.ristorantecavallino.it. Driving directions: from highway A4 exit at Desenzano del Garda. Closed on Mondays; Tuesdays for lunch; and for holidays from November 5 to 25. Forty seats. Cost: EEE.

Esplanade

Esplanade sits directly on the lakeshore with an enchanting view across to Sirmione. In the dining room, generously spaced tables and light flooding in through the windows create a tranquil atmosphere. The cooking style is original and creative, making use of ingredients from the surrounding territory and the lake. Start with a rabbit salad with wild mustard greens or a gratin of zucchini, ricotta, chard, and crisp pancetta. The pasta courses include dishes like pumpkin gnocchi with goose liver, radicchio, and toasted hazelnuts, or whole-wheat tagliatelle with gilthead bream and spring vegetables. For an entrée, choose from a beef filet baked in a salt crust with thyme oil, suckling pig with marjoram and roasted potatoes, or farm-raised rabbit with rosemary and black olives. Desserts include a mascarpone cheese tart with fresh whipped cream and caramel sauce and a chocolate fondant mousse with rum cream. The wine includes excellent Italian labels as well as international wines.

ESPLANADE, Via Lario 10, 25015 Desenzano del Garda (BS), tel. +39 030 914 3361, email esplanade1@libero.it. Driving directions: from highway A4 exit at Desenzano del Garda. Closed on Wednesdays, Christmas Day, New Year's, and Easter. Forty seats; reservations recommended. Cost: EEE.

GARDA

Locanda San Vigilio

This little restaurant is on one of the most beautiful stretches along Lake Garda. It's reached by a tree-lined lane, then a tiny cobblestone street, which leads to the private lakeside pier. The restaurant, part of a charming inn (see page 53), occupies its own little point on the lake and has a covered veranda for dining with a view.

LOCANDA SAN VIGILIO, 37016 Garda (VR), tel. +39 045 725 6688, fax +39 045 725 6551, email info@punta-sanvigilio.it, www.punta-sanvigilio.it. Driving directions from Verona: take highway A22 and exit at Garda. Continue west on the lakeshore highway S249 to Punta San Vigilio. Cost: EE.

GARDONE RIVIERA

Lidò 84

Lidò 84 is right on the shore of Fasano del Garda, not far from the monumental former residence of the poet Gabriele D'Annunzio. On the restaurant's refined, sunlit waterfront terrace you can taste lake specialties and products from the surrounding farms of Brescia. A specialty of the house is spaghetti *all'astice* (spaghetti with lobster sauce), but you can also try preserved sardine filets, trout with prawns, or perch filet with capers. Finish your meal with a *semifreddo* (semi-frozen) custard flavored with chocolate and hazelnut.

After lunch, take a tour of D'Annunzio's citadel *Vittoriale,* where rooms are left as the poet used them, complete with his blue bathtub and souvenirs from heroic moments in his life, including the SVA aircraft D'Annunzio flew over Vienna in 1918 and the ship *Puglia* given to him by the Italian navy in 1925.

LIDÒ 84, Corso Zanardelli 168, 25083 Gardone Riviera (BS), tel. +39 0365 200 19. Driving directions from Brescia or Verona: from highway A4 exit at Desenzano Garda. Continue north on highway S572 to Salò, connect to highway S45 north, and exit at Gardone. Closed on Tuesdays and from December to February 15. Reservations recommended. Cost: EE.

Villa Fiordaliso

The Ristorante Fiordaliso is part of the elegant Villa Fiordaliso hotel (see page 54), situated in a green cove on the Lake Garda shore. In the kitchen, chef Riccardo Camanini carefully prepares an original menu. Excellent dishes to try include scallops roasted with artichokes and olives, risotto with river prawns and garden watercress, fatted duck liver with Spello beans and black radish salad, and grilled porcini mushrooms with celeriac and foie gras vinaigrette.

VILLA FIORDALISO, Corso Zanardelli 150, 25083 Gardone Riviera (BS), tel. +39 0365 201 58, fax +39 0365 290 011, email info@villafiordaliso.it, www.villafiordaliso.it. Driving directions from Brescia or Verona: from highway A4, exit at Desenzano Garda. Continue north on highway S572 to Salò, connect to highway S45 north, and exit at Gardone. Closed on Mondays; on Tuesdays for lunch; and from November 20 to February 10. Eighty seats; reservations recommended. Cost: EEEE.

SALÒ

Belle Époque

The dining room of the aptly named Belle Époque restaurant is filled with neoclassical columns and frescoes. The restaurant is part of the Romantik Hotel Laurin, a Liberty-style villa filled with romantic frescoes located in Salò, on Lake Garda's western shore. Under the restaurant's lofty ceilings you can enjoy a leisurely meal of swordfish carpaccio with roasted asparagus and sorrel, *farfalle* (butterfly) pasta with fresh hake puree and littleneck clams, and spit-roasted homemade lamb sausage with *farro* (spelt). For two, the kitchen is happy to offer specially prepared entrées to share, such as John Dory fish baked with olives, pear tomatoes, and potatoes, or lamb loin in myrtle with fava bean puree. The list of local and regional wines is ample. In the summer, reserve a table in the villa's quiet park. Since 1964, the Belle Époque has been a member of the Ristoranti di Buon Ricordo (see page xiii).

BELLE ÉPOQUE (Hotel Laurin) Viale Landi 4/9, 25087 Salò (BS), tel. +39 0365 220 22, fax +39 0365 223 82, email laurinbs@tin.it, www.laurinsalo.com. Driving directions from Brescia or Verona: from highway A4 exit at Desenzano Garda. Continue north on highway S572 to Salò. Forty-five seats; reservations recommended. Cost: EE. Hotel: EE to EEE.

SIRMIONE

La Rucola

Inside the Scagliere walls of old Sirmione, La Rucola is housed in an old stone building that was once used as a stable. Three intimate dining rooms hold romantic tables set with long white tablecloths and tall candles. Chefs Gionata and Elena Bignotti offer a variety of seasonal tasting menus. Dishes change often, but you might begin with a composition of marinated fish that includes a salmon *millefoglie* with soy rice, a terrine of swordfish, and seared tuna in lemon oil. If you chose a *grande degustazione* tasting menu, you will be offered a lemon raspberry *sorbetto* (ice) to prepare your palette for roasted lamb in an herb crust. The chefs prepare special desserts daily, and the excellent bread is made on the premises.

LA RUCOLA, Vicolo Strentelle 7, 25019 Sirmione (BS), tel. +39 030 916 326, www.ristorantelarucola.it. Closed on Thursdays. Twenty-six seats; reservations essential. Cost: EEE.

Vecchia Lugana

Along the state road from Verona to Brescia, the Vecchia Lugana has been managed since 1969 by the Ambrosi family. The restaurant's building was used in earlier days as a station for changing horses. The menu is updated seasonally to incorporate the freshest local ingredients. Pastas are made each day, and fresh fish from the lake is simply prepared. Some of the specialties are forest mushroom soup with river shrimp, *tortelloni* filled with eggplant and zucchini in thyme sauce, sea bass prepared Lombard style with beans and potatoes, and a venison filet with thyme and watercress with artichoke puree. For dessert, fresh fruit tarts are made by owner Pierantonio Ambrosi's mother, Alma, along with other delicious offerings. Pierantonio has carefully selected the wines that fill his cellar, including an especially cultivated selection of wines from Garda.

> VECCHIA LUGANA, Piazzale Vecchia Lugana 1, 25019 Lugana di Sirmione (BS), tel. +39 030 919 012, fax +39 030 990 4045, email vecchialugana@libero.it. Driving directions from Verona: take highway S11 and exit at Peschiera del Garda. During the month of November open only on Friday, Saturday, and Sunday evenings. Closed on Mondays and Tuesdays and from January 9 to February 22. Cost: EE.

Watching the Sunset

Torri del Benaco

Along the lakeshore, Torri del Benaco's paved pedestrian promenades offer some of the best spots to watch the sunset over Garda's surrounding mountains. For a perfect evening *passeggiata* (stroll) stroll, begin in front of the Castello Scaligero. The walkway passes under the castle walls, then continues onto the tiny harbor filled with sailboats. From the harbor, a tree-lined walk leads to the beach at the north end of town, a perfect sunset vantage point.

> TORRI DEL BENACO is on Garda's eastern shore, just ten minutes north of Garda.

Varenna's Lovers' Walk

Varenna's position on Lake Como's eastern shore makes this charming town a natural spot to enjoy a sunset over the lake. Along the waterfront, a pretty pedestrian walk called the *Passeggiata degli Innamorati* (Lovers' Walk) links Varenna's center with Olivedo, the ferry departure point. Varenna is famed for its demonstrative lovers; as you skirt the waterfront, you may see many young couples holding hands.

As an alternative, the Castello di Vezio, above the town, sets its closing hour by the sunset. The thirteenth-century castle is complete with turrets, knights' armor, and a drawbridge; for additional medieval flavor, in the summer there are falconry demonstrations.

From the castle's strategic perch there is a spectacular view over the lake. The castle is reached by a steep, but brief, footpath that departs from Via della Croce, to the left of the Hotel Monte Codeno. At the top of the climb you will reach the small piazza directly in front of Sant'Antonio Abate church and cemetery. At the end of the piazza is a green gate, beyond which lies the entrance to Castello di Vezio.

For information on seasonal opening and closing hours and for additional directions, see www.castellodivezio.it.

Romantic Lore and Local Festivals

The Legend of the Fiumelatte—Varenna

Varenna's Fiumelatte is the shortest river in Italy, just 250 meters from source to end. This tiny river, named after the milky color of its frothy water, is famous for its elusiveness. It's visible only between March and the first Sunday in October; then it disappears, imprisoned once more in the depths of the mysterious grotto from which it intermittently springs. The strange river has long fascinated scientists and adventurers; reportedly, even Leonardo da Vinci described it in his *Codice Atlantico.*

A sixteenth-century legend about the river tells the story of three local youths, all vying for the love of the same girl. Unsure how to choose between them, the maiden decided that whomever of the three could discover the source of the Fiumelatte would be her future mate. To prove their worthiness and courage, they lowered themselves into the cavern beneath the source. Days, weeks, months, and years passed before the three emerged, recounting fantastic tales of the world inside the mountain. The first youth told a tale of being offered a goblet filled with a magical potion by a siren. As long as he drank, he was transported to heavenly places filled with delights, but as soon as the elixir was gone, he found that he was in a deep abyss with no way out. The second youth told of following glowing lights down a long corridor to a place filled with beautiful dancing maidens. Here, too, the story did not end well, for at the end of their song he found he was in a cold and ugly cavern surrounded by toads and bats. The third youth was so shaken by his experience that he could only remain mute and trembling. Needless to say, since then no one has ever attempted to discover the river's mysterious source.

After you see the Fiumelatte, it's a short walk to the ruins of the old Baluardo, an ancient military observation point. From the fortress's highest lookout, there is a perfect panorama of the lake, and it's a great spot for watching the sun go down over the lake.

Each year on March 25 the villagers honor the return of the Fiumelatte on the *Festa dell'Annunciazione* (Feast of the Annunciation). Villagers carry a sacred Madonna through the tiny village streets to the source.

Nodi d'Amore (Love Knots)—Valeggio sul Mincio

Valeggio sul Mincio, just south of Peschiera sul Garda, is known for a specialty pasta called the *nodo d'amore* (love knot), based on a local legend. People come from all over to taste these golden tortellini, which have been made in Valeggio for centuries.

Once upon a time, locals say, the Mincio river was populated by beautiful water nymphs. At night they liked to dance on the river banks under the castle walls, but always disguised themselves as ugly old witches to prevent any passersby from falling under the spell of their beauty. One day, a group of soldiers led by a local count arrived at the castle and camped along the river banks. That night, while they slept, the water nymphs danced between the sleeping men in the firelight. One of the soldiers, a young captain named Malco, was awakened by the witches and jumped up, chasing them back toward the river. The nymph Silvia lost her cape and revealed that she was actually a beautiful water nymph. Malco fell madly in love with her, and she with him. At sunrise, Silvia was forced to return to the river, but she left behind a token of her love in the form of a golden handkerchief tied in a knot.

The next day the camp was visited by a group of mysterious emissaries who treated the soldiers to a feast and entertained them with dancing. Malco immediately recognized one of the veiled dancers as Silvia the water nymph, and the two began exchanging furtive glances. Isabella, a young noblewoman who was traveling with the group of soldiers, became jealous, as she had always hoped to win Malco for herself. She immediately denounced Silvia as a witch; upon hearing this, the Count ordered that Silvia be arrested. To save her, Malco created a distraction and the two escaped to the river. The soldiers searched everywhere, but the only trace they ever found was the knotted golden handkerchief, dropped on the riverbank.

Today, over forty restaurants in Valeggio produce *nodi d'amore,* the specialty inspired by this ancient love story. Each restaurant adapts the recipe slightly, adding their own signature to the dish. You can also find the *nodi d'amore* at Valeggio's *pastifici* (pasta makers) shops, along with many other local varieties of tortellini and specialty pastas.

Pastifici in Valeggio where you can find *nodi d'amore*:
AL CASTELLO, Via Jacopo Foroni 22. tel. +39 045 795 1301
AL PONTE, Via Michelangelo 6 Borghetto. tel. +39 045 637 0074
AL RE DEL TORTELLINO, Via S. Rocco 25. tel. +39 045 795 0523
ARTIGIANALE TORTELLINO DI VALEGGIO, Via Sala 24. tel. +39 045 795 1630
ARTIGIANALE MENINI, Via S. Rocco 6. tel. +39 045 795 0003
LA TAIADELA, Via Murari 33. tel. +39 045 795 1712

Palio del Baradello—Como

The Palio del Baradello is held in Como the first two weeks in September each year. This historic palio commemorates the arrival of Barbarossa in Como in 1159. To Como, Barbarossa's defeat of Milan meant protection from the sieges and heavy taxation they had been subjected to by Milan.

Each year the town celebrates with two weeks of music, theatrical events, and feasting which lead up to the medieval palio. Five hundred costumed participants are led by Barbarossa and his consort Beatrice di Borgogna for the opening of the event. During the contest, teams compete for a silk banner in three contests: jousting on horseback, a three-kilometer wooden wheelbarrow race, and a classic regatta on the lake.

For more information, contact: APT—Azienda di Promozione Turistica di Como, Piazza Cavour 17, 22100 Como, tel. +39 031 330 0111, www.lakecomo.it.

Palio delle Contrade—Garda

Each year on the Feast of Madonna Assunta (August 15), the Palio delle Contrade is held on Lake Garda. Teams compete in a regatta with rowers who dramatically paddle the boats while standing. Each *contrada* (district) bears a colored banner with their team's colors and one of the lake's fish as their symbol. Before the regatta the rowers march through the streets of the town, proudly bearing their long oars on their shoulders. At nine o'clock, it's *"Barche in acqua"* (boats in the water) and the race begins. After three rounds, a winner emerges and is celebrated with fireworks over the lake.

The Palio delle Contrade is organized by the Comune di Garda, tel. +39 045 620 8428.

Picnic Spots

Il Bastione (The Fortress)—Riva del Garda

Riva del Garda is at the north end of Lake Garda in a position naturally protected by the surrounding mountains. Above the town are the ruins of an ancient bastion built in 1507 to protect the citizens of Riva. Although the fortress successfully protected the town through many battles, in the 1700s the garrison was almost completely destroyed by invading French troops. Today, most of the fortress lies in ruins and is a picturesque and secluded spot to enjoy a picnic with a view over the northern part of the

lake. The bastion can only be reached by a footpath from northeastern Riva. The climb takes fifteen minutes.

Monte Baldo—A View from Fifty-Seven Hundred Feet

Monte Baldo's peaks make up the highest mountain chain surrounding Lake Garda. From the medieval town of Malcesine, an updated funicular climbs the mountain's slopes, bringing passengers to fifty-seven hundred feet in a matter of minutes. The Tratto Spino summit has unparalleled views of the Dolomites to the west and Lake Garda to the south. It's the departure point for hikes throughout the mountains, to idyllic wildflower-filled meadows, perfect for a picnic above the lake. For adventure seekers, paragliders and bicycles are also allowed inside the funicular.

Before or after exploring the mountain, you can learn about the natural habitat by visiting Malcesine's medieval Scaliger castle, which houses a museum dedicated to the flora, fauna, and geology of Mount Baldo.

The funicular is open April to November and departs every half hour starting at 8 A.M.

ALPINE PICNICS—ADDRESSES AND PRACTICAL INFORMATION

All of the lakes are surrounded by natural parks and protected hiking trails. For your authentic alpine picnic, you'll need rustic peasant-style bread, *speck* (a dried cured beef often spiced with juniper), cheeses from alpine pastures, and some fresh woodland fruits or berries. The farmers' markets held every day in various towns around the lakes are among the best places to find picnic provisions.

Farmers' Markets on Lake Garda

LIMONE SUL GARDA: First and third Tuesdays of the month along Via Lungalago Marconi.

TIGNALE: Tuesday mornings in Via Badiale Gardola.

GARGNANO: Every other Wednesday in Via Zanardelli.

SALÒ: Each Saturday morning.

DESENZANO DEL GARDA: Tuesdays.

BARDOLINO: Thursdays.

GARDA: Fridays.

MALCESINE: Saturdays.

RIVA DEL GARDA: In winter, the second Wednesday of the month; from June to September, the second and the fourth Wednesday of the month.

Farmers' Markets on Lake Como

BELLAGIO: The third Wednesday of the month.

Tremezzo, Moscazzano: Thursdays (these markets specialize in cheeses).

Romantic Excursions

From Bardolino to Valpolicella Along the Wine Route

Each September the lakeshore town of Bardolino hosts the *Festa dell'Uva* (Grape Festival) where vintners set up booths in the town's square and offer *degustazioni* (tastings) of Bardolino's famous wines.

During the rest of the year, you can taste regional wines by following the road that winds through the Colli Lessini and between Bardolino and Valpolicella's vineyards. Departing from Bardolino, the road that passes through the hamlets of Sant'Ambrogio di Valpolicella, San Pietro in Cariano, Pedemonte, Fumane, Negrar, and then on to Verona is surrounded by vineyards. Along the road you will find some of the region's best wineries.

FROM BARDOLINO TO VALPOLICELLA—ADDRESSES AND PRACTICAL INFORMATION

Valpolicella.it is the official portal of the Valpolicella region. The site has information about the region's varietals, wines, and wine makers. www.valpolicella.it.

WINERIES

BARDOLINO

GUERRIERI-RIZZARDI offers tours of the estate's lakeside gardens, the palace orchards, and the winery's ancient cellars from April to October. Afterward, you can taste the estate's wines in the cellar museum. Guerrieri Rizzardi, Via Verdi 4, Bardolino, tel. +39 045 721 0028, fax +39 045 721 0704, email visite@guerrieri-rizzardi.it, www.guerrieri-rizzardi.it.

SANT'AMBROGIO DI VALPOLICELLA

The SERÈGO ALIGHIERI estate is owned by descendants of the poet Dante Alighieri. On the farm, wines and other products are available for sale. Tastings for groups can be organized on the premises. Serègo Alighieri, 37020 Gargagnago di Valpolicella (VR), tel. +39 045 770 3622, fax +39 045 770 3523, email serego@easyasp.it, www.seregoalighieri.it. (See page 122 for more information about accommodations at Serègo Alighieri.)

FUMANE

The ALLEGRINI estate dates back to 1557, when Allegrino Allegrini acquired the right to use waters from local springs to irrigate his vines. By 1616, the Allegrini family was among the largest landholders in the region. Since those days the family has continued to cultivate and manage its Valpolicella estate, with vines in Fumane, Sant'Ambrogio, and San Pietro in Cariano, from which they blend some of the region's most esteemed Amarone wines. Allegrini, Via Giare 9/11, 37022 Fumane, tel. +39 045 683 2011, fax +39 045 770 1774, email info@allegrini.it, www.allegrini.it. The winery is open for visits Monday through Friday, 8:30 A.M. to 12:30 P.M. and 2:30 P.M. to 6:30 P.M. Tours are by appointment only.

LE SALETTE has been operating as a wine estate since the early 1900s. Their vineyards are in the northern section of Fumane, directly below the convent of Madonna della Salette. Le Salette, Via Pio Brugnoli 11/C, 37022 Fumane, tel. +39 045 770 1027, fax +39 045 683 1733, email lesalette@valpolicella.it. The winery is open for visits Monday through Saturday, 8:30 A.M. to 12:30 P.M. and from 2:00 P.M. to 7:00 P.M.

NEGRAR

GIUSEPPE QUINTARELLI's family came to this small hamlet just outside of Negrar in 1924. The winery is down a hidden lane amid olive and cypress trees. Quintarelli still uses the traditional methods of winemaking passed down to him by his father. His Alzero wines, blended from Cabernet Franc, Cabernet Sauvignon, and Merlot grapes, are aged in Slavonian casks—a signature of the Quintarelli style. As in the old days, wine labels are still hand glued onto the bottles. Giuseppe Quintarelli, Via Cerè 1, 37024 Negrar, tel. +39 045 750 0016. Visits to the winery are by appointment only.

LE RAGOSE enjoys one of Valpolicella's prettiest views. In 1969 the estate was rescued by enologist Arnaldo Galli and his wife Marta Bortoletto. Their estate extends over forty acres of vineyards situated in an ideal climate for the *appassimento* (drying) of the grapes. The family produces highly rated quality wines that include Amarone, Valpolicella Classico, and Chardonnay. Le Ragose, Via Ragose 1, 37024 Arbizzano di Negrar, tel. +39 045 751 3241, fax +39 045 751 3171, email leragose@leragose.com, www.leragose.com.

VILLA SPINOSA is in the heart of the village of Jago, at the foot of the Masua hills. The villa at the center of the estate dates to the 1800s and is surrounded by an elegant Italian garden. During the summer, the garden is open to the public and is used for summer concerts. Behind the villa, the *rustici* (traditional rural farm buildings) house the cellars. Enrico Cascella

Spinosa has been running the estate since the 1980s. The wines are complex and aromatic, blended from the estate's thirty-five acres of vineyards. Varietals include Corvina Veronese, Rondinella, and Molinella. Villa Spinosa, Località Jago, 37024 Negrar, tel. and fax +39 045 750 0093, email villaspinosa@valpolicella.it. Visits to the winery are by appointment only.

SAN PIETRO IN CARIANO

BRIGALDARA is just outside the village of San Floriano, at the entrance of the Marano valley, atop a hilly knoll. To reach the neoclassical villa, you follow a long tamped-earth drive through the lower sections of the estate's Corvina and Corvinone vines. Next to the villa, centered in a large park, are the farm houses with the recently restored wine cellars. Brigaldara, Via Brigaldara 20, 37020 San Pietro in Cariano, tel. +39 045 770 1055, fax +39 045 683 4525, email brigaldara@valpolicella.it. Visits to the winery are by appointment only.

PEDEMONTE

The SPERI family has been producing wines since 1874, and they are considered a bellwether in the evolution of winemaking in the region. Their Amarone wines are among the region's most highly rated wines, and they also produce an excellent Recioto. Speri, Frazione Pedemonte, Via Fontana 14, 37020 San Pietro in Cariano, tel. +39 045 770 1154, www.speri.com.

Gardens at Villa Melzi

Just a few minutes walk from the center of Bellagio, Villa Melzi is a pearl-like summer residence built in the 1800s. One of many villas that sit right on the lakeshore, it was built with double staircases that conduct visitors arriving from the lake up to the villa. Today, most come to the villa to take a quiet stroll through the gardens, which have views of the Grigna mountains across the lake. Broad grass esplanades flank each side of the villa and lead to the family's private chapel. Shady paths skirt the water's edge, lined with pollarded trees. The terraced gardens above the villa feature giant azaleas, twenty-foot-tall rhododendrons (in full bloom beginning in April or May), and Japanese maples, with ferns flourishing in their

cool shade. Under the tulip trees you might discover archeological relics, such as Roman sarcophagi or hidden grottoes.

VILLA MELZI, Lungolario Marconi, Bellagio (Co), tel. +39 02 869 98647 and +39 02 869 11307, email villamelzi@infoparchi.com. Open March through October from 9 A.M. to 6 P.M. daily.

Summer Concerts at Villa Carlotta

One of the most famous of the villas on the western edge of Lake Como, Villa Carlotta is surrounded by seventeen acres of gardens. It was built in 1690 as a summer house for Marquis Giorgio Clerici, an important figure during the Spanish and Austrian occupation of Milan. He is responsible for the villa's baroque-style interior decorations and the oldest sections of the Italian garden. Later, the villa was given as a wedding present to Carlotta, daughter of princess Marianna di Nassau and prince Albert of Prussia. Carlotta greatly expanded the villa's gardens, and the villa has carried her name ever since.

In the luxurious gardens, giant sequoia, banana palms, citrus pergolas, orchids, rhododendrons, azaleas, jasmine, roses, and Japanese maples flourish. Among them are neoclassical statues and marble staircases.

In the summer, classical concerts are held in the villa's monumental Marble Hall. The Marble Hall is just one of the recently restored halls that are part of the villa's museum, which includes works by Canova and Hayez.

The summer concert series begins at the end of June and continues throughout the summer months. VILLA CARLOTTA, Via Regina 2, 22019 Tremezzo (Co), tel. +39 0344 404 05, fax. +39 0344 436 89, www.villa carlotta.it.

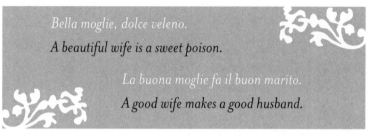

Bella moglie, dolce veleno.
A beautiful wife is a sweet poison.

La buona moglie fa il buon marito.
A good wife makes a good husband.

Weddings on Lake Como

CIVIL CEREMONIES

Palazzo Cernezzi and Villa Olmo—Como

The city of Como holds civil wedding ceremonies in two historic venues. Weddings held Monday through Friday are conducted in the Sala Consiliare in Palazzo Cernezzi, the city hall. Weddings held on Saturdays at noon are conducted in Villa Olmo's *Sala Ovale* (Oval Room) in Via Cantoni.

Since 1853 Palazzo Cernezzi has housed the city's municipal offices. The palace consists of a group of seventeenth-century palazzos unified with a central courtyard surrounded by archways. The halls on the palace's upper floors have coffered ceilings, and one of the rooms on the ground floor is decorated with seventeenth-century frescos depicting Como's military prowess.

Built at the end of the 1700s for the Odescalchi family, Villa Olmo is a palatial complex in neoclassical style, with spacious formal Italian gardens between the villa and the lake. The gardens feature geometric box hedges and topiary, a marvelous fountain with cherubs and water creatures sculpted by the Milanese artist Oldofredi, and statues of ancient deities. The villa is filled with richly decorated halls, but the Oval Room, where wedding ceremonies are held, is regarded as one of the most beautiful. The semi-elliptical room's large fresco depicts the marriage of a young maiden to the God of War, with Mount Olympus in the background—a symbolic representation of Napoleon's union with the Cisalpine Republic.

For civil weddings in Como, please contact the marriage office at Ufficio matrimoni, PALAZZO COMUNALE, Via Bertinelli, tel. +39 031 252 240, fax +39 031 252 247, email guanci.leonardo@comune.como.it. Cost: EE.

PALAZZO CERNEZZI, Via Vittorio Emanuele II 97, 22100 Como (CO). Weddings at Palazzo Cernezzi are held Monday through Friday, 9:00 A.M. to 1:30 P.M.

VILLA OLMO, Via Cantoni 1, 22100 Como (CO). Weddings at Villa Olmo are held Saturday only, from 8:30 A.M. to 12:30 P.M. The villa's public gardens are open for visits year-round.

CEREMONY AND RECEPTION LOCATIONS

Villa Camilla

Santa Maria Rezzonico is one of the prettiest towns on Lake Como. Red-tile-roofed houses cascade down to the lake's northwestern shore, and porticos, archways, and narrow winding streets invite exploration. There is even a grey stone castle with characteristic battlements. Near the village, the ancient Roman road, the Via Regina, crosses Santa Maria Rezzonico's territory through chestnut woods and vineyards. Along one stretch you can find the incised stone marker on the outskirts of Castellaccio, commemorating the scene of a crime of passion that dates to 1612. According to local legend, a country squire named Ficano had planned to lay a claim of *jus primae noctis* (the right of first night) on a local girl.

When he arrived, the young girl's husband-to-be lay in wait disguised as the girl. To defend her honor, he slew the squire.

Villa Camilla lies just south of the town center in the hamlet of Molvedo. An iron gate draped with climbing roses opens to reveal a pretty villa on a green hill. The modest ninteenth-century villa has always belonged to the same Milanese family, who, like many others, chose to summer in Como. The villa faces southeast, ensuring warm sunny days and mild evenings for summer weddings on its grounds. The garden, filled with sequoia, cedar trees, and palms, offers a view that encompasses all three legs of Lake Como.

Inside, the villa rooms are decorated with original mosaic floors and carefully crafted marquetry. Large picture windows and grand glass doors open onto the garden and lake. The villa has been recently restored and has seven comfortable bedrooms that can be used as guest rooms for the bridal party. The villa is managed by Vieffe Studio, an organization that specializes in wedding and event planning. They can assist you with catering, floral arrangements, music, and even wedding clothes.

> The villa can accommodate 120 guests for seated dinners indoors or up to 80 guests in the park. VILLA CAMILLA, Frazione Molvedo, 22010 Santa Maria Rezzonico (CO), tel. +39 02 781 503, fax +39 02 445 0690, email vieffestudio@tiscali.it, www.villacamilla.it. Seven rooms; doubles from EE. Cost: EE to EEE.

Villa del Bono

Just south of Lake Como, Villa del Bono is a nineteenth-century villa built in Renaissance revival style. Its expansive interiors are filled with Tuscan-inspired architectural details, which include marble archways, sculpted columns, colored marble inlaid floors, and carved fireplaces with painted heraldic emblems.

The villa was built for a wealthy manufacturing family who owned it until the Conti dei Bono purchased it in 1936. A warm, inviting atmosphere extends to every space. Inside, the corridors are lined with old family portraits of former counts who spent their holidays here. Tuscan-style antiques grace the halls. A grand entrance staircase leads to the large dining room, which has parquet floors and rich wood wainscoting encircled by a golden Roman inscription. Sit-down receptions can be held either here or outside in the villa's twelve-acre park. The park and gardens have large expanses of green lawns and original specimen plantings. The large upper terrace offers views over the pre-Alps and the tiny lakes of the Alta Brianza.

> The villa can accommodate receptions of 50 to 180 guests and is open year-round. VILLA DEL BONO, Via Cadorna 38, 23894 Cremella (LC), tel. +39 02 760 23764, email amdelbo@tin.it, www.villadelbono.it.

Villa Perego di Cremnago

Villa Perego is part of a vast landed estate that has belonged to the Perego family since the sixteenth century. In 1740, the illustrious humanist Don Giovanni Perego initiated work on the villa, which utilized part of foundations of a preexisting building that stood on the site. Three important architects had a hand in shaping the complex. Carlo Giuseppe Merlo laid the plans for the villa, while the facade and the splendid staircase that joins the Italian garden to the English park are attributed to Piermarini, who also designed the Scala theater in Milan. Piermarini often collaborated with Simone Cantoni, who assisted with the construction of the villa's horse stables, its outbuildings, and the surrounding gardens' design. The villa's interiors are filled with precious artworks, original furnishings, and a magnificent library, all well preserved by the Perego family.

On the palace grounds is a luminous glassed-in greenhouse (the *limonaia*) and majestic neoclassical stables. The splendid Italian garden has geometric parterres planted with vibrant red begonia and sage among a multitude of other flowers. A boxwood parterre leads to ornate balustraded terraces overlooking the village. The terraces are lined with statuary by Orazio Marinali, considered to be the most important Venetian sculptor of the 1600s. From here, the garden rises to a wood of cypress, magnolia, Lebanese cedar, and weeping European beech.

> The entire complex (villa, chapel, greenhouse, and stables) is available to visit by appointment by contacting Amministrazione Nobili Perego di Cremnago, tel. +39 031 696 078 and +39 02 760 03694. The garden is open

for visits year-round, while the Palazzo is open from April 1 to October 3. The villa can host receptions for up to 150 guests. VILLA PEREGO DI CREMNAGO, Via Perego 2, 22044 Cremnago di Inverigo (CO), tel. and fax +39 02 760 03694 and tel. +39 031 696 078, www.unistoric.org. Driving directions from Milan: take highway P5 toward Monza and connect to highway S36 at Carate Brianza. Continue to Inverigo and exit at Viale Zara.

Villa Serbelloni

The Villa Serbelloni holds weddings either in its beautiful gardens or indoors in one of the villa's sumptuously decorated halls (see page 48).

Sites for ceremonies and receptions include two elaborately decorated halls and the villa's rambling gardens. The villa can accommodate receptions for eighty to four hundred guests.

GRAND HOTEL VILLA SERBELLONI, Via Roma 1, 22021 Bellagio (CO), tel. +39 031 950 216, fax +39 031 951 529, email inforequest@villaserbelloni.it, www.villaserbelloni.com. Driving directions from Milan: take the P5 highway to Monza, then continue north on highway S36 to Civate. Transfer to highway S639 for Malgrate, then to S583 to Bellagio. Open from April through late November. Eighty-five rooms; doubles from EEE to EEEEE. Cost: EEEE.

Villa d'Este

The Villa d'Este holds weddings in its monumental halls and majestic gardens (see page 51).

Sites for ceremonies and receptions include four reception halls with a capacity of up to four hundred guests and the villa's elegant garden.

VILLA D'ESTE, Via Regina 40, 22012 Cernobbio (CO), tel. +39 031 348 1, fax +39 031 348 844, www.villadeste.it. Driving directions from Milan: take highway A8 and connect to highway A9, exit at Cernobbio. One hundred sixty-one rooms; doubles from EEEE to EEEEE. Cost: EEEE.

Villa delle Rose

Villa delle Rose is a small patrician villa on Como's eastern shore. Small weddings can be held in the villa's dining room or in the lakefront garden (see page 52).

Sites for ceremonies and receptions include a large interior hall, with room for forty seated guests, and the large lakeshore garden. The villa can accommodate receptions for 40 to 120 guests.

RELAIS VILLA DELLE ROSE, Via Statale 125/127, 23826 Mandello del Lario (LC), tel. +39 0341 731 304, fax +39 0341 731 304, email villadellerose@villadellerose.com, www.villadellerose.com. Driving directions from Milan: take the P5 highway to Monza, then continue north on highway S36 toward Civate, exit at Lierna. Six rooms; doubles from E to EEE. Cost: upon request.

Practical Information—Lago di Como

GETTING THERE
By air: The closest airports are Milano Malpensa (airport code MXP) and Milano Linate (airport code LIN). Both airports in Milan post information online at www.sea-aeroportimilano.it.

By car From Milan highway A9 leads to Como. Ring roads circle the entire lake.

By train: Regular rail service connects Como and Lecco with Milan. Schedules and information are available on the official site for Italy's state railway, www.fs-on-line.com.

By boat: Hydrofoil and ferry service is available from many cities along the lake to Como. Operated by Navigazione Lago di Como, Via per Cerbobbio 18, Como. tel. +39 031 579 211. See www.navigazionelaghi.it for maps and timetables.

WHEN TO GO
Most lake resorts close for winter December through February. High season begins in late May and continues through the end of September.

Official Tourist Information Offices and Websites

APT—Azienda di Promozione Turistica (Tourist Promotion Agency)

IAT—Ufficio Informazione e di Accoglienza Turistica (Tourist Information and Hospitality Office)

Como: A.P.T. Piazza Cavour 17, tel. +39 031 330 0111, fax +39 031 261 152, email lakecomo@tin.it, www.lakecomo.it.

Bellagio: I.A.T. in Piazza Mazzini and at Pontile Imbarcadero, tel. +39 031 950 204.

Cernobbio: I.A.T. Via Regina 33/B, tel. and fax +39 031 510 198.

Lecco: A.P.T. Via N.Sauro 6, tel. +39 0341 362 360, fax +39 0341 286 231, email info@aptlecco.com, www.aptlecco.com.

Tourism Websites

Lago di Como portal: www.comolago.com. Available in English with information on local events, itineraries, excursions, and hiking and mountain biking routes.

Comune of Bellagio: The city of Bellagio maintains a very informative site in English, www.bellagiocomune.it.

Practical Information—Lago di Garda

Getting There

By air: Milano Malpensa (airport code MXP) and Milano Linate (airport code LIN) are both just over an hour away from Desenzano del Garda. Both airports in Milan post information online at www.sea-aeroportimilano.it. Connections within Europe can be made to Verona's Vallerio Cattullo airport (airport code VRN); schedules are available at www.aeroportidelgarda.it.

By car: from Milan or Verona, take highway A4 and exit at Peschiera del Garda, Desenzano, or Sirmione.

By train: Regular rail service connects Peschiera del Garda, Desenzano, and Sirmione with Milan and Verona. Schedules and information are available on the official site for Italy's state railway, www.fs-on-line.com.

By boat: Hydrofoil and ferry service connects many of the towns along the lake. Operated by Navigazione Lago di Garda, Piazza Matteotti - 25015 Desenzano (BS), tel. +39 030 914 9511. See www.navigazionelaghi.it for maps and timetables.

When to Go

Most lake resorts close for winter, December through February. High season begins in May and continues through September.

Helpful Addresses

Official Tourist Information Offices and Websites

APT—Azienda di Promozione Turistica (Tourist Promotion Agency)

IAT—Ufficio Informazione e di Accoglienza Turistica (Tourist Information and Hospitality Office)

APT Garda Veneto www.aptgardaveneto.com. This is the official website for the Garda tourist board. It offers information on accommodations and events and also has area maps.

Gardone Riviera: I.A.T. Corso Repubblica 35, tel. and fax +39 0365 203 47.

Sirmione: I.A.T. Viale Marconi 2, tel. +39 030 916 114, fax +39 030 916 222.

Tourism Websites

Lago di Garda Magazine (www.lagodigardamagazine.com) is an excellent source for information about the individual towns that encircle the lake.

CHAPTER 3

VENETO

Venetian Palazzi and Patrician Garden Villas

VENICE

Venice has always been a favorite destination for romantic travelers. The city's floating islands, with their graceful palazzi and gentle waterways, have beautiful vistas in every direction and quiet squares where you can watch the world go by. To make the experience even more delightful, you can stay in a historic Gothic palazzo. The palazzi are extravagant by today's standards, but they were originally designed to serve as a practical combination of family home and warehouse, accommodating the needs of Venetian merchant families. The Ca', as the palaces are called in dialect, were constructed for an arrival by boat, where heavily decorated façades greeted visitors. The ground floor was simply appointed for business and storage, while the second floor (*piano nobile*) was elaborately decorated to impress and entertain guests. Many of the palaces still have working *porte d'acqua* (water doors), which allow a dramatic arrival by gondola.

Some of the most famous palaces, like the Palazzo Dandolo, have been restored into hotels; others, like the Palazzo Pisani Moretta, open their doors for gala occasions as they did in the heyday of the Venetian Republic.

Once you've settled in to your own Venetian palace, spend an afternoon wandering through the city's *bacari* (wine bars), or plan a day trip to tour the Lido by bicycle.

Accommodations in Venetian Palazzi

Palazzi at the Hotel Cipriani

When the Hotel Cipriani first opened in the 1950s, it was treasured as a summer escape from the heat and crowds of the main islands. Today it is still one of the most luxurious places to stay in the lagoon, surrounded by gardens and its own swimming pool. The Cipriani offers every conceivable luxurious amenity to its guests, including chauffeured *motoscafi* (speed boats) from the airport and a docking pier for luxury yachts. In recent years the Cipriani took over two historic palaces on the Giudecca and now opens them to guests who desire to stay in a Venetian palazzo. Palazzetto Nani Barbaro and Palazzo Vendramin are on the opposite side of the Giudecca from the Cipriani, in a privileged position that looks directly across the canal to Piazza San Marco. Between both villas there are a total of fifteen spacious rooms, each individually furnished with Venetian antiques. There are five deluxe junior suites in the Palazzetto Nani Barbaro and a special junior suite in the Palazzo Vendramin. Some of the apartments have private terraces and gardens and each has a kitchenette and a bar. As if it weren't enough just to be living in an atmosphere of privilege, you can use the hotel's butler service—at the touch of a button you'll be attended by your own staff of white-gloved maids, valets, and butlers.

Next to the palazzi, Hotel Cipriani has renovated three large buildings, which are now used for gala events and sumptuous wedding feasts. The *Granai della Repubblica*, as they are called, are three cavernous interconnecting buildings built by the Venetian republic as storehouses for trade goods that moved in and out of the port in the nineteenth century. Acquired by the Cipriani, they have been completely renovated to provide elegant venues for meetings and wedding receptions for as many as four hundred guests. For smaller parties, the *Piccola Terrazza* (Little Terrace) can accommodate dinners for up to fifty, and an outdoor garden gazebo can host gatherings of up to four hundred guests.

PALAZZI AT THE HOTEL CIPRIANI, Guidecca 10, 30133 Venezia (VE), tel. +39 041 520 7744, fax +39 041 520 3930, email info@hotelcipriani.it, www. hotelcipriani.it. Vaporetto stop: Zitelle. Fifteen luxury rooms; doubles from EEEEE.

Palazzo Dandolo (Hotel Danieli)

Palazzo Dandolo is a spectacular palace built by Doge Enrico Dandolo at the end of the twelfth century. The palace is just steps from St. Mark's Square, with a view across the water to Palladio's San Giorgio Maggiore. In the early 1800s, Giuseppe dal Niel transformed it into a hotel called the Hotel Danieli. Famous personalities have always stayed here, and the hotel was the setting for the tumultuous love affair between Alfred De Musset and George Sand, who conducted their Venetian drama from room number 10.

The hotel, with its red ochre facade and white marble trefoil windows, is truly a landmark on Venice's grandest promenade. Even if you are not staying there, it's worth stopping in for cocktails in the lounge or dinner on the top-floor terrace. The main entrance leads directly to the palazzo's dramatic central staircase, which anchors the palazzo's construction. When you book your stay at the Danieli, you may prefer to request a room in the original Dandolo palace, rather than the newly renovated wing, whose rooms lack the feeling of old-style palazzo. The most extravagant room, the Doge's Suite—filled with giant baroque mirrors, gilt period chairs and settees, a grand fireplace, console tables, terrazzo floors, and marble door frames—is a place where you can live like a doge in modern Venice. On the hotel's top floor, the Terrasse restaurant commands some of the best views of Venice and is one of the best places in the city to watch the sun set behind San Giorgio Maggiore and the Giudecca.

HOTEL DANIELI, Riva degli Schiavoni, Castello 4196, 30122 Venezia (VE), tel. +39 041 522 6480, fax +39 041 520 0208, www.luxurycollection.com/danieli. Vaporetto stop: San Marco. Two hundred thirty-three rooms; doubles from EEEE to EEEEE.

Pensione Accademia—Villa Maravege

David Lean's 1955 film *Summertime* cast Katharine Hepburn as a love-starved American on her first trip to Venice. The Pensione Accademia, also known as the Villa Maravege, was her character's hotel in Venice in the film. Today it's still the perfect place to be on a first trip to Venice, whether you come looking for love or you bring your *amore* with you. The villa-hotel was once a private Venetian palazzo, belonging to the Maravege family. The hotel boasts two gardens—a rarity in greenery-deficient Venice—one at the entrance that faces the Grand Canal, and a quiet rear garden where breakfast is served in the summer. The hotel's interior is still that of an elegant Venetian family dwelling, with soaring ceilings on the second floor the (*piano noble)* hung with vintage Murano glass chandeliers. Stairs from the ground floor lead to the *Androne*, a large drawing room, now used by the hotel as a common room where guests can relax on comfortable settees, surrounded by Venetian artworks and antiques. Each of the large rooms on the first floor opens off of the Androne, and those with views over the front or rear gardens are all excellent choices for a stay here. We stayed in room 16, which has a nineteenth-century antique bedroom set, elegant antique sitting chairs, and a view of the rear garden.

Pensione Accademia is just a short walk from the Accademia Bridge, which connects the Dorsoduro district with that of San Marco. A short walk leads to the Accademia Gallery and the Peggy Guggenheim museum. The hotel's service is cordial, and the management offers guests organized excursions to Murano's glassmaking factories.

PENSIONE ACCADEMIA—VILLA MARAVEGE, Fondamenta Bollani, Dorso-duro 1058, 30123 Venezia (VE), tel. +39 041 521 0188, fax +39 041 523 9152, email pensione.accademia@flashnet.it, www.pensioneaccademia.it. Vaporetto stop: Accademia. Twenty-seven rooms; doubles from E to EE.

Hotel Flora

Hotel Flora, down a small *vicolo* that opens off the posh Calle Larga XXII Marzo, is a delightful hotel just steps from Saint Mark's Square. The hotel was designed by the architect Guido Costante Sullam, a popular early-twentieth-century designer in Venice and the Lido. His Venetian Deco design for the Flora's interiors has been carefully preserved over the years. A central staircase, which brings guests to the upper floors, is filled with decorative iron balustrades and richly painted deco motifs along the casework. The family that manages this hotel is especially charming and cordial, and they will make sure your stay is a comfortable one.

Most rooms in the hotel have been recently renovated and updated, but the owners have carefully preserved the original style. Each guest room has hardwood floors, exposed heavy wood-beamed ceilings, gilt iron sconces, antique bed frames, and brocade coverlets. The bathrooms have modern fixtures and marble floors. The rear corner rooms enjoy views over Venice's rooftops and the Chiesa della Salute's pretty Gothic facade and its carefully groomed grounds.

One of the most popular features of the Flora is its charming outdoor garden, which offers guests a welcome respite from the bustle of Venice's crowded squares.

The hotel's building actually dates back to the seventeenth century and is believed to have been the location for a school of painting directed by an apprentice of Titian. A mosaic portrait over the hotel's entrance pays homage to the celebrated painter. Next door, Palazzo Contarini is the legendary home of Shakespeare's tragic heroine, Desdemona.

> HOTEL FLORA, Calle Larga XXII Marzo, San Marco 2283/A, 30124 Venezia (VE), tel. +39 041 520 5844, fax +39 041 522 8217, email info@hotelflora.it, www.hotelflora.it. Vaporetto stop: San Marco. Forty-four rooms; doubles from EE.

Locanda Leon Bianco

Locanda Leon Bianco is a small hotel between the Ca' d'Oro and the Rialto bridge in Cannaregio. Just seven rooms are available in this hotel, which has been hosting guests since 1500 when it was called the Albergo Leon Bianco (White Lion). Its most famous guest was Emperor Joseph II of Austria, who was a great patron of Mozart, although in the film *Amadeus* he accuses Mozart's music of having "too many notes." The palazzo sits directly on the Grand Canal, and from its perch next to the Ca' da Mosto it enjoys a view across the canal to the Rialto green market. Some of the hotel's finer rooms enjoy this same view over the waterway, and all are wonderfully appointed with Venetian antiques and oriental carpets. In one of the larger guest rooms, one entire wall is frescoed with a powerful scene of the Magi arriving on camelback. The hotel has a central, but quiet location.

> LOCANDA LEON BIANCO, Corte Leon Bianco, Cannaregio 5629, 30131 Venezia (VE), tel. +39 041 523 3572, fax +39 041 241 6392, email info@ leonbianco.it, www.leonbianco.it. Vaporetto stop: Ca' d'Oro. Seven rooms; doubles from E to EE.

Ca' Zanardi

Ca' Zanardi is a sixteenth-century baroque palace five minutes from the Ca' d'Oro. Zanardi's apartments can be rented for weeklong stays in Venice. The palace is located on a quiet *calle* in Cannareggio, behind its own secret gate, and is filled with authentic period charm, with gilt work, terrazzo floors, and eighteenth-century Venetian antiques.

The palace can be rented for weddings and special events; see page 115 for more information. At Carnevale, Ca' Zanardi hosts a baroque masked ball; see page 105 for information about the event.

CA' ZANARDI, Calle Zanardi, Cannaregio 4132, 30121 Venezia (VE), tel. +39 041 241 0220, fax +39 041 523 7716, www.best-of-italy.com/zanardi/, email ecgroup@tin.it. Vaporetto stop: Ca' d'Oro.

Tables for Two in Venice

Antico Martini

Housed in what was once the residence of Admiral Vettor Pisani, the Antico Martini was first opened in 1720 as the Caffè San Fantin. When the Fenice Opera House opened next door in 1792, the spot became the favorite meeting place for performers and patrons of the opera who came here for after-theater parties. Sadly, La Fenice is still missed in the piazza since it was lost to a fire in 1996, but the city of Venice is busily rebuilding the theater, so someday soon the after-theater crowd will again flock to the Antico Martini. Meanwhile, the restaurant has always been a favorite for couples in Venice, who come here to dine tête-à-tête in the candlelit Belle Epoque dining room, to propose marriage, celebrate a honeymoon, or commemorate their anniversaries. Since 1921 it has been continuously managed by the same family, whose members have consistently maintained a high level of service. The dining area, which once looked upon La Fenice's staircase, has been decorated in period style, with candles that cast a romantic glow and tables carefully spaced to provide an intimate experience. The menu changes weekly, and the restaurant also offers tasting menus. The wine list includes a well-researched complement of wines and champagnes for celebrating those special occasions.

ANTICO MARTINI, Campo San Fantin, San Marco 1983, 30124 Venezia (VE), tel. +39 041 522 4121, email info@anticomartini.com, www.anticomartini.com. Closed Tuesdays, and Wednesdays for lunch. Vaporetto stop: San Marco or Sant'Angelo. Fifty seats; reservations essential. Cost: EEEE.

Antica Trattoria Poste Vecie

The Poste Vecie was founded in 1500 as a trattoria for the mail dispatchers and is among Venice's oldest restaurants. It can be incredibly difficult to find, as the restaurant is tucked behind a hidden corner at the end of the Rialto market, reached by its very own tiny wooden bridge. Inside, the rooms are warmed with original sixteenth-century fireplaces. The dining room has heavy wood beams, and there is an enclosed garden in the back for eating in the summertime. Its proximity to the fish market guarantees that the fish they serve is among the freshest in Venice.

ANTICA TRATTORIA POSTE VECIE, Rialto Pescheria, San Polo 1608, 30125 Venezia (VE), tel. +39 041 721 822, fax +39 041 721 037, email postevecie@tiscalinet.it, www.postevecie.com. Vaporetto stop: Rialto. Closed Tuesday. Cost: E.

Da Fiore

Da Fiore will forever stay in my memory as one of Italy's most romantic spots. Many years ago I enjoyed one of the most sublime meals I have ever experienced here, and although I didn't know it then, my date was to become my future husband. Was it the *risotto alle seppie* that cast the spell? I have sent many people to Da Fiore for that very dish, and the restaurant has offered to make it even when it wasn't on the evening's menu, which further enchanted my American friends.

Da Fiore is off the beaten path, near the Campo San Polo, and has an elegant dining room with soft lighting. Reservations can be made on their website, making it easy to plan your evening in advance. Da Fiore is extremely popular with Venetians and foodies, so be sure to book ahead.

DA FIORE, Calle del Scaleter, San Polo 2202, 30125 Venezia (VE), tel. +39 041 721 308, fax +39 041 721 343, www.dafiore.com. Open for dinner only; closed Sundays and Mondays. Vaporetto stop: San Tomà. Forty-five seats; reservations essential. Cost: EEEEE.

Ristorante Fiaschetteria Toscana

Along a characterist *calle* (narrow street) in the Cannarregio district, the Fiaschetteria Toscana is a haven for gastronomes. Managed by the Busatto family, it offers warm and welcoming service, and the food is among the best in Venice. The restaurant's signature dish, the *Frittura della Serenissima,* is one of the lightest and most flavorful *fritto misto* (mixed fry) I have ever tried, combining fried julienned zucchini, fresh grey shrimp, and cuttlefish. The *tagliolini neri con astice* (black pasta with lobster) is a classic dish found on many Venetian menus, but here each bite is a perfectly balanced collection of flavors. The wine list includes a vast assortment of Italian wines, with over five hundred labels on the list. Fiaschetteria Toscana is a member of the Ristoranti di Buon Ricordo (see page xiii).

RISTORANTE FIASCHETTERIA TOSCANA, Cannaregio 5719, 30131 Venezia (VE), tel. +39 041 528 5281, fax +39 041 528 5521, www. fiaschetteriatoscana.it. Closed Tuesdays and the month of July. Vaporetto stop: Ca' d'Oro. Eighty seats; reservations recommended. Cost: EEE.

Vecio Fritolin

At one time this spot was a *friggitoria* (fried fish shop), where fishermen from nearby Rialto market could stop in and buy a package of fried fish to go. The restaurant still maintains a friendly rustic aspect and fish (though not always fried) is central to the menu. Everything is fresh and the prices are extremely fair. We tasted *capesante al pomodoro* (large scallops in their shells with fresh tomato), a perfectly made *sarde in saor* (marinated sardines with raisins and pine nuts), and a delicious *risotto per due* (for two) with squash, spinach, and tiny scallops. The dining room has rustic wood beam ceilings and terrazzo floors, and there is a small bar where locals stand to down a quick glass of wine on their way home.

VECIO FRITOLIN, Calle della Regina, San Cassiano, Santa Croce 2262, 30135 Venezia (VE), tel. +39 041 522 2881, www.veciofritolin.it. Closed Sunday evenings and Mondays. Vaporetto stop: San Stae. Cost: EE.

ISOLE DI VENEZIA

Al Vecio Cantier

Once you have had enough of the tourist throngs on Venice's main island, head to the Lido for a relaxing day at one of the island's private beaches or take a bike ride along the tree-lined canals. Afterward, stop for a bite at Al Vecio Cantier, one of the island's most romantic spots. Under the shade of the pergola you can enjoy fresh pasta, such as the restaurant's homemade *tagliolini*. The restaurant is extremely popular during the film festival, when it becomes a great spot for people watching on the Lido.

Al Vecio Cantier is located at the end of the island near the sand dunes and pinewoods of the Alberoni.

AL VECIO CANTIER, Via della Droma 76, 30126 Lido di Venezia (VE), tel. +39 041 526 8130. Closed Mondays, Tuesdays (except open Tuesday evenings from July to September), and for holidays the months of February and October. Vaporetto stop: Casino or Pallestrina. A five-minute walk from the ferry landing for Pellestrina, and just before the entrance to the Lido's exclusive Golf Club. Cost: EEE.

Da Romano

In the first years of the twentieth century, Romano Barbaro opened a trattoria on Burano to cater to the island's first tourists. The island quickly became a favorite subject for painters, many of whom became regulars at Da Romano. Inside, the walls are lined with framed artworks, an homage that reads like a who's who of artists from the era. The cuisine is faithful to the traditions of the lagoon, with light pastas and risottos prepared with seafood and fresh, locally caught fish.

DA ROMANO, Piazza Galuppi 221, 30012 Burano (VE), tel. +39 041 730 030, www.daromano.it. Closed Sunday evenings and Tuesdays, and for holidays from December 15 to February 15. Vaporetto stop: Burano. Cost: EE.

Trattoria al Gatto Nero

Surrounded by Burano's brightly painted houses, Trattoria al Gato Nero is a pleasant spot to sit and enjoy the scene. There are just a few tables under the awning in front alongside a quiet canal. Everything is prepared with the greatest respect to traditional recipes. Try the *pâté di dentice* (a pâté of the Mediterranean dentex fish), *gnocchetti* with zucchini and prawns, or *branzino all'acqua pazza* (sea bass in "crazy water"; that is, salt water). For dessert, choose between ricotta cake and homemade fruit tarts.

TRATTORIA AL GATTO NERO, Via Giudecca 88, 30012 Burano (VE), tel. +39 041 730 120. Closed Mondays, and for holidays from November 15 to December 5. Vaporetto stop: Burano. One hundred seats; reservations recommended. Cost: EE.

Locanda Cipriani

On the sparsely populated island of Torcello, the Cipriani maintain another exclusive property called the Locanda Cipriani. Founded by Giuseppe Cipriani in 1934, over the years this spot was a favored haunt of Hemingway, who stayed here while he wrote *Across the River and Through the Trees*. Two large dining rooms are decorated in a rustic, elegant style; their large windows overlook a garden filled with tulips and roses. In the warm months, tables are set on a terrace so guests can eat outdoors. If you decide that you'd like to stay here, note that the inn has six elegant rooms, and when the day-trippers leave on the last vaporetto, you'll have the entire island to yourselves.

LOCANDA CIPRIANI, Piazza Santa Fosca 29, 30012 Torcello (VE), tel. +39 041 730 150, fax +39 041 735 433, www.locandacipriani.com. Vaporetto stop: Torcello. Closed Tuesdays, and from January 1 to February 18. Cost: EEE. Hotel: six rooms from EE to EEE.

Ai Frati

Ai Frati is one of the oldest *osterie* (taverns) on Murano and sits directly on the Canale degli Angeli. In the summer you can sit at a table in front of the restaurant with a view over the canal and the Ponte Vivarini. The traditional Venetian menu includes typical specialties like *sarde in saor*, *baccalà mantecato* (creamed codfish), *frittura mista* (mixed fried fish), and *risotto di pesce* (risotto with fish).

AI FRATI, Fondamenta Venier, 30141 Murano (VE), tel. +39 041 736 694. Vaporetto stop: Venier. Open for lunch only; closed Thursdays and the month of February. One hundred seats; reservations recommended. Cost: E.

Trattoria 'Busa alla Torre' da Lele

After wending your way through the glassblower's shops on the island of Murano, you'll be ready for a relaxed lunch. This popular trattoria sits directly on the Campo San Stefano, one of Murano's most charming squares. The building is reportedly one of the oldest on the island, with a stark white second-story colonnade that stands out against red masonry. In the summer months the restaurant serves lunch under shady umbrellas that stretch out into the piazza. Fresh seafood from local fisherman dominates the menu, and the *fritto misto* prepared with calamari, turbot, and Mediterranean shrimp is well worth the trip.

TRATTORIA BUSA ALLA TORRE, da Lele, Campo San Stefano 3, 30141 Murano (VE), tel. and fax +39 041 739 662. Vaporetto stop: San Zaccharia to Venier or Museo. Open for lunch only; closed Mondays. Cost: EE.

Watching the Sunset

Venice along the Riva degli Schiavoni

The Riva degli Schiavoni is named after the ancient mariners from Schiavonia (the western Balkans) who used this area to dock their ships and trade along the waterfront. The hundred-foot-wide promenade is lined with luxury hotels on one side and vaporetto landing stages and souvenir stands on the other.

At this point, the Canale di San Marco opens ever wider, and the view stretches across the water to Santa Maria della Salute's pretty domes and Palladio's monumental San Giorgio Maggiore.

To watch the sunset, grab a spot along the promenade or have a sunset cocktail at the Hotel Danieli's Terrasse restaurant, perfectly positioned to enjoy the view of the western lagoon.

Romantic Lore and Local Festivals

La Festa della Sensa (Lo Spozalizio)—Venice's Marriage to the Sea

One of the oldest Venetian ceremonies, the Festa della Sensa (Feast of the Ascension), commemorates a great naval victory made by Doge Pietro Orseolo on Ascension Day in 998. The original festival was celebrated with a procession led by the doge upon his magnificent ship the *Bucintoro,* followed by a fleet of boats to the entrance of the port at the Lido. There, at a point in the lagoon off San Nicolò, he was blessed together with the sea by the bishop. In 1177, Pope Alessandro III gave the doge a blessed ring to symbolize Venice's domination over the sea and pronounced that Venice should "...marry the sea as a man marries a woman and thus be her Lord." From then on the festival has always involved the commitment of a blessed ring into the lagoon as a sign of Venice's eternal fidelity. In the modern festival, each year on Ascension Day the mayor of Venice leads a flotilla of boats to San Nicolò, near the Lido. Following tradition, he throws the gold ring and a garland of flowers into the lagoon to symbolize the eternal union of Venice and the sea.

Festa del Redentore (Feast of the Redeemer)—Venice

On the third Saturday in July, the city of Venice celebrates the Festa del Redentore with a spectacular night of fireworks reflected in the waters of the lagoon. Hundreds of decorated boats gather in the lagoon to await the fireworks, and Venetians make a big party out of the event with feasts and regattas.

The festival commemorates the end of one of the worst plagues in Venice's history in 1577. In gratitude, Doge Sebastiano Venier vowed to build a temple dedicated to Christ the Redeemer (Redentore) on the Giudecca Canal. On the site where the church was to be built, a temporary altar was erected and eighty galleys were placed side by side, creating a floating bridge across the canal. Venetians who had survived the terrible epidemic made a symbolic crossing across the temporary bridge to the altar to celebrate and give thanks. Once the church was built, the doge decreed that the third Sunday in July should be set aside for thanksgiving. As a part of the modern celebration, a bridge of boats is still built each year across the Giudecca Canal to the Redentore Church.

Picnic Spots

A Picnic on the Island of Torcello

Torcello, at the northern end of Venice's lagoon, is an almost uninhabited island with a seventh-century basilica known for its fantastical doomsday mosaics. Torcello was among the lagoon's first inhabited islands; archeological remains on the island have shown evidence of Roman settlements. During the seventh century the bishop of Altino relocated to Torcello, and in time the population grew to twenty thousand inhabitants. Today, there are perhaps a hundred people living on the island, and there are few traces left of the once thriving community.

As you tour around the island, look for the heavy marble throne in the grassy area in front of the churches. Although the chair was most likely used by the island's tribunals for handing down edicts, it's a popular spot for hopeful brides- and grooms-to-be. Legend has it that if you take a seat in the throne, you'll be married within the year.

Torcello has many spots for picnicking; the ferry ride from Venice takes about forty-five minutes.

Giardini Pubblici—Parco delle Rimembranze

Verdant picnic spots in Venice are few and far between, but the shady gardens at the eastern end of Castello are full of quiet spots where you can share a picnic for two. During the summers of odd-numbered years the park is used for the Biennale's pavilions, at which selected contemporary artists represent nations from all over the world. At other times, the park is quiet and enjoys views of San Giorgio Maggiore and across to the Lido.

Romantic Excursions

Wandering through Venice's Best Wine Bars

Venetians have a wonderful custom of pausing in the early evening for a quick glass of wine and a stand-up snack at their favorite neighborhood wine bar. Venice's traditional wine bars are called *bacari* (each is a bacaro), and they are designed with few (if any) seats—just a bar or counter where wine is served by the glass and a variety of *spuntini* (snacks) are displayed. The wines offered in the *bacari* range from humble *vini rossi* with very moderate prices to the noblest Italian wines. In Venetian dialect the glass of wine is called an *ombra* (shade) and the savory snacks that accompany it are called *cicchetti*. Some believe that the origin of the *ombra* goes back to a time when gondoliers used to enjoy a glass of wine in the shade of the Campanile. Regardless of how it got started, it's a great custom, and it provides a perfect romantic outing that will take you through winding *calle*, over bridges, and across *campielli*, in search of those elusive back alleys where the wine bars hide. Most of the best *bacari* are within a short walk of the Rialto Bridge, making it fun to visit a few before you sit down to dinner. As you linger at the bar, you'll see the locals dart in, down a glass of wine (as they would an espresso), and quickly eat a nibble or two before they dash home for supper.

Venetian cicchetti include a range of dishes like marinated fish, seasonal vegetables *sott'olio* (in oil), fried croquettes, meatballs, crostini, and typical lagoon dishes like *baccala mantecato* (creamed salt cod), *sarde in saor* (sardines marinated with raisins and pine nuts), and polenta.

BACARI IN AND AROUND THE RIALTO MARKET

Cantina do Mori

It would be easy to miss the narrow opening that leads to do Mori (to find it, look for the Sottoportego do Mori that opens off of Ruga Rialto). It's inevitably full of working-class *operaii* in their navy quilted jackets, who come in to toss back an *ombra* and catch up on the day's gossip. The atmosphere is positively medieval, and in fact, Do Mori is one of the oldest of the *bacari*, dating back to 1462. There are no tables, just standing room at the wood bar. Almost the entire ceiling is covered with old hammered copper pots, which add to the *bacaro's* warm tones and atmosphere. Behind the bar, demijohns await customers who bring their own bottles to fill. Chalkboards list wines by the glass, which range from a humble Malvasia to the noble Tignanello. The *cicchetti* are delicious, with a variety of fried treats like *olive* and *arancini* (rice balls), *polpette* (meatballs), and hard-boiled eggs topped with salty anchovies.

CANTINA DO MORI, Calle dei Do Mori, San Polo 429, 30125 Venezia (VE), tel. +39 041 522 5401. Closed on Sundays and Wednesday afternoons. Hours: 8:30 A.M. to 10:30 P.M. Vaporetti stop: Rialto or S. Silvestro.

al Bancogiro

Facing the Erboria, this bacaro-restaurant is carved out of the ancient Banco Giro, the building that held Venice's first revolving credit bank. Inside, the building's old framework is now exposed with ancient masonry, floor joists, and huge paving stones revealing the essence of the structure's architecture. The atmosphere is jovial and friendly, and the owner is likely to be enjoying some wine with friends on the patrons' side of the bar. On the wall, the names of a well-chosen selection of wines, available by the glass, are written on brown paper signs. Traditional cicchetti include mortadella and *salumi a taglio* (cured meats by the slice), a nice variety of cheeses, and crostini. The tiny restaurant also has a small intimate dining room with a cross-vaulted ceiling that sits directly above the bar. In the warmer months, the space between the Banco Giro and the Grand Canal is filled with wooden tables, the perfect spot for a *brindisi* (toast) if you've just tied the knot at nearby Palazzo Cavalli.

OSTERIA DA ANDREA—BANCO GIRO, Campo San Giacometto, San Polo 122, 30125 Venezia (VE), tel +39 041 523 2061. Closed on Sunday evenings and Mondays. Hours: 10:30 A.M. to 3 P.M. and 6:30 P.M. to 12 A.M. Vaporetti stops: Rialto or S. Silvestro.

Ostaria Antico Dolo

The Antico Dolo dates back to the 1400s, when the restaurant was opened to cater to patrons of the building's upper-floor brothel. *Trippa* (tripe) has been the specialty of the house since those early days. The bacaro's narrow entrance is easy to miss in the constant hustle of the Ruga Rialto. The walls are painted deep red, and there is a rustic atmosphere inside. Antico Dolo is more of a restaurant-bacaro than wine bar, with most of the space dedicated to tables. During lunch and dinner, Antico Dolo operates as a traditional restaurant, but during the twilight hours between 4 P.M. and 7 P.M., it's a bacaro where you can enjoy a quick glass of wine and taste *cicchetti* like *polenta con siepie in nero* (polenta with cuttle fish and their ink) and various croquettes such as tasty fried olives.

OSTARIA ANTICO DOLO, Ruga Rialto (Ruga Veccia San Giovanni), San Polo 778, 30125 Venezia (VE), tel. +39 041 522 6546, www.anticodolo.it. Closed on Sundays and Tuesdays and for holidays the third week in January and the first two weeks of July. Hours: 11 A.M. to 11 P.M. Vaporetto stop: Rialto or S. Silvestro.

ON THE SAN MARCO SIDE OF PONTE RIALTO

al Volto

Al Volto is another narrow spot with a warm and inviting atmosphere, a vast selection of wines, and lots of *cicchetti*. You can depend on a good recommendation as to what to drink and which *cicchetti* to pair with your wine. Founded in 1936, this bacaro is still a popular hangout for gondoliers and oarsmen from the nearby *traghetto* stop. Inside, the walls and the ceiling are papered with labels from wine bottles, and in the back there are long rustic tables with benches so you can sit down if you like. A large window opens from the bar area to the *calle* in front, where a single table is usually filled with a few locals engaged in a lively debate with the bartender.

AL VOLTO, Calle Cavalli, San Marco 4081, 30124 Venezia (VE), tel.+39 041 522 8945. Closed on Sundays. Hours: 10 A.M. to 2:30 P.M. and 5 P.M. to 10 P.M. Vaporetto stop: Rialto.

Vino Vino

Vino Vino is an "uptown" *bacaro* with tables. If you are lucky enough to get a seat by the window, you can watch the gondolas pass under the marble Ponte Sartor bridge. Vino Vino has a broad and well-chosen selection of wines by the glass, from both the Veneto region and the peninsula. During lunch and dinner, the bacaro offers a small selection of reasonably priced Venetian dishes like roasted quail with polenta or beef braised in Barolo wine. You can also buy full bottles of wine here, as well as a good selection of grappas.

VINO VINO, Calle del Cafetier, San Marco 2007/A, 30124 Venezia (VE), tel.+39 041 241 7688, www.vinovino.co.it. Closed on Tuesdays. Hours: 10:30 A.M. to midnight. Vaporetto stop: S. Angelo.

ON THE CANNAREGIO SIDE OF PONTE RIALTO

Candela—alla Bomba

Down a small *calle* that departs from the Strada Nova in Cannaregio, Candela alla Bomba has a narrow bar and a side room with a single long communal table for eating full meals. The atmosphere is friendly and the place is often packed with locals. Here you will find one of the broadest ranges of *cicchetti*, with marinated fish like *alici sott'olio* (fresh anchovies cured in oil), traditional dishes like *sarde in saor,* and baccala (salt cod) in all its incarnations. There are many varieties of *fritti* (fried dishes) to choose from as well.

CANDELA ALLA BOMBA, Calle dell'Oca, Cannaregio 4297, 30121 Venezia (VE), tel.+39 041 523 7452. Closed on Wednesdays. Hours: 10:30 A.M. to 2 P.M. and 5:30 P.M. to 10:30 P.M. Vaporetto stop: Ca' d'Oro.

ACROSS THE ACCADEMIA BRIDGE IN DORSODURO

Vini al Bottegon (Cantine del Vino—già Schiavi)

If you are staying near the Accademia at the *Villa Maravege* (see page 88), you are apt to become a regular at this authentic *bacaro* and wine shop. When the bar is crowded, patrons take their glasses outside and sit by the canal or on the Ponte di Trovaso's steps. The *cicchetti* include a wide range of crostini with interesting combinations of fresh ingredients like fresh ricotta with walnut paste and currants, wild mushrooms in oil and parsley, and black olive tapenade garnished with whole green olives. The establishment is run by a friendly Venetian family, and the sons speak excellent English. If you are looking for wine advice, this is the place to come.

VINI AL BOTTEGON, Ponte San Trovaso, Fondamenta Nani, Dorsoduro 992, 30123 Venezia (VE), tel. +39 041 523 0034. Closed Sunday afternoons. Hours: 8:30 A.M. to 2 P.M. and 3:30 P.M. to 8:30 P.M. Vaporetto stops: Accademia or Zattere.

Un Ballo in Maschera—A Masked Ball

Venice is well known for its vibrant Mardi Gras festival, Carnevale, with revelers dressed in ancient costumes and papier-mâché masks. Throughout the year, gala events and weddings are often celebrated as masquerade balls, with wait staff, musicians, and guests all dressed in seventeenth-century costumes. The Venetian tradition of the masquerade goes back to the *ridotti* (gambling halls), when wealthy patrons wishing to conceal their identities wore the *bauta*, the traditional long black cape and white mask. Today, Venetian costumers stock costumes for characters from Goldoni's *Commedia dell'Arte* and personalities from Italian history, providing a vast choice of period guises.

Each year during Carnevale, the Consorzio Comitato per il Carnevale di Venezia organizes masked balls in some of Venice's most exclusive palazzi. These gala evenings are a way to experience the palaces as they were in the high times of the seventeenth and eighteenth centuries when the Carnival celebration came into its greatest popularity. The list of venues and themes may change slightly each year; check with the Consorzio beforehand for ticket information and dates. Consorzio Comitato per il Carnevale di Venezia, tel. + 39 041 717 065, fax + 39 041 722 285.

A MASKED BALL—ADDRESSES AND PRACTICAL INFORMATION
Carnevale Balls

BALLO TIEPOLO—PALAZZO PISANI MORETTA The Ballo Tiepolo is referred to as the "Official Ball" of the Venice Carnevale. The event is hosted at one of the best-preserved Venetian palazzi, Palazzo Pisani Moretta. The palazzo's facade is immediately recognizable from its position on the Grand Canal, with its two levels of lacey mullioned windows standing out against a red-orange background. A specialty at Pisani Moretta is staging events in which the richly decorated rooms are illuminated solely by hundreds of candles, creating an authentic old world ambience. In true Venetian style, guests arrive at the palace's *porta d'acqua* (water door) while through the open windows the sounds of a string quartet waft out. Costumed acrobats, jesters, and mimes welcome arriving guests whether they enter the palace from the *calli* (alleyways) or through the Grand Canal *porta d'acqua*. Dinner is served in one of the palace's grandest salons, illuminated by candlelight. After dinner, guests are led to the ceremonial opening of the Ball. Waltzes and classical music are played on the upper floor, while on the ground floor a modern band plays contemporary dance music. In the early morning hours, *cioccolata calda* (hot chocolate) is served, a welcome treat that prepares guests to brave the cold night on their way home to sleep. For tickets, contact: Club Culturale Italiano, tel. +39 041 717065.

IL BALLO DI CASANOVA—PALAZZO NANI BERNARDO The Palazzo Nani Bernardo (also known as Palazzo Nani Lucchesi) is a sixteenth-century palazzo with a famous garden in its rear courtyard. Tragicomica, a theater group based in Venice, organizes a Carnevale gala in this venue along the Canal Grande. The palace is in front of Palazzo Grassi and next door to Ca' Rezzonico, the Venetian museum of the baroque era. The halls of the palazzo are frescoed in period Venetian style, and for the event they are lit with candles, just as they were when the legendary Casanova tried to woo potential conquests with an elixir or two. The gala includes a banquet dinner, and tickets cost around E300 per person. For information, contact: Compagnia Pantaleon c/o Tragicomica (www.tragicomica.it) tel. +39 041 721 102, fax. +39 041 524 0702, email info@tragicomica.it.

I BALLI DELLA SERENISSIMA—CA ZANARDI The delightful Ca' Zanardi (see page 90) hosts a masked ball each year in its exclusive halls. Revelers are welcomed by the sounds of a baroque quartet; ticket prices are around E250 per guest. For information, contact: Associazione Culturale Ca' Zanardi, www.best-of-italy.com/zanardi, tel. +39 041 241 0220, fax +39 041 523 7716, email ecgroup@tin.it.

Tickets for Carnevale Balls

CLUB CULTURALE ITALIANO offers tickets to most Carnevale events for purchase over the internet. C.C.I., Santa Croce 1714, 30135 Venezia, tel. +39 041 717 065, fax +39 041 722 285, email clubit@meetingeurope.com, www.meetingeurope.com.

Costume Rentals

ATELIER PIETRO LONGHI rents and sells carefully researched replicas of costumes from the various eras of Venice's past. San Polo 2604/B, 30125 Venice, tel. +39 041 714 478, pietrolonghi@ rialto.com, www.pietrolonghi.com.

LA VENEXIANA ATELIER sells handcrafted masks, period costumes, shoes made from eighteenth-century designs, and velvet cloaks. Frezzeria San Marco 1135, Venice 30124, tel +39 041 528 6888, www.lavenexiana.it.

TRAGICOMICA is dedicated to the faithful reproduction of period costumes, from the characters of the Commedia dell'Arte to your favorite historic personalities. The group also organizes the annual "Mascheranda" ball held on the last Sunday of Carnevale. Calle dei Nomboli, San Polo 2800, Venezia, tel: +39 041 721 102, fax +39 041 524 0702, email info@ tragicomica.it, www.tragicomica.it.

A Bicycle Ride on the Lido

Venice's Lido, that green strip of island that protects the lagoon from the Adriatic, is best known for miles of exclusive beach resorts and a glitzy international film festival. While the rest of the crowds flock to the beaches, take a break with a quiet bicycle tour through the island's green center. Between the Adriatic side of the island, with its eight-mile strip of fine sand beaches, and the lagoon side, are the Lido's own waterways. The canals on the Lido separate tree-lined streets, along which you will find Liberty-style villas set in rose-and-wisteria-filled gardens.

A short vaporetto ride from San Marco brings you to Piazza Santa Maria Elisabetta. Three bicycle rental shops are within walking distance of the landing; if a speedier mode of transportation is more appealing to you, note that one also rents scooters. Off the Piazza, the Grand Viale stretches east toward the beaches, while Via Sandro Gallo runs toward the south. Both streets are lined with shops where you will find plenty of picnic provisions.

Three itineraries on the Lido are worth exploring. The first route takes you through many of the island's most beautiful art nouveau villas, built in the early twentieth century in what is referred to in Italy as "Liberty" style. Departing from Piazza Santa Maria Elisabetta, ride two blocks down the busy Grand Viale to Via Lepanto. This street will take you south to the Quattro Fontane (Four Fountains). Once, a fortress that protected the Lido was located here; the Casino and the Palazzo del Cinema have taken its place. The two-mile loop continues back up the shady Via Dardanelli and winds up back where you started; along the way you will see many other smaller streets that are worth exploring.

A second itinerary takes you to the southern part of the island to the village of Malamocco, called Metamaucus in ancient times. Before it was destroyed by a seaquake and tidal wave in the twelfth century, it was the seat of the first doges' governments. The ancient city now lies somewhere at the bottom of the Adriatic, and local fisherman tell tales of getting their nets caught in the ruins of the lost city. The Malamocco of today is typically Venetian, with its own *calli* and *campielli* (alleyways and squares), and a central square lined with fifteenth-century Gothic buildings. Although its monuments pale against the grandeur of those across the lagoon, they offer a charming and refreshing look at a small Italian town untouched by tourism.

The third itinerary lies at the north end of the isle, in San Nicolò, a spot that has always thrilled visitors because of its breathtaking views looking back toward Venice. A shady promenade runs along the lagoon side, where more Liberty villas were built to benefit from the view. Two of the oldest sites on the island are here: the Jewish Cemetery and the church of San Nicolò. Dating back to 1356 and sheltered under a cypress and cedar wood, the Lido's *Cimitero Ebraico* (Jewish Cemetery) gives testimony to the once thriving Jewish community in Venice. The inscriptions on the headstones are a patchwork of languages, symbols, city emblems, and family crests that recount the ever-changing story of Jewish Venezia. If you happen to be here on the Sunday after Ascension Day (in early May) you can be on hand to witness the festival of La Sensa, when Venice reaffirms her marriage to the sea. Each year, after a candlelit mass is held in St. Mark's, a flotilla of richly decorated boats follows the *Bucintoro* (a large ceremonial ship) to a spot in the lagoon directly in front of the church of San Nicolò.

At the end of your bike ride you might want to take a break on the Lido's famous beaches. All along the beachfront, exclusive resorts rent everything you need for a day at the beach, from towels and umbrellas to thatched-roof beach cabanas. In high season, beaches are crowded with international tourists, so if you want a front-row cabana it's a good idea to make a reservation in advance.

A BICYCLE RIDE ON THE LIDO—ADDRESSES AND PRACTICAL INFORMATION

Bicycle Rentals

GIORGIO BARBIERI, Via Zara 5, tel. +39 041 526 1490, has bicycles and multipassenger pedal vehicles. Daily rentals start at E9.

ANNA GARBIN, Piazzale S. Maria Elisabetta 2, 30126 Venezia-Lido, tel. +39 041 276 0005.

DITTA BRUNO LAZZARI, Gran Viale 21, tel. +39 041 526 8019, has bicycles and scooters available to rent.

Picnic Provisions

PASTICCERIA MAGGION, Via Dardanelli 46 C, tel. +39 041 526 0836. Open 8:30 A.M. to 1:00 P.M. and 4:00 P.M. to 7:30 P.M. Closed Mondays and Tuesdays.

LA BOTTIGLIERIA, Via Sandro Gallo, 110/a, tel. +39 041 526 5363. Wine shop.

SALUMERIA DA CIANO, Via S.Gallo, 156/A, tel. +39 041 526 0991, is an *alimentari* (large deli-type shop) with a large variety of *salumi* and cheeses.

STANDA, Gran Viale S.M. Elisabetta, tel. +39 041 526 2898. The Standa is a large supermarket where you can find just about everything you'd need for a picnic.

IL GRANDE FRATELLO Via S. Gallo, 159/b, tel. +39 041 526 0315. A fresh fruit stand.

Sights on the Lido

CIMITERO EBRAICO Riviera San Nicolò, tel. +39 041 715 359.

CHIESA DI SAN NICOLÒ, tel.+39 041 526 0241. Open every day from 9 A.M. to noon and 3:30 P.M. to 7 P.M.

CHIESA DELL'ASSUNTA, Ramo Merceria 2, Malamocco, tel.+39 041 770 715.

Beaches

VENEZIA SPIAGGE manages two beaches. The first is at San Nicolò Piazzale Ravà; the second is farther up near the airport along Lungomare D'Annunzio Piazzale Ravà, tel. +39 041 526 0236 or tel. +39 041 526 1346. Beach umbrellas start at E15, and changing rooms and cabanas range from E25 to E35.

The most exclusive beach resorts on the Lido are located on the Lungomare Marconi, which runs from the Hotel des Bains to the Casino. The HOTEL DES BAINS beach, tel. +39 041 271 6808, is one of the nicest, with lines of white thatched huts. Changing rooms start at E30, but a cabana in the first line costs E137.

The QUATTRO FONTANE is farther down the beach, almost to the casino. Changing rooms start at E45, front row cabanas are E102. Tel. +39 041 271 6862.

The EXCELSIOR, tel. +39 041 271 6836, rents chaise lounges for E32 and mini-cabanas for E37, and the MIRAMARE, Lungomare Marconi, 61/C, tel. +39 041 526 0193, has front-row cabanas for E90.

BAGNI ALBERONI, Strada Nuova dei Bagni 26, Alberoni, tel. +39 041 731 029. This beach is at the southern end of the island in the most natural setting on the Lido. They rent beach umbrellas for E13, chaises for E11, and changing rooms and cabanas from E15 to E53.

Gondola Rides

Gondola rides in Venice are among the most touristy experiences, but just like a hansom cab ride through Central Park, they are a romantic necessity. The most romantic rides will be through the side canals, away from the waterbuses and speedboats on the Grand Canal, and it's better to hire a gondolier in one of the quieter neighborhoods, rather than directly in front of St. Mark's Square. It's a good idea to negotiate the price and the route before you set off. Although the city of Venice sets an official rate for gondola rides, in reality it is only used by gondoliers as a loose starting point. Expect to pay E80 to E100 for a fifty-minute ride. Singing and accordion-playing is extra and most gondoliers do not offer a serenade as part of the package.

Love Letters

Printing and papermaking have a long history in Venice. As early as the fifteenth century, the first printing presses were stamping out volumes such as Petrarch's sonnets, and paper mills sprang up in and around Venice to keep the presses supplied. In the spirit of ancient book arts, you can still find handcrafted marbled paper, hand-sewn leather books, wax seals, and heavy cotton letter-pressed note cards—perfect for leaving a poem on your sweetheart's pillow.

Il Pavone (Dorsoduro 721, 30124 Venezia, tel. +39 041 523 4517) sells silk-screened cards, wrapping paper, and books that look like they are hand-painted with watercolors. The store also sells wonderful initial stamps, each set against a stenciled Venetian background.

Il Papiro has multiple locations in Venice, Florence, and other major Italian cities. The shop in Calle del Piovan, San Marco 2764, tel +39 041 522 3055, is on the main path to Saint Mark's Square.

Paolo Olbi Venezia sells gift items in paper and leather from its shop in Calle della Mandola, San Marco 3653, tel. +39 041 528 5025.

Venice Film Festival

The Mostra Internazionale d'Arte Cinematografica, known internationally as the Venice Film Festival, is the oldest annual film festival in the world, first held on the Lido in 1932 as part of the Venice Biennale. Louis Lumiere, one of the earliest founders of the medium, was in honorary attendance at the first official festival. In 1952, the highest jury prize at the festival became known as the Golden Lion of Saint Mark, after Venice's patron saint, while the acting awards are known as the Coppa Volpi after Count Giuseppe Volpi di Misurata, an entrepreneur and political figure who backed the early festivals. Over the years the festival has been attended by a roster of Italian and international stars, professionals from the world media, and film aficionados. The festival is held each year at the end of August and early September in several venues on the Lido, including the historic Palazzo del Cinema near the Moorish Hotel Excelsior.

For ticket information and a schedule of events, visit the Biennale di Venezia's web site, www.labiennale.org; for general information see the Mostra del Cinema di Venezia at www.mostradelcinemadivenezia.com.

Weddings in Venice

A Venetian palace can be a magical location for a gala wedding reception with all the trappings of the Venetian baroque style, including period costumes for bride, groom, and guests, an elaborate doge's banquet, and a classical string quartet. In the quieter squares, away from the bustle of the Grand Canal, are some of the oldest remaining synagogues in Europe, where wedding ceremonies are still performed today much as they have been for the last five hundred years. For couples eloping, a civil ceremony at Venice's Grand Canal city hall, Palazzo Cavalli, followed by a romantic gondola ride and a sumptuous dinner by candlelight, is an intimate way to celebrate just for two.

Venetian wedding banquets are celebrated as lavishly today as they were in the days of the doges. Venetian cooks pride themselves on their simple presentation of seafood, abundantly available from the lagoon and the nearby Adriatic Sea. The *Bellini,* invented at Harry's Bar, is a delicious concoction of white peach purée and prosecco, a perfect Venetian cocktail to welcome your guests. After cocktails, the antipasti might begin with *stoccafisso,* creamy salt cod spread on crisp crostini; succulent baby octopi; and *sarde in saor* (marinated sardines). Typical *primi* (first courses) are risotto served *alla pescatore* (with seafood) or *alle seppie* (with black cuttlefish ink), followed by a fresh pasta with scallops or crabmeat. The main course may begin with a simply prepared fillet of turbot, sole, or lobster, then continue with roasted leg of lamb or veal.

If a doge's banquet is too much for your taste, you'll be glad to know that the Venetians have a wonderful custom of pausing in the late

afternoon for stand-up snacks at their favorite neighborhood wine bar, a tradition easily adapted to cocktail receptions. This can give you the chance to focus on the region's excellent wines: the sparkling prosecco from the Valdobbiene, the fragrant Tocai, and the robust Amarone. Of course, you'll want to finish with a selection of local grappas, including *grappa con la ruta,* infused with a sprig of rue.

A note on Catholic weddings in Venice:

Stemming from the immense popularity of weddings in Venice for foreigners and natives alike, the Catholic Diocese in Venice has currently placed a prohibition on marriages of foreigners in Venice's Catholic churches. As with many things in Italy, if you really have your heart set on a Catholic wedding in Venice, it can't hurt to ask. Regardless of the diocese, for Catholic weddings in Italy, your parish priest should make inquiries for you directly with the appropriate parish priest in Italy.

CIVIL CEREMONIES

Palazzo Cavalli

Civil ceremonies are held in the beautiful sixteenth-century Palazzo Cavalli, a Gothic palace on the Grand Canal that overlooks the Rialto Bridge. If you are eloping to Venice, or are planning an elegant and informal ceremony, this is a perfect location to arrive at with your own flotilla of gondolas, serenaded by an accordion. As is customary, a city official wearing the classic Italian tricolored sash will greet you at the palazzo's water door. A broad marble staircase leads upstairs to a sunny private hall where you can exchange your vows while surrounded by original stucco paintings from the 1700s and a later work by Luigi Nono entitled *The Golden Wedding.* After the ceremony, hop back into your velvet-lined gondola for a ride to Harry's Bar for a Bellini cocktail or to Florian for a glass of sparkling prosecco.

PALAZZO CAVALLI, Ufficio Stato Civile di Venezia Centro, San Marco 4089, 30124 Venezia (VE) tel. +39 041 274 8331, www.comune.venezia.it. Directions: take the vaporetto to Ponte Rialto. Walk along the Via do Aprile past the church of San Salvatore. Continue along the same direction, now the street will be called Calle dell'Ovo. Follow the signs for Palazzo Loredan.

Water taxis may arrive directly at the palace's main entrance on the Grand Canal. Cost: EEE.

CEREMONY AND RECEPTION LOCATIONS

Ca' Zanardi

In one of the oldest parts of the city, Ca' Zanardi is a small, refined palace on the island of Cannaregio, just a five-minute walk from the Ca' d'Oro. The original tribunes who governed the city built their first palaces here, including Angelo Partecipazio, who was elected doge in 810. In popular Venetian lore, Angelo's beautiful daughter, Estella, rode in a luminous white boat to make a plea for peace with the ferocious Frankish King Pipino. Pipino had driven the Venetians into hiding deep in the lagoon, but it is said that on seeing Estella he was instantly smitten and abandoned his ruthless campaign. Estella's boat may have been one of the earliest incarnations of that most important of Venetian icons, the gondola. For weddings at Ca' Zanardi, guests arrive at the palace water door through a canal that may very well have been Estella's launching place.

As your own gondola arrives at the palazzo, torchlight from the palace's footmen will sparkle in the waters of the Rio Santa Caterina. Your guests can arrive in similar style, greeted by three costumed trumpeters and a red carpet at the palace's *porta d'acqua*. The entire three-story palace at Ca' Zanardi can be rented for weddings; here you can host your own masked ball or an evening *al Casanova*. Its elegant golden salons include a ballroom, a music room, and a dining room, each decorated with gold brocade, gilt-framed mirrors, crystal chandeliers, and intricately patterned terrazzo floors. A spectacular terrace faces onto the canal, offering a rare outdoor space where you can dine while gazing at the gondoliers navigating the waterway.

The ballroom offers a sumptuous space where a banquet can be set, or you can use the room as it was intended, for after-dinner waltzing to the sounds of a classical quartet.

The palazzo has the added benefit of three elegantly appointed guest suites that can accommodate up to six guests. The rooms are sumptuously decorated with silk damask walls and romantic antique furnishings.

CA' ZANARDI, Calle Zanardi, Cannaregio 4132, 30121 Venezia (VE), tel. +39 041 241 0220, fax +39 041 523 7716, email ecgroup@tin.it, www.best-of-italy.com/zanardi/. Directions: take the vaporetto (waterbus) to Ca' d'Oro. Directly across the Strada Nova you will see Calle delle Vele. Continue on this street until you cross the first canal. The street name will change to Calle Corrente. After you cross the second canal, turn right on Fondamenta Sant'Andrea and then left on Calle Zanardi. Cost: EE to EEE.

Ca' Zenobio

Along the Rio dei Carmini, in the quiet Durosduro neighborhood, Ca' Zenobio is one of the largest patrician palaces ever built in Venice. Its lavish seventeenth-century ballroom, private garden, and guest suites can be rented for receptions in the heart of one of Venice's prettiest neighborhoods. A simple façade facing the canal reveals few clues to the richness of the palace's interior spaces, which were built in the late 1600s for the counts of Zenobio. The Zenobio were wealthy landowners from Verona when they arrived in Venice, and although they had titles and property, to enter into the Venetian patriciate they were required to make a large donation. To gain the respect of the other noble families, they hired Antonio Gaspari, an architect who was well respected for his civic works, to build their Venetian palazzo.

Entering the palace, you will pass through a *portego* (small passageway) lined with landscape paintings by the artist Luca Carlevarijs, works so important to his career that he was later known as Luca da Ca' Zenobio. Above your head the ceiling is covered with lively frescoes painted by the French artist Louis Dorigny. The *portego* leads into the grand ballroom through an elegant gilded archway, above which is a gallery where orchestras once played.

The ballroom, called the Sala degli Specchi, is one of the most opulent in all of Venice; it can host banquets for up to two hundred guests. A feminine whirl of sculpted moldings and baroque *putti*, garlands, and shells completely covers the walls, while the ceiling is boldly painted with allegorical stories. The room is named for its floor-to-ceiling mirrors, which are elaborately framed by stucco cherubs busily decorating the walls with garlands, adding to the enchanting atmosphere. The Zenobio coat of arms—birds, beasts, and lions surrounding a wandering saint—is repeatedly featured among the mythological figures and flowered urns.

In the summer months, receptions can be held in the rear courtyard and characteristic Venetian palace garden. The ornamental garden is filled with characteristic baroque arabesque hedges and is the site of an elegant lodge, arranged like a scenographic backdrop. In the 1800s, to suit the romantic tastes of the times, part of the garden was planted with a small grove of yews and laurels, which offer a welcome bit of shade in a city where natural settings are at a premium.

The palace chapel, which can be requested for wedding blessings, still has its original frescoes, precious works by Abbondio Stazio (1685–1750).

In the palace's foresteria, the guest quarters include twelve rooms on the lower floors and twenty-two on the third floor, providing accommodations for over sixty guests under the roof of this sumptuous residence. The rooms are simply decorated, and a few have views over the gardens.

Palazzo Zenobio degli Armeni is situated in the heart of Venice and is accessible by a water door on the canal or by a ten-minute walk from the Accademia.

CA' ZENOBIO, Dorsoduro 2596, 13023 Venezia (VE), tel. +39 041 522 8770, fax +39 041 520 3434, email mooratr@tin.it. Directions: take the vaporetto to Ca' Rezzonico. Walk along the canal (Rio di San Barnaba) and continue until you reach Rio Terra Scoazzera. Turn right and continue past Santa Maria dei Carmini, then turn left and walk along the Fondamento del Soccorso. The palace will be on the left. Reception capacity ranges from fifty to two hundred guests. The palace's private chapel may be requested for wedding blessings. Accommodations are available inside the palace foresteria (guest quarters), where there is room for over sixty guests. Cost: EE to EEE.

Synagogues

Venice has a rich Jewish past and retains five ancient synagogues within its Old and New Ghettos. Offering the opportunity to hold a wedding in some of the oldest remaining temples in all of Europe, the *scole* (religious schools) of Venice are sumptuously decorated with carved gilded moldings, ornate wrought-iron lanterns, plush red fabrics, and bold marble stonework. Jewish wedding ceremonies in Venice, as elsewhere in Italy, are celebrated according to Orthodox traditions. While rabbis in Italy are allowed to legally marry only Italian citizens, the synagogues are available for blessings that may be combined with a civil ceremony in Venice or a ceremony in the States to make your wedding legal. Fees for the use of the synagogues vary according to the size and type of ceremony.

The two oldest *scole* are the Scola Tedesca and the Scola Canton, founded in the early 1500s by Ashkenazim, émigrés from Germany and Eastern Europe. In those years, heavy restrictions placed on the community severely limited construction in what is now the Ghetto Vecchio. Finding an ingenious solution to the problem, architects built both temples on the uppermost floors of existing buildings, with the added benefit that there would be no obstructions between the congregations and the heavens. While their exterior architecture is almost austere, inside they are ornately decorated with jewels and retain their original antique arks.

Of the three Sephardic synagogues, the Scola Spagnola and the Scola Levantina, constructed in the seventeenth century, are the largest and most splendid. Their bold baroque architecture reflects the growing confidence that the Jewish community began to experience in the seventeenth century. Both were designed by the architect Baldassarre Longhena, who is also responsible for the magnificent Ca' Rezzonico. Longhena's *scole* are both decorated with polychrome marbles, elegantly carved walnut benches, and finely hand-detailed wainscoting. Still functioning as religious centers today, each can host ceremonies for over one hundred guests.

For Orthodox blessings at any of Venice's synagogues, contact: Office of the Chief Rabbi, Ghetto Vecchio, Cannaregio 1189, Venezia (VE), tel. +39 041 715 118.

Scola Tedesca, Campo di Ghetto Nuovo, Cannaregio Venezia (VE). Ashkenazi, ceremony capacity: Sixty.

Scola Canton, Campo di Ghetto Nuovo, Cannaregio Venezia (VE). Ashkenazi, ceremony capacity: sixty. Directions: take the vaporetto to Ponte delle

Guglie. Follow the Calle del Ghetto Vecchio to the Campo di Ghetto Nuovo.

SCOLA SPAGNOLA, Campiello delle Scole, Cannaregio Venezia (VE). Sephardic, ceremony capacity: two hundred.

SCOLA LEVANTINA, Campiello delle Scole, Cannaregio Venezia (VE). Sephardic, ceremony capacity: One hundred twenty. Directions: take the vaporetto to Ponte delle Guglie. Follow the Calle del Ghetto Vecchio to Campiello delle Scole (Ghetto Vecchio).

Practical Information—Venice

GETTING THERE

By air: The nearest airport is Venezia Marco Polo (airport code VCE), with daily flights connecting through most major European cities; flight times and information are available on the airport's official website, www.veniceairport.com. From the airport, the Alilaguna motorboat service departs hourly; travel time to San Marco is approximately one hour and costs about E10. Information and timetables are available at www.alilaguna.it. The ATVO airbus travels from the airport to Piazzale Roma, departing every twenty minutes between 8:20 A.M. and 11:50 P.M. The trip takes about twenty minutes; information is available at www.atvo.it. You will also find car taxis outside the arrivals hall; these can take you to Piazzale Roma.

By car: from Milano, take highway A4 and exit at Tronchetto. Cars are not allowed in Venice and must be left at the parking lots in Piazzale Roma or on the island of Tronchetto. Information on the two largest parking facilities can be found at www.asmvenezia.it and www.garagesanmarco.it.

By train: Venice's railway station is Santa Lucia.

By boat: Vaporetti: Venice maintains a waterbus service linking stops along the main canal and many of the lagoon islands. The vaporetti are run by the ACTV (Azienda del Consorzio Trasporti Veneziano), which maintains an information office at 3880 Corte dell'Albero, San Marco Venezia +39 041 528 7886. See www.actv.it for maps and timetables. Tickets can be purchased at the main landing stages, or from tobacconist shops (*tabaccaio*) where the ACTV sign is posted. Unlimited passes are available for twenty-four-hour, seventy-two-hour, weekly, and monthly time periods.

Water taxi: Venice's water taxis operate as convential land taxicabs do. From the airport the ride into Venice takes twenty to forty minutes, depending on your destination. Water taxi stands can be found at the rail station, San Marco, Rialto, Piazzale Roma, and the Lido. Taxi service is expensive, and supplements are charged for luggage, call service, and traveling at night.

WHEN TO GO
During high season (May to September) and Carnevale, Venice is packed with tourists from all over the world. While July and August are popular months, temperatures and humidity can make a summer visit less than pleasant. Hotel reservations for these time periods should be made well in advance. The best time to visit Venice is March, April, and early May.

HELPFUL ADDRESSES
Official Tourist Information Offices and Websites

APT—Azienda di Promozione Turistica (Tourist Promotion Agency)

IAT—Ufficio Informazione e di Accoglienza Turistica (Tourist Information and Hospitality Office)

IAT—San Marco, 71/f 30124 Venezia tel. +39 041 529 8711, +39 041 523 0399, email apt-06@mail.regione.veneto.it, www.turismovenezia.it.

VENICE PAVILION—APT di Venezia, Ex Giardini Reali—San Marco,Venezia, tel +39 041 5225150, fax +39 041 5230399.

IAT—Ferrovia Santa Lucia, 30121 Venezia, tel. +39 041 529 8711 and tel. +39 041 529 8727, fax +39 041 523 0399.

IAT—Lido, Gran Viale 6/a, 30126 Lido di Venezia, +39 041 529 8711 and tel. +39 041 526 5720, fax +39 041 523 0399.

REGIONE VENETO ASSESSORATO AL TURISMO
http://turismo.regione.veneto.it. This comprehensive site offers a variety of tourist information, from accommodations to recipes.

MEETING VENICE www.meetingvenice.it has information on restaurants, special event information, maps, and a directory of Carnevale-related events.

THE VENETO

Just inland from Venice the patrician mansions built as summer homes by wealthy Venetians await you. The *ville delle delizie* (villas of delights), as they are called, are found throughout the Veneto near historic cities like Padova, Vicenza, and Verona.

The expansion to the mainland dates to the sixteenth century, when noble Venetian families seeking a refuge from the demands of life in the lagoon began building quiet provincial estates throughout the countryside. They hired celebrated Italian architects such as Andrea Palladio and Vicenzo Scamozzi to construct their palaces and renowned artists to complete the interior decorations. The Renaissance and baroque architects who designed these villas added gardens intended to be the natural extension of a villa's architecture. Outdoor rooms were created by varieties of textured foliage and multiple hues of green hedges laid out in a formal geometry. Hedges, groomed into lacy arabesques, scrolls, or geometric shapes are often the central element in the garden. Fanciful labyrinths and playful fountains provide the entertainment, while flowers and color are downplayed. Today, these outdoor theaters continue to be perfect backdrops for living and celebrating life's important moments.

Romantics visiting the Veneto may want to visit the birthplace of the real Romeo and Juliet in Montecchio Maggiore, plan an operatic picnic under the stars in Verona's Roman arena, or explore the waterways that connect the plains to Venice's lagoon by houseboat, stopping along the way to visit the region's historic villas.

Accommodations in Patrician Garden Villas

GARGAGNAGO DI VALPOLICELLA
Foresteria Serègo Alighieri

Here, in the gentle countryside of the Valpolicella, you can actually have a holiday under roofs where Dante not only slept but also lived out part of his exile from Florence. While Dante was a guest of what was then called the Casal dei Ronchi, he finished work on the *Inferno* and *Purgatorio,* the first two sections of his masterwork. Perhaps inspired by fond childhood memories, his first son, Pietro Alighieri, purchased the property here in Gargagnago in 1353 and it became the Alighieri ancestral home. Today, twenty generations later, the *Foresteria* (guest house) Serègo Alighieri is owned by one of his descendants, the Count Pieralvise Serègo Alighieri.

For centuries the family's primary business in Valpolicella has been the cultivation of vineyards, which produce some of this area's esteemed wines. In the center of the Alighieri family's vineyards is a restored fourteenth-century manor house with symmetrical gardens. The old granaries and stables surround the house's central courtyard. Today, the complex has been carefully restored and adapted to the needs of an agricultural tourist complex. Eight apartments furnished in "lordly country style" (as described by the owners) have been created in the farm's buildings. A large reception room and a tasting room are used to organize viticultural events and cooking courses for guests. Serègo Alighieri wines are among some of the region's most noteworthy, and here you can sample them firsthand in the farm's tasting rooms.

Apartments are available for weekly rentals and accommodate from two to four persons. Oseleta is a three-floor apartment in the estate's old watch tower, reached by climbing a winding staircase. The larger apartments have fireplaces, and some have exposed wood beam ceilings. The estate also produces jams made from their own cherries, chestnuts, and

apricots, acacia honey from beehives in the orchards, and olive oil from a small grove on the hillside above the farm.

Verona is twenty kilometers from the estate, and Lake Garda is fifteen minutes away.

FORESTERIA SERÈGO ALIGHIERI, Possessioni di Serègo Alighieri, 37020 Gargagnago di Valpolicella (VR), tel. +39 045 770 3622, fax +39 045 770 3523, email serego@seregoalighieri.it, www.seregoalighieri.it. Driving directions: from Verona, take highway S12 to exit S. Ambrogio di Valpoli-cella. Eight apartments; available for weekly rentals.

MIRA

Villa Margherita

On one of the most scenic bends of the Brenta Canal, Villa Margherita is a beautiful fifteenth-century noble residence that has been lovingly transformed into a romantic hotel. Arriving at the villa, you pass through a tree-lined viale (avenue) that leads from the road through the villa's large park. The shady drive is lined with statuary and blooming hydrangea, beyond which you can see the hedges of the verdant park. Inside the villa, common areas have the feel of aristocratic drawing rooms and salons, with frescoed ceilings, broad fireplaces, antiques, and oil paintings. Guest rooms overlook the garden and are decorated in period style, with floor-to-ceiling drapes, velvet-covered chairs, brocade bed coverings, sconces, and chandeliers. During the warmer months you can enjoy breakfast on the quiet garden terrace behind the villa. For quiet dinners for two, the highly rated Ristorante Margherita is located just across the road from the villa (see page 130).

Villa Margherita is situated in Mira, a canal town that was born during the Middle Ages when the Brenta was an active trade route between the plains and Venice. This section of the canal was an immensely popular spot for Venetian nobles to build summer estates. Today, some of the most famous examples of noble patrician villas are located here. Palladio's mas-terpiece La Malcontenta, Villa Valmarana, and Villa Widman are nearby and can be easily reached from Villa Margherita. The villa-hotel is just fifteen kilometers from Venice, making it a convenient departure spot for day trips to the lagoon islands.

> VILLA MARGHERITA, Via Nazionale 416, 30030 Mira (VE), tel. +39 041 426 5800, fax +39 041 426 5838, www.dalcorsohotellerie.it. Driving directions: from Padova, take highway A4, exit at Mira. Nineteen rooms; doubles from EE.

FINALE DI AGUGLIARO

Villa Saraceno

It is impossible to travel anywhere within the inland Veneto and not find the influence of Andrea Palladio. Revered as one of the most influential architects of all time, his civic works, inspired by ancient Roman and Greek architecture, continue to inspire designers to this day. The simple solutions he devised for the Venetian villas, with their dramatic exterior motifs and harmony within their natural settings, provided the answer to the nobles' need to combine the function of a working farm with the lavish tastes of their class. Palladio valued open views, elevated positions, and gardens—which he referred to as the "soul of the villa"—as well as the practical function of easy access to the city. Of the eighteen Palladian villas that survive today, many are open for tours and visits, and one offers the rare possibility to plan a holiday stay under the roof of a national monument.

The Villa Saraceno in Finale di Agugliaro (1545) is one of Palladio's earlier works. Recently restored by its current owner, the British Landmark Trust, it can accommodate sixteen guests in its refurbished rooms. Palladio's original plan called for two lateral wings that would frame the central construction in a *U* formation, but only the central pavilion was completed. A classic example of the farm-villa, its simply designed façade has three tall archways symmetrically framed by a Greek pediment. In the main hall, stark white walls lead up from a warm terra-cotta floor to a surround of frescoes in the trompe l'oeil style. Above, the beamed ceilings are delicately filigreed with fine painted details.

The villa was a commission by Biagio Saraceno, who was an important political figure in Vicenza during the late 1500s. His son, Pietro, commissioned the interior decorations, which have been attributed to the artist Felice Brusasorzi, an important mannerist artist from Verona. Villa Saraceno is set in Agugliaro, a small town twenty-seven kilometers south of Vicenza. To the east, the Colli Euganei and the thermal spas at Abano Terme are twenty kilometers away, and Venice can be reached in an hour. The villa is managed by the British Landmark Trust and is available for weekly rentals.

VILLA SARACENO, Via Finale 8, 36020 Finale di Agugliaro (VI), www. landmarktrust.co.uk. Private villa available for weekly rentals; sleeps sixteen. Driving directions: from Vicenza, highway S247, exit at Agugliaro. From $1870 to $9500 depending on the season. The villa is also open by appointment for group visits; tel. +39 0444 891 371.

SCORZÉ

Villa Soranzo Conestabile

Surrounded by its own three-acre park, the Villa Soranzo in Scorzé is a renovated sixteenth-century villa. This charming hotel and restaurant is forty-five minutes from Venice. Its private park is filled with giant magnolia trees, statuary, and a pond directly in front of the pretty three-story villa. This was once the summer home the Soranzos, one of Venice's founding families.

Inside you will find grand halls, the family's dining room with its original walnut paneling, and a library with a trussed ceiling and fireplace decorated with the Soranzo heraldic shield. A dramatic marble staircase, decorated with columns and Corinthian capitals, leads to a loggia gallery and a small first-floor salon with a view of the garden and the pond. The individually decorated guest rooms on this floor are the most spacious in the villa, with high ceilings and period antiques. Some rooms have fireplaces, and many have views over the quiet park.

The English-style park, the work of the Venetian architect and landscape designer Giuseppe Jappelli, is filled with ancient magnolias, lindens, oaks, plane trees, and horse-chestnut trees—it's a great place for a quiet walk or to sit and enjoy a good book.

After falling into a period of neglect at the beginning of the twentieth century, the villa was rescued by Mario Martinelli, a restaurateur from Cortina d'Ampezzo, who restored the villa in 1960 and turned it into the comfortable inn it is today. Now his descendants continue the tradition of hospitality, offering guests the opportunity to sleep in this noble house.

VILLA SORANZO CONESTABILE, Via Roma 1, 30037 Scorzé (VE), tel. +39 041 445 027, fax +39 041 5840 088, email info@villasoranzo.it, www. villasoranzo.it. Driving directions: from Venice, highway S245, exit at Scorzé. Twenty rooms; doubles from E to EE.

DOLO

Villa Ducale

The Villa Ducale is a palatial complex with a statuary-lined drive and monumental facade along the Brenta Riviera in Dolo. The patrician estate was built over the foundations of a more antique villa by Count Giulio Rocca, a Venetian nobleman, in 1884. The villa's beautiful park contains statues, cultivated hedges, shady pergolas, and its own small church, which was built in the 1600s. Today, the villa has been lovingly restored and remade into an intimate hotel and restaurant filled with Murano glass chandeliers, Venetian antiques, and original frescoes. The eleven guest rooms have frescoed ceilings; some have private balconies that look over the park.

This stretch of the Brenta Canal, just thirteen miles from Venice, was a beloved subject for scene painters like Canaletto, who immortalized the Dolo lock in a 1780 painting. Dolo's sixteenth-century mills, also captured in Canaletto's painting, can still be visited today.

The villa's restaurant, Le Colonne, has Venetian travertine floors, empire-style crystal chandeliers, and a dining room with damask-covered tables and fresh flowers. The menu consists of Venetian style dishes and focuses primarily on fresh fish from local sources.

VILLA DUCALE, Via Martiri della Libertà 75, 30031 Dolo (VE), tel. +39 041 560 8020, fax +39 041 560 8004, email info@villaducale.it, www. villaducale.it. Driving directions: from Padova, highway S11, exit at Dolo. Eleven rooms; doubles from EE to EEEE.

VESCOVANA

Villa Pisani Bolognesi Scalabrin

Villa Pisani in Vescovana is an enchanting private home that offers bed-and-breakfast style accommodations. The proprietress, Mariella Bolognesi Scalabrin, also offers full-service wedding planning (see page 145). Weddings at Villa Pisani can be held in the classical hedge-filled garden, which guests staying at the villa are invited to enjoy. Vescovana is just fifty minutes from Venice and twenty minutes from the medieval walled city of Montagnana.

VILLA PISANI BOLOGNESI SCALABRIN, Via Roma 19, 35040 Vescovana (PD), tel. +39 0425 920 016, fax +39 0425 450 811, www.villapisani.it, email info@villapisani.it. Driving directions: take the A13 (Padova-Bologna) highway and exit at Boara Pisani. At the exit, continue to the left toward Padova, continuing three kilometers until the Stanghella stop. Continue toward the left, following the signs indicating Vescovana; continue for three kilometers until the stop sign and from there descend to the left, skirting the park. To enter the villa, ring the bell at Via Roma, 19 (directly in front of the Municipio).

Tables for Two

ARQUÀ PETRARCA

La Montanella

Immersed in the verdant countryside of the Euganean Hills, La Montanella is an idyllic spot to enjoy a meal in one of the most beautiful Venetian country landscapes. The restaurant is situated in Arquà Petrarca, a pretty medieval town famous as the last home of the poet Petrarch. The cuisine at La Montanella follows the traditions of Padova; the menu is built almost exclusively upon products indigenous to the area. Here you will find staples of Padovan cooking: polenta, pasta *fatta in casa* (made at home), asparagus, radicchio, wild greens like *bruscandoli* (wild asparagus) and *ortiche* (nettle), and wild fowl like pigeon and pheasant. The wines of the Colli Euganei include fragrant Tocai Italico, refreshing Pinot Bianco, Cabernet, Merlot, and the *fior d'arancio,* a special moscato made from grapes from these vineyards. The desserts are excellent; the restaurant makes its own gelato flavored with amaretto, grappa, or coffee.

La Montanella, Via Costa 33, 35032 Arquà Petrarca (PD), tel. +39 0429 718 200, fax +39 0429 777 177, www.montanella.it. Closed Tuesday evenings and Wednesdays. Driving directions: from Padova, highway S16, exit Arquà Petrarca. Ninety seats; reservations recommended. Cost: E.

SELVAZZANO DENTRO

Relais La Montecchia

Relais La Montecchia is housed in a beautifully restored tobacco-drying barn at the exclusive Golf Club La Montecchia, just twenty minutes from Padova. Next door, the wine estate of La Montecchia is a great spot to stop for a *degustazione di vino,* and while you are there, you might get to visit the graceful Villa Emo Capodilista.

The cuisine at the Relais is original and harks back to Venice's history in the spice trade. The tasting menu follows the spice route, with offerings like tandoori red prawns and lentil cream, garbanzo bean puree with red rice and spice powder, rack of lamb in herb crust with shallot *agrodolce* and roasted potatoes, and, for dessert, *panforte* semifreddo with coconut-black pepper sauce. On the excellent wine list, look for the wines of La Montecchia, from grapes grown in the surrounding vineyards.

Relais La Montecchia, Via Montecchia 12, 35030 Selvazzano Dentro (PD), tel. +39 049 805 5323, fax +39 049 805 5368, email relais@calandre.com, www.calandre.com. Closed Sundays and Mondays, and for holidays January 1 to 8, and August 6 to 30. Driving directions: from Padova, take the state road SS11 and exit at Sarmeola. Continue, following indications for Selvazzano Dentro. Eighty seats; reservations recommended. Cost: EEE.

ASOLO

Villa Razzolini Loredan

Just outside historic Asolo is a little jewel full of history and tradition. Villa Razzolini Loredan, now an elegant restaurant, is an eighteenth-century villa surrounded by an old park. Once used exclusively to receive noble families, today the villa's beautiful main floor halls are filled with elegantly set tables. A large entrance hall decorated with graceful capitals leads to the dining room, which is circled by a balustraded gallery and a ceiling painted with the crowning of a triumphant Venus, frescoed in the early 1900s by Noè Bordignon. The setting alone makes it worth coming to the villa, but the food, which exalts the products grown in the Treviso hills, adds to the experience. Seasonal menus highlight fresh local crops like white asparagus from Bassano and wild mushrooms from the Venetian woods. Although the restaurant is refined, the cooking style is based in the classic home style cooking of the region. The wine list includes some of the best labels the Veneto has to offer.

VILLA RAZZOLINI LOREDAN, Via Schiavonesca Marosticana 15, 31011 Asolo (TV), tel. +39 0423 951 088, fax +39 0423 521 127, www.villarazzolini.it. Closed: Monday evenings and Tuesdays. Driving directions: from Treviso, highway S348 to Montebelluna, continue west on highway S248, exit at Casella. Sixty seats; reservations recommended. Cost: E.

MIRA

Ristorante Villa Margherita

This restaurant, with its three small classical dining halls, is situated in a nineteenth-century villa in a vast private park. The dining room is decorated with garden-like frescoes, pretty chairs, and lots of fresh flowers. For service, the waiters arrive in coat tails and bow ties. In the summer you can enjoy the park-like setting dining at one of the restaurant's outdoor tables. Chef-owner Remigio dal Corso skillfully prepares old Venetian

recipes. For couples, the chef offers a tasting menu, which includes courses like a delicate carpaccio of salmon and scampi, fresh spider crabs, seafood risotto, gilt-head bream with artichokes, and the classic *fritto misto*. The excellent wine list has many delightful sparkling wines, perfect for toasting, and many interesting wines from northeastern Italy. Ristorante Villa Margherita is also available for parties and wedding banquets. Just across the road is the Villa Margherita, a hotel set in a patrician mansion (see page 124).

RISTORANTE VILLA MARGHERITA, Via Nazionale 416, 30030 Mira Porte (VE), tel. +39 (041) 426 5800, fax +39 (041) 426 5838, www. dalcorsohotellerie.it. Closed Tuesday evenings and Wednesdays, and for holidays January 7 to 27. Driving directions: from Venice, highway S11, exit at Malcontenta. One hundred twenty seats; reservations recommended. Cost: EEEE.

ISOLA RIZZA

Perbellini

Perbellini is one of the highest-rated restaurants in all of Italy. The dining room is quite formal, with soft lighting, tall candles, and a patrician aura. The menu leans toward fish and seafood, and each day's *menu del giorno* (daily menu) is presented verbally to diners. Some highlighted dishes include tuna carpaccio marinated in olive oil and lemon and served with panzanella and crab salad, and smoked ricotta gnocchi with tomato confit and basil. Desserts are exquisitely prepared and include Perbellini's signature dessert, the *millefoglie stracchin,* made from layers of pastry filled with a vanilla soufflé. This dessert's name derives from the dialect expression *la se straca* (it tires), because the original method used to prepare the confection meant that it had to be consumed immediately after preparation. The wine list includes the best names in Italian and French wines.

The Perbellini company is well known for its *pasticceria*, producing gourmet versions of holiday sweets like *pandoro, panettone,* and for Easter the dove-shaped *colomba* cake. The restaurant is forty kilometers south of Verona, along the route to Rovigo.

PERBELLINI, Via Muselle 10/11, 37050 Isola Rizza (VR), tel. +39 045 713 5899, fax +39 045 713 5352, email ristorante@perbellini.com, www. perbellini.com. Closed Sundays and Mondays. Driving directions: from Verona take highway S12, connect to highway S434, exit Isola Rizza. Forty-five seats; reservations essential. Cost: EEEE.

VERONA

12 Apostoli

In the oldest part of Roman Verona, the 12 Apostoli is a classic restaurant that has been open since the eighteenth century. Although the name would seem to be a biblical reference, it's actually a reference to the restaurant's first group of regulars—twelve merchants from Piazza delle Erbe who came here every day to settle their business affairs in the 1750s.

The restaurant has changed somewhat since those rustic days. Today the dining room is elegantly painted with warm medieval-style frescoes, which cover the walls and the barrel-vaulted ceilings. The service is impeccable and formal, yet unobtrusive—perfect for an intimate dinner. Specialties include porcini mushrooms *al forno*, sturgeon and Swiss chard, fresh tagliatelle with prawns in saffron sauce, squash gnocchi with truffles, filet of beef with taleggio and chanterelles, and the specialty of the house, *vitello alla Lessinia* (veal from the mountains of Lessini). The restaurant is one of the founding members of the Ristoranti di Buon Ricordo (see page xiii).

12 APOSTOLI, Corticella San Marco 3, 37121 Verona (VR), tel. +39 045 596 999, fax +39 045 591 530, email dodiciapostoli@tiscalinet.it, www. 12apostoli.it. Closed Sunday evenings and Mondays, and for holidays from January 2 to 7 and from June 14 to July 6. Cost: EEEE.

VALEGGIO SUL MINCIO

Antica Locanda Mincio

This old inn along the Mincio River was used by Napoleon's troops as a horse-changing station during their advances against the Austrians in 1796. In the 1950s, Luchino Visconti chose this spot to stage scenes for his epic romance, *Senso*, the tumultuous love story of an Italian countess and an Austrian officer. Today the historic spot is a charming restaurant where you can enjoy local specialties next to a roaring fire in the *Sala del Camino* (hearth room) or sit under the shade trees of the riverside garden. The dining room is decorated with frescoes by a local artist, who painted them in the spirit of the mannerist frescoes common to the area's patrician villas. The Locanda is renowned for its *agnolotti*, a romantic specialty made following an ancient recipe indigenous to Valeggio sul Mincio. To finish your meal, you can try regional cheeses like the fermented *bruss delle Langhe,* the alpine cow's milk *toma ossolana,* or the *ubriaco trevigiano,* a cheese from Treviso flavored with grape must.

ANTICA LOCANDA MINCIO, Via Michelangelo 12, Località Borghetto, 37067 Valeggio sul Mincio (VR), tel. +39 045 795 0059, fax +39 045 637 0455, email anticalocandamincio@libero.it, www.anticalocandamincio.it. Closed Wednesdays and Thursdays, and for holidays from November 14 to 30 and from February 1 to 15. Driving directions: from Verona, take highway S11 to Castelnuovo del Garda, connect to highway SS249, exit Valeggio sul Mincio. One hundred seats; reservations recommended. Cost: E.

Watching the Sunset

Teolo, Colli Euganei—Teolo in the Euganean Hills

The Euganean Hills were first discovered by the Romans, who came here to take advantage of the area's curative thermal springs. Over the centuries, the hill's quiet vistas have inspired poets from Petrarch, who came here to work on his love sonnets, to Percy Shelley, who wrote longingly about the sunset over the Euganean Hills.

The hills are circled by quiet villages and linked by roads, which wind through vineyards and wooded hillsides. Montegrotto, Galzignano, and Arquà Petrarca are among the area's more famous sights, but to the north, the route that connects Torreglia, Treponti, and Teolo is particularly scenic. The three northern villages are filled with ancient sanctuaries and churches, and in Teolo a mountain rises to one of the highest points in the range (over seventeen hundred feet), offering one of the best spots to take in the view.

The Santuario e Monastero di Monte della Madonna (Sanctuary and Monastery of the Madonna's Mountain) stands atop its own hill northwest of Teolo. The first mention of the sanctuary dates to 1253, but it was greatly expanded in the sixteenth century after Pope Julius II ceded it to the Benedictines. The monastery conserves a fourteenth-century stone Madonna, carved from *pietra di Avesa* (a stone quarried near Verona), which has been attributed to the fourteenth-century sculptor Andriolo de Santi.

From the monastery's terrace, one of the best panoramas of the gentle verdant hills opens before you. If you are here for sunset, you can catch the sight of Shelley's "crimson light."

SANTUARIO MONTE DELLA MADONNA, 35037 Teolo (PD), tel. +39 049 992 5087.

Places to Propose

Ponte degli Alpini (Alpine Corps Bridge)—Bassano del Grappa, Vicenza

The Ponte degli Alpini at Bassano is a graceful wooden bridge designed by Palladio in 1569 to span the Brenta River. Since its completion in 1575, the covered, pedestrian-only bridge has been destroyed by destructive floods and bombardments, but always rebuilt according to Palladio's design. The most recent reconstruction of the bridge was carried out by the Alpine division of the Italian army after World War II, which is how the bridge came to be called the Ponte degli Alpini.

Perhaps due to the solitude of its setting and the romantic views from the bridge's edge, this spot has attracted lovers since it was first built. For years, couples have come to the Ponte degli Alpini to stroll across its cobblestone walk and to exchange a kiss or a solemn promise. The bridge was also immortalized by a World War I song, "Sul Ponte di Bassano," which recounts the story of the parting between a soldier and his beloved. The wooden bridge is open only to pedestrians, making it a naturally quiet setting above the reflective river. If you come here to propose, you can toast to your future just across the bridge in the tasting rooms of Bortolo Nardini Steam Distillery, where they have been producing grappa since 1779 (www.nardini.it).

Romantic Lore and Local Festivals

Villa Valmarana ai Nani

Romantics planning a visit to Vicenza shouldn't miss the famous Villa Valmarana, built in 1669 and frescoed by Tiepolo in 1757. An ancient story says that a rich and powerful prince built this lugubrious castle and circled it with high walls to protect his only daughter, Jana, from the cruelties of the outside world. Jana was born a deformed dwarf, and the prince wanted to spare her from seeing other people more beautiful than she. To further this end, all the servants hired in the household were loyal dwarves. As Jana grew, many youths, attracted by the prince's riches and the young girl's beautiful face, requested her hand in marriage, but as soon as they discovered her deformity they fled the villa's walls. Finally, the young girl fell hopelessly in love with one of the suitors, who, like all the others before him, made a hasty retreat from the villa after seeing her. Brokenhearted, she ran to a balcony that overlooked the street and, as she called out to him, slipped and fell to her death. The dwarves, having climbed the wall to watch the scene, were turned to stone by sheer grief. Their statues still guard the walls of the villa today.

VILLA VALMARANA, Via S. Bastiano, Vicenza, tel. +39 0444 543 976. Open March 15 to November 5, from 10 A.M. to noon and from 3 P.M. to 5 P.M. Closed Mondays and Friday mornings.

Romeo and Juliet's Castles

Any Venetian will tell you that Shakespeare's tragic play was actually inspired by an Italian novella written by Luigi da Porto. Locals in his home town of Montecchio Maggiore believe that the source of da Porto's inspiration for *Giulietta e Romeo* are two Scaligero-era castles built on opposite hillsides of the town, which the townspeople have nicknamed "Romeo" and "Juliet." Popular lore says that da Porto took shelter here in Montorso (a hamlet of Montecchio Maggiore) after a war wound left him disfigured and in failing health. After writing his novella, he lived here until his death, and some of the townsfolk believe his ghost still roams the hillsides. Almost nothing remains of the writer's own ancestral home except an ancient portico and a large tower. In its place sprang up the beautiful Palladian villa Da Porto Barbaran, a work of the French architect Cherrette. Each year on the first of May, the town holds a medieval festival in which characters play the parts of the two feuding houses, the Montagues (Montecchi) and the Capulets (Capuleti). The historic event is opened by an elected Romeo and Juliet and includes a medieval market, archery demonstrations, and sword fights.

MONTECCHIO MAGGIORE is just seventeen kilometers west of Vicenza. For more information about the festival, contact: Gruppo Storico Medievale Giulietta e Romeo, Via L. Da Vinci 50, 36075 Montecchio Maggiore (VI), tel. +39 0444 497 147, fax +39 0444 491 758, www.faida.it.

A Chess Match for a Princess

North of Vicenza, in the walled city of Marostica, a chess match is held every other year in the castle square with live characters dressed as the game pieces. The origins of this festival go back to the fifteenth century, when two rival knights sought to win the hand of the lord of Marostica's beautiful daughter Lionora. The lord, not wanting to lose either of his valuable knights, forbade the duel in favor of a live chess match complete with mock kings, queens, bishops, knights on horseback, and pawns. The winner also won Lionora's hand, and the tradition has been replayed here ever since.

Five hundred years after the first challenge, the game is replayed every two years and involves almost four hundred figures—practically the entire population of Marostica. Information and photos of past games can be found at www.marosticascacchi.it.

Picnic Spots

Operatic Picnic in Verona's Roman Arena

Plan a dinner picnic under the starry summer night in Verona's ancient arena. The summer opera series begins in June and always includes classic romantic operas like *La Boheme*, *Turandot*, and *Aida*. The unnumbered spaces on the arena's steps (rent a cushion, as the stone steps haven't been modified since Roman times) are the best spots to settle on with a decanted bottle of wine (no glass is allowed) and a basket full of Venetian specialties. Tickets can be reserved online through the Arena's website (www.arena.it).

Romantic Excursions

Exploring the Lagoon by Houseboat

A novel way to intimately explore the Venetian lagoon and the Brenta Canal is by renting your own houseboat. No prior boating experience or license is required to rent a boat in Italy. A houseboat gives you access to the more secluded lagoon islands and surrounding fishing villages like Chioggia and Caorle, where you can buy fish directly from the fishermen's nets. Local boat-rental agencies provide detailed nautical charts and a short lesson on how to operate and dock the boat. Most of the agencies dock their boats in Chioggia, a colorful fishing village at the south end of the lagoon. From Chioggia, the entrance to the Brenta Canal is nearby, along which you can trace the route followed by the seventeenth-century *burchielli* (canal barges) past Palladian villas all the way to Padua. Along the canal you can visit historic villas like the elegant Villa Foscari, the Villa Widmann-Foscari in Mira, and the palatial Villa Pisani at Stra (see "Villas to Tour by Houseboat," page 139).

Exploring the Lagoon by Houseboat—Addresses and Practical Information

Houseboat Rentals

CROWN BLUE LINE rents two-, four-, six-, and eight-person cruisers with sun decks, showers, and kitchens. Boats are usually rented by the week, but you can reserve for other time periods. Crown Blue Line, Venetian Lagoon, Chioggia, tel. 1-888-355-9491, email crownbluelineus@att.net, www.crownblueline.com. Prices start at E700 per week for a two-person boat.

RENDEZ-VOUS FANTASIA rents two-, four-, and six-person boats with sun terraces and outdoor showers. Rendez-Vous Fantasia, Via San Marco 1720, 30019 Sottomarina (VE), tel. and fax +39 041 554 0016, email rendez@cbn.it, www.rendez-vous-fantasia.com. Prices start at E627 per week.

HOUSEBOAT HOLIDAYS ITALIA rents four- to ten-person boats in a variety of configuration and amenities. Houseboat Holidays Italia, tel +39 0426 666 025 and +39 0425 213 57, fax +39 0425 421 733, email: info@houseboat.it, www.houseboat.it. Weekly rentals start at E880.

Villas to Tour by Houseboat—Brenta Canal

THE BRENTA RIVIERA has been enchanting poets and travelers since the first *burchielli* traveled along its waters in the sixteenth century. Rich Venetian families built their summerhouses here, commissioning the greatest architects and artisans to build their villas and *foresterie* (guest houses). The most famous of the villas that line its shores are Villa Foscari, also called La Malcontenta, a monumental masterpiece by the architect Palladio; Villa Widmann-Foscari in Mira, with its extensive frescoes; and Villa Pisani in Stra, a national monument with lavish frescoes by Giambattista Tiepolo and Jacopo Guarana, extensive classical gardens, and a famous labyrinth.

STRA

VILLA SAGREDO (sixteenth century) The Sagredo family hired a famous architect, Jacopo Sansovino, to transform an ancient Roman castle into their country villa. The villa was famed for its gardens and for having hosted Galileo Galilei during the summers of 1592 to 1608. Villa Sagredo,

Via Sagredo 3A, Vigonovo (PD), tel. +39 049 503 174 and +39 041 412 967, fax. +39 041 410 664, www.villasagredo.it. By appointment only. Hours: Tuesday through Friday, 5 p.m. to 10 p.m., Saturday and Sunday, 2 p.m. to 10 p.m. Admission is free. The villa is also available for special event and weddings. The villa's reception capacity is 20 to 120 guests.

Villa Foscarini (seventeenth century) Built by the architect Vicenzo Scamozzi between 1617 and 1635 and inspired by a design of Palladio's, the Villa Foscarini is now owned by the Rossi family, who have filled its halls with an interesting shoe museum that chronicles fifty years of haute couture shoe history. In its *foresteria* there is a richly frescoed ballroom with paintings attributed to Domenico Bruni and Pietro Liberi. The ballroom is often used for wedding receptions (see page 152). Villa Foscarini Rossi, Via Doge Pisani 1/2, 30039 Stra (VE), tel. +39 049 980 1091, www.villa foscarini.it. Open Tuesdays and Sundays. Hours: 9:00 A.M. to 12:00 A.M., 2:30 P.M. to 6:00 P.M. Admission E5.

Villa Pisani (also called Villa Nazionale or Villa Reale, ca. 1720) This palatial complex was the grandest of the villas built by the powerful Pisani family. Over the centuries, other rulers adopted the palace as their own, among them Napoleon, and Francis I, emperor of Austria. In 1866 the villa became a property of the Savoy, kings of Italy, who twenty years later ceded it to the state. Inside, the main ballroom has a fantastic ceiling decorated by Giambattista Tiepolo, which celebrates achievements of the Pisani family. Villa Pisani (Villa Nazionale, Villa Reale), Stra (VE), tel. +39 049 502 074. Closed on Tuesdays. Hours: April through September, 9 a.m. to 6 p.m. and October through March, 9 A.M. to 4 P.M. Admission for the park and museum is E5.16.

FIESSO

Villa Soranzo (also called Villa Fracasso, sixteenth century) A typical sixteenth-century Venetian villa whose facade, though simple in design, is richly decorated with period frescoes. Villa Soranzo, Via Naviglio, 30032 Fiesso. The villa's garden and park are always open to visitors.

SAMBRUSON DI DOLO

VILLA BADOER (eighteenth century) The villa houses a collection of antique agricultural tools. In addition, you can visit the park, the antique cellars, and a few of the ground-floor rooms. Villa Badoer, Via Tito 2, Sambruson di Dolo. Open: May, June, September, and October on Sundays; July and August open for group visits by appointment. Hours: 3 P.M. to 7 P.M.

MIRA

BARCHESSA ALESSANDRI (seventeenth century) Built at the end of the seventeenth century and frescoed by Pellegrini and del Busaferro. Barchessa Alessandri, Mira (VE), tel. +39 041 415 729. Open daily from May through the summer months; otherwise open on Saturdays and Sundays. Hours from 10:30 A.M. to 12:30 P.M. and 3:30 P.M. to 6:00 P.M. Admission is free.

VILLA CONTARINI (1558) The Villa Contarini dei Leoni, built in 1558 by Francesco Contarini, procurator of San Marco, once boasted magnificent frescoes painted by Giambattista Tiepolo. Tiepolo's frescoes were removed and taken to a palace in Paris and are now part of the Jacquemart-André museum. Villa Contarini dei Leoni is the seat of Mira's public library and theater. The park is always open for visits. Theater information is available at tel. +39 041 426 6545, fax +39 041 560 9910, www.teatrovilladeileoni.it.

VILLA WIDMANN FOSCARI (eighteenth century) This villa was modernized in 1705 and decorated in elegant French rococo style. The decorations include paintings by Giuseppe Angeli (a pupil of Giambattista Piazzetta) and stucco and polychrome decorations. Villa Widmann Foscari, Mira Porte (VE), tel. +39 041 424 156 and +39 041 560 9350. Open on Sundays in March, and Tuesday through Sunday from April through October. Hours: 10:00 A.M. to 5:00 P.M.

BARCHESSA VALMARANA (seventeenth century) Barchessa Valmarana is all that remains of a famous villa built in the seventeenth century, frescoed by a pupil of Tiepolo, Michelangelo Schiavoni Il Chiozzotto (of Chioggia). The villa is situated on a curve along the Brenta; it contains a great hall with frescoes of architectural trompe l'oeil, allegories, and landscapes. Barchessa Valmarana, Mira Porte (VE), tel. +39 041 426 6387 and

+39 041 510 2341. Open Tuesday through Sunday, from April through October. Hours: 9:30 A.M. to 12:00 A.M., 2:30 P.M. to 5:30 P.M.

ORIAGO

VILLA GRADENIGO (sixteenth century) is a classic villa of the period, decorated with historical and mythological frescoes. Villa Gradenigo, Oriago di Mira (VE), tel. +39 041 429 631. Group visits by appointment only.

VILLA MOCENIGO (eighteenth century) This villa was built as a summer residence by the Mocenigo family; today it is owned by the city of Oriago and is the seat of a university. Villa Mocenigo, Riviera San Pietro, Oriago di Mira (VE). The villa is not open for visits.

MALCONTENTA

VILLA FOSCARI (1560) A masterpiece by Palladio built in 1560 and frescoed by Giambattista Zelotti and Battista Franco. According to local lore, the villa's name comes from a "malcontented" Foscari ancestor, a noblewomen who was confined to the villa after she had embarrassed the family with unbecoming behavior. Villa Foscari, "La Malcontenta," Via Dei Turisti 9, Malcontenta—Oriago (VE), tel. + 39 041 547 0012 and +39 041 520 3966. Open Tuesdays and Saturdays, from April through October. Hours: 9 A.M. to noon.

Weddings in the Veneto

There's something seductive about a wedding dinner in the classical garden of a patrician villa. Enveloped in the heady scent of night-blooming jasmine, one long table is elegantly set. The only illumination comes from baroque candelabras, their beeswax candles dripping onto the linen tablecloth. An endless parade of crystal water and wineglasses are the remnants of an unhurried meal marked by a succession of savory delicacies, each paired with the perfect wine. Scintillating conversation and a jovial mood keeps the guests lingering into the wee hours of the morning, until they finally wander off to sleep in one of the villa's bedrooms.

Most of us don't have our own villas. Fortunately, if your heart is set on a spring wedding set in a lush baroque garden, Italy's *Ville delle Delizie,* or Villas of Delights, can provide the perfect setting. Once the ancestral homes of the Veneto's most illustrious families, they are set among the verdant hills and dramatic landscapes surrounding the historic towns of Verona, Vicenza, and Padua. Named for the doges, counts, and former aristocracy of the Venetian Republic, the villas feature impressive architecture and gardens. Some still retain their original family chapels, allowing you to plan both a religious ceremony and a reception on the grounds of the same splendid estate.

CEREMONY AND RECEPTION LOCATIONS

Villa Allegri Arvedi

Driving along the ancient road that divides the vineyards of the Valpantena Valley, leading from Verona to Trento, you'll feel your anticipation build as you see a landmark, the Villa Allegri Arvedi, rising against the horizon. The grandeur of this palace-villa dominates the idyllic valley, and while its scale should be overwhelming, its architecture is so perfectly integrated into the landscape that it achieves a calming harmony of color and shape.

Designed in 1656 by the architect-sculptor Giovanni Battista Bianchi, the Villa Allegri Arvedi might not be standing today if it were not for the vagaries of the nineteenth-century silk trade. An ancestor of the current owners acquired the villa and its properties in 1824 with the intention of razing it to make way for a state-of-the-art silk factory. Fortunately,

Chi non ha moglie non ha padrone.
A man without a wife is without a master.

La moglie é la chiave di casa.
The wife is the key to the house.

although plans were drafted and designs laid, the destruction never took place, due to a decline in the silk market, and today the villa remains standing in its commanding position overlooking the vineyards and olive groves of the Valpantena.

When staging a wedding here, a couple can make a grand entrance through the villa gates, walking along the hedge-lined lane and finally up the stairs through the remarkable Italianate garden. The ornamental garden parterre in front of the villa has the look of embroidery, formed by 250-year-old boxwood hedges in a symmetrical butterfly-wing design, each wing opening off of the garden's circular central fountain. A grass esplanade joins the garden with the villa, creating a perch that makes a perfect stage for an outdoor wedding ceremony in this classical atmosphere.

At the end of the lawn, the garden's baroque grotto, with faux stalactites and mythological mosaics, is a charming space for cocktails. Alternatively, the villa's two reception rooms, the Sala Gialla (Yellow Room) and the Sala Blu (Blue Room), can also be used for toasting. The Sala Gialla has a wood-beamed ceiling, hand-painted with scrolls and cherubs, and frescoes that depict scenes of fantasy gardens, each with its own fountains, grottoes, and gazebos. In the adjoining Sala Blu, allegorical representations of the four seasons adorn the four walls. The intimate spaces of these smaller rooms are reached by passing through the impressive Hall of Caesars, lined with framed portraits of the Roman Caesars, and antique banquettes delicately painted with interior scenes from the 1700s.

A majestic marble staircase leads up from the first floor to the villa's grandest space, the Hall of Titans. A lovely collection of silk stencils and printing rollers along the staircase are reminders of the family's former foray into the silk trade. Designed for entertaining, the monumental Titan's Hall is named for the large-scale painted figures that stand like sentinels circling the room, each giant representing one of the twelve signs of the zodiac. The ceiling rises forty feet overhead, with trompe l'œil paintings creating a play of illusion and perspective. Architectural motifs are shaped into balconies, windows, and colonnades that rise to an imaginary gallery. During gala dinners, the play of candlelight on the scenes creates an otherworldly atmosphere. The hall's massive doors open onto a wide balcony that overlooks the garden, cultivated fields, and green expanses encircling the villa. The room can comfortably accommodate a seated dinner for three hundred guests.

Behind the villa, a gravel courtyard leads to the small baroque family chapel. The chapel is dedicated to San Carlo Borromeo, who visited the villa in 1562 on his way to the Council of Trent. Completely frescoed by Dorigny, the little church has room for fifty guests and may be requested for small Catholic weddings.

The villa's proximity to Verona makes it possible to plan your civil ceremony in Romeo and Juliet's romantic city, and ensures that there will be plenty of sightseeing to keep your guests entertained. The Arvedi family maintains a charming bed-and-breakfast inn across the valley from Villa Arvedi, in a nineteenth-century villa called Borgo 27, where there are accommodations for twenty guests.

VILLA ALLEGRI ARVEDI, Località Cuzzano, 37023 Grezzana (VR), tel. +39 045 907 045, fax +39 045 908766, email arvedi@sis.it, www.villarvedi.it. Driving directions: take the A4 (Milano-Vicenza) highway and exit at Verona Est. Continue straight. At the intersection with the state highway Verona-Vicenza, turn left toward Verona. After five kilometers, turn right and follow the signs for Boscochiesanuova-Grezzana. Continue, following the road to Quinto. After passing through Quinto, you will see the villa on the left. Available for guided tours by appointment. Accommodations are available at Borgo 27; information is available on the villa's website. Cost: EE to EEE.

Villa Pisani

Passing through the gates of the enchanting Villa Pisani, you will fall immediately under a spell that transports you to the past. Shaded by noble trees, a park lined with beguiling marble figures leads to the villa's door. Once inside, there's hardly time to notice the elegant interior, as a second pair of doors beckons you down a hallway to the irresistible lure of the expansive rear gardens. Outside, the quiet of the setting is interrupted only by the cooing of doves and the occasional rapping of woodpeckers.

Though the villa was built in the fifteenth century by Cardinal Pisani as the central manor house to a vast farm estate, its gardens weren't completed until the Victorian era, when its then-owner Evalina van Milligan Pisani, a half-English, half-Turkish countess, expanded them to their current form. Countess Evalina, a fascinating personality, was raised in the Grand Sultan's seraglio at Topkapi Palace. Her Oriental style made her quite popular with the glitterati of Venetian society, and her engaging spirit is still felt within the garden walls. In fact, the villagers of Vescovana believe that Evalina's ghost returns to stroll through the gardens each year in September—and after spending time here, it's not hard to believe that her inviting presence is still nearby.

Spanning the length of the saffron-hued neoclassical façade, a vine-covered arbor offers a shady spot for wedding guests to enjoy an early-evening glass of prosecco before dinner. Two majestic marble peacocks stand guard atop matching balustrades, marking the formal entrance to the Italian and English gardens. Boxwood topiaries, groomed into finials of varying heights, invite you to wander back through the fan-shaped garden and down its paths.

After your guests enjoy aperitifs, they can take a seat at tables around the neoclassical fountain in the intimate spaces created by the hedges, or you can seat them at one long table dramatically illuminated with candelabras. After dinner, guests can steal a romantic moment of their own, taking a seat on the sheltered stone benches that flank the garden or disappearing along the statuary-lined paths.

The delights of Villa Pisani don't end with its carefully groomed gardens. The interior rooms are graced with priceless Venetian antiques, frescoes, marble fireplaces, and delicate Murano glass chandeliers. The decor achieves a style of timeworn elegance that immediately puts you at ease. Despite the villa's aristocratic characteristics, it has a welcoming soul.

You and your guests can choose to spend the night under the villa's sumptuously decorated ceilings. The villa has a long history of hosting illustrious guests—such as the queen of Sweden, Lord Byron, and Henry James—all at the invitation and hospitality of the captivating Countess Evalina. The current owner, Mariella Bolognesi Scalabrin, welcomes guests with the same style and flair as one imagines would have been de rigueur in Evalina's day.

Signora Bolognesi Scalabrin brings her impeccable taste to planning events at the villa and can be at your disposal for all the wedding details. She can help you with a variety of services, from assistance with the legal documents for civil or religious ceremonies to arranging the catering and choosing the gifts for the guests, the floral arrangements, and what the wait staff should wear. If you want an occasion where you can be as relaxed as if you were in your own home and trust that every detail will be attended to, Villa Pisani is the choice for you.

Easily reached from Venice, the villa can accommodate eighteen guests in its superbly appointed suites. Guests may prefer to relax inside the villa's gates, but if they get the urge to venture forth, the Euganean Hills, historic Padua, Venice, and the Brenta Canal are all close by, offering many great sights to keep them entertained.

VILLA PISANI BOLOGNESI SCALABRIN, Via Roma 19, 35040 Vescovana (PD), tel. +39 0425 920 016, fax +39 0425 450 811, email info@villapisani.it, www.villapisani.it. For driving directions see page 128. Available for guided tours by appointment. Reception capacity ranges from 50 to 350 guests; accommodations for 18. Catholic chapel available upon request. Cost: EE.

Castello del Catajo

Although Castello del Catajo has been known as a castle for centuries, it wasn't built to fend off marauding hordes. This awe-inspiring complex—with its 350 rooms, acres of parkland filled with roaming deer, two-hundred-year-old magnolias, and water-lily fishponds with paddling swans—was the vision of one man, Pio Enea degli Obizzi, who built his own version of Xanadu over a three-year period beginning in 1570. Obizzi's single-minded quest was to create a residence worthy of his ancient family's name. In colors so vivid that they seem to have been created yesterday, the frescoed interior halls chronicle four hundred years of Obizzi glories and achievements, from 1007 to 1422, through marriages, battles, and political victories. So passionate was Obizzi about his architectural-genealogical undertaking that he hired the then-famous Gian Battista Zelotti (a student of Paolo Veronese) to begin frescoing the halls with chapters from the family's history before the palace's construction was even finished.

The stark monolithic structure rises in a lush green park above a canal that was once a busy trading route between Battaglia Terme and Padua. The castle entrance passes through a stately triumphal arch with heraldic bas-reliefs and statues. The scale of the castle is evident in the Cortile dei Giganti, the Giant's Courtyard, once used to entertain castle visitors with weeklong theatrical presentations that included tournaments and, after flooding the space, mock naval battles. Today, the Cortile has a splendid lawn and can comfortably accommodate over 350 guests for a seated dinner. This gargantuan space is connected to the main body of the castle by an intimate staircase with mysterious hidden niches. Under the shade trees, orientalized waterspouts and exotic stone beasts lurk in stone grottoes nestled under the stairs. Climbing up the castle's external staircases, which were constructed as horse ramps so returning lords could enter the castle on horseback, you arrive at an expansive terrace with a view of the Euganean Hills. For cocktails and outdoor dinners, the sunny

terrace can be set with wide umbrellas, creating a perfect setting in this dreamlike atmosphere.

On entering the castle from the terrace, you will find six vividly frescoed halls awaiting receptions. The rooms can accommodate events of many sizes, and the paintings are so rich with historical and allegorical references that you may want to offer your guests a tour before dinner.

The green park below the castle offers a natural respite from the majesties of the castle rooms. Under the lofty branches of age-old specimen trees, the gardens are filled with roses, peonies, and lavender, offering a fragrant setting for a wedding ceremony or after-dinner strolls. A procession of potted lemon trees leads to an enormous rectangular fishpond, flanked on two sides by sixteen towering magnolias. The garden is at its best in May, when the magnolias are in bloom, although the rare botanical trees make the shady paths a delight year-round.

Arquà Petrarca, named for the medieval poet Petrarch, and the thermal springs of Abano and Montegrotto Terme are all nearby, so you can plan to "take the waters" or relax with mud baths and spa treatments before or after your big day.

Castello del Catajo, Via Catajo 1, 35041 Battaglia Terme (PD), tel. +39 049 875 9326, fax +39 049 910 0411, www.castellodelcatajo.it, email info@castellodelcatajo.it. Driving directions: take the A13 (Padova-Bologna) highway and exit at Terme Euganee. Just before you reach the town of Battaglia Terme, you will see the castle on a hill to the right. Available for guided tours Tuesdays and Sundays; closed in December. You may select your own catering. Reception capacity ranges from 100 to 350 guests. Cost: E to EE.

Villa Capodilista—La Montecchia

Originally conceived as a hunting lodge for the counts of Emo Capodilista in 1568, Villa Capodilista, with its symmetrical façades and double-storied loggias, is an intimate and luxurious setting for small weddings. Like a Fabergé egg, the elegant white lines of the villa's architecture reveal few clues as to the delights of its interiors, which seem to have been designed for fairy-tale occasions. The architect-painter who designed the villa, Dario Varotari, created an intensely symmetrical plan for the villa and its gardens, and set his jewel box on a plateau above the count's vineyards. Four identical clover-shaped gardens, one on each side of the villa, are reached through the four identical gates that once provided an entrance for visitors on horseback. The gardens, with their shady lawns and circular hedges, offer a quiet setting where you can exchange your vows; alternatively, the estate's church at the bottom of the hill can be requested for Catholic ceremonies.

The cocktail hour can be spent wandering through the villa's fanciful rooms, where the walls and ceilings are covered in Mannerist frescoes with cherubs, vignettes, and scenes from mythology recast with the Emo Capodilista family members in the starring roles. As you sip a glass of wine pressed from grapes grown on the estate's surrounding vines, you can enjoy the Vineyard Room, where frescoes celebrate the foremost occupation of the family with paintings of winged cherubs harvesting and pressing grapes. Three other whimsical rooms are connected on the first floor, each adorned with paintings in a particular theme. The four rooms on the ground floor and those on the upper floor are connected by a splendid four-ramp staircase in a Greek cross formation, completely decorated with a fresco of the *Four Ages of Man.* An intimate candlelit dinner can be set within the adjoining upstairs rooms, which are reached by a ramp. The large doors can be left open, allowing guests to wander out onto the covered loggias; this is also a perfect spot for tossing the wedding bouquet.

Villa Capodilista is just one facet of the La Montecchia estate. At the end of the evening, the bride and groom can lead guests on a promenade down the winding drive to the inviting rooms of La Montecchia's *agriturismo,* set on the grounds of the family's medieval castle. Castello di Mottollo, characterized by its massive keep, has been converted into a spacious apartment with a kitchen, dining area, and terrace, with room for ten guests. Other apartments are located in the ancient priests' quarters and the old farm buildings where the workers once lived. All have been carefully renovated and are wonderfully appointed in a relaxed Italian style. The *agriturismo*'s apartments have room for a total of twenty-two guests and can be rented by the week.

The current count of Emo Capodilista continues his family's commitment to fine wine making and opens his cellars for guests to taste La Montecchia's esteemed wines. Under the rustic wood-beamed ceilings of the former castle granary, the Cantinone is a perfect space to hold a rehearsal dinner, where you can dine on local rustic specialties accompanied with La Montecchia's delicious wines.

VILLA CAPODILISTA (La Montecchia), Via Montecchia 16, 35030 Selvazzano Dentro (PD), tel. +39 049 637 294, fax +39 049 805 5836, email Agriturismo@LaMontecchia.it, www.lamontecchia.it. Driving directions from Venice: take the A4 (Venezia-Milano) highway and exit at Padova Ovest. Follow the signs for Padova, which will take you onto the bypass road called Corso Australia. Follow the indications for Abano-Vicenza. Take the exit for Padova Aeroporto. On the overpass (which passes above the road you have just exited), follow the directions for Colli Euganei and the Hotel Piroga. Continue through Tencarola and Feriole, after which there will be a sign for La Montecchia. Driving directions from Milan or Verona: Take the A4 (Milano-Venezia) highway and exit at Grisignano. Continue on the state road toward Padova. After approximately three kilometers, take the road for Selvazzano Dentro and follow the indications for "Golf della

Montecchia." The entrance to the estate is next to the entrance to the golf club, on the same side of the street. Available for guided tours on Wednesdays and Saturdays, from March 15 to November 15. You may select your own catering. Reception capacity ranges from 50 to 120 guests. Next door, the estate's Castello del Mottolo has accommodations for twenty-two guests. Cost: EE.

Villa Foscarini Rossi

Just outside Venice's lagoon, the Brenta Canal stretches twenty-two miles from Venice to the northern city of Stra. The canal was originally constructed to help prevent the silting of the Venice lagoon, but noble families realized the convenience of the canal's proximity to Venice and soon began constructing baronial homes along its banks. At the top of the canal, in Stra, Villa Foscarini-Rossi is a seventeenth-century patrician villa, with its own sixteenth-century *foresteria:* a guest house built to host elegant receptions.

The building was designed to be a sumptuous spot where the Foscarini family could receive illustrious visitors and entertain them in style. Over the years the family has hosted many important visitors, such as Gaspare Gozzi, the founder of one of the earliest Italian newspapers, and the duke of Modena, Francesco Maria d'Este, who spent a long sojourn here with the members of his court in 1772.

Today, the foresteria hosts gala events and weddings in the spirit of that genteel era. The sweeping portico along the building's façade can be used for serving the first toast, or for seated dinners with a view of the garden. Inside, a grand ballroom with forty-foot ceilings can host seated dinners for 230 guests. Amusing frescoes in vibrant colors completely cover the walls and ceiling. The depictions of heroic feminine virtues (Fame, Virtue, Knowledge, and Wisdom) may have been inspired by an earthly muse, perhaps even a former Foscarini. The painter Pietro Liberi, nicknamed Il Libertino—ostensibly for the erotic style of his paintings—made many visits to the foresteria before it was discovered by Signore Foscarini that he was also interested in Signora Foscarini. Following Liberi's departure, many other artists collaborated on the rest of the room's decorations, which are completed by rows of vine-covered Corinthian columns, and balconies painted in an illusion of perspective.

The park and gardens that surround the villa and its guest house provide a verdant setting for outdoor dinners. On the estate's grounds is a private chapel that can be used for Catholic ceremonies on request.

Next door, the marvelous Villa Foscarini Rossi, an architectural masterpiece designed by Vicenzo Scamozzi, is home to the Calzaturificio Rossimoda (the Rossimoda Shoe Museum). The villa, with its wealth of frescoes, can be visited by wedding guests, who may enjoy wandering through the museum's collection of over fifteen hundred pairs of couture shoes. The Rossi family, who own the villa and its estate, were the founders of the museum and have been manufacturers to Italy's premier designers for over fifty years. Shoes produced for such couturiers as Yves Saint Laurent, Fendi, Givenchy, and even Andy Warhol are on display in the museum.

The villa's proximity to the Brenta Canal creates the perfect opportunity to plan for your guests to arrive by boat from Venice. The *Battelli di Brenta* (river tour boats) leave daily from Venice and Padua, touring through the same route that inspired so many Venetian painters.

VILLA FOSCARINI ROSSI, Via Doge Pisani 1/2, 30039 Stra (VE), tel. +39 049 980 0335, fax +39 049 960 1589, email info@villafoscarini.it, www.villafoscarini.it. Driving directions from Venice: take state road S11 and exit at Dolo. Continue toward Fiesso and Stra and follow the indications for the Villa Reale/Villa Pisani. After you pass Villa Pisani's enclosing wall you will see Villa Foscarini. Driving directions from Milan: take the A4 (Milano-Venezia) highway and exit at Padova Est. Continue on the Padova-Venezia state road, following indications for Ponte di Brenta, Vigonza, and Stra. The villa and the Rossimoda Calzature museum are open for public visits. Information on boat tours is available online at www.antoniana.it. Cost: EE to EEE.

Castello Porto-Colleoni

The eastern area of the Veneto plain, from Vicenza to Verona and north, is filled with castles and medieval walled towns unchanged since the days of the legendary Montagues and Capulets. The province's indigenous medieval culture is preserved in the festivals of the local villages, offering the opportunity to combine a castle wedding with age-old romantic traditions.

You can celebrate your own romantic occasion at Castello Porto-Colleoni in Thiene. A breathtaking example of the northern castle, it bears a strong resemblance to the Gothic palaces that line the Grand Canal in Venice. The gleaming white structure, with delicate Ghibelline crenellations, along the roofline, began as the center of an agricultural estate built to help ensure a steady food supply to neighboring Venice. In 1507, Francesco Porto inherited the castle and its properties and began working toward transforming the estate into a luxury palace. The roof was raised, decorative Renaissance windows were added to the towers, marble staircases were built next to the loggias, and the walls surrounding the garden and courtyard were built. Wedding receptions can be held in the stupendous main hall on the ground floor.

In the summer months, you may prefer to set tables within the castle's verdant park. Fifteen grand magnolias, planted over a century ago, surround a grand grass esplanade where outdoor receptions can be set in warm weather. The romantic garden, planted in the 1840s, includes huge shade trees and a fragrant cedar grove.

Another beautiful venue for receptions is the opulent eighteenth-century stables, built by Francesco Muttoni and lined with marble statuary and ornate wood casework. Receptions are now held in this lavish spot, which was originally reserved for the horses of the Porto-Colleoni family. No expense was spared to create these palatial quarters. Even the troughs are decorated with sculpted leaves and arabesques, while the floors are elegantly paved with interlocking chains of red and white stones. Inside the castle's museum, a wonderful collection of equestrian paintings chronicles the family's cavalry background.

The castle can accommodate large weddings in its gardens during the spring and summer months, while in the winter the interior halls are best suited for weddings of one hundred guests or fewer.

CASTELLO PORTO-COLLEONI DI THIENE, Corso Garibaldi 2, 36016 Thiene (VI), tel. +39 0445 366 015, email info@castellodithiene.com, www. castellodithiene. com. Driving directions: take the A31 (Vicenza-Piovene Rocchette) highway and exit at Thiene. The castle is located at the center of the city. Available for guided visits from March 15 through November 15. You may select your own catering. Reception capacity ranges from 50 to 350 guests. Cost: EE to EEE.

Castello di Bevilacqua

Just south of Verona, Castello di Bevilacqua is a wonderful fourteenth-century fortress located just outside medieval Montagnana. Circled by a large moat and fortified walls, Castello di Bevilacqua was built as a defensive tribute to the Veronese court of Can Grande della Scala, the infamous Ghibelline ruler. Before Venice took control of the inland territories, the Can Grande and his northern Ghibellines ruled the region with an iron fist, using outposts such as Bevilacqua to maintain control of the area. As Venice sought to assert its dominance in the area, the castle became the prize in many stormy battles and skirmishes, ultimately suffering heavy damage under Venice's rule. In 1756, Gaetano Ippolito Bevilacqua restored the interior, creating the elegant first-floor rooms, but just a century later, during the Napoleonic Era, the castle was burned by occupying Austrian troops. Ten years later Countess Felicita Bevilacqua restored the castle, adding medieval crenellations atop the castle walls and giving the complex its neo-Gothic look, in line with the nostalgic taste of the Victorian era.

Despite its many restorations, the castle exudes medieval charm, especially when its courtyard and halls are filled with revelers celebrating in period style. The proprietors host themed events throughout the year, from theatrical presentations to pageants. For wedding banquets, Bevilacqua can offer you and your guests your choice of their carefully researched medieval menus, and authentic entertainment provided by jugglers, drummers, fire-eaters, and magicians. The porticos in the central courtyard can be illuminated by torchlight for outdoor banquets, and the elegant interior halls can offer ample space for indoor dining. Sit-down dinners can be held in either the Sala di Musica or the Sala Rosa, both elegantly appointed with chandeliers and polished terrazzo floors.

The castle is surrounded by six acres of parkland, created in part by the appropriation of the moat as garden space. A long tree-lined walkway leads into the castle, creating a romantic promenade for guests as they arrive or take a stroll after dinner.

For receptions, guests are free to roam through the castle's museum-like halls. The old castle kitchen, the subterranean cellars (complete with dungeons), and various other halls are filled with antiques, suits of armor, and period artworks. Additional sections of the castle are currently being restored to offer guest accommodations.

CASTELLO DI BEVILACQUA, Via Roma 2, 37040 Bevilacqua (VR), tel. +39 0442 936 55, fax +39 0442 649 420, email info@castellodibevilacqua.com, www.castellodibevilacqua.com. Driving directions from Padova: take the A13 (Padova-Bologna) highway and exit at Monselice. Connect to the state road S10 and follow the signs to Montagnana. Open for public visits Wednesdays and Sundays. Catering is managed on the premises. Reception capacity ranges from 50 to 350 guests. Cost: E to EE.

Practical Information—Veneto

GETTING THERE

By air: There are two airports with service to the Veneto region. Venezia Marco Polo (airport code VCE) has daily flights connecting through most major European cities; flight times and information are available on the airport's official website, www.veniceairport.com. Connections within Europe can be made to Verona's Vallerio Cattullo airport (airport code VRN); schedules are available at www.aeroportidelgarda.it.

By car: highway A4 links Verona, Padova, and Vicenza with Milan and Venice.

By train: Regular rail service connects most cities in the Veneto region. Schedules and information are available on the official site for Italy's state railway, www.fs-on-line.com.

Boat travel along the Brenta Canal: Two companies offer guided tours of the canal and its villas. Il Burchiello, tel. +39 049820-6910, www.ilburchiello.it, offers daily tours between Venice and Padova with an optional catered lunch. I Battelli del Brenta, tel. +39 049 876 0233, www.antoniana.it, offers a variety of daily tours for individuals and groups.

When to Go

Spring and autumn are particularly pleasant times of the year to visit the Veneto region. High season begins in May and continues through September.

Helpful Addresses
Official Tourist Information Offices and Websites

APT—Azienda di Promozione Turistica (Tourist Promotion Agency)

IAT—Ufficio Informazione e di Accoglienza Turistica (Tourist Information and Hospitality Office)

Battaglia Terme: I.A.T. Via Maggiore 2, tel. +39 049 526 909, fax +39 049 910 1328.

Chioggia: A.P.T. Lungomare Adriatico 101, tel. +39 041 401 068, fax +39 041 554 0855.

Mira: I.A.T. Villa Widmann Foscari—Via Nazionale 420, tel. +39 041 529 8711. Open June to the end of September.

Montagnana: I.A.T. Castel S. Zeno, tel. and fax +39 0429 81320.

Padova: A.P.T. Riviera dei Mugnai 8, tel. +39 049 876 7911, fax +39 049 650 794, email info@turismopadova.it, www.turismopadova.it.

Verona: I.A.T. Via Degli Alpini 9 (Piazza Bra), tel. +39 045 806 8680, fax +39 045 800 3638, email info@tourism.verona.it, www.tourism.verona.it.

Vicenza: A.P.T. Piazza dei Signori 8, tel. +39 0444 544 122, fax +39 0444 325 001, www.vicenzae.org.

Vicenza: I.A.T. Piazza Matteotti 12, tel. +39 0444 320 854, fax +39 0444 327 072, www.vicenzae.org.

Tourism Websites

Turismo Regione Veneto, http://turismo.regione.veneto.it. Available in English. Helpful information for travelers to the Veneto region, with recipes, history, and weather forecasts.

CHAPTER 4

TOSCANA
Medieval Castles and Hamlets

For a fairytale wedding, honeymoon, or romantic trip, Tuscany's castles, hamlets, and fortified villas offer the perfect setting to surround your stay with the chivalry and pageantry of the Renaissance. Set in the heart of enchanted forests, tranquil valleys, and sun-drenched hills, Tuscany's remaining castles show little evidence of the stormy history that created them. Today, their ancient battlements are draped in creeping vines, their moats are filled with fragrant lavender gardens, and their drawbridges have been dismantled. The defensive spirit of a medieval past has been replaced with the warmth and hospitality of local residents who welcome visitors with open arms.

A century of conflict between Florence and Siena created the need for fortified positions along the frontier between the two republics. As battle lines were drawn and redrawn, it became prudent for noble families to fortify their country homes, creating safe havens where they could wait out the storm. Eventually, at the hands of the Medici family, a time of peace and prosperity was reached in Tuscany, and a passion for arts and letters spread through the territory. Families began turning their castles into country villas, adding creature comforts and filling their banquet halls with paintings by the masters. The ever-growing Medici family added to their vast property holdings, creating villas and hunting retreats for every season and converting municipal buildings into palaces suitable for entertaining visiting heads of state. Today, many of the properties have been transformed into hotels or *agriturismi*, providing locations that can be rented for a relaxed week amid the vineyards and rolling Tuscan hills.

Accommodations in Medieval Castles and Hamlets

FIRENZE

Loggiato dei Serviti

In a quiet square surrounded by delicate arcades, the Loggiato dei Serviti is a charming old-world style hotel near the Galleria dell'Accademia. In the sixteenth century, this building welcomed traveling prelates under its roofs. For over three hundred years it remained part of the religious order called the *Servi di Maria* (Mary's Servants), a name that was later shortened simply to Serviti. A grand loggia leads to the entrance of the hotel. Inside, rooms are large and comfortable, many with high ceilings. Each room is uniquely decorated in Florentine Renaissance style with canopied beds, plush furniture, antique dressing tables, hand-painted coffered ceilings, and white-tiled bathrooms with modern fixtures. In the lobby is a 1920s style bar where you can sip a Campari soda after a day of sightseeing, and a comfortable breakfast room for savoring morning cappuccinos. The hotel shares the Piazza della Santissima Annunziata with Brunelleschi's Spedale degli Innocenti, Florence's first orphanage, built in 1444.

> LOGGIATO DEI SERVITI, Piazza SS. Annunziata 3, 50122 Firenze (FI), tel. +39 055 289 592, fax +39 055 289 595, email info@loggiatodeiservitihotel.it, www.loggiatodeiservitihotel.it. Driving directions: from the A1 highway, exit Firenze Nord and follow the indications for "Centro—Viali Circonvallazione" until you reach Piazza della Libertà. Turn right on Via Cavour and continue to Piazza San Marco. From here, turn left on Via Battisti and continue five hundred meters to Piazza SS. Annunziata. Twenty-nine rooms; doubles from EE to EEE.

Torre di Bellosguardo

The aptly named Torre di Bellosguardo ("tower of the beautiful view") is the perfect hillside hideaway for those who can't decide between vacationing at a villa in the Tuscan countryside or a week in Florence. This castle-like luxury hotel, set on a perfect hill above the Boboli gardens, offers the best of both worlds. The former patrician manor is surrounded by classic views of Florence and hazy Tuscan hills. A twenty-minute stroll down the hill through streets lined with olive groves brings you to the center of Florence. The central section of Bellosguardo is a fifteenth-century watchtower, built by a contemporary of Dante's. The villa that surrounds it is filled with old Renaissance-era frescoes and carefully selected antiques. The palazzo's former ballroom, with soaring ceilings and frescoes from the 1500s, is now the reception area. The guest rooms—some with high cross-vaulted ceilings, others with fading frescoes—are spacious and filled with heavy Renaissance furniture. From June to September you can laze by the pool or stroll through the villa's secret gardens and enjoy the roses, camellias, and wisteria-laden arbors.

Torre di Bellosguardo, Via Roti Michelozzi 2, 50124 Firenze (FI), tel. +39 055 229 8145, fax +39 055 229 008, email info@torrebellosguardo.com, www.torrebellosguardo.com. Driving directions: from the A1 highway, exit Firenze Certosa, and continue toward Porta Romana. Sixteen rooms; doubles from EE to EEE.

FIESOLE

Fattoria di Maiano

Next to the fortified Villa Maiano, where weddings are held (see page 208), the same owners manage a comfortable *fattoria* (farm) with thirteen individual apartments. Olive groves and quiet winding roads lead from Fiesole to Maiano's own tiny hamlet. The apartments, furnished with country charm, accommodate from two to ten persons each and are available for weekly rentals.

Fattoria di Maiano, Via Benedetto da Maiano 11, 50014 Fiesole (FI), tel. +39 055 599 600, fax +39 055 599 640, email maiano@contemiarifulcis.it, www.fattoriadimaiano.com. Driving directions: take the A1 (Milano-Roma) highway and exit at Firenze sud. Follow the signs to Fiesole. Once you have passed San Domenico, turn right onto Via Benedetto da Maiano, which leads to the villa. Thirteen apartments available for weekly rentals; doubles from E.

MONTESPERTOLI

Castello di Montegufoni

Castello di Montegufoni is seventeenth-century medieval castle in the countryside twelve miles south of Florence. Its most distinctive feature is a central tower, a copy of the one belonging to Florence's Palazzo Vecchio. A loyal following of guests return year after year to sleep in the castle's charming rooms. The guest accommodations are carved out of the old functional castle rooms, and many have original frescoes. The ground-floor La Grotta apartment sleeps as many as five persons under elaborately frescoed ceilings. La Grotta, like many of the other flats, has a view of the castle gardens and has its own small kitchen. All the flats are available for weekly rentals, and guests are invited to enjoy the gardens and use the castle swimming pool. The castle also hosts wedding receptions; see page 214.

CASTELLO DI MONTEGUFONI, Via Montegufoni-Montagnana 18, 50025 Montagnana, Montespertoli (FI), tel. +39 0571 671 131, email info@ montegufoni.it, www.montegufoni.it. Driving directions: take the A1 (Milano-Firenze) highway and exit at Firenze-Certosa. Follow the road toward Montagnana-Montespertoli. Fifteen apartments available for weekly rental; doubles from E to EE.

ARTIMINO

Paggeria Medicea—Villa Medicea La Ferdinanda

The Paggeria Medicea, now a fully renovated hotel, was once the medieval quarters for the court of Ferdinando Medici, Grand Duke of Tuscany. The grounds include the Villa Medicea La Ferdinanda, also known as "the villa of one hundred chimneys," where wedding receptions can be held (see page 216). The villa, the hotel, its restaurants, and the cantina are all set in the charming hamlet of Artimino, just north of Florence. If you stay here, plan a meal at Da Delfina, one of Tuscany's best restaurants (see page 181).

PAGGERIA MEDICEA—VILLA MEDICEA LA FERDINANDA, Viale Papa Giovanni XXIII no.1, 59015 Artimino (PO), tel. +39 055 875 141, fax +39 055 875 1470, email hotel@artimino.com, www.artimino.it. Driving directions: take the Firenze-Pisa highway and exit at Montelupo Fiorentino (Artimino is also indicated). Continue on state road SS 67 toward Firenze for five kilometers to the entrance of Camaioni. On the left, signs lead to Artimino. Thirty-seven rooms; doubles from EE.

BUCINE

Castelletto di Montebenichi

At the top of a hill in the Chianti countryside, Castelletto di Montebenichi was once charged with protecting the southernmost edge of Florence's territory with Siena. Across the valley, Castello di Montalto (see page 167), stood ready to defend Siena's interests along the frontier. Rivalries aside, the Castelletto of today is nestled in the tiny medieval village of Montebenichi, one of those quintessential Tuscan towns where locals play soccer in the central piazza and everyone knows each other. A typical medieval facade greets you, with crenellated towers, gothic windows, and ancient heraldic shields. Any potential misconceptions about drafty medieval castles disappear as you walk into the interior, which has been carefully appointed with the proprietor's antique collections. The castle rooms are elegantly filled with original medieval frescoes, coffered ceilings, black stone fireplaces, and terra-cotta pavements. Individual guest rooms have antique bedsteads, and some have their own fireplaces. In recent years, a swimming pool was added to the castle garden, where there are views over the surrounding sunflower-filled valleys. Montebenichi is just twenty-eight kilometers from Siena in a wooded section of the Chianti winemaking region.

CASTELLETTO DI MONTEBENICHI, Località Montebenichi, Piazza Cinque Giornate 6, 52021 Bucine (AR), tel. +39 055 991 0110, fax +39 055 991 0113, email info@castelletto.it, www.castelletto.it. Driving directions from Florence: take the A1 highway south and exit at Valdarno. Follow indications to Montevarchi. Continue through Montevarchi then in direction Arezzo. At the traffic light in Levane, follow signs to Ambra-Siena. You will pass Bucine, Capannole, Ambra, and Pietraviva; after two kilometers, turn right, following the sign to Montebenichi. Nine rooms; doubles from EE.

SAN GIUSTINO VALDARNO

Il Borro

Il Borro, a tiny hamlet thirty-eight miles south of Florence, has been completely restored by the Ferragamo family. As with many of the country hamlets, nearly all its residents had moved to the city, and the entire place was in a state of neglect before it was rescued by the owners and turned into a charming country retreat. The estate includes eight apartments and four farmhouses, all created out of the old stone buildings that make up this storybook medieval village. The old village mill and a former barn have also been renovated, creating comfortable quarters with rustic beamed ceilings, Tuscan country furniture, and private kitchens. One apartment, La Penna, even has a pizza oven, for those who'd like to try their hand at Italian pizza making. All apartments are available for weekly rentals, and many have their own private gardens. You can shop at local markets and cook in your own kitchen, or walk over to the Osteria Il Borro for a relaxed Tuscan dinner on the candlelit terrace. There is also a small shop in the hamlet where the farm's wines, honey, and other products are sold.

The hamlet is centered in seventeen hundred acres of farmland and nature reserves; interested guests can take horseback rides through the estate. The owners can also organize cooking classes for those who long to learn to make classic Tuscan dishes like homemade ravioli and *panzanella* (Tuscan bread salad).

While you stay at Il Borro, you'll want to check out two elaborate miniatures modeled by the village priest, Don Pasquale Mencattini. Two rooms at Il Borro are devoted to his detailed representations of the story of Pinocchio and of the Nativity.

IL BORRO, Frazione Il Borro, 52020 San Giustino Valdarno (AR), tel. +39 055 977 053, fax +39 055 977 055, email ilborro@ilborro.it, www.ilborro.it. Driving directions from Florence: from the A1 highway take the Valdarno exit. Follow the road through Terranuova Bracciolini toward San Giustino Valdarno. From there you will see indications for Il Borro. Eight apartments and four farm houses available for weekly rentals; doubles from E to EEE.

MONTE SAN SAVINO

Castello di Gargonza

Castello di Gargonza is a charming hamlet in southern Tuscany that has been completely refurbished as a hotel. All the rooms are carved out of the old medieval village's shops and stores that surround a tiny piazzetta with its own church and guard tower. There is a delightful restaurant just outside the hamlet walls, where you will also find the bocce court and a swimming pool with a sweeping Tuscan view. For additional information about the hotel and weddings at Gargonza, see page 210.

CASTELLO DI GARGONZA, 52048 Monte San Savino (AR), tel. +39 0575 847 021, fax +39 0575 847 054, email gargonza@gargonza.it, www.gargonza.it. Driving directions: take the A1 (Firenze-Roma) and exit at Monte San Savino. Proceed on state road SS73 and follow the signs to Gargonza. Twenty-three apartments and seven double rooms available for both weekly and nightly stays. Doubles from E to EE.

CASTELNUOVO BERARDENGA

Castello di Montalto

In the summer of 2000, my husband and I were married on the grounds of this enchanting tenth-century castle. Montalto's castle, centered in a rustic hamlet, was one of the southern Tuscan fortresses built for the defense of Siena. The center of many battles, it was destroyed and refortified many times before it became a noble residence in the fifteenth century. The current owners, Giovanni and Diana Coda-Nunziante, a charming husband-and-wife team, have owned the castle and its farm since the early 1970s. The hamlet's former schoolhouse, guard's quarters, "bishop's" tower, and farmhouses have been refurbished into holiday apartments, where guests are invited to come and stay in the quiet of this country hamlet.

In this secluded enclave, hidden in its own woods, you can spend a relaxed week for two or plan a trip with a group of friends. Montalto's apartments are available in a variety of sizes; each has its own kitchen and access to a private or shared garden space. The *Torre del Vescovo* (Bishop's Tower) is a grand multistory apartment filled with eclectic country furnishings. It can accommodate as many as six guests and has its own hydrangea-filled terrace with views of the Tuscan hillsides. Perfect for two, the hamlet's original one-room schoolhouse, *La Scuola,* is a charming stone cottage with a red tile roof.

Off the castle's tiny piazza, the restored granary is used for serving breakfast to guests. There is also a bocce court and a secluded swimming pool.

From Monalto, it's a twenty-minute drive to Siena, and the Chianti wine route is just steps away. If you stay here, you might want to plan a dinner for two at nearby Da Antonio, one of Italy's best seafood restaurants (see page 183).

CASTELLO DI MONTALTO, Località Montalto, 53019 Castelnuovo Berardenga (SI), tel. +39 0577 355 675, fax +39 0577 355 682, email info@montalto.it, www.montalto.it. Driving directions from Florence: from the A1 highway exit at Firenze-Certosa and continue on the road to Siena. When you reach Siena, do not enter the town; instead, follow the signs for Arezzo. Once on the road to Arezzo, disregard signs for Castelnuovo Berardenga but pay attention to the kilometer indications on the right side of the road. When you reach kilometer sign number 17, turn left toward Arezzo-Bucine and follow the signs for Ambra-Bucine. After about three kilometers you will see a sign for Montalto. Ten apartments available for weekly rentals; doubles from E.

SINALUNGA

Locanda dell'Amorosa

Locanda dell'Amorosa (the lovers' inn) is just north of Montepulciano in a postcard-perfect Tuscan landscape where broad cultivated plots are edged by cypress trees, and hillsides are blanketed with rows of vines. In the fourteenth century, Amorosa was a lively medieval village. Its castle is depicted in Lippo Vanni's painting *Battle for the Val di Chiana* (now housed in the Sala del Mappamondo in Siena's Civic Museum). Since 1971, this authentic hamlet has been a luxury hotel. The old hamlet's stables, cellars, and farm houses have been restored into this charming hotel.

The spacious guest rooms enjoy gentle views over the vineyards. Although the setting is rustic, the furnishings are an elegant mixture of antiques and art. One of the best features of the hotel is the romantic Le Coccole del Amorosa restaurant, set in the hamlet's old stables. Inside, old stone vaults are a backdrop for elegantly set tables. The menu consists of Tuscan delicacies like pecorino cheese from nearby Pienza, prized Chianina beef, and white truffles from San Giovanni d'Asso. For a more relaxed atmosphere, there is also a wine bar, where you can enjoy a glass of local wine and a bruschetta or two. Although you may never want to leave the comforts of the hamlet, the famous vineyards of Montepulciano are just twenty-five kilometers away, and Siena is forty kilometers from Sinalunga.

> LOCANDA DELL'AMOROSA, Località l'Amorosa, 53048 Sinalunga (SI), tel. +39 0577 677 211, fax +39 0577 632 001, email locanda@amorosa.it, www.amorosa.it. Driving directions from Florence or Rome: take the A1 highway to the Valdichiana exit. Follow the signs to Sinalunga. Once you arrive in town, follow the signs to Amorosa. Twenty rooms; doubles from EE to EEE.

CASOLE D'ELSA

Relais La Suvera

This vine-covered tower with three stories of graceful loggias was once a papal palace. Suvera (the sovereign) takes its name from the medieval queen, a certain Countess Ava Matilde dé Franzesi, who once owned the estate. After passing through many noble hands, it is now owned by descendants of the Marquis of Ricci, who have turned it into a museum-like hotel. Marquis Giuseppe Ricci and his wife, the Princess Eleonora Massimo, have filled the Relais with their vast collection of antiques gathered from all over Europe. Each of the hotel's princely suites is themed to a particular historical style, from neo-Gothic to Empire. The only dilemma is choosing between the Maria Gabriella of Savoy suite, with its empire chaise and crystal chandeliers, or the Camera degli Angeli, with its frescoed walls and red canopied bed. Rooms are spread throughout the estate's restored stables, farmhouses, and *frantoio* (olive mill).

Guests are invited to enjoy the regal rooms of the papal villa, where three open loggias overlook Italian gardens and verdant hills pierced by dark green cypress. Inside the villa, rooms are decorated with grand pianos, huge painted canvases, marble sculptures, and leather-bound books. Each room still carries the name of its original role in the villa: Biblioteca (library), Sala del Papa (Pope's hall), and Sala della Musica (music room).

On one side of the grounds is a small church dedicated to San Carlo Borromeo with a glistening white interior and carved stucco altar.

A subterranean medieval cistern has been renovated to house the hotel's health center, where you can enjoy a variety of spa treatments, from hydro massage to Turkish baths in a setting that seems to date to Roman times.

An elegant restaurant in the estate's olive mill, Ristorante Oliviera, offers sumptuous dinners in its celadon dining room, where guests are seated on high-backed chairs surrounded by gilt mirrors and candlelight. There is also an outdoor terrace for dining under the stars.

RELAIS LA SUVERA, Pievescola, 53030 Casole d'Elsa (SI), tel. +39 0577 960 300, fax +39 0577 960 220, email reservations@lasuvera.it, www. lasuvera.it. Driving directions from Florence: take the Superstrada Firenze-Siena and exit at Colle Val d'Elsa sud. Proceed toward Grosseto on the SS 541. After fifteen kilometers, take the left turn for Pievescola. Just past the village you'll find Relais La Suvera. Ten rooms; doubles from EE to EEEEE.

GAIOLE IN CHIANTI

Castello di Spaltenna

Gaiole is one of the small Tuscan villages on the Strada Chiantigiana, the wine route that winds through Chianti's vineyards. Above the tiny village, an ancient fortified monastery, with its own eleventh-century Romanesque chapel and square bell tower, is noted in historical records as far back as 1030. Castello di Spaltenna, now a charming hotel, enjoys a view over wooded hillsides and is itself surrounded by vineyards. The old grey stone buildings include the imposing fortified monastery, the church and tower, and rambling farm buildings; all have been restored to provide thirty guest rooms and a charming restaurant. A small stone courtyard, with a central well, leads to the inn's elegant restaurant. Breakfast is served in the monastery's subterranean *cantine* (cellars), which open onto the garden. In warm weather, umbrellas are set along the garden's edge. As you enjoy a cappuccino, you'll be enveloped by the scent of lavender and the hum of bees. The elegant restaurant, with its high coffered ceiling, medieval tapestries, and heraldic shields, offers creative Tuscan dishes like lamb dressed in herbs from Spaltenna's own gardens or veal braised in Chianti Classico. In the summer, the stone courtyard is used for candlelit dinners.

The guest rooms are elegantly decorated, but maintain a rustic feeling with wood-beamed ceilings and terra-cotta tiled floors. Each of the rooms have a view either over the valley or of the surrounding hillside. Two swimming pools, both indoor and outdoor, with views over the valley, are available for guests.

CASTELLO DI SPALTENNA, 53013 Gaiole in Chianti (SI), tel. +39 0577 749 483, fax +39 0577 749 269, email info@spaltenna.it, www.spaltenna.it. Driving directions: from Florence, take the A1 highway toward Rome and exit at Incisa in Val d'Arno. Connect to state road SS408, following indications for Gaiole. Thirty rooms; doubles from EE to EEEEE.

GREVE IN CHIANTI

Villa Vignamaggio

The fourteenth-century manor house at the center of this estate is the birthplace of Mona Lisa Gherardini, who was born at Vignamaggio in 1479. When she was sixteen, she was married to the twice-widowed Francesco di Bartolomeo di Zanobi del Giocondo, who reportedly hired Leonardo da Vinci to paint her famous portrait. More recently, Kenneth Branagh chose this romantic villa for the sun-drenched setting of his film *Much Ado About Nothing.* If you've seen the film, you'll immediately recognize the estate's topiary-filled Italian gardens, which ramble through the grounds and lead to a secluded swimming pool.

Today, the villa is part of a wine estate and *agriturismo* just outside Greve, one of the most charming villages along the Chianti wine route. Vistas in every direction are typically Tuscan, of rolling vineyards and cypress-dotted hillsides.

The property's stone farmhouses—Cenobio, Casolese, Fienile, and Casaccia—accommodate from two to four guests each. Casaccia is a small independent villa for two, set in its own secluded garden. Rooms are furnished with terra-cotta tiled floors, lacy iron bed frames, and simple country antiques.

The cellars are open for small groups to taste Vignamaggio's wines, accompanied by select Tuscan *rustici* like brushetta, crostini, cheeses, and cured meats. Two swimming pools, tennis courts, a gym, and hiking paths are available to guests.

VILLA VIGNAMAGGIO, Via Petriolo 5, 50022 Greve in Chianti (FI), tel. +39 055 854 661, fax +39 055 854 4468, email agriturismo@vignamaggio.com and info@vignamaggio.com, www.vignamaggio.com. Driving directions: from Florence, follow state road SS222 south to Greve. Twenty rooms; doubles from EE.

SAN GIMIGNANO

L'Antico Pozzo

San Gimignano's mysterious towers were most likely built by rival noble families engaged in a bout of one-upmanship in the thirteenth century. In another explanation, a legend recounted by San Gimignano locals, the towers were the end result of the quest for a local maiden's hand, in which the young lords of San Gimignano were challenged to build the city's tallest tower. Many tried, and many even succeeded in building lofty towers—but they all eventually crumbled over their narrow bases. Finally, one smart engineer came up with a solution. He would build two identical towers, whose combined heights would surpass that of any other single tower. In doing so, he won the maiden's hand. In the San Gimignano skyline, you can still distinguish two identical towers that stand to this day.

San Gimignano has remained almost unchanged since those days, making it one of Tuscany's best-preserved medieval towns. During the day, buses bring tourists from all over to roam through its narrow streets and piazzas, but at night, when the last buses leave, once again it becomes a quiet village. L'Antico Pozzo (the old well) is a tiny gem in the heart of San Gimignano, not far from the Piazza del Duomo. The hotel is set in a fifteenth-century town house once inhabited by a religious order and reportedly the scene of religious trials during the Inquisition. In the eighteenth century, the house's Sala Rosa (Pink Room) was the setting for high society gatherings; now it is used for morning breakfast. All the rooms are charming, and the "superior" rooms have high ceilings and delicate period frescoes. Bathrooms are newly renovated with marble counters and modern fixtures. A central vine-covered courtyard has chaises and tables for relaxing and is used for serving breakfast in the summer months.

L'ANTICO POZZO, Via San Matteo 87, 53037 San Gimignano (SI), tel. +39 0577 942 014, fax 39 0577 942 117, email info@anticopozzo.com, www. anticopozzo.com. Driving directions: from Florence, take the highway for Siena and exit at San Gimignano. Eighteen rooms; doubles from E to EE.

SAN GIOVANNI D'ASSO

Lucignanello Bandini

San Giovanni d'Asso lies thirty miles south of Siena, just north of Montalcino and Pienza. The hamlet that houses the Azienda Agrituristica Lucignanello Bandini is made up of a castle, two churches, and a variety of old farm houses connected by two tiny stone roads. The hamlet's buildings have been artfully renovated, but they retain the patina of time, in a palette of ochre, grey stone, and terra-cotta. All around are the sights and smells of the Crete Senesi, the limestone hills south of Siena known for their rich pastures. Five houses within the hamlet hold guest accommodations: Casa Maria, Casa Severino, Casa Clementina, Casa Amedeo, Casa Remo, and one independent villa, Casale Sarageto (with its own private swimming pool). Each house sleeps from two to eight guests, for a combined maximum of twenty-eight guests. Casa Maria is a perfect honeymoon cottage, complete with a romantically draped canopy bed and shuttered windows that open onto Tuscan vistas. Its antique-filled living room has a fireplace, and it has its own kitchen with a private outdoor garden. All of the houses are similarly charming, with old stone floors, country kitchens, and antique furniture. A small store in the hamlet sells the farm's cold-pressed olive oil, which is carefully extracted from olives grown on the property. On the hilltop, the swimming pool floats like a sheet of glass, reflecting views that stretch all the way to Monte Amiata. The houses are available for weekly rentals.

SAN QUIRICO D'ORCIA

Castello di Ripa d'Orcia

Ripa d'Orcia is the sort of medieval castle that immediately evokes images of chivalrous knights on horseback. A *ripa* is a steep place, and this imposing castle is set high above a river gorge. From the air, Ripa d'Orcia resembles a miniature medieval city perched on a wooded cliff. Its massive castle keep was built as part of Siena's defenses in 1271. In 1484 the castle became a holding of the Piccolomini family, who also once owned the hamlet of Lucignano.

Descendants of this family still own the castle today, which they have turned into a country residence with thirteen renovated rooms and apartments. The seven apartments have large living rooms, independent kitchens, rustic Tuscan furniture, and panoramic views. Inside the walled hamlet, there are also six double rooms that share the grounds and terrace.

San Quirico d'Orcia, just north of the castle, is an old medieval city and the famous site of the historic meeting between Barbarossa (Red Beard) and papal delegates in 1153. It is full of medieval flavor, and its southern position makes it a great starting point for visits to Pienza, Montalcino, and Montepulciano. Bagno Vignoni, just five kilometers away, is a village built around the thermal sulfurous springs where Lorenzo de' Medici once bathed.

SORANO

Hotel della Fortezza

The Maremma is a still largely undiscovered part of Tuscany, filled with medieval hill towns steeped in history. Sorano, near Lake Bolsena and along Tuscany's southernmost edge, is one such medieval jewel. The city is dominated by the Orsini fortress, which, due to its position on the fringes of the Tuscan territory, is a remarkably well-preserved castle. A section of this testament to medieval military architecture is inhabited by the Hotel della Fortezza (the Fortress Hotel). Rooms have been renovated inside the old castle, and from their position high above the valley floor they offer unrivaled views of the countryside. The rest of the castle houses a museum, which holds medieval and Renaissance objects from the area as well as the medieval codices of Sorano and Castell'Ottieri.

The castle is reached by a steep medieval lane, once trod by knights on horseback. At one point in its history, the castle and all its holdings were presented as a wedding gift to Romano Gentili Orsini and Anastasia Aldobrandeschi. The intertwined heraldic shield of the two families still hangs over the entrance to the oval castle keep. Sheer cliffs descend on two sides of the castle, falling to the Lente River valley. Traces of the original drawbridge and moat lead to the Castelletto, the original residence of the Aldobrandeschi family.

Sorano is near the thermal baths at Saturnia, and from its southern position it is easy to visit the neighboring regions of Umbria and Lazio.

HOTEL DELLA FORTEZZA, Piazza Cairoli, 58010 Sorano (GR), tel. +39 0564 632 010, fax +39 0564 633 209, email fortezza@fortezzahotel.it, www.fortezzahotel.it. Driving directions: from the A1 highway, exit at Orvieto. Continue southwest on state road SS71 in the direction of Bolsena, then onto SS 74, following indications for Grotte di Castro. When you reach Grotte di Castro, follow the indications for Sorano. Sixteen rooms; doubles from E to EE.

Tables For Two in Florence and Province

BAGNO A RIPOLI

Centanni

Just a few miles south of Florence, Centanni is a homey country restaurant with a pretty summer garden overlooking the hills. The view over vineyards, cypress trees, and olive groves is equally enjoyable from the sunny dining room or the summer terrace. Pastas are made fresh each morning in this family-style restaurant. The rabbit and chicken for sauces and main courses come from nearby farms. The cuisine is quintessentially Tuscan, with dishes like *sfogliatine calde* (warm savory pastries), *ribollita* (Tuscan soup), beef filet served with *fagioli al fiasco* (beans cooked in a "flask"), and of course, the classic steak *alla fiorentina,* an extra thick T-bone steak grilled Tuscan style. The carefully researched cellar includes an excellent list of Tuscan wines.

> CENTANNI, Via di Centanni 8, Località Croce a Varliano, 50012 Bagno a Ripoli(FI), tel. +39 055 630 122, fax +39 055 651 0445, email info@ residence-centanni.it, www.residence-centanni.it. Driving directions from the A1 highway: exit at Firenze sud. Continue to Bagno a Ripoli, then to Meoste, and finally to Croce a Varliano. Closed on Sundays, and for holidays the months of February, August, and November. One hundred twenty seats. Cost: EE.

CERTALDO

Osteria del Vicario

Osteria del Vicario (the Vicar's Tavern) is set in a former monastery that dates to the 1200s. Certaldo itself is one of Tuscany's most well-preserved medieval cities, and if you venture there for a day of sightseeing this restaurant should be on your list. In the summer, meals are served from the quiet of the cloisters, with vine-covered archways that lead to incredible views down over the plains below. The food is elegantly prepared, each dish presented as a *piccolo capolavoro* (a small masterpiece).

Tagliolini with scampi, fresh daily risotto and handmade *gnocchetti*, turbot *al forno* with littleneck clams, and *tagliata* (chopped) steak are a few of the offerings. A wine list with an excellent selection of Tuscan Cru wines provides ample choices to accompany your meal.

OSTERIA DEL VICARIO, Via Rivillino 3, 50052 Certaldo (FI), tel. +39 0571 668 228, email info@osteriadelvicario.it, www.osteriadelvicario.it. Driving directions from Florence: take the S2 highway south, exit at Tavarnelle Val di Pesa. Follow indications for Tavarnelle, then Barbarino Val d'Elsa, and then on to Certaldo. Closed on Wednesdays, and for holidays in January and February. Forty seats; reservations recommended. Cost: EEE.

La Saletta di Dolci Follie

La Saletta di Dolci Follie (the little room of sweet follies) is a small enoteca with a few tables and an intimate, casual atmosphere. Near Piazza Boccaccio, in the center of medieval Certaldo, this osteria offers simple Tuscan cuisine following antique regional recipes, accompanied by a cellar replete with more than five hundred of the region's most prestigious wines.

LA SALETTA DI DOLCI FOLLIE, Via Roma 35, 50052 Certaldo (FI), tel. +39 0571 668 188. Driving directions from Florence: take the S2 highway south, exit at Tavarnelle Val di Pesa. Follow indications for Tavarnelle, then Barbarino Val d'Elsa, and then on to Certaldo. Cost: E.

FIRENZE

Alle Murate

Alle Murate is a popular spot with Florentine locals and tourists alike. The decor is modern, along the lines of a restaurant you might expect to find in Manhattan, and some nights there is live jazz. The owners came to Florence by way of Basilicata, and their menu stretches beyond the usual Tuscan *ribollita* and *bistecca fiorentina*. Southern Italian ingredients are central to the cooking, with fava beans, orecchiette, and fish cooked in *acqua pazza* among the typical offerings. The well-prepared dishes include plates like bean soup with giant prawns and truffle oil, braised octopus, and *maccheroncetti* pasta with rabbit sauce. Desserts are light and innovative. There is a well-furnished wine cellar. Umberto Montano also owns the elegant Caffè Italiano, in via della Condotta 56/r, tel. +39 055 291 082, and the Osteria del Caffè Italiano, inside the fourteenth-century Salviati Palace in Via Isole delle Stinche 11/13r, two other solid bets for dining in Florence.

ALLE MURATE, Via Ghibellina 52-54/r, 50122 Firenze (FI), tel. +39 055 240 618, fax +39 055 288 950, email info@caffeitaliano.it, www.caffeitaliano.it. Closed on Mondays, and two weeks at Christmas. Cost: EEE.

Beccofino

Beccofino is a trendy restaurant with a big-city look, across the river in the Oltrarno (the "other" side of the Arno). Beccofino also has an adjoining wine bar where you can order small dishes and excellent wines. The atmosphere is welcoming and elegant, with great care taken in the restaurant's design. In the summer, there is outdoor service with a lovely view of the Arno. A young and renowned chef, Francesco Berardinelli, heads the kitchen. The fare is a creative reinterpretation of classic Tuscan cooking, with dishes like seafood soup with ginger and pancetta, fresh pasta in a sauce of milk-fed lamb and asparagus, and roast suckling pig with fava-bean puree and chicory. There are many tempting desserts and an excellent list of Italian and French wines, many of which are offered by the glass.

BECCOFINO, Piazza degli Scarlatti 1R, 50125 Firenze (FI), tel. +39 055 290 076, fax +39 055 272 8312. Closed on Wednesdays, Thursdays at lunch, and for holidays the month of August. Reservations are essential. Cost: EE.

Cibreo

Intimate and elegant, Cibreo is a perennial favorite in Florence. Fabio Picchi and company offer creative Tuscan cuisine—but don't come here looking for pasta; it's not on the menu. Instead, first courses include thick pureed soups like yellow pepper and tomato, ricotta flan, or goat-cheese mousse, and for main courses there are squab filled with *mostarda di Cremona* (preserves for game meats) and *zampa di vitella alla parmigiana* (veal trotters in parmesan). For dessert, choose from dishes like bitter chocolate and caramel pudding and cheese cake with orange marmalade. The wine list is rich in national and international labels. For a more relaxed atmosphere, Osteria del Cibreo is just next door and offers a similarly creative menu at lower prices.

CIBREO, Via dei Macci 118r, 50122 Firenze (FI), tel. +39 055 234 1100, fax +39 055 244 966, email cibreo.fi@tin.it. Closed Sundays and Mondays, for holidays December 31 to January 7, and for the month of August. Sixty seats; reservations essential. Cost: EEE.

Enoteca Pinchiorri

Pinchiorri is one of Italy's finest restaurants, with one of the world's best wine cellars. The restaurant occupies a refined patrician palazzo, and in the dining room, tables are elegantly set with fine crystal, porcelain, and silver. This is a place to spend an unhurried evening savoring the entire experience of carefully prepared dishes, impeccable service, and refined atmosphere. The cooking by French chef Annie Féolde is elegant and sumptuous, with a seamless blending of both esteemed and humble ingredients. Tasting menus propose either a "Fantasy" or a "Seasonal" selection of courses, each paired with wines from the cellar. Giorgio Pinchiorri's admirable wine list includes thirty-seven hundred famous and rare wines from all over the world.

ENOTECA PINCHIORRI, Via Ghibellina 87, 50122 Firenze (FI), tel. +39 055 242 777, fax +39 055 244 983. www.pinchiorri.it. Closed on Sunday and Monday, and for holidays at Christmas, Easter, and the month of August. Seventy seats; reservations essential. Cost: EEEEE.

Il Latini

Il Latini is a convivial restaurant where locals and tourists alike are seated together at long rustic banquet tables. While this isn't a spot for a romantic tête-à-tête—as you're likely to be seated next to either Italian businessmen or families enjoying a hearty dinner—it is a place to enjoy warm Tuscan hospitality and cuisine. If you go, bring a hearty appetite and say "Si, si, si" to everything they offer you. Si, to an antipasto of crostini toscani (toasts topped with chicken livers and sage), si to the fresh pasta, and a definite *si* to the *bistecca alla fiorentina,* the charcoal-grilled extra-thick T-bone steak.

IL LATINI, Via dei Palchetti 6R, 50123 Firenze (FI), tel. +39 055 210 916, fax +39 055 289 794, email info@illatini.com, www.illatini.com. Closed on Mondays, and for holidays from December 24 to January 5. Cost: EE.

Trattoria Garga

Giuliano Gargani and his wife Sharon Oddson manage this amiable trattoria in the heart of Florence. The walls of the fourteenth-century palazzo, now inhabited by the restaurant, have been vibrantly painted with murals by Garga and his artist friends. His artistry extends to the kitchen as well, where he perfumes his Tuscan dishes with the scents of fresh local herbs (basil, mint, thyme, sage, laurel, fennel, juniper, and parsley). The owners also offer one-day cooking classes in Florence and week-long lessons on *la cucina povera* (country cooking) at Villa Margherita in southern Tuscany.

TRATTORIA GARGA, Via del Moro 48, 50123 Firenze (FI), tel. +39 055 239 8898, email garga@fol.it, www.garga.it. Cost: EEE.

SANT'ANDREA IN PERCUSSINA

L'Albergaccio di Machiavelli

San Andrea in Percussina is famous as the city where Niccolò Machiavelli, author of the famous political treatise *Il Principe* (*The Prince*), spent his years in exile. While working on his masterwork, he reportedly spent many hours at this inn, no doubt blowing off steam and playing cards. The Albergaccio dates to 1450 and is on the national historical register. Here you will find classic Tuscan cuisine prepared *alla casalinga* (housewife's style), accompanied by local Chianti wines.

L'ALBERGACCIO DI MACHIAVELLI, 50026 Sant'Andrea in Percussina (FI), tel. +39 055 828 471 and +39 055 820 027. Closed on Mondays. Cost: EE.

Tables For Two in Grosseto and Prato Provinces

SATÚRNIA

I Due Cippi

Two Roman funerary altars, *cippi* in Italian, mark the entrance to the historic building that houses I Due Cippi. The building is noted as a national monument and was once a residence of the Portugese Marquis of Ximenes. During the winter, a crackling fire on the hearth welcomes diners into the cozy stone dining room; in the summer, meals are served on an outdoor terrace. The restaurant features the cuisine of the Maremma and highlights local ingredients like wild boar and hearty vegetables. Specialties of the house include lamb and goat carpaccio, ricotta gnocchi with walnuts and artichoke hearts, and chestnut-filled tortelli in fennel sauce.

I Due Cippi, Piazza Vittorio Veneto 26, 58050 Saturnia (GR), tel. +39 0564 601 074, fax +39 0564 601 207. Closed on Tuesdays and for holidays from December 10 to 25. Driving directions: from the A 12 highway, exit at Rosignano Marittimo. Eighty seats. Cost: E.

ARTIMINO

Da Delfina

Da Delfina is found in Artimino, a charming fortified hamlet that is also home to the Villa Artimino "La Ferdinanda" (pages 163 and 216). Surrounded by a striking panorama of green Tuscan hills, this country house has been the stomping ground for food-a-philes and gastronomes who drive up from Florence just to sample a few select dishes. Everything is fresh and flavorful, and old standbys take on new dimensions with the care and attention they receive from da Delfina's kitchen. The key to da Delfina's success is the careful preparation of simple dishes like *ribollita* (classic Tuscan soup), baccalà with garbanzo beans, *stracotto con fagioli all'uccelletto* (pot roast with beans prepared like a roasted bird), and pheasant in vin santo. Desserts include classics like *zuccotto* served with fresh cream. Da Delfina is also a member of the Ristoranti del Buon Ricordo, and if you try their signature dish, rabbit with olives and pine nuts, you will receive a charming commemorative plate.

DA DELFINA, Via della Chiesa 1, 59015 Artimino (PO), tel. +39 055 871 8074, fax +39 055 871 8175, email posta@dadelfina.it, www.dadelfina.it. Closed on Sunday evenings, Mondays, and for holidays the month of August. Seventy-five seats; reservations recommended. Cost: EE.

Tables For Two in Siena Province

CASTELLINA IN CHIANTI

Osteria del Laghetto

Just steps from the Chianti wine route, Osteria del Laghetto is situated along the shore of Lake Vallechiara in the village of Quornia. A view over Tuscan hillsides and the peace and serenity of a quiet country location are among the charms of this country restaurant. You can dine in the quaint stone dining room or on the outdoor terrace. The menu includes typical Tuscan dishes and pizzas prepared in the restaurant's wood-burning oven. Tradtional fare includes specialties like linguine with lobster and a triple-filled raviolone in a truffled pecorino sauce. The wine cellar has 150 wines from the region and elsewhere.

OSTERIA DEL LAGHETTO, Località Quornia, Strada Comunale delle Masse n. 112, 53011 Castellina in Chianti (SI), fax +39 0577 743 125, email osteriadellaghetto@ristoratori.it. Closed on Mondays. Cost: EE.

L'Albergaccio di Castellina

In a tiny restored hamlet, L'Albergaccio is a rustically elegant restaurant, set in a refurbished stable. The buildings are all constructed of local stone, with heavy wood beams and loads of country charm. What was once a threshing floor is now a pretty outdoor terrace, where guests dine under canvas umbrellas in the summer. The chef's motto is "the territory on the table," and to accomplish this, only the freshest local ingredients are used to prepare the seasonal menu. Among the dishes to taste: garbanzo bean *gnocchetti* with fresh cherry tomatoes, pancakes filled with pigeon and crispy leeks, and wild boar braised in Chianti wine with chestnuts and wild fennel. The cellar offers a wide variety of wines to try with each dish, including many of the best Tuscan labels. Dessert includes offerings like apple pine-nut cake, and pistachio flan with saffron cream. L'Albergaccio di Castellina is situated in the center of Castellina in Chianti, between the valleys of Pesa, Elsa, and Arbia. The town is dominated by an ancient medieval *rocca* (fortress) and is in the heart of the Chianti wine route.

L'ALBERGACCIO DI CASTELLINA, Via Fiorentina 63, 53011 Castellina in Chianti (SI), tel. +39 0577 741 042, fax +39 0577 741 250, email posta@ albergacciocast.com, www.albergacciocast.com. Closed on Sundays, Tuesdays, Wednesdays, and Thursdays at lunch, and for holidays from November 17 to December 6. Driving directions from Florence: from the A1 highway, exit at Firenze-Certosa. Connect to the superstrada Siena-Firenze and continue south to the San Donato exit. Follow the indications for Castellina in Chianti. Eighty seats; reservations recommended. Cost: EEE.

CASTELNUOVO BERARDEGNA

Da Antonio

In Castlenuovo Berardegna's central square (twenty kilometers east of Siena), Da Antonio is an unusual find in the heart of Tuscany. Even though the restaurant lies two hundred kilometers from the sea, the menu consists only of dishes based on fresh fish, which are brought in daily directly from the Tuscan waterfront. The dining room and covered terrace are elegant, quiet, and romantic. The menu is a fixed *degustazione* of delights, and this is a place to spend an unhurried evening enjoying a dinner for two. Dishes change daily, based on the local catch and the season. Some past offerings have included arugula salad with scampi and porcini mushrooms, sea-bass ravioli with baby calamari and sage, scampi stewed with Sorana beans, and Catalan style lobster. There is an excellent selection of cheeses, and the wine list includes an ample selection of interesting wines.

Da Antonio, Via Fiorita 38, 53019 Castelnuovo Berardenga (SI), tel. +39 0577 335 321. Open for dinner only. Closed on Mondays and for holidays from November 10 to 25. Forty-five seats; reservations essential. Cost: EEE.

CETONA

Frateria di Padre Eligio

Padre Eligio founded this monastery in 1975 to house a Mondo X community of youths rescued from a life of drugs and homelessness. Together, as a community, they restored the thirteenth-century convent, which has become a dream-like oasis, filled with flowers and gardens. An elegant, spiritual atmosphere greets you immediately as you enter the quiet of the hermitage. An old Roman road leads to the cloisters that house the brotherhood's renowned restaurant. The restaurant was initially founded with the humble intention of supporting the community, but its reputation quickly grew largely due to a passionate approach to cooking and ingredients. Today, this is a spot worthy of a culinary pilgrimage. The fixed menu changes each day and includes produce grown on the premises as well as house-cured prosciutto, pancetta, and coppa, as well as daily baked breads. The convent's old cellars are stocked with prestigious Italian wines. The monastery also offers a small number of elegant guest accommodations.

Frateria di Padre Eligio, Convento di San Francesco, 53040 Cetona (SI), tel. +39 0578 238 015, tel. and fax +39 0578 238 261, www.lafrateria.it. Driving directions: from highway A1, exit at Chiusi, Chianciano Terme. Follow the indications from Cetona. Closed on Tuesdays, and for holidays from November 5 to December 5, and January 7 to February 15. Thirty-five seats; reservations required. Cost: EEE.

COLLE DI VAL D'ELSA

Ristorante Arnolfo

For an elegant meal in a historical setting, Arnolfo, situated in the center of Colle Val d'Elsa, is hard to beat. Its home is an elegant patrician palazzo from 1500, with a pretty garden that looks over the Tuscan hillsides. The creative cuisine prepared by chef Gaetano Trovato has won the restaurant two Michelin stars. Dishes are light and inventive and include delights like seared scallops with oysters in lemon and citrus salad, a puff pastry *millefoglie* with goose liver and Norcia truffles accompanied by red-wine steeped pears, pigeon with hazelnuts and figs in vin santo, ravioli filled with purple artichokes in a Pienza pecorino and yellow squash sauce, and for dessert, orange cake with white chocolate mousse and dark chocolate gelato.

RISTORANTE ARNOLFO, Via XX Settembre 50/52, 53034 Colle di Val d'Elsa (SI), tel. +39 0577 920 549, email arnolfo@arnolfo.com, www.arnolfo.com. Driving directions: from Florence, take the superstrade Firenze/Siena toward Siena and exit at Colle di Val d'Elsa. Closed on Tuesdays and Wednesdays, and for holidays from January 10 to February 10. Thirty-five seats; reservations essential. Cost: EEEEE.

GAIOLE IN CHIANTI

Badia a Coltibuono

Lorenza de' Medici, author of many cookbooks on Tuscan cuisine, owns this ancient Vallombrosan abbey, set high in the Chianti hills. Apart from dining in the abbey's elegant and comfortable restaurant, you can take a tour of the abbey, buy Coltibuono's wine from their gift shop, or participate in cooking classes offered on the premises.

The kitchen is under the careful direction of chef Paolo Stucchi Prinetti, who serves freshly prepared Tuscan style dishes with a creative flair. Offerings include dishes like duck salad with balsamic vinegar, fresh pappardelle pasta with lamb sauce, roasted suckling pig with fennel apple puree, and roasted pigeon stuffed with pears. Desserts include traditional almond *cantucci* biscotti with a glass of vin santo, or more unusual delights like chocolate pear cake or honey chestnut ice cream. Guided tours of the abbey are available daily from May through July and the months of September and October. Tours begin every half hour from 2:30 to 4:30 P.M.

BADIA A COLTIBUONO, Località Coltibuono, 53013 Gaiole in Chianti (SI), tel. +39 0577 749 424, fax +39 0577 749 031, email ristbadia@coltibuono.com, www.coltibuono.com. Driving directions: from highway A1, exit at San Giovanni Valdarno, connect to state road S408, then S429, always following the indications for Coltibuono. Closed on Mondays (except open every day from April through October), and for holidays from January 10 to March 10. Eighty-five seats; reservations recommended. Cost: EE.

Osteria del Castello

Castello di Brolio is a perfectly preserved Tuscan castle with stout walls, turrets, a drawbridge, and a view across vineyards all the way to Siena. It was a day at this castle that inspired my husband and me to plan our wedding at a Tuscan castle. Just down the hill from Brolio, where the drive begins a climb through Brolio's shady woods, a transplanted Irish chef, Seamus de Petheny O'Kelly, has opened a restaurant and cooking school. Seamus came to Gaiole by way of London and Paris, and before opening the Osteria del Castello he spent time at Castello di Spaltenna. His passionate approach to Italian cooking marries classical ingredients with his international training.

CASTELLO DI BROLIO (tel. +39 0577 749 066) is open for visits Monday through Saturday from 9 A.M. to noon and from 3 P.M. to 7 P.M.

OSTERIA DEL CASTELLO, Località Brolio, 53013 Gaiole in Chianti (SI), tel. +39 0577 747 277, email www.seamus.it. Driving directions from highway A1: exit at San Giovanni Valdarno, connect to state road S408. Follow the indications for Gaiole. After passing Gaiole, connect to S484, following indications for S. Regolo/Castelnuovo Berardegna. Brolio is just past San Regolo.

della Pieve—Castello di Spaltenna

Castello di Spaltenna's della Pieve restaurant is situated in an old fortified monastery, surrounded by vineyards and woods. The restaurant is part of a refined hotel with thirty rooms (see page 170). In this singular and intimate atmosphere, chef Antonio Perin prepares select dishes with creative combinations of Tuscan ingredients. Menus are inspired by the changing seasons; among the dishes are risotto with asparagus points, fava beans, and black Norcia truffles; saddle of rabbit glazed in vin santo; and for two, lamb loin in herbs from Spaltenna's garden. The restaurant's cellars hold more than 250 wines selected from local producers and national and international labels.

CASTELLO DI SPALTENNA, Via Spaltenna 13, 53013 Gaiole in Chianti (SI), tel. +39 0577 749 483, fax +39 0577 749 269, email info@spaltenna.it, www.spaltenna.it. Driving directions from highway A1: exit at San Giovanni Valdarno, connect to state road S408. Follow the indications for Gaiole. Closed for holidays from January 6 to March 30. Eighty seats; reservations suggested. Cost: EE.

GREVE IN CHIANTI

Locanda "Borgo Antico"

Among a small cluster of stone houses, the Locanda Borgo Antico is a rustic inn and restaurant, set in the tiny hamlet of Dimezzano. The village is reached through a chestnut wood in the hills above Greve. The owners of the Borgo Antico have restored their casa colonica (country home) to include a charming restaurant and three guest rooms. The restaurant's dining room is typically Tuscan in style, with terra-cotta floors, white walls, exposed brick archways, and racks of local wines. A vine-covered terrace, with views of the wooded hills, is used for summer dining. Each day, the owners shop local markets for the fresh seasonal ingredients they use to prepare dishes like pappardelle made from chestnut flour and served with a hearty ragù of wild boar, or grilled meats, and homemade desserts. The wine list offers a good selection of Chianti wines. Although the spot is secluded in the woods, it is still close to the vines and olive trees of the Chianti wine route—just eleven kilometers from Greve.

LOCANDA "BORGO ANTICO," Località Dimezzano—Lucolena, 50022 Greve in Chianti (FI), tel. and fax +39 055 851 024, email info@ilborgoantico.it, www.ilborgoantico.it. Driving directions from Florence: take the S.S. 222 to Strada, then follow the signs for Figline. Continue along this road for about twelve kilometers, passing through Cintoia, Passo della Panca, and Dudda, then turn right to Lucolena. Closed on Tuesdays. Sixty seats. Cost: E.

MONTALCINO

Poggio Antico

This restaurant is part of the Poggio Antico wine estate, set in the heart of five hundred acres of Brunello grapes, olive groves, and woodlands. Roberto and Patrizia Minnetti manage this elegant restaurant in a restored farmhouse whose windows frame the green countryside. The imaginative and expert cooking of this pair of Roman restaurateurs includes dishes like Chianina steak tartare with black truffles, *bucatini* pasta with *guanciale* (cured pork jowl), and tortelli filled with white meats. Most dishes are planned to match with the estate's wines (Brunello di Montalcino, Brunello Riserva, and Rosso di Montalcino), but the wine list extends to other regions and producers as well. There is an excellent assortment of local cheeses, and with dessert you can try a grappa di Brunello. Wine tastings, for groups of a minimum of ten persons, are also offered on the estate by reservation only.

POGGIO ANTICO, Località Poggio Antico, 53024 Montalcino (SI), tel. and fax +39 0577 849 200, email mail@poggioantico.com, www. poggioantico.it. Driving directions from Siena: take the Cassia road (SS 2) south and follow indications for Montalcino and Rome. After Buoncon-vento, follow signs for Montalcino on the right. When you reach an inter-section at the top of the hill in Montalcino, the fortress will be on your right. Take the road toward Grosseto; after about 4.5 kilometers you will see the turn for Poggio Antico. There are stone walls on both sides of the road entrance to the property and signs on each side for Poggio Antico. The unpaved cypress-lined drive takes you straight to the estate. Closed on Monday and Sunday evenings, and for holidays the months of November and March, and from January 7 through January 31. Reservations required. Cost: EEE.

Re di Macchia

In the heart of Brunello country, Re di Macchia occupies a seventeenth-century stone house in the center of Montalcino. The elegant dining room has intimately spaced tables under brick archways and beamed ceilings. Try fresh pastas in wild boar ragu, rabbit stewed with black olives, spelt with saffron and *lardo di Colonnata* (aged fatback), and rabbit in honey and hazelnuts. Re di Macchia is near Piazza Garibaldi and just steps away from the Enoteca La Fortezza, a wine shop that offers sales and tasting of Montalcino's wines from its location inside the city's fourteenth-century fortress (Piazzale Fortezza, tel. +39 0577 849 211, www.enotecalafortezza.it).

RE DI MACCHIA, Via Soccorso Saloni 21, 53024 Montalcino (SI), tel. +39 0577 846 116. Driving directions from Siena: take Via Cassia (S2) south and exit at Montalcino. Closed on Thursdays, and for holidays from January 9 to February 9. Thirty seats. Cost: EE.

Osteria del Vecchio Castello

In a small former convent, which for eight hundred years stood guard over the Romanesque Pieve di San Sigismondo, is the renowned restaurant Osteria del Vecchio Castello. A very intimate dining room in a thirteenth-century parish church among the Brunello vineyards forms the evocative setting for this haven of elegance and culinary expertise. Susanna Fumi and Alfredo Sibaldi preside over the small dining room with just five tables. The innovative cuisine takes advantage of all the products in the region and the old traditions of the Tuscan table. Dishes like broccoli flan with fresh pecorino and crisp *guanciale,* pheasant ravioli in a wine reduction sauce with black truffles from the Crete Senesi, and lamb wrapped in lardo from Greve with braised vegetables have won the owners a prestigious Michelin star. The notable wine list includes the best from Montalcino, Italy, and elsewhere, with over four hundred labels and particular attention to historic vintages.

Pieve di San Sigismondo is located on a hillside outside Montalcino, the heart of the wine growing region.

Osteria del Vecchio Castello, Pieve di San Sigismondo, S.Angelo Scalo, 53024 Montalcino (SI), tel. +39 0577 816 026, email osteriavecchio castello@virgilio.it. Closed on Tuesdays, and for holidays from February 15 to March 15. Twenty seats; reservations essential. Cost: EEE. Four apartments in the converted convent are available for weekly rental and accommodate from two to six guests each. Doubles from E.

SINALUNGA

Le Coccole della Locanda dell'Amorosa

Locanda dell'Amorosa is a restored fourteenth-century hamlet, encircled by vineyards and woods (see page 168). The charming hotel's restaurant, Le Coccole, is housed in the hamlet's old stone stables. In this rustic ambience, which is also elegant and welcoming, chef Davide Canella presents a menu based on typical Tuscan dishes, yet reinterpreted in a modern key. Some of his specialties: duck terrine with pistachios served with spelt crepes, and saddle and thigh of rabbit with fennel flowers.

In the cantina there are more than 130 wines, from the best Tuscans to choice wines from other Italian regions. They include the wines produced by Amorosa's farm, including Borgo Amorosa and Rosso dell'Amorosa.

La Locanda dell'Amorosa, Località l'Amorosa, 53048 Sinalunga (SI), tel. +39 0577 677 211, fax +39 0577 632 001, email locanda@amorosa.it, www.amorosa.it. Closed Monday and on Tuesdays at lunch, and for holidays from January 1 to March 1. Sixty seats; reservations essential. Cost: EEE.

RADDA IN CHIANTI

La Bottega di Volpaia

The cuisine of the Chianti area is tied to the simple habits of the farmers who have worked the hillsides for centuries. Their ingredients: cold-pressed olive oil, hard grains like durum wheat, fresh garden herbs, and the wines of Chianti. Carla Barucci and her mother Gina use these very elements to fashion the dishes at their Bottega di Volpaia restaurant. The charming restaurant they manage is set in a medieval village, amidst the spectacular panorama of the Chianti hills. At Volpaia you can even learn the secrets of Tuscan cooking, from *ribollita* (Tuscan vegetable and bread soup) to hand-cut pastas, under the expert guidance of Gina and Carla. Cooking classes are offered for groups by appointment.

La Bottega di Volpaia, Piazza della Torre 2, Località Volpaia, 53017 Radda in Chianti (SI), tel. +39 0577 738 001. Reservations are suggested for dinner. Closed on Tuesdays.

Watching the Sunset

Pienza—Via dell'Amore

There is poetry to the street names in Pienza's carefully designed city. At the end of the day, you can wander along *Via della Fortuna* (Street of Fortune), *Via dell'Amore* (Street of Love), and *Via del Bacio* (Street of the Kiss). It is no wonder that the streets bear poetic epithets, as the city center was the brainstorm and inspiration of humanist poet Enea Piccolomini, who was born in Pienza in 1405 and later became Pope Pius II. Piccolomini's vision for Renaissance Pienza was to create a harmonious city plan filled with ideal squares, streets, and monuments. The city he created with architect Bernardo Rossellino remains one of Italy's most perfectly preserved Renaissance cities.

Departing from the Via della Fortuna and the Via dell' Amore, the walk arrives at the old city walls, which overlook the dramatic Orcia Valley—a perfect spot to watch a romantic sunset.

From Piazza Pio, follow Corso Rossellino east to Via della Fortuna, Via dell'Amore, and Via del Bacio.

Volterra—Viale dei Ponti

Volterra is a magical Tuscan town with a blend of Etruscan, Roman, and medieval roots. Perched on a plateau above the Val d'Elsa and the Val di Cecina, the city enjoys views that extend, on clear days, to the Ligurian Sea. Volterra is probably best known as an important center for alabaster, first mined by the Etruscans. The city is also rich with precious archeological monuments, including a Roman amphitheater and baths and an Etruscan acropolis. Volterra's Piazza dei Priori is one of Italy's prettiest medieval squares, circled with thirteenth-century palaces.

Along the city's southwest edge, the Viale dei Ponti promenade is one of the best spots in town to catch the sunset. The walk was created by the city in 1846 and looks over the *Colline Metallifere* (metal-bearing hills). Towering over the promenade is Volterra's fourteenth-century Medici *fortezza*, with impressive circular towers and a massive keep.

The Comune of Volterra maintains an informative website at www.comune.volterra.pi.it.

Places to Propose

On the Walls of Brolio Castle—Gaiole in Chianti

Castello di Brolio is a well-preserved Tuscan castle that dates to 1141. The castle allows visitors to wander through its Italianate gardens and to visit the pristine family chapel, painted with celestial frescoes. From its massive walls there is a view over rolling vineyards with Siena in the distance. If you are looking for a romantic spot in Tuscany to make a marriage proposal, Castello di Brolio has some of the prettiest views.

The gardens, walls, and chapel are open for visits during the summer from 9 A.M. to noon and 3 P.M. to 6 P.M. and during the winter from 9 A.M to noon and 2 P.M. to 5 P.M. Closed on Christmas Day, New Year's Day, and every Friday during winter. Brolio is also a wine estate and offers wine tastings by appointment in its historic cellars; call tel. +39 0577 7301 or email shop@ricasoli.it for an appointment. CASTELLO DI BROLIO, 53013 Gaiole in Chianti (Siena).

Two elegant apartments inside the castle are available for weekly rentals. Il Maniero can accommodate six to ten guests, and Cavaliere on the second floor has room for six. Rates upon request. Contact: Stagioni del Chianti: tel. +39 055 265 7842, fax +39 055 264 5184, email info@stagionidelchianti.com, www.stagionidelchianti.com.

Driving directions from highway A1: exit at Valdarno and follow highway S408 until the crossroads for S484 signed for Brolio.

Romantic Lore and Local Festivals

Giostra del Saracino—Arezzo

The Giostra del Saracino is an annual jousting tournament held in the city of Arezzo. The name of the festival hails from the twelfth-century crusades against the Saracens (as Muslims were called by Europeans in the Middle Ages). The contest is a game of skill in which riders from different quarters use a lance to hit a target, dubbed the *saracino*. The first known *giostra* in Arezzo dates back to 1535. Today, the tradition continues on the second to last weekend of June, when flag-bearers, trumpeters, and townsfolk in medieval costumes fill the streets of this beautiful city.

ISTITUZIONE "GIOSTRA DEL SARACINO," Via Porta Buia (ex Caserma Cadorna), Arezzo, tel. +39 0575 377 462, fax +39 0575 377 464, email giostradelsaracino@comune.arezzo.it, www.giostradelsaracino.arezzo.it.

Ferie delle Messi—San Gimignano

Each year, on the third Saturday and Sunday in June, the town of San Gimignano celebrates the Ferie delle Messi. During this two-day medieval festival, the streets are filled with jugglers, acrobats, and jousting knights—all in authentic costumes. On Sunday afternoon, the Giostra dei Bastoni tournament is held, in which the contesting *contrade* (districts) compete in sword fights and archery contests. Afterward, a victory parade is held for the winners and festivities continue late into the night.

The FERIE DELLE MESSI is organized by Cavalieri di Santa Fina, Piazza Duomo 1, 53037 San Gimignano (Siena), tel. +39 0577 940 008, fax +39 0577 940 903.

Palio—Siena

The city of Siena runs its historic Palio horse race on July 2 and August 16 every year. Sixteen competing *contrade,* each representing a different neighborhood, parade through the streets in team colors and demonstrations of pageantry. Weekend displays and feasting lead up to the dangerous, epic, ninety-second race, in which bareback riders make three daring circuits around the Piazza del Campo.

Siena's Palio is organized by the Comune di Siena (www.comune.siena.it). Tourist assistance is available at Siena APT, Piazza del Campo 56, tel +39 0577 280 551, fax +39 0577 270 676, email aptsiena@siena.turismo. toscana.it.

Bravio delle Botti—Montepulciano

The last Sunday in August, eight ancient contrade compete in Montepulciano's Bravio delle Botti. The Bravio began in 1372 as a horse race dedicated to the city's patron saint, San Giovanni Decollato. The city archives still hold the original edict that set the game's medieval rules. In the seventeenth century, in the interest of public safety, the dangerous horse race was banned. Revived in 1974, the modern contest involves teams of *spingitori* (pushers) who roll two-hundred-pound barrels along a hazardous uphill course.

Magistrato delle contrade di Montepulciano, Via dell'Opio nel Corso 1, 53045 Montepulciano (SI), tel. +39 0578 757 575. PRO-LOCO di Montepulciano, Via di Gracciano nel Corso 59/a, 53045 Montepulciano (SI) tel. and fax +39 0578 757 341, email info@braviodellebotti.it, www. bravio dellebotti.it.

Picnic Spots

Fiesole Above Florence

Start by gathering picnic provisions at Florence's San Lorenzo market, then enjoy a day of picnicking and exploration in the hills above Florence. Once in Fiesole, you can picnic on the grassy, overgrown stone stairs of Fiesole's first-century B.C.E. Roman amphitheater, or find a quiet spot in town and enjoy the view over Florence. If you are in the mood for some hiking, you can follow the hiking trail that leads up the hill from

Fiesole to Monte Ceceri, where in 1505 Leonardo da Vinci conducted his famous experiments on flight. Alternatively, follow the road from Fiesole to Settignano and find a quiet olive grove along the way for a picnic for two.

Maps of the hiking trails that run from Fiesole to Maiano, Vincigliata, and Settignano are published by Kompass maps (available through www. omnimap.com), or from Carte dei Sentieri *Dintorni di Firenze e Mugello*, available in Italian bookstores.

Monte Senario—Vaglia

Just north of Florence, near the small village of Vaglia, is a sacred sanctuary atop Mount Senario. Founded by the original members of the *Servi dei Maria* (Servants of Mary), the Santuario di Monte Senario stands 2,673 feet above sea level and enjoys peaceful views over the valley below. The monastery is still used for spiritual retreats and is surrounded by grassy meadows and deep woods, with many shady spots for picnicking. In the woods around the monastery you can visit the monks' cells, where they found solace in isolation, and the *ghiacciaia* (icehouse) where they stored winter ice. The icehouse, a large building with a stone cupola, dates to the 1800s when monks would make regular trips to nearby hospitals with mule carts filled with ice.

Driving directions from Florence: take highway S65 north and exit at Pratolino. Continue, following indications for Monte Senario.

Romantic Excursions

A Food Lover's Holiday—Cooking Courses in Tuscany

Food in Tuscany is inherently romantic. The cuisine is simple and straightforward, yet full of sensual flavors and aromas. For food lovers, a holiday in Tuscany doesn't have to be limited to gazing longingly at the bountiful outdoor markets or through the windows of every butcher's shop you pass. Instead, you can master the art of Tuscan cooking by spending part or all of your holiday at one of the region's excellent cooking schools. Fortunately for those who long to master the art of crafting fresh pasta by hand or stewing up a perfect *ribollita,* many of Tuscany's schools are directed by internationally recognized experts on Tuscan cuisine, so you're sure to return home with secrets you can use for a lifetime.

Cooking Schools

BADIA A COLTIBUONO, an enchanting eleventh-century abbey in the Chianti countryside, is the setting for courses in Tuscan cuisine. The abbey is owned by Lorenza de' Medici, who started her culinary career as the food editor for Vogue Italia, then went on to write over twenty works on Italian cooking. One-day courses include a hands-on cooking class, a tour of the historic abbey, and lunch at the abbey restaurant (see page 185). For committed cooks there are five-day courses, taught by Francesco Torre, chef at the Badia's restaurant. During the extended course, participants are guests at the historic abbey and venture into the field with Francesco to regional markets and local farms in search of Tuscany's best ingredients. Classes are limited to sixteen participants. Detailed schedules and class itineraries are available by contacting Badia a Coltibuono. Badia a Coltibuono, Località Coltibuono, 53013 Gaiole in Chianti (SI), tel. +39 0577 749 424, fax +39 0577 749 031, email info@coltibuono.com, www.coltibuono.com.

IL FALCONIERE is a romantic seventeenth-century villa and luxury hotel in the valley below Cortona. Cooking courses at Il Falconiere are taught by Titi Richard, chef of Il Falconiere's restaurant, and by Silvia Regi, the hotel's owner and professional sommelier. Students can participate in either three- or six-day courses, which include hands-on cooking classes, lunches, dinners, and a winery tour and tasting. Class size is limited to fourteen students. Il Falconiere, Località S. Martino 370, 52044 Cortona (Arezzo), tel. +39 0575 612 679, fax +39 0575 612 927, email ilfalcon@il falconiere.com, www.ilfalconiere.com.

TENUTA DI CAPEZZANA winery, located west of Florence, serves as the setting for a cooking school directed by food writer Faith Heller Willinger. During her five-day courses, students learn to make pizza and focaccia in a wood-burning oven; make trips to outdoor markets; and practice pairing

Tuscan wines with their culinary creations. The classes are limited to fourteen participants; guests stay at the secluded Carmignano farm. Capezzana Wine and Culinary Center, Tenuta di Capezzana, Via Capezzana 100, 59015 Carmignano (PO), tel. + 39 055 870 6005, fax + 39 055 870 6673, email agriturismo@capezzana.it, www.capezzana.it.

Restaurant Cooking Schools

BOTTEGA DI VOLPAIA is a charming restaurant in a small medieval hamlet above Radda in Chianti. Managed by a mother-and-daughter team, the restaurant opens its kitchen to those who desire to learn the secrets of Tuscan cooking. Cooking classes are offered for groups by appointment. La Bottega di Volpaia, Località Volpaia, 53017 Radda in Chianti (SI), tel. +39 0577 738 001.

TRATTORIA GARGA is one of Florence's most popular restaurants. Proprietors Giuliano Gargani and wife Sharon Oddson offer one-day cooking classes in Florence and week-long lessons on *la cucina povera* (country cooking) at Villa Margherita in southern Tuscany. From the farm, students make excursions to local producers to taste extra-virgin olive oil and pecorino cheese. La Cucina del Garga Cooking School, Via del Moro 48, 50123 Firenze, tel. +39 055 211 396, email garga@fol.it, www.garga.it.

OSTERIA DEL CASTELLO in Gaiole di Chianti is managed by an energetic Irish chef, Seamus de Petheny O'Kelly. On Tuesdays and Fridays, Seamus opens his kitchen to a limited number of participants and provides hands-on demonstrations and lessons in Tuscan cooking. Osteria del Castello, Località Brolio, 53013 Gaiole in Chianti (SI), tel. +39 0577 747 277, email www.seamus.it.

Taking the Waters—Ancient Etruscan Spas

Since Etruscan times, the natural springs throughout Tuscany have been revered for their curative powers. While our modern idea of spas involves pampered treatments like massages and seaweed wraps, traditional Italian spas have focused on the curative properties of the water itself and emphasize regimens that involve a regulated intake from the source. When you visit Tuscany's thermal springs, you will find the source's waters labeled with their mineral properties, with an explanation of potential cures they are believed to provide.

The most glamorous spas in Tuscany are Montecatini Terme and Saturnia. Both springs were known in ancient times and have a rich history.

Montecatini's heyday was during the Belle Epoque era at the turn of the twentieth century. During the 1920s, many of the baths were expanded with monumental pavilions circled by glorious colonnades and marble fountains. Visiting the oldest of Montecatini's spas, Tettuccio and Leopoldine, is like stepping into a Fellini film. Their plazas are filled with an amazing cast of characters who sit at tables and sip the waters while listening to old Italian standards played by a live band. Spa goers looking for more modern wellness and beauty treatments can find them at the Excelsior, which offers Turkish baths, massage, mud treatments, and a selection of beauty treatments.

The ancients believed that the god Saturn created Saturnia's thermal springs. To calm warring Tuscan tribes, Saturn threw a bolt of lightning into a volcano and released calming waters from beneath the earth. Saturnia's waters were a popular attraction for both Etruscans and Romans. Today, much of Saturnia has been modernized to cater to the needs of modern spa travelers. There are four thermal outdoor pools, each with a constant temperature of 98°F. Thermal therapies range from mud treatments to hydromassage, and beauty treatments include a wide range of aromatherapy, mud, and massage services.

Taking the Waters—Addresses and Practical Information

Terme di Montecatini

Montecatini is twenty-seven miles north of Florence in the rolling hill country near Pistoia. The city maintains an informative website with information about the thermal springs at www.termemontecatini.it.

> Terme Excelsior, Viale Verdi, tel. +39 0572 778 511
> Terme Tettucci, Viale Verdi, tel. +39 0572 778 501
> Terme Leopoldine,Viale Verdi, tel. +39 0572 778 551

> The Grand Hotel e La Pace is a classic hotel that has often been used as location for films. Over the years, it has been a favorite stopping point for celebrities like Audrey Hepburn, Orson Welles, and Spencer Tracy. The hotel has 136 rooms, eight suites, and six junior suites all centrally located and steps away from the historic spas. Grand Hotel & La Pace, Via della Torretta 1, 51016 Montecatini Terme (PT), tel. +39 0572 924 0, fax +39 0572 784 51, www.grandhotellapace.com. Doubles from EE to EEEE.

Terme di Saturnia

The *Saturnia Spa Resort* has 140 rooms, three restaurants, and updated spa facilities. There are also tennis courts, golf, and gym facilities. Saturnia Spa Resort, tel. +39 0564 600 111, fax +39 0564 601 266, email info@termedisaturnia.it, www.termedisaturnia.it. Doubles from EEE to EEEEE.

Mercati Antiquariato—Antiquing in Tuscany

Tuscany is known for its rich collection of antique markets. Some of our favorite souvenirs from vacations abroad have come from picking our way through treasures that came from *Nonna's* attic. An old Roman coin from the market in Arezzo became a symbolic token of payment for our minister when we got married in Tuscany. We've proudly hung a 1940s advertising poster for Vampa pasta in our kitchen at home—another souvenir that will always remind us of Italy.

Most of the antique markets in Italy include a combination of the rare and the mundane, from priceless Roman artifacts to 1930s electronics. Among the sellers, you will find dealers who specialize in numismatics and antiquarian books, as well as families getting rid of old junk from their attics.

In Tuscany the largest monthly markets are those held in Arezzo (five hundred sellers) and Lucca (two hundred sellers). There are many smaller markets in other cities and villages.

For serious antiquarians, the city of Florence holds a biannual fair at the princely Palazzo Corsini (at the end of September and early October of odd-numbered years). For this serious antiques show, over thirteen thousand square feet of exhibition space is filled with exhibitors who are renowned experts in the field of precious antiques. The museum quality objects on display are from varied periods and provenances.

ANTIQUING IN TUSCANY—ADDRESSES AND PRACTICAL INFORMATION

There are many other markets throughout Tuscany in both large and small towns. Most close for July and August holidays; check with the tourist boards for updated schedules before you go. For contact information and a schedule of all the markets by weekend, see page 202.

A few of Tuscany's Monthly Antique Markets

AREZZO

FIERA ANTIQUARIA (Antiques Market) Held the first Saturday and Sunday of the month in Piazza San Francesco, Piazza Grande, and the adjacent streets, Arezzo's antique fair is central Italy's largest market, with more than five hundred exhibitors. The entire historic center of the town is filled with booths, and most of Arezzo's antique shops are also open during the fair. Among the treasures you'll find are antique books, eighteenth- and nineteenth-century paintings and furniture, scientific instruments, glass, old posters, art deco objects, and jewelry.

FIRENZE

Three monthly antiques markets and one biannual fair are held in the city of Florence. On the second Sunday of the month (except in August), Piazza Santo Spirito's normally quiet square is filled with the MERCATO DELL'ANTIQUARIATO, a small market of arts and crafts, bric-a-brac, and small antiques. On the third Sunday of the month (except in July and August), an antiques market is held in the gardens of FORTEZZA DA BASSO (in Viale Filippo Strozzi, just a short walk from the train station). Furniture, lamps, and decorative pieces are on sale from 150 exhibitors. On the last Sunday of the month (except in July) the PIAZZA DEI CIOMPI flea market boasts nearly a hundred exhibitors from all over Italy. Paintings, antique furniture, ceramics, and jewelry are among the offerings. The biannual MOSTRA MERCATO INTERNAZIONALE DELL'ANTIQUARIATO is held in odd-numbered years at Palazzo Corsini. See www.mostraantiquariato.it for information.

LUCCA

MERCATO DELL'ANTIQUARIATO is held the third Saturday and Sunday of each month in the city's historic center. Antiques, furniture, rare items, jewelry, marble sculptures, and collectibles are offered by two hundred exhibitors alongside Lucca's most noteworthy monuments.

MONTEPULCIANO

MERCATINO DELL'ANTIQUARIATO is held the second Sunday of the month and the Saturday that precedes it in the historic Piazza Grande. Fifty exhibitors offer antiques, furniture, and collectibles.

PISTOIA

MERCATO DELL'ANTIQUARIATO is held on the second Saturday and Sunday of the month (closed in July and August) in Viale Pacinotti. Antiques and collectibles are displayed by 130 exhibitors.

SIENA

L'ANGOLO DEL COLLEZIONISTA is held on the third Sunday of the month (closed in August) near Piazza del Campo (Loggiati di S. Domenico). Antiques, furniture, numismatics, and collectibles are offered by eighty exhibitors.

Antiques Markets by Weekend — First Weekend of the Month

CITY / MARKET	LOCATION	DATE	EXHIBITORS	CONTACT
AREZZO: Fiera Antiquaria	Piazza Grande	First Sunday of the month and the Saturday that precedes it	500 exhibitors	A.P.T. Arezzo Piazza della Repubblica 28, tel. +39 0575 208 39, email info@arezzo.turismo.toscana.it.
CARMIGNANO (FI): Mercato dell'Antiquariato e dell'Usato	Piazza Vittorio Emanuele II	First Sunday of the month	30 exhibitors	Associazione Turistica Pro Loco di Carmignano Piazza Vittorio Emanuele II 1, 59015 Carmignano (PO) tel. +39 055 871 2468
LIVORNO (LI): Mercato del Passato	Quartiere Venezia	First Saturday and Sunday of the month	70 exhibitors	A.P.T Livorno Piazza Cavour 6, 57125 Livorno tel. +39 0586 898 111, fax +39 0586 896 173 email info@livorno.turismo.toscana.it
ORBETELLO (GR)	Centro Storico	First Sunday of the month	60 exhibitors	
PIETRASANTA (LU): Antiquità in Piazza	Piazza Duomo	First Sunday of the month	70 exhibitors	
SAN MINIATO (PI)	Centro Storico	First Sunday of the month (closed in July and August)	50 exhibitors	Ufficio Turismo Comune di San Miniato Piazza del Popolo 3, 56027 San Miniato (Pi) tel. +39 057 142 745
SCARPERIA (FI): Mercato dell'Antiquariato	Centro Storico	First Sunday of the month	60 exhibitors	
SESTO FIORENTINO (FI): Mercatino dell'Antiquariato	Piazza Comune	First Sunday of the month	30 exhibitors	Comune di Sesto Fiorentino Via Barducci, 2 tel. +39 055 449 6260, fax +39 055 449 6267 www.comune.sesto-fiorentino.fi.it
VINCI (FI): Mercatino dell'Antiquariato	Centro Storico	First Sunday of the month	90 exhibitors	

Antiques Markets by Weekend — Second Weekend of the Month

CITY / MARKET	LOCATION	DATE	EXHIBITORS	CONTACT
BARGA (LU): Mercato Antiquariato	Centro Storico	Second Sunday of the month	40 exhibitors	
FIESOLE (FI): Fiesole Antiquaria	Centro Storico	Second Sunday of the month	60 exhibitors	
FIRENZE	Piazza Santo Spirito	Second Sunday of the month	60 exhibitors	A.P.T. Firenze Via Manzoni 16, 50121 Firenze tel. +39 055 233 20, fax +39 055 234 6286 email info@firenze.turismo.toscana.it
MONTEPULCIANO (SI): Fiera delle Arti e Artigianato	Centro Storico	Second Sunday of the month	40 exhibitors	
PIOMBINO (LI): Mercatino dell'Antiquariato	Corso Italia	Second Sunday of the month and the preceding Saturday	40 exhibitors	Comune di Piombino, Assessorato Attività Produttive e Turismo tel +39 0565 633 52
PISA (PI): Mercato dell'Antiquariato	Centro Storico	Second Sunday of the month and the preceding Saturday (closed in July and August)	120 exhibitors	A.P.T. Pisa Via Benedetto Croce 26, 56125 Pisa tel. +39 050 400 96, fax +39 050 409 03
PISTOIA (PT): Mercato dell'Antiquariato	Viale Pacinotti	Second weekend of the month (closed in July and August)	130 exhibitors	A.P.T. Pistoia Via Marconi 28, 51028 San Marcello Pistoiese tel. +39 0573 630 145, fax +39 0573 622 120 email aptpistoia@comune.pistoia.it
SEANO (PO): La Soffitta In Piazza	Via XX Settembre	Second Sunday of the month		Pro Loco Carmignano tel. +39 055 871 2468
TERRANUOVA BRACCIOLINI (AR): Fiera Antiquaria del Valdarno	Piazza della Repubblica (Via Roma)	Second Sunday of the month (closed in August)	100+ exhibitors	

Antiques Markets by Weekend — Third Weekend of the Month

CITY / MARKET	LOCATION	DATE	EXHIBITORS	CONTACT
ANGHIARI (AR): Mercatino dell' Antiquariato	Centro Storico	Third Sunday of the month	45 exhibitors	Ufficio Turistico "Pro Anghiari," Corso Matteotti 103, Anghiari (AR), tel. +39 0575 749279
DICOMANO (FI): Mostra Antiquariato Artigianato	Centro Storico	Third Sunday of the month	45 exhibitors	Comune di Dicomano email assessori@comune.dicomano.fi.it— tel.+ 39 055 838 541, fax+39 055 838 5423
FIRENZE	Giardini Fortezza da Basso	Third weekend of the month		A.P.T. Firenze Via Manzoni 16, 50121 Firenze tel. +39 055 233 20, fax +39 055 2342 86 email info@firenze.turismo.toscana.it
LUCCA (LU): Mercato Antiquario di Lucca	In Piazza Antelminelli, Piazza San Giovanni, Piazza San Martino, Via del Battistero	Third Sunday of the month and the preceding Saturday	200 exhibitors	A.P.T. Lucca Via Guidicciani 2, 55100 Lucca tel. +39 0583 919 91, fax +39 0583 490 766 email aptlucca@lucca.turismo.toscana.it www.lucca.turismo.toscana.it
QUARRATA (PT): L'Antiquariato in Piazza	Piazza Risorgimento	Third Sunday of the month	80 exhibitors	
SIENA (SI): L'Angolo del Collezionista	Piazza del Mercato	Third Sunday of the month	90 exhibitors	A.P.T. Siena Via di Città 43, 53100 Siena tel. +39 0577 422 09, fax +39 0577 281 041 email aptsiena@siena.turismo.toscana.it

Antiques Markets by Weekend — Fourth Weekend of the Month

CITY / MARKET	LOCATION	DATE	EXHIBITORS	CONTACT
BIENTINA (PI): Mostra Mercato dell'Antiquariato	Centro Storico	Fourth Sunday of the month and the preceding Saturday	40 exhibitors	
PRATO (FI): Collezionare in Piazza	Piazza San Francesco	Fourth Sunday of the month—from September through May		A.P.T. Prato Via Luigi Muzzi 38, 59100 Prato tel. +39 0574 351 41, fax +39 0574 607 925 email apt@prato.turismo.toscana.it
VIAREGGIO (LU): Mercato dell'Antiquariato	Piazza d'Azeglio	Fourth Sunday of the month and the preceding Saturday	55 exhibitors	

Antiques Markets by Weekend — Last Weekend of the Month

CITY / MARKET	LOCATION	DATE	EXHIBITORS	CONTACT
BUONCONVENTO (SI): Mercatino dell'Antiquariato e Cose del Passato	Along the old walls of the Cassia	Last Sunday of the month (closed in December)		Comune di Buonconvento tel. +39 0577 809 71, fax +39 0577 807 212 email info@comunedibuonconvento.net
FIRENZE	Piazza dei Ciompi	Last Sunday of the month (closed in July)	80 exhibitors	A.P.T. Firenze Via Manzoni 16, 50121 Firenze tel. +39 055 233 20, fax +39 055 234 6286 email info@firenze.turismo.toscana.it
MONTECATINI TERME (PT): La Piazza dei Ricordi	Piazza XX Settembre	Last Sunday of the month		A.P.T. Montecatini Valdinievole Viale Verdi 66, 51016 Montecatini Terme (PT) tel. +39 0572 772 244, fax +39 0572 701 09 email apt@montecatini.turismo.toscana.it
SCANDICCI (FI): Fiera Antiquaria	Centro Storico	Last Saturday and Sunday of the month	80 exhibitors	

Weddings in Tuscany

If you plan a wedding in Tuscany, you can tie the knot in one of the region's city halls, housed in the centuries-old public buildings that date back to the time of the Guelphs and Ghibellines. In the large city centers, these *uffici di stato civile* are usually centered in the most famous and prestigious palaces, like the Palazzo Vecchio in Florence. Alternatively, in the historically rich medieval villages of San Gimignano and Poppi, smaller city halls host quiet, intimate ceremonies away from the crowds. For religious weddings, many Tuscan castles and hamlets have their own chapels where ceremonies are permitted, or weddings can be held at one of the region's Romanesque country churches or monumental city cathedrals.

Large receptions can be held in the patrician villas in and around Florence, while more secluded hamlets along the Chianti and Montalcino wine routes are well suited to smaller occasions. Either way, if you want a storybook event, many locations offer authentic medieval or Renaissance banquets. Fire-eaters, magicians, jugglers, and trumpeters can welcome and delight your guests before you feast on medieval-style dishes. If your wedding is held during the summer months, the ancient medieval tournaments reenacted in many Tuscan cities are great events to keep guests busy before your wedding. By celebrating your wedding in Tuscany's Renaissance churches, medieval city centers, or country castles, you can

Chi si marita per amore, di notte ha piacere,
e di giorno ha dolore.
If you marry for love you'll have happy nights and painful days.

Chi si marita in fretta, stenta adagio.
He who marries in haste struggles at leisure.

surround your event with centuries of culture, warm hospitality, and an unforgettable setting.

CEREMONY AND RECEPTION LOCATIONS

Castello di Vincigliata

After winding along a cypress-lined lane through silver olive groves, at last you will see an unmarked gate. Passing through the portcullis where a drawbridge might once have stood, and climbing up the bridle path, you reach the castle's secret garden, enclosed by ramparts and surrounded by views of the cultivated Fiesole hills. In 1840, the British expatriate Lord John Temple Leader, while wandering the hills of Fiesole, stumbled upon the ruins of Castello di Vincigliata. He climbed the still-standing tower and was overcome by the view of Florence at his feet. Hiring the best local craftsmen, he painstakingly restored the castle and made it into a lavish summer residence, where today receptions and events are held.

It's easy to envision what might have been in Lord John's mind's eye, when during the summer months lush creeping vines engulf both the castle walls and the battlements of the towering keep, adding a soft, natural contrast to the stone construction. Bordered by the castle walls, the English-style castle garden offers a sunny spot to exchange your vows, surrounded by the fragrance of lemon trees and lavender.

While the garden is the ideal setting for ceremonies, the central castle courtyard—complete with medieval style fortifications is an impressive location for a wedding dinner. Guests enter from the garden through massive wood doors with hand-forged hinges and wrought-iron latches. A staircase leads up to the gallery that surrounds the courtyard and then to the upper landing with its sweeping view of Florence. During receptions, the gallery, garden, and castle ramparts are romantically lit with Roman torches.

Adjoining the courtyard, a covered gallery with glassed-in twenty-foot archways, a vaulted ceiling, and a stately fireplace can be used for after-dinner dancing or cocktails. On one side, the windows look into the courtyard; on the other side, the view is through cypress trees down to Florence.

Inside, the classically appointed castle rooms are decorated with framed fresco panels—fragments of a fourteenth-century fresco cycle rescued from a Vallombrosan chapel by Lord John. Of course, no castle would be complete without an armory, and Vincigliata's swords, jousting lances, and suits of armor are displayed in a museum-like setting. Two additional permanently tented spaces have room for a total of three hundred seated guests and are available when the weather doesn't allow for outdoor dining. A wonderful tower room is at the bride's disposal, where she and her attendants can dress before the wedding.

Just fifteen minutes from Florence, the castle is best reached by a shuttle service, as the roads are quite narrow and parking is limited.

You may select your own catering. Reception capacity ranges from seventy-five to three hundred guests. The castle offers accommodations for six guests inside the castle and in the attached farmhouse.

CASTELLO DI VINCIGLIATA, Via di Vincigliata 13, 50014 Fiesole (FI), tel. +39 055 599 556, fax +39 055 599 166, email vincigliata@fol.it, www. castellodivincigliata.it. Driving directions from Milan: take the A1 (Milano-Firenze) highway and exit at Firenze nord. Follow the signs to Fiesole. Once you reach Fiesole, follow the signs to Vincigliata. Driving directions from Rome: Take the A1 (Roma-Firenze) highway and exit at Firenze sud. Follow the signs to the Centro Tecnico di Coverciano. After passing through Coverciano, take the second road on the left, which will be the Via di Vincigliata. Follow this road two kilometers until you arrive at the castle. Cost: EE to EEE.

Villa di Maiano

James Ivory couldn't have picked a more accurate setting when he cast the Villa di Maiano as the home-away-from-home for Brits on the Grand Tour in his film, *A Room with a View*. In the early part of the century, the villa was owned by the British expatriate Lord John Temple Leader, who remodeled it and its adjoining abbey to create a suitable country retreat for his visiting friends and family. Lord John, who made a second career of rescuing and restoring ancient landmarks in Fiesole, purchased the villa, the adjoining Benedictine convent, and church of San Martino in 1873, and carefully restored them into the buildings we see today.

The fortified villa, with its golden three-story façade, colonnaded entranceway, and central watchtower, sits on a hillside above Florence in a landscape dominated by cypress trees and olive groves. Part of a vast agricultural estate, Maiano is surrounded by 740 acres and eighteen thousand olive trees that produce the prized Laudemio olive oil. Next door, a fifteenth-century cloister is now the central structure to the adjoining Fattoria di Maiano, where the nuns' cells have been lovingly restored and converted into eight comfortable holiday-stay apartments, which will accommodate fifty guests.

The villa's impressive outdoor spaces have an unsurpassed view of Florence and the valley. Outdoor wedding receptions are often set on the broad lawn directly in front of the villa, with tents providing shade from the warm summer sun. The Italianate garden on the lower terrace, with its lattice-shaped arrangement of hedges, is one of the best locations for a wedding ceremony. An altar can be set in front of the wrought-iron garden gate, where you'll be framed by a backdrop of olive groves that wander down the valley. Alternatively, you can hold your ceremony under the

canopy of the two-hundred-year-old oak tree at the garden's edge, with Brunelleschi's dome punctuating the background.

Lord John enclosed the villa's open courtyard to create a grand banquet hall, the Sala Arazzi. Named for the tapestries that hang on both stories, it has room for one hundred guests for dinner in front of the inviting fire. Francesco Giovannozzi created the huge Florentine sandstone fireplace carved with florets and beasts for the Temple Leader family. The room has a forty-foot ceiling and a stately balustraded gallery that circles the perimeter.

While the villa's interior starred as the Florentine Pensione Bertolini, the romantic outdoor scenes in *A Room with a View* were filmed in the spectacular landscape just outside its gates. It would be hard to have a wedding in Fiesole and not also plan a lazy picnic in one of the nearby barley fields, like the one Mr. Beebe, Lucy, Miss Bartlett, and the Misters Emerson enjoyed so many years ago. Access to the villa is by a narrow road from Florence that winds through olive groves, gardens, and gentle meadows, leading to the tiny village of Maiano and the villa, just ten minutes from downtown Florence.

Available for guided visits by appointment. Sites for ceremonies and receptions include four halls and a formal Italian garden with a panoramic view of Fiesole and Florence. You may select your own catering. Reception capacity ranges from fifty to three hundred guests. Accommodations for fifty guests are available at the adjoining Fattoria Maiano.

VILLA DI MAIANO, Via Benedetto da Maiano 11, 50014 Fiesole (FI), tel. +39 055 599 600, fax +39 055 599 640, email villa@contemiarifulcis.it, www. fattoriadimaiano.com. Driving directions: take the A1 (Milano-Roma) highway and exit at Firenze sud. Follow the signs to Fiesole. Once you have passed San Domenico, turn right onto Via Benedetto da Maiano, which leads to the villa. Cost: EE to EEE.

Castello di Gargonza

Inscribed over Gargonza's castle gate, a passage from the *History of the Life of Dante* chronicles the poet's stay in 1304 as a guest of the Ubertini family. When Dante stopped in this tranquil hamlet on his way home from an unsuccessful ambassadorial envoy to Rome, he learned that he

had been exiled from Florence, thus beginning a journey that would never bring him back to the city of his birth.

At the end of a gently winding road, nestled in its own forest, the medieval hamlet of Gargonza may have served as inspiration for the opening lines of Dante's epic poem, *The Divine Comedy:*

> *Midway upon the journey of our life*
> *I found that I was in a dusky wood;*
> *For the right path, whence I had strayed, was lost.*

Happily, Dante's story ends in Paradise beside his beloved Beatrice, where "love . . . moves the sun and the . . . stars." A wedding at Gargonza could begin a similar journey for you.

Walking in Dante's footsteps past the building that once housed the baker's ovens, you'll enter into Gargonza's charming *piazzetta* with its towering castle keep and thirteenth-century church. Today, Gargonza has been transformed into a wonderful hotel complex; the old shops and storerooms of the hamlet are now cozy rooms with fireplaces and comfortable furnishings. Gargonza offers the unique possibility of hosting a wedding in true medieval style, at which you and your guests can experience the flavor of living in the thirteenth century. The tiny village's narrow cobblestone streets, closed to car traffic, wind past garden plots and window boxes to each of the twenty-three apartments.

The Lemonaia, where the hamlet's prized lemon trees are grown, has a spiritual, almost pagan, feeling and is an ideal setting for outdoor weddings in the summer months. The silence of the surrounding woods envelops the intimate asymmetrical cross of lawn, which is enclosed by a short wall. The dividing lines between the four sections of lush green grass suggest ancient foundations or some long-forgotten archaic ritual setting. Like a theatrical backdrop, the altar space is framed by the church bells and the crenellated watchtower, both elegantly lit at night.

The warm-spirited and highly professional staff delight in assisting with wedding details, especially when it comes to deciding what to serve for your wedding banquet. The hotel's chef at the Torre di Gargonza restaurant is an expert in the preparation of intensely Tuscan dishes like *pappardelle al sugo di lepre* (fresh pasta with wild rabbit sauce) and *bistecca alla Chianana* (steak cut from prized grass-fed beef). Sitting just outside the castle walls, the restaurant can seat 150 outside and 100 inside. Its broad, covered veranda overlooks a garden of fruit trees, while the inviting dining room has rustic stone walls and brick archways.

The staff can also help you plan your own medieval festival at Gargonza, filling the hamlet once more with blacksmiths, peddlers, tinkers, tanners, and potters performing their crafts.

The village church, Chiesa dei Santi Tiburzio e Susanna, will bless Christian weddings, even non-Catholic ones, on request. The church was founded in the thirteenth century and carefully restored in 1928; its doorway is crowned with a sweet terra-cotta lunette depicting the Madonna and Child with angels. Inside, one large arched window illuminates the simple altar with natural light. A heavy wood ceiling decorated with sawtooth edgework shelters the simple wooden pews.

The Castle of Gargonza is situated high on a hill, midway between Arezzo and Siena, in the Comune of Monte San Savino, easily reached by the A1 highway from Rome or Florence. The twenty-three renovated private apartments have room for over seventy people and are rented by the week.

Catering is provided by the Torre di Gargonza restaurant on the premises. Reception capacity ranges from 50 to 150 guests.

CASTELLO DI GARGONZA, Località Gargonza, 52048 Monte San Savino (AR), tel. +39 0575 847 021, fax +39 0575 847 054, email gargonza@gargonza.it, www.gargonza.it. Driving directions: take the A1 (Firenze-Roma) and exit at Monte San Savino. Proceed on state road SS73 and follow the signs to Gargonza. Cost: E to EE.

Castello il Palagio

In the heart of the Chianti countryside, among vineyards, golden hill-sides, and olive groves, the enduring Castello il Palagio offers the possibility of celebrating a wedding in an original thirteenth-century castle. Just south of Florence, the fortress played an important historical role in the defense of the territory, as its occupants battled Siena's Ghibelline army in 1260, the Prince of Orange in 1312, and John Hawkwood's mercenaries in 1381. Despite being in the center of many incursions, the castle's massively thick defensive walls prevented significant damage, and over the centuries its later owners have carefully protected it. Although the crenellations atop the tower and the walls seem authentic, they were added in the late 1800s, when it was fashionable to restore castles in an imagined style of the Middle Ages.

The dense walls surround a wonderful brick-paved courtyard, where wedding banquets are held during the warm summer months. The courtyard is circled by a second story of arched loggias. At the base of the tower, there is a romantic Romeo and Juliet-style balcony where you can toss your bouquet. At one end of the courtyard, a Gothic-arched doorway leads to a diminutive, frescoed chapel with a Florentine golden triptych, available for Catholic ceremonies. The lush surrounding park and garden are also available for nonreligious outdoor ceremonies.

Catering is organized on the premises, and the owners take great pride in the food offered to guests. The castle can create a Renaissance-themed event with waiters dressed as pages, a menu of antique fifteenth-century recipes, and entertainment including heraldry, flag bearers, fire-eaters, musicians, minstrels, magicians, and jesters. They can also organize theatrical presentations of scenes adapted from Boccaccio's medieval *Decameron*.

Accommodations for over thirty guests are available at the rustic Borgo Montefolchi or the elegant Villa Roncognano, both just down the road from the castle. Borgo Montefolchi is a wonderful farmhouse made from one of the castle's military outbuildings. The private garden is a great place to enjoy sunsets over the meadows, while the old threshing floor, with a view of the undulating hills, has become a terrace where a relaxed rehearsal dinner can be organized. The Villa Roncognano, reached by a romantic cypress-lined walkway, has room for thirty guests in rooms decorated in a refined Tuscan style.

The estate is found along the wine route that passes from San Casciano to Greve and has been producing wines under the Il Palagio label for over two hundred years. Its cellars are open for wine tastings and tours.

Catering is managed on the premises. Reception capacity ranges from 50 to 220 guests.

CASTELLO IL PALAGIO, Via Campoli, 124-140, 50024 Mercatale Val di Pesa, tel. +39 055 821 630, tel./fax +39 055 821 8157, email info@ castelloilpalagio.it, www.castelloilpalagio.it. Driving directions: take the Firenze-Siena highway and exit at San Casciano. Continue to San Casciano Val di Pesa and follow the signs toward Greve in Chianti and Mercatale Val di Pesa. From Mercatale Val di Pesa follow the signs toward Greve until you see signs for Il Palagio. Cost: EE.

Castello di Montegufoni

Sir George Sitwell, in his treatise *On Making Gardens,* suggests that rather than struggling to make a garden beautiful around a house, it is easier simply to move a house to a site where a garden is already beautiful. Surely his remark was inspired by his time spent at Montegufoni. Sir George acquired the castle in the 1920s, and while he may have amplified it slightly, the garden's roots had already been laid in the seventeenth century. The stupendous view around the castle, with swaying cypresses, cultivated fields, olive groves, and vineyards, was certainly already there, as it is today.

Rising between the wonderful Val d'Elsa and Val di Pesa valleys, Monte Gufoni (Owl's Mountain) is reached by the Via Volterrana, an ancient Roman road used by Charlemagne to travel from Florence to Rome. Situated on a working agricultural estate, Montegufuni houses a popular *agriturismo,* where you and up to forty-five guests can relax for a week in the country before your castle wedding.

Montegufoni's first owners, the Ormanni family, were mentioned as illustrious citizens by Dante in the *Divine Comedy.* Later, the castle passed to the Acciaioli family, who added the central Palazzo Vecchio-style tower. During the seventeenth century, Donato Acciaoli joined all the outbuildings and added the gardens, fountains, and grottoes, creating an ornamental complex at the height of baroque taste. During these years (1650–1690), the interior fresco decorations—works by some of the most important Florentine baroque painters—were added, turning the castle into a luxurious residence for hosting Florentine nobility.

Cypresses surround the castle perimeter and its spacious Italianate gardens, creating intimate locations for outdoor ceremonies. Just off the castle courtyard, an entrance leads to the beautiful Salone, where a reception for one hundred guests can be held under its sumptuously painted ceilings. Today, the castle is owned and managed by the Posarelli family, who will be happy to help you create the perfect Tuscan menu and can make recommendations for florists, photographers, and other wedding services.

Various parts of the castle have been turned into holiday apartments, including part of the tower, a former chapel, and the old theater. Some of the apartment rooms are frescoed, while others have rustic wood-beamed ceilings and open onto views of the garden. The Galleria, once the castle armory, is the loveliest apartment, full of antiques, frescoed vaulted ceilings, and room for eight. On its ground floor is a large *salotto* (drawing room), with a ceiling decorated with seventeenth-century frescoes and French windows that overlook the Italian garden. The Teatro is a double room fashioned from the original banquet hall, which once hosted performances by the great Italian poets Boccaccio and Petrarch.

The castle and its owners have a long history of promoting and protecting the arts. During World War II, the *Birth of Venus* and the *Primavera,* priceless paintings by Botticelli, were successfully hidden in Montegufoni's cellars, along with many other important works from the Uffizi.

The territory of Montespertoli lies to the southwest of Florence. The Strada del Vino Montespertoli winds through three thousand cultivated acres of historic vineyards that open their cellars for tasting. The area can also be toured by bicycle, and there are many hiking trails.

Catering is managed on the premises. Reception capacity ranges from fifty to one hundred guests.

CASTELLO MONTEGUFONI, Via Montegufoni Montagnana 18, 50025 Montagnana, Montespertoli, tel. +39 0571 671 131, fax +39 0571 671 514, email info@montegufoni.it, www.montegufoni.it. Driving directions: take the A1 (Milano-Firenze) highway and exit at Firenze-Certosa. Follow the road toward Montagnana-Montespertoli. Cost: EE.

Villa Artimino ("La Ferdinanda")

Commonly called La Ferdinanda, the Villa Artimino was designed by the architect Bernardo Buontalenti in 1596 as a prestigious hunting residence for the Medici family. Commissioned by Ferdinando I de' Medici, the fortified house rests in a sylvan setting surrounded by a vast pine forest, the private hunting reserve created by Ferdinando's father, Cosimo I.

The villa's design is characterized by the austere elegance typical of late Florentine Renaissance style. A host of chimneys along the roofline have earned it the name "Villa of the Hundred Chimneys." In truth, there are only forty, and they recall the villa's use as a winter residence for the Medici.

Receptions can be held in either of the villa's grand halls, the Sala dell'Orso (Bear) and Sala Leone (Lion); each has room for two hundred guests. Stark white vaulted ceilings highlight the heavy wood doors and massive stone fireplaces in each room. The grand duke's ancient cellars, the Cantine Granducali, are now used to host gatherings alongside the giant wooden casks. A broad lawn directly in front of the villa can be used for outdoor receptions with a view of the hilly vineyards and olive groves.

For centuries, Artimino has been the center of a great tradition of viniculture, and today the estate manages over 170 acres of vines, including sangiovese, cabernet sauvignon, trebbiano, and mammolo, to name a few. Fattoria di Artimino's wines can be sampled at the Enoteca Cantina del Redi, just inside the village.

Today, the villa is the center of a vast vacation complex with a hotel, restaurants, swimming pools, and tennis courts, all conveniently located twenty minutes outside of Florence and forty-five minutes from Montecatini's thermal spas. The Paggeria Medicea, formerly the servants' quarters, has been transformed into a four-star hotel with accommodations for 180 people.

The hotel's restaurant, Biagio Pignatta, named after the Grand Duke's court majordomo, offers a wide choice of traditional Tuscan dishes and can be a great setting for rehearsal dinners or gatherings before the wedding. Artimino is equipped with its own independent restaurant and in-house catering service. For weddings, the staff offers a wide range of services from flower arrangements, photography, car rental, and musical entertainment.

Reception capacity ranges from seventy-five to two hundred. Catering is managed on the premises by the Biagio Pignatta restaurant.

VILLA ARTIMINO, Viale Papa Giovanni XXIII 3, 59015 Artimino (PO), tel. +39 055 875 1427, fax +39 055 8 75 1490, email villa@artimino.com, www. artimino.com. Driving directions: take the Firenze-Pisa highway and exit at Montelupo Fiorentino (Artimino is also indicated). Continue on state road SS 67 toward Firenze for five kilometers to the entrance of Camaioni. On the left, signs lead to Artimino.Cost: EE.

Palazzo Borghese

Perhaps the most interesting member of the Borghese family, via her arranged marriage to Prince Camillo in 1803, was Napoleon's favorite sister, Paolina Bonaparte Borghese. Paolina left an indelible mark on the social mores of the Empire era and was legendary in her own time for both her beauty and her capricious lifestyle. She was married and widowed at an early age; her first husband, General LeClerc, died of yellow fever on a campaign in the Caribbean. After his death, Paolina entertained a long parade of lovers and suitors before Napoleon hastily arranged her second marriage to Camillo Borghese. Camillo is remembered for shipping half of the family's precious art collection, amassed by his great-uncle Cardinal Scipione Borghese, to France. Possibly to compensate for some of the gaps this created in the collection, he commissioned a sculpture of Paolina as *Venus Victorious* by Canova. The life-size reclining nude, on view at the Villa Borghese in Rome, caused quite a stir among Paolina's contemporaries.

Although they had many properties in Italy and France, Paolina and Camillo spent their last years at their palazzo in Florence. Just behind the Piazza della Signoria, the Palazzo Borghese is a lavish example of the Empire style and today specializes in organizing gala evenings in its lavish halls.

Located in the shade of the Bargello Museum's tower, the palazzo began as a fifteenth-century home for the Salviati family, before falling into the Borghese family's hands. The Borghese coat of arms still hangs over the door below a façade that can be adorned with torches for your wedding event.

Two neoclassical statues representing Egyptian warriors are set into niches, keeping watch over the main entrance. A duo of trumpeters can be placed at the foot of the stairs to announce your guests' arrival in regal style. The grand Scalone d'Onore, a dignified staircase, is the main portal to the world of the palazzo's eighteenth-century halls. At the top of the staircase a succession of sparkling salons, each more richly decorated than the last, opens before guests, quickly transporting them back to the days of the empire.

The first, the Sala degli Specchi, once used as a bedroom and salon by Paolina, takes its name from the ten grandiose mirrors in baroque gold-leaf cornices that surround the room. An enormous chandelier with 150 candles and Bohemian crystal prisms completes the decadent atmosphere. Small dinners can be hosted here, in a space where Paolina once charmed her admirers with brilliant conversation while languid notes were played by musicians hidden behind a curtain.

The Sala degli Specchi is only the first in a magnificent parade of rooms rich with velvet, brocades, gilt stuccos, and frescoes. From here, you pass through the Salotto Rosso, the Sala del Consiglio (characterized by a curious fireplace whose mantel is held up by two female satyrs), the Salotto Giallo, and the Sala di Passo, and finally arrive in the gigantic ballroom, the Salone delle Feste—the true jewel of the palace. In Paolina's day, the orchestra's musicians were hidden in the niches and balconies surrounding the room, leaving the guests to revel in the mysterious atmosphere. You can plan your own event inspired by her style, with your guests dining under the monumental chandeliers, each lit by 147 candles. Music from classical harps, flutes, and violins, or more contemporary piano arrangements can serenade you during dinner.

The palace can provide varied levels of service for your event, from simply renting the halls to planning every last detail.

Palazzo Borghese, Via Ghibellina 110, 50122 Firenze (FI), tel. +39 055 239 6293, fax +39 055 2 38 2042, email info@palazzoborghese.it, www.palazzo borghese.it. Walking directions from the Duomo: follow the Via del Proconsolo to the Bargello. Turn left on Via Ghibellina. Cost: EE to EEE.

CIVIL CEREMONIES

Florence: Palazzo Vecchio

In Florence, civil wedding ceremonies are held in the Palazzo Vecchio, a building that has been the center of Florentine politics for over five hundred years. Intended to reflect Florence's domination over rival cities, it towers over Piazza della Signoria with a rusticated façade and a three-hundred-foot tower. In the belfry, the tower bell (called *vacca,* after its cow-bell tone) once summoned the Florentines to arms or to the piazza to hear political addresses made by the counsel of the Signoria. In between the towers' swallow-tailed machicolations are the heraldic shields of the cities that fell subject to Florentine rule, while over the door the people of Florence added an inscription, "Christ is King," to remind their rulers that human power is fleeting. In the sixteenth century, Cosimo I de' Medici made the palazzo into a family residence and had his court architects add rich decorations to the interiors. In honor of his son Francesco's wedding to Joan of Austria, he had gilded stuccowork and scenes of Austrian cities added to the majestic interior courtyard. After a ceremony in the aptly named Sala Rossa, with its imperial red decor, you can take photos under the piazza's sculpture-filled Loggia dei Lanzi or stroll along the river to watch the sunset from the nearby Ponte Vecchio.

PALAZZO VECCHIO, Piazza Signoria, 50100 Firenze (FI), tel. +39 055 276 8518, fax +39 055 261 6715, www.comune.firenze.it/servizi_pubblici/ anagrafe/celmatci.htm. Walking directions from the Duomo: follow Via dei Calzaiuoli to Piazza della Signoria. Cost: EE to EEE.

Siena: Palazzo Pubblico

Siena's Palazzo Pubblico rises at the end of the Piazza del Campo, the same square where the famed Palio horse race is run in the summer. The shadow of its tower, the tremendous red-and-white Torre del Mangia, has dominated the square since 1344; its bell once called the town council to session. The prestigious building's lower floors still house the city municipal offices, while the upper floors have been made into the Museo Civico, where wedding ceremonies are held. The museum halls are full of important historical works by Siena's master artists, including Lorenzetti's *Allegories of Good and Bad Government,* painted to remind the Council of nine of the dangers of corruption. You'll exchange your vows in the Sala Mappamondo (Hall of the World Map) under fourteenth-century frescoes painted by Simone Martini, including his wonderful portrait of the mercenary Guidoriccio da Fogliano returning on horseback, and his painting of the *Maestà,* considered to be his oldest surviving work. For a quiet moment after the ceremony, you can climb the tower, for a breathtaking view at the top of a mere five hundred steps.

PALAZZO PUBBLICO, Piazza del Campo, 53100 Siena, tel. +39 0577 411 69, fax +39 0577 226 265, www.comune.siena.it. Driving directions from Florence: take the Firenze-Siena highway to Siena. Driving directions from Rome: take the A1 (Roma-Firenze) highway and exit at Sinalunga. Connect to state road S73 and exit at Siena. Cost: EE to EEE.

San Gimignano: Palazzo del Popolo

In the enchanting medieval city of "one hundred towers," weddings are celebrated in the ancient town hall on the main square, the Palazzo del

Popolo. Despite the city's nickname, there were originally only seventy towers in San Gimignano, built to serve the vanities of its noble citizenry. Today only fifteen towers remain, and at the base of the tallest, the Torre Grosso, is San Gimignano's city hall. Built at the end of the 1200s, today the building houses the city's collection of paintings from the Florentine and Sienese schools. Passing through the picturesque center courtyard—a perfect place for photos—you'll climb a covered staircase that leads to the Museo Civico. Weddings are held in one of the museum's rooms, the Sala di Dante, named in commemoration of the poet's ambassadorial visit in 1299. It is exquisitely decorated with frescoes and Renaissance furniture, and one entire wall is covered with the *Maestà,* painted by Lippo Memmi in 1317. After the ceremony, if you don't have enough energy to scale the Torre Grosso, wander the quiet cobblestone streets to a quiet café table where you can toast your future with a glass of sparkling Vernaccia.

PALAZZO DEL POPOLO, 53037 San Gimignano (SI), tel. +39 0577 942 208, www.comune.sangimignano.si.it. Driving directions: take the Firenze-Siena highway and exit at San Gimignano. Cost: EE to EEE.

Montepulciano: Palazzo Comunale

Encircled by walls and fortifications added by Cosimo the First, Montepulciano has one of the highest elevations of any of Tuscany's hill towns. A long, winding street called the Corso climbs up to the summit where the main square, the Piazza Grande, provides sweeping views of the surrounding countryside. Civil ceremonies are held in the Palazzo Comunale, the city's town hall, a building whose tower makes it resemble a smaller version of Florence's Palazzo Vecchio. Michelozzo, a trusted architect to the Medici family, added the tower and machicolated façade to the original Gothic construction in the fifteenth century, while Antonio di Sangallo designed the quaint Renaissance wishing well that stands across the plaza. Montepulciano's streets are lined with Renaissance palaces and churches, but the town is internationally renowned for its namesake Vino Nobile wines. Appropriately, in the town's own *palio,* the Bravio dei Botti, eight teams race up the steep cobbled streets rolling empty wine barrels. Run on the last Sunday in August, the tournament has fourteenth-century origins and culminates with a citywide feast. An intimate location for a

wedding, Montepulciano can also be a great starting point for exploring Tuscany's southern wine routes.

PALAZZO COMUNALE, Piazza Grande 1, 53045 Montepulciano (SI), tel. +39 0578 712 213, fax +39 0578 712 213, www.comune.montepulciano.si.it. Driving directions from Florence: take the A1 (Firenze-Roma) highway and exit at Sinalunga. Continue on state road S327 for six kilometers to Torrita di Siena. Connect to state road S326 and follow the indications toward Montepulciano. Driving directions from Rome: Take the A1 (Roma-Firenze) highway and exit at Chiusi. Take state road S146 to Montepulciano. Cost: E to EE.

Poppi: Castello dei Conti Guidi

Set in the center of the magnificent valley of Casentino, the grandiose Castello dei Conti Guidi dominates the quiet hamlet of Poppi. The scale of this thirteenth-century feudal palace allegedly inspired Arnolfo de Cambio's design for the Palazzo Vecchio in Florence. Built for the powerful counts of Guidi, it remains one of the most important examples of Tuscan feudal architecture and today hosts weddings in its superb rooms. Locations for ceremonies depend on the number of guests and include the grand Salone, decorated with frescoes and paintings from the fifteenth century; the Riliana library, which houses a precious collection of medieval manuscripts; and the covered courtyard. An Escher-style medieval staircase zigzags through the center of the castle, surrounded by heraldic relics.

The Castello dei Conti Guidi is at the center of many legends. At one time the esplanade below the castle was used for tournaments and duels—fought to the death. The villagers believe that when the full moon rises, gallant ghosts still try to scale the castle walls. Another particularly dark legend involves a beautiful but evil countess who, after becoming a widow, lured the town's young men into the castle for a single night of love, followed by a plunge into the dungeon. After a few too many disappearances, the inhabitants of Poppi stormed the castle and sealed the countess inside the tower forever.

CASTELLO DEI CONTI GUIDI, 52014 Poppi (AR), tel. +39 0575 502 224, fax +39 0575 502 222, www.comune.poppi.ar.it. Driving directions from Florence: take state road S67 toward Pontassieve. Connect to state road S70 and follow to Poppi. Cost: E to EE.

CATHOLIC CEREMONIES

Chiesa Ognissanti

At the western end of the Lungarno near the Arno, in the quiet old Ognissanti neighborhood now populated with luxury hotels, stands Florence's magnificent fifteenth-century All Saints Church. Chiesa Ognissanti was once the parish church of the wealthy Vespucci family, and the family's patronage is evident in Domenico Ghirlandaio's altar painting of the Pietà, which depicts Vespucci family members as mourners. The church is one of the earliest examples of Florentine baroque. The pediment of its white marble façade is simply decorated with a grand cartouche at its top, and its interior is graced with green, red, and white marble archways, luminous artworks, and stained-glass windows. The church faces a grand paved plaza; its convent, reached through a tranquil cloister, has a refectory decorated with masterworks, including Botticelli's *Saint Augustine.* Under the arcade is a wonderful depiction of the *Last Supper,* another work by Ghirlandaio.

CHIESA OGNISSANTI, Borgo Ognissanti 42, 50123 Firenze (FI), tel. +39 055 239 8700. Walking directions from Santa Maria Novella: from Via della Scala turn left on Via del Porcellana. Continue to Il Prato Borgo Ognissanti. Ceremony capacity: Two hundred.

Santa Maria Maddalena de' Pazzi

Before she became Florence's most revered saint, Mary Magdalene de' Pazzi spent a quiet childhood in the hills of Fiesole. Caterina de' Pazzi, the child of a Florentine noble family, was born in 1566 at the Villa Maiano, a beautiful villa where you can have a reception after you wed in her namesake church. Located in the center of Florence, the church has a beautiful entrance cloister with an Ionic portico, a lovely spot for photos. The church and the adjoining Benedictine monastery were first built in the thirteenth century, with additions made in 1480 and 1492 by Giuliano da Sangallo. Entrance to the church is made through the Cappella del Giglio, a sixteenth-century structure frescoed by Poccetti with *Scenes from the Lives of the Saints*. The interior of the church has a single aisle and six arches, with chapels full of distinguished works from the sixteenth and seventeenth centuries.

SANTA MARIA MADDALENA DE'PAZZI, Borgo Pinti 58, 50122 Firenze (FI), tel. +39 055 247 8420. Walking directions from the Duomo: from the Duomo walk two blocks along the Via dell'Oriuolo. Turn left at Borgo Pinti. Ceremony capacity: 150.

Pieve di San Lazzaro

In 990, Sigeric, archbishop of Canterbury, traced a route from England to Rome that came to be known as the Via Francigena. Followed by millions of pilgrims, the road was marked by refuges, shrines, and milestones that indicated the safest path for travelers. Since long journeys were fraught with danger in the Middle Ages, before setting out, pilgrims would receive a blessing and a walking stick from their parish priest. Along the section of the road that passes from San Gimignano to Certaldo, an ancient chapel dedicated to St. Lazarus continues to await passing travelers. Mystical and silent, its ancient origins were documented as early as 780 in a map drawn as part of a deed made by Charlemagne to the Novantole Abbey. The humble sandstone church has a simple, unadorned early-Christian floor plan. Its small village, Lucardo, was the center of a Longobard *comitatus* (stronghold), and the church's design reveals the mysterious characteristics of Longobard designs. Its clean lines are punctuated by preternatural faces topping the pediments in the presbytery. The noteworthy fifteenth-century frescoes in between the pilasters are attributed to Cenno di Francesco di Ser Cenni.

PIEVE DI SAN LAZZARO, 50050 Lucardo (FI), tel. +39 0571 669 125, www.pieveslazzaro.com. Driving directions: take the A1 (Milano-Firenze) highway and exit at Firenze-Certosa. Follow the road toward Montagnana-Montespertoli. From Montespertoli take Via Volterrana, also known as

Provinciale 79, toward Certaldo. When you reach Il Pozzo, follow the signs indicating Pieve di San Lazzaro. Ceremony capacity: 150.

CHURCH WEDDINGS: OTHER FAITHS

Non-Roman Catholic religious sites in Florence are relatively new, as the city did not allow construction of churches for other faiths until the grand duke of Tuscany was exiled in 1849, and the Tuscan parliament passed legislation permitting other denominations to build their own churches. Two churches in the heart of Florence offer the possibility of a ceremony conducted in English.

Florence's American Church, St. James Anglican Episcopal, was designed and built by an English architect in the nineteenth-century Gothic Revival style. Centrally located, not far from Piazza Santa Maria Novella, the church maintains a helpful website with information on how to plan your wedding blessing at St. James.

ST. JAMES ANGLICAN EPISCOPAL CHURCH, Via Bernardo Rucellai 9, 50123 Firenze (FI), www.dinonet.it/stjames. Walking directions from Santa Maria Novella: follow Via della Scala four blocks to Via Bernardo Rucellai.

Crossing the Ponte Santa Trinità to the Oltrarno, St. Mark's English Church is found in a converted fifteenth-century palazzo. The church was founded by the English community living in Florence in 1877, whose members adapted the ground floor of the palazzo into a house of worship.

ST MARK'S ENGLISH CHURCH, Via Maggio 16-18, 50125 Firenze (FI), tel./fax +39 055 294 764, email info@stmarks.it, www.stmarks.it. Walking directions from Ponte Vecchio: cross the bridge to the Oltrarno. Continue on the Via Giucciardini to Piazza Pitti. When you arrive at the piazza, turn right on Via Pitti. Walk one block to Via Maggio.

Practical Information

Getting There

By air: Tuscany has two airports, Pisa G. Galilei (airport code PSA) and Florence-Peretola (airport code FLR). Schedules and information are available at www.aeroporto.firenze.it.

By car: Highway A1 links Florence with Milan to the north and Rome to the south.

By train: Regular rail service connects most of Tuscany's cities. Schedules and information are available on the official site for Italy's state railway at www.fs-on-line.com.

When to Go

High season begins in May and continues through September.

Helpful Addresses

Official Tourist Information Offices and Websites

APT—Azienda di Promozione Turistica (Tourist Promotion Agency)

IAT—Ufficio Informazione e di Accoglienza Turistica (Tourist Information and Hospitality Office)

Tourism in Tuscany, the official website for the tourist board in Tuscany has information on history, travel within the region, and special events: www.turismo.toscana.it.

Arezzo: A.P.T. Piazza Risorgimento 116, 52100 Arezzo, tel. +39 0575 239 52, fax +39 0575 280 4, email info@arezzo.turismo.toscana.it.

Firenze: A.P.T. Via Manzoni 16, 50121 Firenze, tel. +39 055 233 20, fax +39 055 234 6286, email info@firenze.turismo.toscana.it.

Lucca: A.P.T. Via Guidicciani 2, 55100 Lucca, tel. +39 0583 919 91, fax +39 0583 490 766, email aptlucca@lucca.turismo.toscana.it.

Pisa: A.P.T. Via Benedetto Croce 26, 56125 Pisa, tel. +39 050 400 96 and +39 050 402 02, fax +39 050 409 03.

Pistoia: A.P.T. Via Marconi 28, 51028 San Marcello Pistoiese, tel. +39 0573 630 145, fax +39 0573 622 120, email aptpistoia@comune.pistoia.it.

Prato: A.P.T. Via Luigi Muzzi 38, 59100 Prato, tel. +39 0574 351 41, fax +39 0574 607 925, email apt@prato.turismo.toscana.it.

Siena: A.P.T. Via di Città 43, 53100 Siena, tel. +39 0577 422 09, fax +39 0577 281 041, email aptsiena@siena.turismo.toscana.it

Grosseto: A.P.T. Via Monterosa 206, 58100 Grosseto, tel. +39 0564 462 611, fax +39 0564 454 606, email aptgrosseto@grosseto.turismo. toscana.it.

CHAPTER 5

Umbria

Bucolic Country Farms and Monasteries

*I*n the seclusion of undulating green landscapes and ancient hill towns, you can enjoy a quiet country retreat in Umbria's converted farms, country houses, and monasteries. Dubbed "Italy's green heart," the territory alongside the Tiber River as it cuts through the divide between the Apennines and the Pre-Apennines is characterized by verdant hills and open green expanses that become golden in the summer. Along the mountain ranges, forests protect the old hermit retreats, prized for centuries for the quietude of their natural settings. If you are hoping for an intimate holiday with the one you love, or a relaxed occasion with family and friends surrounded by both history and a natural landscape, Umbria is the place for you.

While Umbria is filled with beautiful medieval towns, Romanesque churches, and fine artworks, it has come to be appreciated for its spiritual contributions to Italian culture. Its rocks and air exude a mystical aura, immortalized by the teachings and wanderings of St. Francis. Assisi's patron saint came from a long hermetic tradition in Umbria, where followers initially found religious seclusion within its forests or atop the craggy mountains. Later, as the movement grew, monasteries were founded in the most isolated settings, guaranteeing reflection and meditation. Set on wooded hilltops, many of these monasteries have become charming retreats for secluded holidays.

The rich pastoral tradition in Umbria dates back to the *mezzadria*, whereby feudal lords cultivated vast tracts of land through tenant farmers, a system that defined rural life here for centuries. Today, these country farms are perfect places to recharge in the fresh, clean air in a bucolic setting.

The cuisine is dominated by the *tartufo* (Umbrian truffle), the *caccia* (the hunt for game birds and wild boar), and the tradition of *norcineria* (pork products from Norcia), all providing ample material for a culinary journey or a succulent wedding feast. The art of making sausages from domestic pork and wild boar is a prized tradition passed from generation to generation, and the results add a hearty flavor to many dishes. The truffles of the region, both black and white, are less known than those of Alba, but equally prized. They are often served with a hand-cut pasta, like the shoestring-shaped *strangozzi,* or in a simple omelet so that the earthy flavor of the truffle is highlighted. The savory tradition of spit-roasted meats and breads cooked on the hearth typifies Umbrian woodsman cuisine.

The region is full of romantic lore and rich medieval festivals. In the south, the city of Terni dedicates the month of February to celebrating the memory of its patron saint and former bishop, St. Valentine. On Valentine's Day couples come from all over Italy to receive a blessing in Terni's Basilica. In Bevagna, Narni, and Foligno, the spirit of the middle ages is kept alive through lively re-enactments of chivalrous events and oldcustoms.

Accommodations in Monasteries and Farms

SPOLETO

Eremo delle Grazie

Since Roman times, Monteluco's dense woods have been a protected, sacred place. In the solitude and cover of this same holy wood, a monastic hermitage was founded by St. Isaac in the sixth century. Today in this spot, known as Eremo delle Grazie (hermitage of the Graces), guests are offered hospitality in what once were the friars' cells.

The Eremo of today has more of the aspect of a private villa than of a traditional monastery. From its ochre exterior there is a lovely view of Spoleto's panorama. Inside, the interior is filled with dark wood antiques, artworks, and old leather tomes. A long gallery leads to the eleven individually decorated and comfortable guest rooms. The monks' ancient subterranean grotto has been appropriated for a wine cellar, filled with the owner's collection of prestigious vintages.

The Eremo shares the mountaintop with the tiny monastery of San Francesco, where St. Francis and his followers came to meditate in the thirteenth century. You can still visit the seven penitent cells they built for themselves. From the mountain, an old mule track leads down the mountain to the Ponte delle Torri, a 260-foot-tall aqueduct that spans the Tressino river valley and leads to Spoleto.

Eremo delle Grazie, Monteluco, 06049 Spoleto (PG), tel. +39 0743 496 24, fax +39 0743 496 50, email info@eremodellegrazie.it, www. eremodellegrazie.it. Driving directions: from the A1 highway, take the Orte exit. Continue on SS3 to Terni, then onto Spoleto. Once you reach Spoleto, look for indications to Monteluco. Eleven rooms; doubles from EE to EEE.

Le Logge di Silvignano

Le Logge di Silvignano is a mysterious medieval building, once annexed to the castle of Poreta for a hundred florins. Although there is some evidence that the building might have been used as part of the village's defense, its signature architectural feature, a covered loggia with an arcade of octagonal pillars, harks back to the cloisters of a convent. There are just five individually appointed suites in the converted inn. Each is carefully furnished with local antiques and beautiful linens woven on Montefalco's medieval looms. The rooms all have sitting areas and kitchenettes, and each enjoys a view of either the valley or the garden. The Loggiato suite is paved with handmade tiles and has doors that open out onto the covered loggia. Archi, named after its stone vaulted archways, has its own entrance from the garden, and the Elia suite has a romantic working

fireplace and a tiny medieval dungeon that has been converted into a dressing room. The pretty garden in front of the house has a broad lawn circled by fruit trees, and a view over the Montefalco valley. The owners speak English and pride themselves in offering home-style hospitality and often invite guests to share an aperitif along with some lively conversation in their private living area.

The tiny village, Silvignano, has some interesting undiscovered architectural treasures, including a fourteenth-century frescoed chapel. Just a few kilometers away are the Clitunno springs (see Campello sul Clitunno, page 233).

LE LOGGE DI SILVIGNANO, Frazione Silvignano 14, 06049 Spoleto (PG), tel. +39 0743 274 098, fax +39 0743 270 518, email mail@leloggedi silvignano.it, www.leloggedisilvignano.it. Driving directions from Florence: take highway A1 and exit at Bettolle-Sinalunga. Continue on the highway toward Perugia-Assisi-Foligno. After reaching Foligno, proceed on the state road SS3-Flaminia toward Spoleto, for about eighteen kilometers. When you arrive at Clitunno Springs (Campello), turn left, leaving the SS3 Road, and continuing toward Campello-Pettino. Cross Campello's residential area, and after about three kilometers turn right to Silvignano. Six rooms; doubles from EE.

CAMPELLO SUL CLITUNNO

Il Vecchio Molino

Campello sul Clitunno is a small village between Spoleto and Trevi. The village is famous for its natural springs, at the source of the Clitunno River. At its source the river widens to a spacious lake, strewn with green islets and encircled by verdant banks lined with poplars and weeping willows. These waters were sacred to the Romans, who built temples along the banks in honor of the river god Clitumnus and celebrated the Festival of Jupiter here. Pliny the Younger, Virgil, and Propertius (ancient Rome's greatest love poet) wrote poems and odes to the bucolic beauty of Clitunno's landscape.

Along the river bank just one kilometer from the springs of Clitunno is a singular building, the Tempietto del Clitunno. Although it looks like an ancient Roman temple, it has always been a Christian church. The tiny temple's architecture follows the plan of a Roman temple, with a Corinthian colonnade supporting a peaked pediment. Next to the Tempietto is a mill built in medieval times by the community of Spoleto for grinding flour and extracting oil from local olives. After painstaking restoration work, the Vecchio Molino (Old Mill) has been made into a comfortable bed-and-breakfast inn. The original gears and wheels are still on display on the hotel's grounds. Vine-covered stone buildings that once housed the workings of the mill now hold thirteen guest rooms, comfortably furnished with rich wood antique beds and armoires.

IL VECCHIO MOLINO, Via del Tempio 34, Località Pissignano, 06042 Campello sul Clitunno (PG), tel. +39 0743 521 122, fax +39 0743 275 097, email info@vecchio_molino.it, www.vecchio-molino.it. Driving directions from Florence: take highway A1 and exit at Bettolle-Sinalunga. Continue on the highway toward Perugia-Assisi-Foligno. After reaching Foligno, proceed on the state road SS3-Flaminia toward Spoleto, for about eighteen kilometers. Exit at Campello sul Clitunno. Thirteen rooms; doubles from E.

ORVIETO

La Badia

La Badia, a beautiful hotel and restaurant just outside Orvieto, began as a Benedictine abbey dedicated to the saints Severo and Martirio. The abbey's most striking architectural feature is a twelve-sided tower, added at the behest of Countess Matilde di Canossa in the twelfth century.

Few women in Italian history have had as important a role as that of Matilde di Canossa. The daughter of Boniface of Canossa and his wife Beatrice, at the age of thirty she inherited vast feudal holdings, territories equivalent to almost half of Italy. In part because of her wealth, she became a powerful ally of Pope Gregorio VII, playing a significant role in the political battle between the pope and Henry IV.

Matilde owned castles and palaces throughout her fiefdom. She was an extremely devout Catholic, and she used her wealth and influence to contribute to her favorite charity, the Church. At her death, she ceded all her holdings to the Papal State.

Eventually the abbey passed into private ownership, and since the 1900s it has been owned by the Counts Fiumi di Sterpeto, an Umbrian noble family. The abbey's sand-colored tufa stone gives it an authentic medieval air. The architecture combines Romanesque and Lombard elements, with high stone archways and delicately carved marble pilasters. The vaulted church is decorated with frescoes painted by various artists over the twelfth, thirteenth, and fourteenth centuries. The Fiumi di Sterpeto family has carefully restored the property and decorated the interior with comfortable antiques. The guest rooms have beautiful double-arched windows with views over the abbey's wooded park. Suites are quite spacious, and a few have views of Orvieto.

The hotel's restaurant offers classic Umbrian dishes, accompanied by Orvieto Classico wines produced on the family's farm. Dishes include hearty fare like roast suckling pig, meats roasted on an open hearth, and fresh pasta with local truffles.

LA BADIA, Località La Badia 8, 05019 Orvieto (TR), tel. +39 0763 301 959 and +39 0763 301 876, fax +39 0763 305 396, email labadia.hotel@ tiscalinet.it, www.labadiahotel.it. Driving directions: From Florence or Rome take highway A1 and exit at Orvieto. At the first traffic light, turn left toward Viterbo. At the first junction turn left toward Bagnoregio. After a few meters, you will see indications for the hotel. Twenty-six rooms; doubles from E.

FERENTILLO

Abbazia San Pietro in Valle

San Pietro in Valle is a protected national monument high atop a hillside above Ferentillo. The abbey's adjoining buildings are privately owned and have been restored as a charming inn and restaurant. Rooms have been created from the old monks' cells, with simple and comfortable furnishings. For more information, see page 267.

Abbazia San Pietro in Valle, S.S. 209 Valnerina, Località Macenano, 05034 Ferentillo (TR), tel. +39 0744 780 129, fax +39 0744 435 522, email abbazia@sanpietroinvalle.com, www.sanpietroinvalle.com. Driving directions: Take the A1 (Roma-Firenze) highway and exit at Orte. Continue along state road S204 to Terni. Once you reach Terni, take the SS209 to kilometer 20 and then follow signs to the abbey. Twenty rooms; doubles from E to EE.

PRODO

Fattoria di Titignano

Titignano is a medieval farm hamlet surrounded by over five thousand acres of farmland. The farm is located along a secluded road that connects Orvieto to Todi. There are twenty-nine rooms altogether between the old castle and the hamlet's farm buildings. Titignano is available to host weddings; see page 262 for additional information.

FATTORIA DI TITIGNANO, Località Titignano, 05020 Orvieto (TR), tel. +39 0763 308 000, fax +39 0763 308 002, email info@titignano.it, www. titignano.it. Driving directions: Take the A1 (Firenze-Roma) highway and exit at Orvieto. Connect to state road S79 and follow the signs toward Prodo. At Prodo, continue toward Todi until you see the sign indicating Titignano. Twenty-nine rooms; doubles from E.

FICULLE

La Casella

La Casella is a quiet farm retreat where you can enjoy the countryside by relaxing on the grounds of your own rented farmhouse or by trekking through the woods on horseback. The farm houses an equestrian center (see page 261) and a rustic restaurant with Umbrian fare. Wedding receptions are often held on the premises; see page 266 for additional information.

LA CASELLA ANTICO FEUDO DI COMPAGNA, Località La Casella, 05016 Ficulle (TR), tel. +39 0763 866 84, fax +39 0763 865 88, email info@lacasella.com, www.lacasella.com. Driving directions: take the A1 (Firenze-Roma) highway and exit at Fabro. Continue left toward Parrano. After seven kilometers, before the hill that climbs up to Parrano, a sign on the right indicates La Casella. Thirty-two rooms; doubles from EE.

BEVAGNA

L'Orto degli Angeli

This romantic inn and restaurant is in the center of medieval Bevagna. The charming owners offer home-style hospitality in their family's ancestral home. All the rooms are individually decorated with eighteenth- and nineteenth-century antiques. Two suites named for angels feature eighteenth-century frescoed ceilings and canopied beds. The inn is also available for weddings; see page 263.

L'ORTO DEGLI ANGELI, Via Dante Alighieri 1, 06031 Bevagna (PG), tel. +39 0742 360 130, fax +39 0742 361 756, email prenotazioni@ortoangeli.com, www.ortoangeli.it. Driving directions from Florence: take the A1 (Firenze-

Roma) highway and exit at Valdichiana. Continue toward Perugia and Foligno. Exit at Foligno Nord-Bevagna (about eighty-five kilometers from the Valdichiana exit). Driving directions from Rome: take the A1 (Roma-Firenze) highway and exit at Orte. Continue toward Terni and Foligno. Exit at Foligno Nord-Bevagna (about seventy-five kilometers from Orte). Once you arrive in Bevagna, enter the town through the Porta Foligno gate; the palazzo will be to your right. Nine rooms; doubles from E to EE.

Tables for Two

ORVIETO

Giglio d'Oro

A miracle visited on a traveling priest was the inspiration for Orvieto's Duomo. The monumental edifice was three hundred years in the making and has been dubbed the *giglio d'oro* (gilded lily) of Italy's cathedrals. Next door, in a fifteenth-century building that was once used to house the canonical staff, is the Giglio d'Oro restaurant. In the summer months, you can feast on Umbrian cuisine while you admire the Duomo's sparkling facade from an outdoor table. The experienced family that runs the restaurant offers prix fixe or à la carte menus filled with authentic dishes that draw upon the typical ingredients of the Umbrian table. Some dishes to try: garbanzo bean puree with fried salt cod flakes, eggplant flan with white truffle velouté, and pasta with boar ragu and melted *caciotta* (ewe's milk cheese). Satisfying desserts are made on the premises and include chocolate mousse with white chocolate rum sauce and *panna cotta* with honey and pears in vanilla. The wine list's selection of Tuscan and Umbrian labels pair well with the menu.

GIGLIO D'ORO, Piazza Duomo 8, 05018 Orvieto (TR), tel. +39 0763 341 903. Driving directions: from the A1 highway, exit at Orvieto. Most of Orvieto is closed to car traffic. Parking can be found either at the train station or in Piazzale Cahen. Closed on Wednesdays. Sixty seats. Cost: EE.

Le Grotte del Funaro

Orvieto is known for its intricate subterranean caves, built from tufa stone by ancient Etruscan settlers. Below the city, in a characteristic expanse of volcanic caves, Le Grotte del Funaro is a place where you can experience Orvieto's underground while enjoying simple, hearty fare. In medieval times this place housed a *funaio* (rope-maker's workshop), but these days it's filled with hungry diners. Dishes are simple and straight-forward, with offerings of *bruschette* topped by seasonal vegetables, local cheeses, and handmade *salumi,* fresh pasta with hearty rabbit sauce or wild boar sauce, and the classic Umbrian *grigliate miste di carne* (mixed grilled meats). When truffles are in season, you can expect to see them paired with eggs or light pastas. The restaurant also has a wood-burning oven where thin-crust pizzas and calzones are prepared. On the wine list you'll find an ample selection of regional Orvieto Classico and Rosso di Orvieto wines. It's one of the few places in town to stay open late and to offer "piano bar" music.

LE GROTTE DEL FUNARO, Via Ripa Serancia 41, 05018 Orvieto (TR), tel. +39 0763 343 276, fax +39 0763 342 898. Driving directions: from the A1 high-way, exit at Orvieto. Most of Orvieto is closed to car traffic. Parking can be found either at the train station or in Piazzale Cahen. Closed on Mondays (excluding July and August). One hundred seats; reservations recommended. Cost: EE.

I Sette Consoli

On the way to Rome from Florence, my husband and I made a specific detour to dine at the Sette Consoli. Highly rated by critics, this serene spot in Orvieto doesn't disappoint, with its intimate dining room, impeccable service, and excellent menu. An able husband-and-wife team manage and own this restaurant set in the sacristy that once belonged to the Church of Sant'Angelo, just across the tiny square. The formal dining room is quiet and intimate; in the summer months, a rear garden filled with flowering vines and fruit trees offers a quiet outdoor spot to linger over lunch. Dishes are elegantly prepared with offerings like *fantasia di fegato grasso d'oca* (fatted goose liver served two ways: cold terrine with dried fruit and seared with a warm pear sauce), asparagus soup with scallops, and bone-less saddle of rabbit stuffed with suckling pig and fennel puree. To finish your meal, try a *millefoglie* with strawberries and pear aquavit cream. The staggering wine list makes great reading for any connoisseur, with selections from all over the world.

I SETTE CONSOLI, Piazza Sant'Angelo 1A, 05018 Orvieto (TR), tel. +39 0763 343 911. Driving directions: from the A1 highway, exit at Orvieto. Most of Orvieto is closed to car traffic. Parking can be found either at the train station or in Piazzale Cahen. Closed on Wednesday and on Sunday evenings, and for holidays from December 24 to 26, and from February 15 to 28. Thirty seats; reservations essential. Cost: EE.

AMELIA

Il Carleni

Amelia lies close to Umbria's border with Lazio. The town is surrounded by pre-Roman walls of uncertain origin and has several pre-Renaissance monuments. The tiny town seems untouched, with an old white marble Porta Romana, tiny piazzettas, and twisting, covered alleyways.

Inside Amelia's medieval walls, just next door to the village church, is the ancestral home of the Carleni family. Il Carleni is a charming inn and restaurant with a welcoming dining room. The owners offer Umbrian home-style cooking, with some French influences. Start with crostini, local cheeses, *salumi*, or smoked duck salad. Heartier fare includes hand-made pastas and grain soups made with spelt or barley, roasted meats, and, when in season, regional game and Umbrian truffles. The inn offers seven simply furnished double rooms, with rustic wood-beamed ceilings and pleasant country furnishings.

IL CARLENI, Via Pellegrino Carleni 21, 05022 Amelia (TR), tel. +39 0744 983 925, fax +39 0744 978 143, email carleni@tin.it, www.ilcarleni.com. Driving directions from Florence or Rome: from highway A1, exit at Attigliano and follow the indications for Amelia. Closed on Mondays and Tuesdays, and for holidays from January 10 to February 9. Thirty seats; reservations recommended. Cost: E.

CIVITELLA DEL LAGO

Trippini

Along the road that winds between Orvieto to Todi—two of Umbria's most glorious hill towns—there is an incredible panorama over acres of verdant parkland and Lake Corbara. Almost at the halfway point, the town of Civitella del Lago rises four hundred meters above the valley. This is home to one of the region's highest-rated restaurants, managed by the Trippini family. In the formal dining room, with white tablecloths and red upholstered chairs, ask for a table near the window where the view over the lake and the Tiber river valley is truly breathtaking. The restaurant offers a tasting menu, which takes the pressure off choosing between dishes like the *millefoglie con pâté di fegatini d'anatra* (puff pastry filled with duck liver pate) and *gnocchi di patate farciti di ricotta e menta* (potato gnocchi stuffed with ricotta and mint). To finish the meal, there is always an excellent selection of cheeses or desserts like pears poached in Sagrantino Passito wine. The cultivated wine list contains labels from all over the world, selected to match the restaurant's cuisine.

TRIPPINI, Via Italia 14, 05020 Civitella del Lago—Baschi (TR), tel. and fax +39 0744 950 316, www.trippini.net. Driving directions from Florence or Rome: take the A1 highways and exit at Orvieto. Continue on the state road SS448, following the indications for Civitella del Lago—Todi. Closed on Mondays. Thirty seats; reservations recommended. Cost: EE.

Vissani

Vissani, housed in a restored country farmhouse, is regarded as one of Italy's top ten restaurants. This is a place to come armed with an appetite and plenty of time to experience a meal. Celebrity chef Gianfranco Vissani says the secret of his cooking is in the ingredients, and when you read through the menu you won't doubt it. Combinations are layered with an innovation that is beyond the bounds of even the most creative cooks. The constantly changing menu includes dishes like *lasagnette* of toasted sweetbreads, black truffles, and foie gras and leek mirepoix (a sautéed mixture of diced vegetables). Or you might try savoy cabbage and soft cow's-milk cheese *polpettine* (dumplings) served with red prawns, and topped with a julienne of *bresaola* (spiced, air-cured beef) and fried leeks. The desserts receive as careful attention as the rest of the menu with combinations like a *millefoglie* with grape must, lime-tree honey, and a mascarpone clove sauce, or golden apple risotto with Calvados and vanilla sauce.

> VISSANI, Strada Statale Todi-Baschi 448, Km 6,600, 05020 Civitella del Lago (TR), tel. +39 0744 950 206, fax +39 0744 950 396. Driving directions from Florence or Rome: take the A1 highway and exit at Orvieto. Continue on the state road SS448, following the indications for Civitella del Lago—Todi. Continue to mile marker Km 6,600. Closed on Sunday evenings, Wednesdays, and Thursdays at lunch. Fifty seats; reservations essential. Cost: EEEEE.

CITTÀ DI CASTELLO

Il Postale di Marco e Barbara

Just outside Città di Castello's city walls, in a building that began as a 1930s coach stop, you will find Il Postale. Heavy trussed ceilings and an old gas pump in front are the last traces of the building's past. The rest of the decor follows an Italian post-modern bent, with minimalist decor and an airy open dining room. In the summer, there is an outdoor veranda for dining al fresco. Three themed tasting menus take some of the anguish out of settling on what to order. The *Alta Valle del Tevere* (the high Tiber valley) incorporates seasonal vegetables like *funghi porcini* and chestnuts with farm-raised meats; *Il Mare* (the sea) makes use of fish selected daily at the Cesanatico fish market, and *Sensazioni* (sensations) takes traditional ingredients and dishes, then reinterprets them based on the creativity and innovation of chef Marco Bistarelli.

Local ingredients from surrounding farms and woods—like pheasant, pigeon, quail eggs, truffles, and wild mushrooms—find their way into the dishes. The wine list perfectly complements the menus, and many good wines are offered by the glass.

IL POSTALE DI MARCO E BARBARA, Viale Raffaele De Cesare 18, 06012 Città di Castello (PG), tel.+39 075 852 1356. Driving directions from Florence or Rome: from the A1 highway exit at Arezzo—Viciomaggio. Continue to Arezzo and then connect to SS73, following indications for Città di Castello. Closed on Mondays and for Saturday lunch. Fifty seats; reservations recommended. Cost: EE.

CORCIANO

Locanda San Michele

Corciano is a fortified hamlet just twelve kilometers from Perugia near Lake Trasimeno. The entrance to the city passes through the castle-like fortifications of the sixteenth-century Porta Santa Maria. Just outside the small hamlet's walls lies the Locanda San Michele. The restaurant's two dining rooms are carved from a medieval building with rustic stonewalls, vaulted and trussed ceilings, and dark wood tables. A terrace with umbrella tables is available for summer dining with a view over the valley. The menu features simple and delicious fresh pastas, grilled meats, as well as homemade desserts like cinnamon *panna cotta* and a long list of flavored sorbets and *gelati* (ice creams). The annexed "country house" offers four renovated suites, with recently frescoed ceilings and views over the valley.

LOCANDA SAN MICHELE, Via Ballarini 1A, 06073 Corciano (PG), tel. +39 075 697 9677. Driving directions: from highway A1, take the Valdichiana exit and continue toward Perugia, then exit at Corciano. Open for dinner only. Closed on Tuesdays. Fifty seats; reservations recommended. Cost: E. Hotel: E.

DERUTA

L'Antico Forziere

Just outside Deruta, in the tiny town of Casalina, is a rustic country house called the Antico Forziere (the antique strongbox). The medieval building overlooks a panorama of green hills. In the spacious dining room, with its large stone archways, you can taste local dishes based on regional ingredients like *umbrichelli* (handmade noodles) with duck speck (smoked duck) and tomato, *risotto di piccione e nero estivo* (pigeon risotto with black summer truffle), grilled lamb offal with Umbrian flat bread, or *cervo al sagrantino e pere* (venison in sagrantino wine with pears). The wine list includes an excellent selection of regional and national wines. The country house offers six double rooms and four apartments for guest accommodations.

L'ANTICO FORZIERE, Voc. Fontana Casalina, 06053 Deruta (PG), tel. +39 0759 724 314, email info@lanticoforziere.com, www.lanticoforziere.com. Driving directions from Perugia: take the E45-S3 south and exit at Deruta. Closed on Mondays, and for holidays January 1 to 15. One hundred ten seats. Cost: E. Hotel: E to EE.

FOLIGNO

Osteria del Teatro

The Osteria del Teatro is set in an elegant, restored cellar of red Assisi stone with vaulted ceilings, dating back to the 1400s. Graced with antiques and paintings, the dining room is comfortable and welcoming for a quiet meal after a day of sightseeing. The creative menu offers new interpretations of pastoral dishes like fried squash blossoms, *baccalà affumicato* (smoked salt cod) with Fossa pecorino, *rigatoni con pajata* (rigatoni with calf's intestine), grilled local spring lamb chops, crispy sweetbreads, and beef filet with field mushrooms and asparagus tips. For dessert, hazelnut mousse in chocolate sauce and Sagrantino wine ice cream with toasted pine nuts are a few of the choices. To finish your meal, you can sample excellent local artisan cheeses, as well as *pecorino di fossa* from Emilia Romagna, *blu del Moncenisio* from Piedmont, the soft cow's milk *scimudin* from the Upper Valtellina in Lombardy, and Sicilian ewe's milk *piacentinu di Enna*. There is an interesting wine list with local and national labels.

OSTERIA DEL TEATRO, Via Petrucci 10, 06034 Foligno (PG), tel. +39 0742 350 745. Driving directions from Assisi: follow state road SS75 south to

Foligno. Closed on Wednesdays. Forty seats; reservations recommended. Cost: EE.

GUBBIO

Taverna del Lupo

After St. Francis tamed a savage wolf that had been terrorizing the people of Gubbio, the town adopted the beast and fed him until he died of old age. The Taverna del Lupo, named for the legendary wolf, is set in the heart of this enchanting medieval city. The restaurant occupies a charming old stone palace, with six barrel-vaulted dining rooms filled with period antiques. Each dining room is elegantly set with white tablecloths and dark wood straight-backed chairs. Guided by an extremely experienced staff, you can choose from such Umbrian specialties as *ventaglio di faraona in salsa di ginepro* (pheasant in juniper sauce), homemade *strangozzi* with local truffles, and *lonzino di maialino con pecorino e tartufo* (pork tenderloin with pecorino cheese and truffles). Truffles, when in season, are often the protagonists of dishes here and should not be missed. The open wine cellar showcases the restaurant's wines and has a long refectory table for group tastings. The Taverna has long been a member of the Ristoranti di Buon Ricordo; on the walls you can see the plates commemorating previous years' dishes (see page xiii).

RISTORANTE TAVERNA DEL LUPO, Via Ansidei 6, 06024 Gubbio (PG), tel. +39 075 927 4368, fax +39 075 927 1269, email mencarelli@ mencarelli group.com, www.mencarelligroup.com. Driving directions: from Florence, take highway A1 and exit at Arezzo, then continue on toward Gubbio. From the south, exit at Orte and continue toward Perugia then Gubbio. Closed on Mondays. One hundred twenty seats. Cost: E.

Villa Montegranelli

Four kilometers from Gubbio, Villa Montegranelli is a massive three-story villa with a patrician aspect. The villa was built for the Conti di Guidi in the 1300s, but later renovations have given it an eighteenth-century feel. Inside, lovely common rooms have vaulted ceilings, massive fireplaces, and original frescoes and stuccowork. The villa's restaurant is housed in the original fourteenth-century cellars, with grand stone archways and a warm rustic decor. You can each choose from the menu of dishes like *girelle di ricotta in salsa di carciofi* (ricotta pastry with artichoke sauce), porcini mushroom soup served in a bread crust, roasted lamb loin with sweet and sour onions and Sagrantino wine sauce, or ask to share a *piatto per due* of risotto with local pecorino and basil cream, followed by a beef sirloin filet with radicchio and grape must. For dessert there are excellent *semifreddi* or *bavarese* custards and homemade pastries to try. The villa's banquet hall and spacious outdoor esplanades are often used for weddings. Seventeen double rooms and four lovely suites are available for guests, with filigreed wrought-iron beds and views over the Umbrian hills.

Villa Montegranelli, Località Monteluiano, 06024 Gubbio (PG), tel. +39 075 922 0185, fax +39 075 927 3372, www.villamontegranellihotel.it. Driving directions: from Florence, take highway A1 and exit at Arezzo, then continue on toward Gubbio. From the south, exit at Orte and continue toward Perugia then Gubbio. Sixty seats; reservations recommended. Cost: EE. Hotel: E to EE.

MONTEFALCO

Villa Pambuffetti

Montefalco, the "falcon's mountain," is a tiny village just south of Foligno. The village sits high above the valley and has a charming center with an interesting civic museum. As the hillside road winds up to the town you will pass vineyards for the renowned Rosso di Montefalco, Sagrantino di Montefalco, and Sagrantino Passito wines.

Just outside of Montefalco, Villa Pambuffetti is a restored noble villa surrounded by its own three-acre park filled with majestic trees. The restored villa has been transformed into a hotel and restaurant that makes its grounds available for wedding receptions. In the restaurant's elegant dining room, the cuisine is relaxed and down-to-earth. Savory Umbrian fare begins with *bruschette al tartufo* (grilled bread with truffles), *vellutata di legumi e castagne* (vegetable and chestnut veloute), followed by home-made pasta dishes like risotto with sagrantino wine, *strangozzi* with seasonal vegetables and local cheeses, and *gnocchi di patate ripieni di ricotta di pecora e tartufo* (potato gnocchi filled with goat's-milk ricotta and truffles). To accompany your meal, choose from the excellent selection of local Sagrantino wines, or from other wines from Umbria. For small groups, the chef offers cooking lessons in the villa's kitchen. For weddings, the villa offers banquet dinners in the tranquil park or intimate sit-down dinners in the formal dining rooms. Guest rooms and suites are equipped with the latest comforts and antique furniture; all face the quiet park. Rooms on the top floor enjoy a magnificent view over the valley's green landscape.

VILLA PAMBUFFETTI, Via della Vittoria 20, 06036 Montefalco (PG), tel. +39 0742 378 823, fax +39 0742 379 245, www.villapambuffetti.com. Driving directions from Rome: take highway A1 and exit at Orte. Connect to highway E45 Narni/Viterbo and then onto Terni, where you will connect to highway SS3. When you reach Villa Faustino, connect to highway S316 and follow to Montefalco. Open for dinner only. Closed on Mondays, and for holidays from January to March. One hundred twenty seats; reservations recommended. Cost: EE. Hotel: E to EE.

PACIANO

La Locanda della Rocca

Just south of Lake Trasimeno, the hamlet of Paciano was founded as a feudal command post in the fourteenth century. La Locanda della Rocca is an elegant inn and restaurant housed in an old Umbrian farm house that dates to the 1300s. The cozy, charming restaurant overlooks the house's garden. Managed by husband and wife Luigi and Caterina Buitoni, the restaurant offers simple, hearty dishes like crostini with game meats, fava bean puree with truffles, homemade pastas like *strappatelle* and *pici,* trout filet in grappa, and pork chops browned in wine and honey. There is a selection of Umbrian wines, as well as Brunello di Montalcino, Chianti Classico, Barbaresco, and Barolo.

The Locanda's seven quiet rooms all have views over the valley or the rooftops of the medieval village. If you stay here, you can enjoy their exquisite homemade preserves at breakfast.

LA LOCANDA DELLA ROCCA, Viale Roma 4, 06060 Paciano (PG), tel. +39 075 830 236, fax +39 075 830 155. Driving directions: from highway A1, exit at Chianciano-Chiusi. Connect to state road SS71 and exit at Paciano. Closed on Tuesdays, and for holidays January 10 to February 28. Thirty-five seats; reservations essential. Cost: E. Hotel: E.

SPELLO

La Bastiglia

Spello, along the road from Assisi to Foligno, was built from red stone quarried from nearby Monte Subasio. At sunset, the hill town seems to glow in warm orange and pink tones.

Spello is home to La Bastiglia, a small town hotel and restaurant with a chef recognized as one of the brightest new chefs in Italy. Originally an old olive mill, the interior spaces are beautifully restored and decorated. The owner's collections of busts and sculptures from antiquity are mixed with period antiques, terra-cotta tiled floors, and trussed ceilings. The dining room is warm and welcoming, and there is also a romantic terrace that opens out to reveal a view over the valley. Chef Marco Gubbiotti offers a menu of dishes based on traditional flavors with inventive additions. In the spirit of the *norcineria,* he house cures *ciauscolo,* a spreadable pork salami with fennel. Adventuresome dishes like salt cod *soufflé* with sundried tomatoes accompanied by a gorgonzola fondue with prunes; spelt and zucchini pie with wild fennel sausage; and pheasant breast in a lentil pecorino crust make a memorable meal here. The wine selection is curated by sommelier Ivan Pizzoni, and the desserts are as creatively fashioned as the rest of the menu.

The hotel has thirty rooms, all elegantly equipped. Junior suites have private terraces and huge bathtubs. All guests are invited to use the swimming pool, set alongside the hotel with an unobstructed view of the landscape.

LA BASTIGLIA SPELLO Piazza Valle Gloria 7, 06038 Spello (PG), tel. +39 0742 651 277, fax +39 0742 301 159, email fancelli@labastiglia.com, www.labastiglia.com. Driving directions: from Assisi, take highway SS75 toward Foligno and exit at Spello. Closed on Wednesdays, and for holidays from January 7 to 14. Sixty seats; reservations recommended. Cost: EE Hotel: E to EE.

TREVI

La Taverna del Pescatore

Trevi began as a Roman settlement. In the Middle Ages the town was encircled with defensive walls, which remain today. Nearby, the famous wells of Clitunno, surrounded by poplars and ash trees, inspired poets from Virgil to Byron.

Not far from the Tempietto on the river Clitunno, this elegant "fisherman's tavern" is set in a tranquil setting surrounded by trees. Even the indoor dining room is romantic, with wide windows that frame the view. The owners pride themselves in the use of local ingredients, predominantly fish from the nearby rivers. The *taglierini tirati a mano con funghi finferli e chiodini e gamberi di fiume* combines fresh cut pasta, river shrimp, and wild local mushrooms, or you can try river shrimp sautéed with olive oil pressed from olives cultivated on the hills of Trevi. If fish is not your fancy, try the restaurant's excellent traditional Umbrian meat dishes, like spring lamb in Sagrantino wine sauce. Truffles, when in season, also figure heavily in the menu. Claudio and Catia Menichelli have passionately researched the wine list and include many offerings from local producers, as well as regional and international wines to pair with the exquisite cuisine. The residence also has rooms where you can stay the night and space to host receptions for up to 150 guests.

LA TAVERNA DEL PESCATORE, Via Chiesa Tonda 50, 06039 Trevi, Pigge (PG), tel. +39 0742 780 920, fax +39 0742 381 599, email info@ latavernadel pescatore.com, www.latavernadelpescatore.com. Driving directions: from Assisi, take highway SS75 toward Foligno—Spoleto and exit at Trevi. Closed on Wednesdays, and the second and third week of June for holidays. Fifty seats; reservations recommended. Cost: EE.

Watching the Sunset

Porta Venere—Spello

Spello's travertine Porta Venere dates to the era of Augustus. Three arches—a broad central arch for carriages, flanked on each side by smaller pedestrian archways—make up the structure of this ancient city gate. The two twelve-sided towers that flank the ancient travertine arch were an early twentieth-century addition to the gate, but they lend a medieval air to the structure. When you stand on the wall above the gate, a view of the valley opens before you, stretching southwest to Montefalco. At sunset, the local stone, quarried from Mount Subasio, takes on a rosy glow.

Ponte delle Torri—Spoleto

Built between the thirteenth and fifteenth centuries, Spoleto's Ponte delle Torri (tower bridge) joined the holy mountain of Monteluco with the city's ancient fortress, La Rocca. The 750-foot span sits atop ten arches and has a height of 250 feet. The pedestrian-only path across is perfect for a twilight *passeggiata*.

Palazzo dei Consoli—Gubbio

The Palazzo dei Consoli sits on one of Umbria's prettiest squares. The red-bricked square is dominated by the white marble town hall, and the entire piazza is built on a shelf, supported by substantial subterranean arches. On one side, the piazza is completely open to an unobstructed view over the rooftops and onto the valley below. After sunset, a blue halo falls upon the battlements of the ancient palace before giving way to the night sky.

Romantic Lore and Local Festivals

Calendimaggio Festival—Assisi

The origins of Assisi's Calendimaggio go back to pagan festivals that celebrated the rebirth of spring each year. In Roman times, the goddess

Flora (who was responsible for the flowering of plants and trees) was feted with the celebration of the Floralia, and Christian peoples folded the ancient celebrations into what became our modern May Day celebrations.

Strangely, this benign festival became interwoven with a dark period in Assisi's history. During medieval times, Assisi was embroiled in the conflict between the Guelph and Ghibellines. Eventually, the conflict divided the city into two parts: Assisi di Sotto (Lower Assisi) and Assisi di Sopra (Upper Assisi). While the ancient division was the line of demarcation for an angry political blood feud between rival factions, today in the modern festival it determines teams for a friendly competition played entirely with cultural events.

For the festival (held on the Thursday, Friday, and Saturday after the first of May) the entire city of Assisi turns out to commemorate the time that was, with spectacular demonstrations of medieval and Renaissance culture. The Upper City and the Lower City challenge each other in skits, concerts, singing and dancing, and processions, as well as archery, crossbow, and flag-throwing demonstrations.

For more information contact: Ente Calendimaggio di Assisi, tel. +39 075 816 868, email entecalendimaggiodiassisi@libero.it, www. calendimaggiodiassisi.it.

Corsa all'Anello (Race for the Ring)—Narni

This festival's medieval origins date to a traditional feast held each year to honor the city's patron saint, San Giovenale. Laws regulating the rules of play were written into the city statutes in 1371, and little has changed since then. The first race was a speed competition among horses; the second, a competition among the riders of the town's three *terzieri* (districts): Mezule, Fraporta, and Santa Maria. Horsemen from each district attempt to catch a silver ring with a jousting lance, while riding at full speed. The race takes place in the town's main square, the present Piazza dei Priori. For two weeks preceding the race, the whole town of Narni prepares for the feast. Flags and torches decorate the squares, and streets and the town's restaurants offer medieval Umbrian dishes. The night before the race, a procession with as many as six hundred costumed participants passes through the city streets in anticipation of the next day's competition.

The event is held each year on the second Sunday in May. For more information contact: Ente Corsa all'Anello, Piazza dei Priori 2, Narni, tel. and fax: +39 0744 726 233.

Corsa dei Ceri (Race of the Candles)—Gubbio

Celebrated each year on May 15 (St. Ubaldo's Eve), the Corsa dei Ceri is one of Italy's strangest medieval tournaments. The festival's origins are uncertain, beginning either with Gubbio's victory in battle over eleven allied cities in 1154 or with candlelight processions held in honor of the passing of the city's bishop in 1160. The "candles" are three enormous wooden totems, each over seven meters tall, which are placed in wheelbarrows and pushed by teams. Each candle is crowned by a statue of a saint: St. Ubaldo, protector of masons; St. Giorgio, protector of merchants; and St. Anthony, protector of farm workers. *Ceraioli* (candle teammates) in bright costumes complete an extremely complex course through the streets of Gubbio. First, they draw for team captains and receive bouquets of flowers; then the teams parade to the Piazza della Signoria. At noon, the bell in the Palazzo dei Consoli rings and each team captain baptizes his candle with water from a sacred jug, which is then smashed against the pavement of the piazza. The crowds gather the broken shards for luck in the coming year. At six o'clock the race begins: down Via Dante, back to the Piazza della Signoria, then finally returning the candles to their resting place inside Ubaldo's cathedral. Strangely, St. Ubaldo is always allowed to win the race; his candle must be the first to reenter the church each year.

Festa della Palombella (Wood Pigeon Festival)—Orvieto

This strange, ritualistic festival seems to have originated with the arrival of a wood pigeon in the rafters of Orvieto's cathedral in the fifteenth century. A noblewoman, Giovanna Monaldeschi, willed her entire estate to the city to guarantee that each year the event would be commemorated with a festival held on Pentecost Sunday. Each year, on the seventh Sunday after Easter, a shrine is created in front of Orvieto's Duomo. A wood pigeon is strapped, with its wings outspread, onto a metal crown, which is attached to a metal cable at the cathedral's roof. Accompanied by a grand display of pyrotechnics and colored smoke, the crown is launched down the wire to the shrine, where, after another burst of fireworks, it is caught by the bishop. The bird is then presented to the city's most recently married couple, who must care for it for the rest of its natural life. The bird is meant to represent the figure of Christ; the descent down the wire is a representation of his descent to the Apostles at the Last Supper.

Festa della Promessa (Feast of the Promise)—Terni

Most scholars agree that the origins of St. Valentine's Day began with a Roman fertility rite, the Lupercalia, celebrated on February 15 in ancient times. During the medieval period, legends arose that connected the holiday to the belief that February 14 was the day on which birds began to mate. Christian records hold the names of three Valentines that were martyred for various reasons. The most famous Valentine, at least in Italy, is the sainted bishop of Terni, who was martyred in 270 C.E. His name became associated with romantic love when he blessed the union between a young Christian girl and a Roman soldier, despite the fact that this was strictly forbidden by Rome. Many other couples sought his blessings after this act, and eventually his continued defiance of Rome led to his martyrdom. Today, the city of Terni commemorates their beloved patron saint with a month of celebration and the solemn Festa della Promessa, which is held February 14 in the Basilica di San Valentino. Over one hundred engaged couples come to the church to seek a blessing for their future unions. For additional information see www.sanvalentinoeventi.com.

Giostra della Quintana (Ring Tournament)—Foligno

Since 1946, the city of Foligno has held a celebration in the spirit of the medieval tournaments in which knights demonstrated their loyalty to ladies of the court. Ten *contrade* represent the various historic city districts: Ammanniti, Badia, Cassero, Contrastanga, Croce Bianca, Giotti, La Mora, Morlupo, Pugilli, and Spada. Riders from each participate in a jousting contest, each attempting to thread rings with a lance in three breathtaking sequences. The rings hang from the arm of a wooden statue that plays the part of a seventeenth-century warrior. The warrior statue turns on a pivot, one arm holding a shield with the crest of Foligno, the other holding a ring that is smaller for each new attempt. In anticipation of the festival, hundreds of participants parade through the streets, and local restaurants offer menus based on baroque dishes.

> The event is held each year on the second and third Sunday of September. Ente Giostra della Quintana, largo F. Frezzi 4, 06034 Foligno (PG), tel. +39 0742 354 000, fax.+39 0742 340 653, www.quintana.it.

Infiorata (The Flowering)—Spello

Spello's Infiorata festival celebrates Corpus Cristi with elaborate floral displays laid like carpets through the streets of the city. A sweet perfume of flower petals surrounds the masterpieces, designed by local artists who spend weeks preparing richly colored designs made exclusively from vegetable and floral elements. Villagers begin collecting flower petals from the surrounding hillsides two weeks before the festival. Flowers are painstakingly separated by color to create a palette for the artists; the petals are stored in the town's subterranean cellars. Religious floral paintings like these have been a part of the Corpus Cristi celebration since the late eighteenth century. Throughout the afternoon and evening of the day before the feast of Corpus Christi, you can watch the artists arrange thousands of petals that will create the design. Corpus Christi Sunday is usually the third Sunday in June.

Mercato delle Gaite (Medieval Festival)—Bevagna

During Bevagna's Mercato delle Gaite, villagers create a living medieval museum in which the ancient trades come to life along the city's streets. Competitions are held among the town's four medieval districts, known as *gaite*. Dressed in period costumes, teams are challenged to perform authentic demonstrations of medieval crafts. In the streets you'll see demonstrations of rope making, silk spinning and weaving, forging, caning and wickerwork, papermaking and printing, glassblowing, and pottery. In the old taverns, set up for the festival, visitors are invited to sample traditional gourmet foods. The festival is held each year during the last week of June.

Picnic Spots

Parco del Monte Subasio and Eremo delle Carceri

For an outing in the spirit of St. Francis, you can trace his footsteps up Mount Subasio. The retreat he made famous, Eremo delle Carceri, is a five-kilometer hike from the city, but it can also be reached with a short drive. The hermitage was named Carceri (prison cells) after the way in which St. Francis and his followers imprisoned themselves in the natural caves along the hillside. You can still see the tiny cells where they came for extended periods of prayer and meditation. St. Francis first came here in 1206 and was a frequent visitor in subsequent years.

Monte Subasio is now a national park, and it is encircled by roads that link Assisi with the villages of Armenzano, Valtopina, and Collepino. From each of the villages, horse paths and hiking trails bring enthusiasts into the wilds of the park.

The park's headquarters, along with a museum dedicated to the mountain's geology, is in Cà Piombino, reached from the state road SS. 444 that departs from Porta Perlici in Assisi. For park information contact: Ente Parco del Monte Subasio, tel. +39 075 815 181, www.parks.it/parco.monte.subasio.

Parco del Trasimeno

Lake Trasimeno, site of the Hannibal's brutal defeat of the Romans, today is occupied mainly by migrating storks, egrets, swans, ducks, and geese. Three tiny islands—Maggiore, Minore, and Polvese—dot the center of the blue green lake. Two of the islands are great spots for excursions, and both have ample natural space for picnicking.

The largest of the islands, Isola Polvese (in the territory of Castiglione del Lago) is a protected wildlife refuge. During the Middle Ages, the island played a defensive role for the territory. Most of the island's medieval buildings have fallen into ruin, but their old stone walls, which have surrendered to the vines and natural undergrowth, make a romantic framework for views of the lake. The Monastero Olivetano (1482) was the center for the island's religious order, until the monks abandoned the "excessive quiet of the island" and relocated to Perugia in 1624. The ruins of the San Secondo church, on the island's summit, provide the perfect spot to watch the sunset over the lake. The entire island can be seen from the three-and-a-half-kilometer ring trail that circles its outer edge. The path leads past the old medieval castle and through olive groves, poplars, and the recently added aquatic gardens. The island's small beach, on the eastern shore, is a good spot for lake swimming. Near the beach there is a self-service restaurant and bar, Casa di Delfo (tel. +39 075 965 9545).

Isola Maggiore, the only inhabited island on the lake today, is situated closer to Tauro on the north end of the lake. The island was founded by fishermen and still retains the feeling of a fifteenth-century village. Its lace makers, like those of Burano in Venice, are famous for their intricate work. On the island, you can see examples in the Museo del Merletto (Lace Museum). The path around the island departs from the inhabited village and passes the tiny Romanesque church of San Salvatore, the medieval Castello Guglielmi rising on the southeast summit, the gothic church of San Michele Arcangelo, and a statue of St. Francis in memory of his visit in 1211. If you are not inclined to bring your own picnic, try the island's restaurant, Da Sauro (Via G. Guglielmi, tel. +39 075 826 168, closed Wednesdays) or the pizzeria, All'Antico Orologio (tel. +39 075 826 188).

> Boats to both islands depart hourly from the port cities around the lake: for Isola Polvese, from San Feliciano on the eastern side; for Isola Maggiore, from Castiglione del Lago on the western shore, and from Passignano and Tuoro on the northern shore. For ferry information, schedules, and fares, contact: Navigazione APM, Lago Trasimeno, www.apmperugia.it.

Cascate delle Marmore

The Marmore falls are the highest waterfalls in Europe, with a spectacular 541-foot cascade. The falls are the product of a Roman public works project executed in 271 B.C.E. by the consul Curio Dentato. To end the continuous flooding of the Sabina valley, the Romans redirected the

Velino River into the Nera by cutting a large canal into the rock. Today the park is one of Umbria's treasured natural settings and a popular place for hiking, river rafting, and canoeing.

> For the last fifty years, the falls have been harnessed to power hydro-electric works, so they can only be seen during the park's opening hours (see www.bellaumbria.net/Terni/Cascata_delle_Marmore_eng.htm for a schedule).

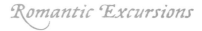

Romantic Excursions

In Search of Truffles

Although northern Piedmont's Alba carries the reputation of being Italy's truffle center, Umbria's woods are particularly rich in truffles. At almost any time of year, you can taste truffles in the region's restaurants, which are usually prepared either with fresh *strangozzi* pasta, egg dishes, or roasted meats. For gastronomes and fans of the elusive fungus, Umbria is a great place to find culinary fairs dedicated to truffles or to participate in guided truffle hunts.

Truffle season in Umbria lasts nearly year round, with a variety of species found in the region. The most prized truffle is the *bianco pregiato* (precious white). This rare and valuable truffle, *Tuber magnatum* Pico, has a season that begins in October and continues to the end of January. Found in the Tevere Valley near Gubbio, Gualdo, and Orvieto, the *bianco* prefers clay soils in the company of oak, poplar, and lime trees. It has a smooth surface and a brown creamy color.

In November the *nero pregiato* (precious black) season begins and continues through March. This truffle, *Tuber melanosporum* Vittadini, competes with the *bianco* for most prized status. The Nero is found in mountainous areas where there are groves of walnut and oak trees. Hunting grounds for the black truffle range from areas bordering the Nera, Corno, and Sordo rivers, the hillsides of Spoleto, and near the Trevi and Subasio mountains.

The *bianchetto* (little white) is found from February to March. It distinguishes itself from the *bianco pregiato* by its smaller size and veined flesh, and its perfume. The *bianchetto* (*Tuber albidum* Pico) prefers to grow in pinewoods.

The *scorzone* (*Tuber aestivum*) is known as the summer truffle, but it can be found all year long. This truffle has a thin, pebbled black surface and white flesh. It grows in rough clay or volcanic soil.

ADDRESSES AND PRACTICAL INFORMATION

Truffle Hunts

Truffle "safaris" are offered by various tour operators. ACTIVITYDAYZ offers one-day truffle hunts from May through October. An experienced guide with a truffle-sniffing dog will take you through the woods. After you find your truffles, you get to enjoy them over fresh pasta. The tour costs about $75 per person. See www.actividayz.com for more information.

Truffle Fairs

Truffle fairs and exhibitions occur throughout the year in Umbria. They include a variety of educational exhibitions and lectures for serious gastronomes, combined with traditional and cultural events. Dates change year to year; please contact the organizers for a current schedule of events.

GUBBIO: Mostra Mercato Nazionale del Tartufo Bianco (National White Truffle Market and Exhibition). This gastronomic competition and fair is held the first weekend in November in Piazza 40 Martiri.

CITTÀ DI CASTELLO: Exhibition and market for truffles and woodland products, the first weekend in November. This fair takes place in the historic center and concentrates on the white truffle. Organized by the Comunità Montana Alto Tevere Umbro, Via Pomerio S. Girolamo, 06012 Città di Castello (PG), tel. +39 075 862 901.

FABRO: Mostra del Tartufo dell'Orvietano (Orvieto Truffle Show). Third weekend in November. Events, held all weekend long, include a medieval banquet and a traditional dinner held in the historic center. Organized by the Comunità Montana di Monte Peglia e Selva di Meana, Via Principe Umberto, San Venanzo (TR), tel. +39 075 875 322, fax +39 075 875 120, www.tartufo.org.

VALTOPINA: Mostra Mercato del Tartufo In Valtopina (on the eastern side of Mount Subasio, twenty-five kilometers from Assisi), the Truffle Market

Exhibition is held at the end of November. For a week, truffle lectures and discussions are held by the region's cooking and hotels schools, with truffle tastings during the last weekend of the month. At the food fair, truffles, chestnuts, and other regional products are sold.

Norcia holds a truffle exhibition in the city's principal square the last Sunday in February. Truffles are the protagonists, but you will also find other products from the Val Nerina, like cured meats, cheese, and trout. The fair is organized by the Comune di Norcia, tel. +39 0743 828 044, fax +39 0743 816 519, email comunedinorcia@libero.it.

Scheggino: This small village on the Nera river is known for its truffle production. The second weekend in March a fair and truffle tasting are hosted by the municipality. Organized by the Comune di Scheggino, tel. +39 0743 613 232, fax +39 0743 613 233.

Trekking on Horseback to Medieval Castles

Umbria offers one of the most varied natural settings for horseback riding in Italy. There are forested mountain trails, paths that wander near crumbling medieval ruins, and broad open plains. You can plan an entire equestrian vacation or just an outing for the day.

Part of the intrigue of horseback riding in Umbria is finding hidden trails where the traces of Umbria's medieval past can be found. Among the vineyards, you might discover the ruins of an ancient fortress or the last remaining stones of a secluded monastery.

ADDRESSES AND PRACTICAL INFORMATION
Equestrian Centers

Centro Ippico—Agriturismo La Somma La Somma riding center is located in the Umbrian Apennines, nine hundred meters high on the summit of Mount Fionchi. Nearby, there are horse trails of varied difficulty levels, along rivers and ascending mountain trails. The center offers lessons and tours to Norcia or Cascia. Departing from the center's base in Montebibico, it's also possible to ride to small neighboring villages, to the falls at Marmore (the highest in Europe), or to Spoleto. All routes pass through spectacular mountain trails with abundant woods and scenery. Centro Ippico—Agriturismo La Somma, Località Aiacucigli, Montebibico—

Spoleto (PG), tel. and fax +39 0743 543 70, email lasomma@val.it, www.lasomma.it.

LA CASELLA La Casella's riding center has forty horses and offers jumping, dressage, rentals by the hour, full day treks, and simulated fox hunting. Overnight rides are organized in spring and autumn and tour through medieval castles, monasteries, and wineries. In June, La Casella offers a romantic night ride that culminates with a candlelit dinner in the woods. (For more about La Casella's wedding services and accommodations, see page 266.) La Casella, 05016 Ficulle, tel. +39 0763 866 84, fax +39 0763 865 88, email info@lacasella.com, www.lacasella.it.

Umbria Jazz Festival

Twice a year, in winter in Orvieto and summer in Perugia, the Umbria Jazz Association hosts a renowned music festival that for thirty years has brought the greatest names in jazz to historic Italian venues. Past guests have included Herbie Hancock, Roy Hargrove, and Chick Corea, along with emerging artists from all over the world. The ten-day festival is hosted in a variety of indoor and outdoor theaters.

For more information contact: ASSOCIAZIONE UMBRIA JAZZ, Piazza Danti 28, 06122 Perugia, tel. +39 075 573 2432, fax +39 075 572 2656, email info@umbriajazz.com, www.umbriajazz.com.

Weddings in Umbria

Umbria's charming rural landscapes are punctuated by medieval hill towns constructed atop ancient Umbrian, Etruscan, and Roman settlements. The characteristic sights and sounds in these villages include medieval nooks and balconies, twisting cobblestone streets that wind past tile-roofed houses, and the sound of church bells ringing through Romanesque piazzas. For weddings, Umbria's city halls are among the oldest civic buildings in Italy. Here, wedding ceremonies can be held in halls surrounded by ancient relics and the layers of a rich past.

Umbria's rustic landscape offers many scenic options for weddings. You can plan your wedding ceremony in an isolated glade, arriving on horseback along the same shaded paths once used by the Romans. Or, plan a ceremony in the silence of a hilltop monastery's ancient cloister.

Ceremony and Reception Locations

Fattoria Titignano

Situated on a high plateau overlooking the Corbara Lake, midway between Todi and Orvieto, the hamlet of Titignano has remained intact for centuries. Grouped around the piazza are Titignano's old castle manor, its church, and the outbuildings, which now make up this rustic and relaxed *agriturismo*. If you plan a wedding at Titignano, make sure your guests come prepared to eat well, as the kitchen is renowned for its authentic Umbrian cuisine. Your wedding menu's ingredients will consist of local specialties like porcini mushrooms and truffles gathered in the nearby woods, tiny wild asparagus foraged from the meadows, local wild boar and pigeon, and pasta hand-rolled in Titignano's own kitchen. In this retreat, where relaxation and eating are synonymous, menus for weddings include the most savory and hearty of dishes presented in a simple, straightforward style. Titignano is surrounded by five thousand cultivated acres of sangiovese, syrah, and cabernet grapes, some of which are blended into the Fattoria Titignano's wines.

The medieval castle manor houses the hotel's offices and the banquet hall where the counts of Titignano once entertained their own guests. Passing across the pebble-patterned stone floor in the entranceway, you will see cross-vaulted ceilings and doors framed by heavy cedar planks leading up the stairs past statues of muses set into niches. The counts inscribed their names under the steps of the stairs and within the door frames of the grand banquet hall, where wedding receptions are hosted before a roaring fire. Here you can entertain your guests at a long table set in front of the immense carved sandstone fireplace, with its scrolled pediments and griffins. Under the coffered ceiling, warm ochre-painted walls glow in the firelight, crowned by a whimsical trompe l'oeil gallery whose birds seem to nest above your head. After dinner, you can toast under the stars on the balcony that opens from the hall, where the view overlooking Lake Corbara seems to go on forever.

The landscape around the hamlet offers many choices for outdoor ceremonies. You can hold a ceremony on the grass esplanade below the castle, framed by the vine-covered foundations and sweeping views toward Orvieto behind you. Near the entrance to the hamlet, a long path leads through tall cypress trees to a hidden shrine, revealing another quiet spot where an altar can be placed. There is also the central church to one side of the *piazzetta,* built at the start of the 1900s, which can be requested for religious ceremonies.

Within this atmosphere of a medieval burg, there are accommodations for over sixty guests. Rooms have been created in the castle's old halls and in the building that faces the plaza, where double doors open right onto the pavement stones of the *piazzetta*. The rooms have a rustic yet refined decor, with exposed heavy-wood-beamed ceilings, clean white walls, fireplaces, and country antiques.

For sightseeing, the historic cities of Orvieto and Todi are just thirty minutes away.

Catering is managed on the premises. Reception capacity ranges from 50 to 120 guests. FATTORIA DI TITIGNANO, Località Titignano, 05020 Orvieto (TR), tel. +39 0763 308 000, fax +39 0763 308 002, email info@titignano.it, www.titignano.it. For driving directions, see page 236. Cost: E to EE.

L'Orto degli Angeli

In the center of Bevagna, a city called Mevania by the ancient Romans, there is a garden oasis hidden from view. Two Renaissance mansions

were built over the ruins of a Roman theater, and in between them lies the Angels' Garden. The counts of Angeli were the first "angels" to care for the garden; today their descendants, Tiziana and Francesco Antonini, graciously tend to guests with the warmest hospitality. L'Orto degli Angeli has been converted into an inviting inn where you will be surrounded by all the comforts of a private Italian home. Centered in the walled medieval town of Bevagna, the hotel offers the possibility to hold an intimate wedding where bride, groom, and guests can stay within the seclusion of a noble residence.

Passing through one of the Roman portals that open along the city walls and walking along the ancient Via Flaminia, you will find the large door that leads into the inviting and spacious halls of the palazzo. A grand staircase, with a delicately carved wooden statue of St. Lorenzo, brings you into the frescoed drawing room. Under a ceiling decorated with the family crest, a large stone fireplace welcomes guests with its inviting glow.

The antique kitchen leads to the hanging garden, below the sixteenth-century loggia and the ruins of the Roman theater. Here small wedding receptions can take place, surrounded by the perfume of the jasmine and wisteria vines, antique roses, and climbing clematis. During the winter season, ceremonies can be held in the salons of the manor house, where an intimate buffet can be arranged in front of a roaring fire. Your event can also make use of the inn's lovely restaurant, with its sunny lemon-tinted walls and its view of ancient temple ruins.

The kitchen garden figures prominently in the working of the house and its menus. Its lavender blossoms are incorporated into one of the desserts, lavender Bavarian cream with warm chocolate sauce. Menus are created weekly, drawing upon a great tradition of cooking and recipes taken from the kitchen diary that belonged to the proprietor's great-grandmother, Nonna Caterina. Her picture hangs in the breakfast room, and while her recipes are treasured, the owners are happy to share them with you. For a wedding menu, you might try her famous hand-cut pasta, *strappatelle;* savory *tortelli di patate ripieni di ricotta* (ravioli filled with potatoes and fresh ricotta cheese); and earthy *tacchinella ai marroni* (turkey stuffed with chestnuts).

The inn offers guests nine sumptuously decorated rooms. Their names follow an angelic theme; suites are named for the archangels Gabriel, Rafael, and Michael, and double rooms are named for other celestial creatures such as *serafini* and *cherubini*. The rooms' heavenly furnishings include delicately frescoed ceilings, antique Italian fabrics, and period antiques.

The proprietors ask that you rent the entire facility for weddings. L'ORTO DEGLI ANGELI, Via Dante Alighieri 1, 06031 Bevagna (PG), tel. +39 0742 360 130, fax +39 0742 361 756, email ortoangeli@ortoangeli.it, www.orto angeli.it. For driving directions, see page 236. Cost: EE.

La Casella (Antico Feudo di Campagna)

Located between two tiny, wonderful medieval villages, La Casella is a splendid country retreat where you can celebrate your wedding in nature. This *antico feudo di campagna* (ancient country fief) consists of one thousand acres of parkland set within a five-thousand-acre forest, making it a green oasis far from the urban hustle and bustle, but still within easy reach of some of Umbria's best sights. (For more about La Casella's equestrian center offerings, see page 261).

In the winter months, wedding banquets (for up to one hundred guests) can be organized in the splendid Le Noci hall. Once the *granaio* (granary), it was built in the 1800s and has a magnificent masonry crossvaulted ceiling and a large hearth where there is always a blazing fire.

A passion for cooking has inspired owners Luciano Nenna and Tommaso Campolmi to research authentic Umbrian country cuisine, which they have updated into a modern menu. For your wedding feast, the kitchen will serve a savory mix of house-made pastas, greens from the farm's garden, hearty soups, and roasted game. In the summer months, dinners can be held out under the trees, after which you can dance under an unobstructed night sky, far from the lights of any city.

Set among the poplars, and oaks of the wooded property, the old stone farmhouses have been converted into wonderful accommodations, tastefully furnished with country antiques; some even have romantic fourposter beds and fireplaces. The farmhouse apartments are spread through four private hamlets; in total, thirty-two rooms are available to guests.

The stone clubhouse has a fireplace and a pool table, a natural spot to gather with friends after a long day of horseback riding, touring, or relaxing by the pool. The farm has a *centro benessere,* a small beauty spa that offers massage therapy and natural treatments. For the more energetic, there is a swimming pool, tennis courts, and hiking trails.

Two wonderful medieval villages are just down the road from the farm. Parrano's old walls surround a medieval castle, and Ficulle is a medieval jewel, with a maze of narrow streets, tiny piazzas, and two towers that once stood watch over the little burg. In Ficulle, master artisans still produce earthenware following an ancient tradition, using clay gathered from local riverbeds and firing their creations in ancient wood-burning kilns.

Hiking through the park trails that wind through the Chiani River, you might see other local inhabitants—the fox, badger, porcupine, and deer—who live undisturbed in the silence of the woods. The Tane del Diavolo (Devil's Dens) just outside the village of Parrano, are vast caves, cut into the walls of the river gorge, that were inhabited in the Bronze Age. If you feel the urge to rejoin civilization, Orvieto is only ten miles away.

La Casella, Località La Casella, 05016 Ficulle (TR), tel. +39 0763 866 84, fax +39 0763 865 88, email info@lacasella.com, www.lacasella.com. For driving directions, see page 236. Cost: E to EE.

Abbazia San Pietro in Valle

The Abbazia San Pietro in Valle is set in a dramatic landscape, between the dense forests that line the Nera River gorge. The white stone abbey, church, and cloisters sit at twelve hundred feet, framed by a densely wooded mountainside.

The abbey's ancient church is a consecrated national monument, cherished for its acoustics. Classical concerts of sacred music are held here, and while it's no longer used for daily or dominical celebrations, it is a popular place for Catholic weddings. Its architecture reflects two ancient styles, Longobardo and Romanesque. Inside, the main altar has two antependiums and four small pilasters, possibly from the ruins of a Roman villa that predated the first hermitage. Even older relics include five Roman sarcophaguses dating from the third century C.E. The church's ancient fresco cycle is regarded as one of the most important examples of

Romanesque art in Umbria. A long succession of subjects from the Old and New Testament cover the wall, its faded pastel colors and tranquil composition befitting the quietude of the setting.

The Costanzi family, proprietor of the adjoining abbey, allows bridegrooms the opportunity to take photos inside the twelfth-century cloister and the abbey's garden. The cloister has an austere succession of pillars and archways, with cross vaults built from local stone. Its floor of terracotta flagstones surrounds a cylindrical pagan altar once used by the Romans and later adapted by the Benedictines.

Receptions can be held in the intimate and elegant abbey restaurant, which has room for fifty guests, or outside on the grass esplanade with its view of the valley. The restaurant, situated in the ancient guardhouse, is an intimate and inviting environment where you can try regional classics that incorporate the prized local truffles. The menus take their names from the abbots and friars who once lived in the abbey and include specialties like *crostini al tartufo e lardo di colonnata* (toasted bread with truffles and *lardo), pappardelle al ragù di cinghiale e ginepro di arborea* (fresh pasta with wild boar sauce and juniper berries), and *faraona alla leccarda* (roasted pheasant with black olives and capers).

The hotel's twenty double rooms, two suites, and romantic junior suite have been tastefully created from the monks' former quarters. Nearby, the Cascata delle Armore is a giant manmade waterfall created by the Romans to redirect the flow of the Velino River. It is found in a national park, which offers the possibility for rafting, canoeing, and climbing. For sightseeing, medieval Ferentillo and Arrone are not far away.

ABBAZIA DI SAN PIETRO IN VALLE, S.S. 209 Valnerina, Località Macenano, 05034 Ferentillo (TR), tel. +39 0744 780 129, fax +39 0744 435 522, email abbazia@sanpietroinvalle.com, www.sanpietroinvalle.com. For driving directions, see page 235. Cost: EE.

CIVIL CEREMONIES

Todi: Palazzo del Popolo

High atop its mountain aerie, medieval Todi watches over the Tiber Valley. The ancients believed that the town was founded after an eagle appeared to a lord who had traveled from the north in search of a new settlement. The lord had planned to build a city on the banks of the Tiber, but the bird snatched a cloth from him and placed it on the hill, guiding him to a safer location. The omen proved propitious, as this city, founded one thousand years before the Romans, has endured three civilizations. Three sets of walls circle the city, each reflecting the succession of settlements—the innermost, Etruscan; the second, Roman; and the last, medieval. In the dignified Piazza del Popolo, two adjoining medieval buildings, the Palazzo del Capitano (1293) and the Palazzo del Popolo (1214), house the city's offices and museums. A massive marble staircase leads up to the building's main floor and to the Sala del Capitano, where wedding ceremonies are held. Illuminated by the same Gothic trefoil windows that decorate the façade, the walls are covered with religious and civic frescoes discovered during renovations in the 1920s. After the ceremony, you can wander down Corso Cavour to the *nicchioni romani,* standing ruins from an ancient basilica where the Romans blessed their weddings.

PALAZZO DEL POPOLO, Comune di Todi, Piazza del Popolo 45, 06059 Todi (PG), tel. +39 075 895 6236, fax +39 075 893 862, www.todi.net. Driving directions from Perugia: take the E45 (Perugia-Terni) highway and exit at Todi. Cost: E to EE.

Gubbio: Palazzo dei Consoli

A charming medieval town, Gubbio is remembered as the site where the wandering St. Francis tamed a savage wolf with prayer. Twisting streets lead to the center of town, the Piazza della Signoria. In a massive feat of engineering, huge archways were constructed to create this wide, flat piazza atop the hill, from which there is a striking Umbrian panorama. The city hall is located in the Palazzo dei Consoli, a brilliant white marble building with a slender campanile and Guelph crenellations framing its roofline. Weddings are held in the section of the palazzo that houses the archeological museum, in the Tablets Hall, where seven ancient bronze tablets, the Tavole Eugubine, were inscribed in the third century B.C.E. with the sacred rites and ceremonies followed by the ancient Umbrians. After the ceremony you can walk among the ruins of Gubbio's Roman amphitheater or pose in front of the Bargello's Renaissance Fontana dei

Matti. The locals believe that three laps around the "Fountain of the Mad" are enough to earn you the honorary title of "fool of Gubbio."

PALAZZO DEI CONSOLI, Comune di Gubbio, Via XX Settembre 1, 06024 Gubbio (PG), tel. +39 075 923 71, fax +39 075 927 5378, www.comune. gubbio.pg.it. Driving directions from Perugia: take state road S298 to Gubbio. Cost: E to EE.

Orvieto: Palazzo Comunale

An ancient volcano created the huge tufa plateau where the Etruscans founded their city of Volsinii, the place we know today as Orvieto. The city floats above the plains of the river valley, making a striking impression even at a distance. On the way up the hill you will pass the remains of a Etruscan necropolis built thousands of years ago within the sheer face of the hillside. The city has remained unchanged for five hundred years, with many of its winding streets still closed to cars. In the past, Orvieto was often a refuge for the popes, and it was from its Sant'Andrea Church that Innocent III proclaimed the Fourth Crusade. Next to Sant'Andrea's twelve-sided medieval campanile is the Palazzo Comunale, where civil weddings are held. Seven giant archways mark the entrance to the halls of the Renaissance palazzo. The palazzo is full of Roman relics, among them a large fragment from a roman sarcophagus depicting an ancient nuptial scene. Ceremonies, usually conducted by the mayor, are held in the council hall, the Sala del Consiglio. The halls of the *comune* are decorated with heraldic shields from cities that once fell under Orvieto's jurisdiction and precious paintings from the Middle Ages.

PALAZZO COMUNALE, Comune di Orvieto, Via Garibaldi 8, 05018 Orvieto (TR), tel. +39 0763 3061, www.comune.orvieto.tr.it. Driving directions: take the A1 (Roma-Firenze) and exit at Orvieto. Cost: E.

Assisi: Palazzo dei Priori

In St. Francis's eternal city, weddings are celebrated in the Palazzo dei Priori, a building facing Assisi's magical center square, the Piazza del Comune. The entire plaza was built over an ancient Roman forum. Excavations in recent years have been made directly under the plaza, allowing for a visit among the relics after your wedding. Across from city hall, the Tempio di Minerva is one of the most perfectly preserved remaining Roman temples. Before the priors built their own hall, they met in the shadows of the temple's colossal colonnade. Today the Palazzo dei Priori houses the Municipio, the city's public offices, and the Pinacoteca Comunale, the art museum. The wedding hall, the Sala della Riconciliazione, has beautiful frescoed walls and large stained-glass windows. Later in the day you can visit St. Francis's forest hermitage at the Eremo delle Carceri, outside Assisi, where his ancient cave has been enshrined.

PALAZZO DEI PRIORI, Comune di Assisi, Piazza del Comune 2, 06081 Assisi (PG), tel. +39 075 813 81, fax +39 075 813 8264, www.comune.assisi.pg.it. Driving directions from Rome: take the A1 (Roma-Firenze) highway and exit at Terni. Connect to state road S3 and continue to Terni. At Terni connect to the E45 (Terni-Ravenna) highway and exit at Assisi. Cost: E to EE.

Città di Castello: Palazzo Comunale

In the northernmost part of Umbria, Città di Castello is a medieval city still surrounded by the wall built in the sixteenth century. The Romans founded the town, which they named Tifernum Tiberinum for its proximity to the Tiber. The boxy Gothic town hall, the Palazzo Comunale, was built in 1328 and has an elegant portal and trefoil windows. Weddings are held in the Sala del Consiglio. In the summer, the main square is the starting point for the evening *passeggiata,* when the entire town turns out to walk, chat, see and be seen, and enjoy an evening gelato. If you plan your wedding in November, you might want to save some euros for the Mostra del Tartufo, or truffle fair, when regional truffles are sold in the main square.

PALAZZO COMUNALE, Comune di Città di Castello, Piazza Gabriotti 1, 06012 Città di Castello (PG), tel. +39 075 852 91, fax +39 075 852 9216, www.cdcnet.net. Driving directions from Perugia: take the E45 (Perugia-Ravenna) highway and exit at Città di Castello.

Practical Information

Getting There

By air: Perugia is a 200-kilometer drive from Rome's Leonardo da Vinci Airport (airport code FCO); to the south, Terni is just 120 kilometers from Rome. Perugia's San Egidio airport (airport code PEG) has flight connections to Milano Malpensa (www.airport.umbria.it).

By car: Highway A1, which also links Florence to Rome, passes through much of Umbria's western territory. The E45 highway runs north to south further inland, passing through Città di Castello, Perugia, and Terni.

By train: Rail lines operated by Italy's state railway, the Ferrovie dello Stato, depart from Florence and Rome with connections to Assisi, Spello, Foligno, Spoleto, Terni, and Orte. Schedules and information are available at www.fs-on-line.com. Within the region, a smaller rail line, Ferrovia Centrale Umbra, has connections to Sansepolcro, San Giustino, Città di Castello, Umbertide, Perugia, Deruta, Marsciano, Fratta Todina, Todi, Massa Martana, Acquasparta, Montecastrilli, Sangemini, Terni. Schedules and information are available at www.fcu.it.

When to Go

Umbria's Mediterranean climate varies considerably due to the changes in elevation throughout the region. Typically, summers are hot and dry, and winters are relatively mild although higher elevations do see snow from time to time. Although it is particularly pleasant in the summer, the popular tourist sites can be crowded during June, July, and August. October marks the beginning of white truffle season and can be one of the nicest times of year to visit.

Helpful Addresses
Official Tourist Information Offices and Websites

APT—Azienda di Promozione Turistica (Tourist Promotion Agency)

IAT—Ufficio Informazione e di Accoglienza Turistica (Tourist Information and Hospitality Office)

Amelia: I.A.T. Via Orvieto 1, 05022 Amelia, tel. +39 074 498 1453, fax +39 074 498 1566, email info@iat.amelia.tr.it.

Assisi: I.A.T. Piazza del Comune, 06081 Assisi, tel. +39 075 812 534, fax +39 075 813 727, email info@iat.assisi.pg.it.

Castiglione del Lago: I.A.T. Piazza Mazzini 10, 06061 Castiglione del Lago, tel. +39 075 965 2484 and +39 075 965 2738, fax +39 075 965 2763, email info@iat.castiglione-del-lago.pg.it.

Città di Castello: I.A.T. Via S. Antonio 1, 06012 Città di Castello, tel. +39 075 855 4817, fax +39 075 855 2100, email info@iat.citta-di-castello.pg.it. Tourist information: Piazza Matteotti, Logge Bufalini, tel. +39 075 855 4922.

Foligno: I.A.T. Corso Cavour 126, 06034 Foligno, tel. +39 074 235 4459 or 074 235 4165, fax 074 2340545, email info@iat.foligno.pg.it.

Gubbio: I.A.T. Via Ansidei 32, 06024 Gubbio, tel. +39 075 922 0790, fax +39 075 927 3409, email info@iat.gubbio.pg.it. Tourist information: Piazza Oderisi 6, tel. +39 075 922 0693.

Orvieto: I.A.T. Piazza Duomo 24, 05018 Orvieto, tel. +39 076 334 1911 or 076 334 3658, fax +39 076 334 4433, email info@iat.orvieto.tr.it.

Perugia: I.A.T. Via Mazzini 6, 06100 Perugia, tel. +39 075 572 8937 or 075 572 9842, fax +39 075 573 9386, email info@iat.perugia.it. Tourist information: Sala San Severo, Palazzo dei Priori, Piazza IV Novembre 3, tel. +39 075 573 6458.

Spoleto: I.A.T. Piazza della Libertà 7, 06049 Spoleto, tel. +39 074 349 890, fax +39 074 346 241, email info@iat.spoleto.pg.it.

Terni: I.A.T. Viale C. Battisti 5, 05100 Terni, tel. +39 074 442 3047, fax +39 074 442 7259, email info@iat.terni.it.

Todi: I.A.T. Piazza Umberto I 6, 06059 Todi, tel. +39 075 894 3395, fax +39 075 894 2406, email info@iat.todi.pg.it.

Tourism Websites

Bella Umbria: www.bellaumbria.it. Available in English. Information on events, hotels, gastronomy, and Umbrian culture.

Argoweb: www.argoweb.it. Available in English. Guides to many of Umbria's individual cities, as well as information on cultural events and itineraries.

CHAPTER 6

LAZIO
Palatial Rome

R ome has always been intoxicating for romantic travelers. Within its heroic streets and monumental plazas, you can traverse centuries in a matter of yards, walking from antiquity into the Renaissance and back again. When you plan a romantic stay in Rome, your backdrop will be the old grand ruins, magnificent churches, colossal obelisks, mythic fountains, and lively squares that compose the Eternal City.

Rome is a series of contrasts. Plazas invaded by throngs of tourists are often just steps away from hidden neighborhoods where barely a soul is on the street. Crumbling ruins stand beside perfectly preserved monuments. Egyptian obelisks are surrounded by glitzy boutiques, and the quiet of the Forum is reached only after crossing a boulevard dominated by the drone of Vespas. The city is a blend of drama and nuance, motion and stillness.

Romantic settings are numberless. Pick any square (Navona, Campo de' Fiori, Santa Maria in Trastevere) and sit at a cafe table with a Campari soda in the late afternoon and watch the world go by. Stand under the central oculus in the Pantheon and allow yourself to be transported back in time, to an age when the Forum was not a crumbling pile of stones, but a bustling city center, and when vestal virgins baked farro cakes in the

Temple of Vesta to bless Roman unions. You can drift in and out of Rome's delicate churches, climb the Colle Oppio to Nero's "Golden House," and shop for the latest fashions along the Via Condotti. Whatever your mood, Rome has an answer.

Accommodations in Rome

Finding Your Own Roman Pied-à-Terre

Having your own apartment in a great European city doesn't have to be a fantasy. While Rome is not without its fair share of luxury hotel accommodations, most come with the high prices and small rooms typical of a large metropolis. For a unique honeymoon or romantic trip to the Eternal City, you can rent your very own apartment steps away from Rome's best sights. Having your own apartment places you at the center of the old adage "When in Rome..." As you return from shopping the bustling Campo de' Fiori market or from the local *macellaio* (butcher's) with treasures in hand, you'll know that you're getting a feel for authentic Roman life.

As in any major city, short-term rental apartments in Rome range from historic buildings to modern renovated buildings. Spaces can vary from studio ateliers to palatial palaces.

The Bed & Breakfast Association of Rome was one of the first organizations in Italy to offer bed-and-breakfast-style accommodations. Their directory contains more than one hundred apartments in Rome's various districts. Most properties require a minimum stay of two nights and still cost far less than comparable hotel accommodations. Among their listings you'll find a sumptuous apartment near Santa Maria Maggiore with coffered ceilings, oriental carpets, and Italian antiques that can sleep up to five guests, and a flat on the Esqualine Hill with a country kitchen, complete with a rustic hearth.

Caffelletto specializes in high-quality bed-and-breakfast-style accommodations throughout Italy. Among their Roman offerings are two apartments, both just a stone's throw from the Trevi Fountain. Both apartments are inside a seventeenth-century palazzo and face onto a garden with orange trees and fountains. Other carefully selected properties include apartments in the fashionable Parioli district, an apartment near the Pantheon, and a luxury palazzetto near the Vatican.

GoToRoma offers an apartment with terraces on Via dei Zingari (just up the hill from the Colosseum) and an apartment with balconies from which there are views of St. Peter's dome.

Before you go, make sure you understand what is included in the daily or weekly rental rates. Cleaning and maid service are often optional and are not always included in the basic fee. Additionally, some firms will require you to pay for insurance and will ask for a refundable security deposit. And be sure to coordinate your arrival and departure times with your hosts.

Addresses and Practical Information

Bed & Breakfast Association of Rome, Via A. Pacinotti 73, Sc.E, 00146 Roma, tel. +39 0655 302 248, fax +39 0655 302 259, email info@b-b.rm.it, www.b-b.rm.it.

Caffelletto: Bed and Breakfast Bon Voyage, Via Procaccini 7, 20154 Milan, tel. +39 02 331 1814, fax +39 02 331 3009, email info@caffelletto.it, www.caffelletto.it.

COMFORT ITALIA rents fully renovated, modern apartments in the heart of Rome. All their apartments have modern kitchens and bathrooms. Comfortitalia, Vicolo del Gallo 3, 00186 Roma, tel. +39 06 686 7932, email info@comfortitalia.com, www.comfortitalia.com.

CROSS POLLINATE offers inexpensive bed-and-breakfast accommodations in Florence and Venice as well as Rome. www.cross-pollinate.com.

DOLCE VITA VILLAS has apartments in a Pompeian red villa above the Colosseum, an eighteenth-century palazzo a few steps from the Pantheon, and on the second floor of a townhouse with a view directly over the Fontana di Trevi. www.dolcevitavillas.com.

VACANZE ROMANE has reasonably priced furnished apartments in Rome's most historic neighborhoods. www.vacanzeromane.com.

If you can plan a longer stay in Rome, AT HOME ITALY specializes in monthly rentals and sales for individuals relocating to Rome. At Home Italy, Via Bisagno 28, 00199 Roma, tel.+ 39 06 863 98549, fax +39 06 860 6244, email info@at-home-italy.com, www.at-home-italy.com.

Tables for Two

Agata e Romeo

Romeo Caraccio and Agata Parisella's elegant Esquiline area eatery is undoubtedly one of Rome's best restaurants. You are sure to share the dining room with Roman VIPs, yet despite its status the restaurant has a comfortable, welcoming atmosphere. Both the food and the wine cellar have been recognized with awards by Europe's toughest critics. Agata minds the kitchen, preparing new takes on old-world specialties like smoked cod with capers, sun-dried tomatoes, and an eggplant flan; crisp sweetbreads with artichokes; and pork medallions with apple chutney. Romeo manages the world-class cellar, filled with exotic labels from around the world as well as vintages from Italy's best winemakers. If you are having trouble deciding what to order, try the restaurant's tasting menu.

AGATA E ROMEO, Via Carlo Alberto 45, 00100 Roma, tel.+39 06 446 6115, fax +39 06 446 5842 (Metro Cavour, Termini). Just southeast of Piazza Santa Maria Maggiore. Closed on Sundays, and for holidays one week at Christmas and the month of August. Thirty seats; reservations essential. Cost EEEEE.

Baja

Ever since Audrey Hepburn and Gregory Peck danced on a river barge along the Tiber, an evening spent on the river has been associated with the most romantic outings in Rome. Baja, near the Ponte Margherita, is a bit fancier than Audrey's floating dance palace, but it offers a combination of dinner, music, and late-night dancing on a hip, completely renovated barge. The decor is a Roman's interpretation of *stile newyorkese*, as it's called in Italy, with polished light hardwood floors, brushed aluminum, ambient lighting, and a wraparound bar. The restaurant-club offers mixed cocktails and straightforward Mediterranean dishes, but caters only to late-night eaters, as service starts at ten. The club gets started at 12:30 A.M.

BAJA, Lungotevere Arnaldo da Brescia (Ponte Margherita) Roma, tel. +39 06 326 00118 (Metro Flaminio). Between Ponte Margherita and Ponte Nenni; access is by a flight of steps at the Ponte Margherita end of Lungotevere Arnaldo da Brescia. Closed Mondays, opens at 10 P.M. Cover charge.

Camponeschi

Camponeschi is one of Rome's most elegant spots for outdoor dining, with impeccably dressed tables that enjoy a view over one of Rome's prettiest squares, the Piazza Farnese. The restaurant shares the square with the monumental Farnese palace, named after Alexander Farnese (Pope Paul III). After Michelangelo had painted the Sistine Chapel at Farnese's behest, Farnese commissioned Michelangelo to expand this palace. Palazzo Farnese is now home to the French Embassy in Rome, and as you sit at a table under Camponeschi's veranda you can admire its gentle facade. A rich menu is composed of regional and international dishes like lobster with black truffles and raspberry vinegar, foie gras with port and sultanas, *tagliolini* soufflé with white truffles, and partridge in a brandy sauce with mushrooms. The well-managed wine list includes famous international wines and the Camponeschi family's own Colli Lanuvini and Carato wines.

CAMPONESCHI, Piazza Farnese 50, 00187 Roma, tel. +39 06 687 4927, fax +39 06 686 5244, www.ristorantecamponeschi.it. Closed on Sundays. During the month of August open evenings only. Seventy seats; reservations recommended. Cost: EEEE.

Il Convivio Troiani

Once you find the door to this exclusive restaurant near the Piazza Navona, you'll feel like privileged aristocracy dining in its cultivated atmosphere. First, you'll be offered an aperitif; then you'll be shown to your intimate table for two under the vaulted ceilings of the ancient palazzo's dining room. Tables are elegantly dressed and carefully spaced to provide a maximum of privacy to each party. The three Troiani brothers who own and manage Il Convivio came to Rome from their native Ascoli Piceno. Since their arrival on the Roman scene, they have been turning out creative menus in a modern key. This is a great spot to choose a menu *degustazione*, then sit back and relax as a parade of carefully prepared courses arrives from the kitchen. The well-researched wine list includes over one thousand vintages from all over the globe.

IL CONVIVIO TROIANI, Via Vicolo dei Soldati 31, 00186 Roma, tel. +39 06 686 9432, www.ilconviviotroiani.com. On a tiny alley, just north of Piazza Navona. Fifty-five seats; reservations essential. Cost: EEEE.

Montevecchio

Part of the fun of spending any amount of time in Rome is navigating the back alleyways in search of those out-of-the-way spots that make the city so intriguing. Montevecchio is one such locale, tucked away in its own piazza, which you will discover after you've wandered through the maze of streets above the Piazza Navona. In a historic Renaissance building, the small dining room has an intimate atmosphere of soft lighting and very few tables. In the summer, the restaurant serves diners in the tiny piazza. The eclectic menu includes specialties like garbanzo terrine with scallops, tagliolini with sea truffles (Venus clams) and truffles, and roasted lamb with shallots and grapes.

Montevecchio, Piazza Montevecchio 22A, 00186 Roma, tel. +39 06 686 1319 (Metro Spagna). Just northwest of Piazza Navona. Closed on Mondays and from August 13 to 20. Twenty-four seats; reservations recommended. Cost: EEE.

Al Moro

Al Moro has been a Roman institution since 1929 and was once a favored lunch spot for Federico Fellini. The restaurant is not far from the Fontana di Trevi where Anita Ekberg danced in *La Dolce Vita* and, according to some, the elder al Moro was cast in Fellini's *Satyricon*. Despite the references to Rome's pop culture, the restaurant embodies that inimitable Roman spirit, and is complemented by a surly proprietor who reportedly enjoys throwing people out of his establishment. Al Moro has always been a popular lunch spot for Rome's *uomini d'affari* (business men). Promptly at 1:00 P.M. the place quickly fills up with serious diners, so it is best to reserve or arrive early to get a table. Once you're in and past the young al Moro, the waiters are friendly and will help guide you through classic Roman specialties like *spaghetti alla carbonara*, roasted *caprettto* (kid) with rosemary, or *abbacchio* (milk-fed lamb). When truffles are in season, decadent diners can spend an extra thirty euro for a few savory shavings over their pasta.

Al Moro, Vicolo delle Bollette 13, 00186 Roma, tel. +39 06 678 3495 (Metro Spagna). From the Fontana di Trevi, Vicolo delle Bollette is one block west, at the corner of Via Muratte. Closed on Sundays and Mondays. Cost: EEE.

da Pancrazio

At da Pancrazio, in the subterranean bowels of the ancient Teatro di Pompeo, you can dine amid unearthed archeological finds that date back to the days of Julius Caesar. It was, in fact, among these very stones that Julius Caesar breathed his last "Et tu, Brute?" In the vaulted stone dining room, bits of marble ruins peak out here and there around an informal arrangement of tables. The food is informal as well, with a mixture of classic Roman favorites like *saltimbocca* (veal scaloppini with sage and prosciutto), *fritto misto* (mixed fish fry), and fresh *paglia e fieno* (green and yellow "hay and straw" pasta).

DA PANCRAZIO, Piazza del Biscione 92, 00186 Roma, tel. +39 06 686 1246 (Metro Spagna). At the southeast end of the Campo dei Fiori. Closed on Wednesdays, and for two weeks in August. Cost: E.

La Pergola

La Pergola is one of Italy's best-regarded restaurants, not only for its enchanting views over the Eternal City but also for the creative cuisine offered by chef Heinz Beck. The luxurious and refined dining room is one of the most romantic spots in Rome. Warm cherrywood columns divide the room's elegantly dressed tables, all of which are positioned to enjoy a view of the illuminated dome of St. Peter's. The service is impeccable, just what you would expect from a restaurant of this caliber. Dishes are an elegant mix of Italian and international cuisines, with offerings like deep-fried zucchini flowers with shellfish and saffron consommé, potato agnolotti filled with caviar and quail eggs, lamb in an olive crust, and for two, a fillet of sea bass in salt crust. The two-story Palladian-styled wine cellar boasts over eighteen hundred labels and a stock of forty-eight thousand bottles.

LA PERGOLA (Hotel Cavalieri Hilton), Via Cadlolo 101, 00136 Roma (Metro Vaticano), tel. +39 06 350 91, www.cavalieri-hilton.it. Open for dinner only. Closed on Sundays and Mondays at lunch, and for the month of January. Ninety seats; reservations essential. Cost: EEEEE.

La Terrazza

The Hotel Eden's rooftop restaurant, La Terrazza, is another great spot to enjoy views over Rome's seven hills. Before coming to the Hotel Eden, Chef Enrico Derflingher was the personal chef to the Prince and Princess of Wales. He describes his menu as *cucina mediterranea moderna* (modern Mediterranean cuisine), including dishes such as goose liver with toast served with grapes and myrtle berries, or lobster medallions with a puree of green apple and black truffle. First courses and entrées include *stracci* (pasta "rags") with lobster and pesto, sea bass steak baked in salt, and duck breast served with artichokes and onions in sweet and sour sauce. Innovative desserts include a *fagottino* (rolled pancake) filled with cherries with lemon ice cream.

LA TERRAZZA (Hotel Eden), Via Ludovisi 49, 00187 Roma (Metro Barberini), tel. +39 06 478 121, fax +39 06 482 1584, www.hotel-eden.it. Seventy seats; reservations recommended. Cost: EEEE.

Vecchia Roma

Sitting outside on a warm summer evening at this classic spot in the old Jewish Ghetto, you'll be surrounded by a combination of medieval and Renaissance architecture in a formula that is quintessentially Roman. One of the best dishes to try, especially since its origins are right here in Jewish Rome, is the *carciofi alla giudia,* tender deep-fried artichokes. The menu also includes typical Roman fare of classic pasta dishes and roasted meats.

VECCHIA ROMA, Via della Tribuna di Campitelli 18, 00186 Roma (Metro Colosseo), tel. +39 06 686 4604. Near Piazza Campitelli, steps from the Teatro di Marcello. Closed on Wednesdays. Eighty seats; reservations recommended. Cost: EE.

Watching the Sunset

The Angels' Bridge—Ponte Sant'Angelo

The Ponte Sant'Angelo was built as a triumphal bridge across the Tiber by Emperor Aelius Hadrian, in 138 C.E. In the Middle Ages, the popes converted Hadrian's tomb into the fortress they dubbed the "Angels' Castle." In the seventeenth century, Bernini was commissioned to decorate the bridge with the angelic statues that line it today.

Two saints (Peter and Paul) and ten baroque angels stand dramatically atop the bridge's balustrade. The bridge is a perfect spot from which to catch the sun as it sets behind the dome of St. Peter's, with the silhouettes of the angels in the foreground.

The Pincio Gardens—Giardini di Pincio

The Pincio gardens, above Piazza del Popolo, are a great place to watch the sun set over Rome's rooftops. The view extends over Piazza del Popolo's twin churches and obelisk down the illuminated Via Cola di Rienzo to the Città Vaticano. You can begin your evening stroll from atop the Spanish Steps, walking past the Borghese gardens, and finally into the gardens of the Pincio.

Romantic Lore and Local Festivals

Natale di Roma—Rome's Birthday

Each year on April 21, the city of Rome celebrates its own birthday with a citywide celebration. The ancients believed that the city was founded by Romulus sometime around 753 B.C.E. While the actual year of Rome's birth has always been a mystery, the ancients seemed to agree that the date was April 21. This was the day the early Romans celebrated the feast of Pales, the goddess of shepherds. For the contemporary event, many of the city's historic sites are opened to the public for free, banners decorate the Campidoglio, and there are fireworks displays.

Festa di San Giovanni—St. John's Eve

In the early days of Christian Rome, the date of St. John the Baptist's feast coincided with ancient pagan celebrations marking the start of summer. Perhaps because of the confluence of the two events, and perhaps because St. John's martyrdom was caused by the temptress Salome, the ritual for his feast became associated with another annual event—the summer witch hunt. It was believed that the evening of June 23 was the night when witches gathered to prepare to make their annual journey to their capital in Benevento. Although they possessed the ability to render themselves invisible to mortals, on this night alone, witches could be seen and therefore hunted.

As the Christian celebration developed, traces of the pagan ideas remained, especially with regard to the subjugation of women. During medieval times, women were not allowed to enter into the church of San Giovanni on this date, as it was thought that all womankind carried culpability for Saint John's martyrdom.

The night continued to be associated with miracles and magic. Couples chose this night to exchange promises of eternal love, and the date

marked the opening of the Tiber baths (*bagni del Tevere*), as it was believed that on this date Saint John conferred magical virtues on water.

Today, the festival, held on June 23 and 24 in the Piazza di Porta San Giovanni, is celebrated with a feast of snails in tomato sauce and suckling pig, and a fireworks display.

Festa della Madonna della Neve—Festival of the Madonna of the Snowfall

This festival originated with a miraculous event that occurred in the early centuries of the Christian church in Rome. On August 5, 356, a snowfall fell upon the Esqualine hill, during what had been a typically warm Roman summer. The Virgin Mary was immediately credited with the event, and the area of the snowfall became the site of the largest shrine dedicated to the virgin, Santa Maria Maggiore. The miraculous snowfall is reenacted each year on August 5, when showers of white flower petals fall from the rafters of Santa Maria Maggiore's basilica.

Maritozzi Romani—Groom's Cakes

Maritozzi are an ancient Roman specialty that dates back to medieval times—sweetened buns, made with pine nuts and raisins, traditionally baked during Lent. Their name derives from *marito* (husband) because they were often given by young grooms-to-be to their future brides. Once upon a time, gold "surprises" like a ring or a piece of gold jewelry would be baked inside them. Although they began as larger loaves, over time they became quite small, inspiring this old proverb:

Er primo è pe' li presciolosi;
er siconno pe' li sposi;
er terzo pe' li innamorati;
er quarto pe' li disperati.

The first is for the hasty;
the second is for the newlyweds;
the third is for the lovers;
and the fourth is for the desperate.

Today they are often filled with cream or chocolate, and you can find them at many Roman *forni* (bakeries) and *pastifici* (pastry shops).

One place you'll find maritozzi is IL MARITOZZARO in Trastevere, Via Ettore Rolli 50, 00153 Roma, tel. +39 06 581 0781.

Picnic Spots

Picnic Along the Appia Antica

The Appia Antica, that most ancient of Roman roads, was started by consul Appio Claudio in 312 B.C.E. as a means of connecting Rome with Campania. Later, in 190 B.C.E., it was extended to link the city with emerging ports in Rome's ever-expanding empire. In its heyday, it was the most modern road of the ancient world and was cleverly designed to allow all types of traffic to pass under almost any weather condition.

The section of the Appia Antica closest to Rome's gates became an important Christian and Jewish burial place for both commoners and the wealthy. Early Roman law forbade burials within the city's limits, and soon both sides of the Appia were lined with tombs and subterranean catacombs.

In medieval times, the lands along the Appia were ceded to Rome's most important families. The families became feudal overlords and developed the area for agriculture. During this period, many of the Appia's sepulchral relics were looted or moved to churches and museums.

Fortunately for the preservation of the Appia Antica, in the Napoleonic era an emerging interest and fascination with archeology led to first steps toward the restoration of the Appia and its monuments.

Today, the first ten miles of the Appia Antica are at the center of a protected park reserve filled with ruins and monuments of the road's Roman past. Both sides of the road are lined with Christian catacombs, wistful ruins, and grassy meadows. The protected park area extends over eighty-six hundred acres and is a great spot for a picnic, a quiet walk, or a bicycle tour through Rome's ancient past.

Each Sunday the park management offers guided tours of the park. On Saturdays and Sundays, bicycles are available to rent for children and adults, near the park office. Two-hour bicycle tours of the park are led each Sunday by the park ranger, from via Appia Antica and in the Valle della Caffarella. Park Headquarters, Via Appia Antica 42, tel. +39 06 512 6314, fax +39 06 518 83879, www.parcoappiaantica.org. Open Monday through Friday, 9 A.M. to 6 P.M.

Park at the Villa Sciarra

The ancient Romans chose this spot in Trastevere to erect a nymphaeum, a sanctuary dedicated to water nymphs. The Caesar gardens were located here; at one time they stretched all the way to the river. Today, the park is frequented mainly by local Romans who come to enjoy its quiet, flower-laden paths and views of the city. An American diplomat who lived here in the early 1900s restored much of the original garden and added statuary and fountains to the grounds. Throughout the park you will find fountains dedicated to cherubs, goddesses, and sirens, and plenty of quiet benches for sitting and enjoying the scene or sharing a picnic for two.

The park's monumental entrance is on Via Calandrelli, and its south and western sides are delimited by a section of the Aurelian wall.

Villa Doria Pamphilj

The park around this seventeenth-century villa is favored by native Romans for lazy Sunday picnics. Originally designed for a prince, the gardens surround the Casino del Bel Respiro (house of the good breath) that was built for Pope Innocent X. There are numerous fountains, shady paths, bridges, and a central lake in this, the largest of Rome's historic parks.

VILLA DORIA PAMPHILJ, Via San Pancrazio, Via Aurelia Antica 183, Roma. In the summer, I Concerti nel Parco organizes open-air jazz concerts in the park. I Concerti nel Parco, Villa Doria Pamphilj - Palazzina Corsini Via di Porta San Pancrazio 10, Roma, www.iconcertinelparco.it.

Romantic Excursions

The Pope's Thermal Springs—Terme di Papi (Viterbo)

The thermal waters in Viterbo have been known since ancient times. When the Romans came to these parts in the third century B.C.E., they found that the waters had already been harnessed by the Etruscans, who prized their curative effects. The Romans developed the area, and the springs became known as Aquae Passeris, Paliano, and the most famous, Bullicame.

In the Middle Ages, the spas became a place of privilege for the Popes. The springs were used by Pope Gregory IX in the thirteenth century and in 1404 Boniface IX came to Viterbo to try to cure his *gravi dolori delle ossa* (serious bone pains) in the sacred waters and mud. A third pope, Nicholas V, is credited with the renaming of the springs. He chose to build his papal palace in Viterbo so that he could more easily avail himself of the "cure."

There is a two-thousand-square-meter pool heated by underwater springs, and other cures include sulfurous baths, mud baths, and vapor baths. There are two hotel facilities at the springs. The Grand Hotel Salus e delle Terme—Pianeta Benessere has thermal pools and Hotel Niccolò V has a large outdoor thermal pool. Both offer a comprehensive list of services, from mud baths and saunas to beauty treatments.

THE POPE'S THERMAL SPRINGS—ADDRESSES AND PRACTICAL INFORMATION

GRAND HOTEL SALUS E DELLE TERME—Pianeta Benessere, Via Tuscanese 25, Viterbo, tel. +39 0761 358 1, fax +39 0761 354 262, email info@grand hoteltermesalus.com, www.grandhoteltermesalus.com.

HOTEL NICCOLÒ V DELLE TERME DEI PAPI, Strada Bagni 12, 01100 Viterbo, tel. +39 0761 350 1, fax +39 0761 352 451, email info@termedeipapi.it, www.termedeipapi.it. Driving directions: the Terme dei Papi are situated two kilometers west of Viterbo. From highway A1, exit at Attigliano or Orte. Continue in the direction of Orte-Civitavecchia until you reach Viterbo Sud. Follow Via Bagni to the Terme.

Summer Cinema—Cinema all'Aperto

In the summer months, many Italian cities offer *cinema all'aperto*, vintage and first-run films screened under the stars. Recalling the one in *Cinema Paradiso*, the open-air theaters range from impromptu screenings on the sides of buildings to expertly equipped outdoor theaters. In Rome, the city holds the Estate Romana festival (Roman Summer) and outdoor cinema figures heavily in the cultural offerings. Foreign films are often shown in their original languages, with Italian subtitles.

One of the most enchanting venues for outdoor theater in Rome is Tiberina Island, where films and multimedia are screened nightly between the two flows of the ancient river. During the *L'Isola del Cinema* (Cinema Island) film festival, the island becomes a multimedia film set, with images projected on the surrounding travertine walls.

Passeggiate Romane (Roman Strolls) recaptures the spirit of Rome's film heritage, with themed projections held throughout the city. For nine years the organizers of this festival have selected classic films from the archives of Italian cinema and shown them in the locations where they were originally shot. Past offerings have included a screening of Roberto Rossellini's *Roma Città Aperta* (Rome Open City) in via Montecuccoli and Vittorio de Sica's *Ladri di Biciclette* (The Bicycle Thief) in Valmelaina, on the outskirts of Rome.

Piazza Vittorio's arcaded square is the location for the films shown during *Notti di Cinema a Piazza Vittorio*. First-run films are screened amid the square's mysterious ruins.

In the San Lorenzo neighborhood, first-run films are shown from late June through August in the park of the Villa Mercede public library as part of the *Sotto le Stelle di San Lorenzo* (Under the Stars of Saint Lawrence) festival.

Giallo (yellow) has become shorthand in Italian for detective and crime stories, thanks to publisher Mondadori's early yellow-jacketed pulp titles. Appropriately, during *Giallo Estate*, film noir classics are screened amid the atmospheric ruins of the Roman Forum. Past programs have included films like *Scarface, Asphalt Jungle, Anatomy of a Murder*, and *Whatever Happened to Baby Jane?*

Summer Cinema—Addresses and Practical Information

L'Isola del Cinema—Tiberina Island, Piazza S. Bartolomeo, tel. +39 06 583 33113 and +39 06 581 1060, fax +39 06 581 1060, email cineland@tin.it, www.isoladelcinema.com. Held in July and August.

Passeggiate Romane is organized by Roma Città di Cinema, tel. +39 06 700 9305, fax +39 06 704 52713.

Giallo Estate, Belvedere Antonio Cederna, Via dei Fori Imperiali Roma, (Metro Colosseo) tel. +39 06 332 22132. Held in July.

Cinema Fuori 2002...E Cose Che Capitano, Via Filoteo Alberini, Roma, tel. +39 06 871 36693. Held in July.

The Estate Romana Festival begins each June 21 and continues through August. The festival is organized by the city of Rome, and events are posted on the city's website. Contact: Estate Romana, Piazza Campitelli 7, 00186 Roma, tel. +39 06 671 03168 and +39 06 360 04399, www.comune.roma.it/cultura.

Sotto le Stelle di San Lorenzo, Villa Mercede, Via Tiburtina 113, Roma, tel. +39 06 996 2946, fax +39 06 996 74413. From the end of June to the end of August.

From July to September, Cineporto screens first-run films with digital sound in Viale Antonino di San Giuliano (near Ponte Milvio). Tel. +39 06 324 3903, email info@cineporto.com, www.cineporto.com.

Love and Art—Amore e Arte

While you are in Rome, you can chase down the best examples of art that celebrates the theme of "love's triumph."

The idea has a long history in Italian decorative arts and is evident in the gallery Raphael painted for Agostino Chigi's Villa Farnesina and in Annibale Carracci's gallery in the Palazzo Farnese—both palaces that you can visit in Rome.

The Villa Farnesina, on the Trastevere side of the river, was commissioned by a wealthy banker in the sixteenth century. In addition to Raphael's *Cupid and Psyche,* you can see a delightful rendition of the *Wedding of Alexander and Roxanne* by Sodoma.

Palazzo Farnese was built for a cardinal who later became Pope Paul III. Today, the majestic Renaissance palazzo hosts the French Embassy in Rome. On the ceiling, Carracci's painting, *The Triumph of Bacchus and Ariadne*, rivals Rome's more famous painted ceilings and the lines are a lot shorter.

VILLA FARNESINA, Via della Lungara 230, Roma, tel. +39 06 688 01767. Open Monday through Saturday, 9 A.M. to 1 P.M.

PALAZZO FARNESE, Piazza Farnese. Visits by special permission of the French Cultural office, tel. +39 06 686 011.

Weddings in Lazio

Two thousand years of history and the refined tastes of Rome's patrician citizens have created a rich profusion of palaces, cathedrals, and castles in the city of Rome and its surroundings. In these locations, among the grandest in all of Italy, opulent weddings can be celebrated in lavish style. Once, many of the grandiose residences in Rome's vicinity belonged to Catholic cardinals and bishops who lived at a level of luxury that rivaled that of even the most prominent Italian noble families. Today, many former palaces have been conserved as museums, some are hotels, and many are preserved private residences in which parties can be held.

Civil ceremonies in Rome are still celebrated on the Capitoline hill, the same spot where the ancient Romans sanctified patrician weddings.

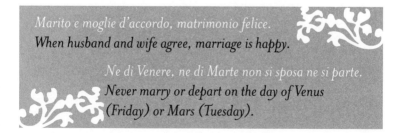

Marito e moglie d'accordo, matrimonio felice.
When husband and wife agree, marriage is happy.

Ne di Venere, ne di Marte non si sposa ne si parte.
Never marry or depart on the day of Venus (Friday) or Mars (Tuesday).

Rome's churches, often erected over pagan temples and incorporating marble discovered among vine-covered ruins, offer an unparalleled variety of styles and settings for ceremonies. Catholics also have the option of consecrating their marriages in the sovereign state of the Holy See, at St. Peter's Basilica.

For wedding photos, Rome offers an unrivaled stage: you can chose historical monuments like Constantine's Arch for your backdrop, or plan a contemporary *Roman Holiday* Vespa tour with your very own paparazzi in tow.

Despite the stateliness of the city, Rome's cuisine is characterized by a hearty straightforwardness, not unlike its stalwart population. Recipes are based on a tradition of cooking with pastoral ingredients like spring lamb, ewe's-milk pecorino, *mozzarella di bufola*, and oxtails. Yet despite the simple presentation of traditional dishes, Roman wedding banquets are lavishly arranged, befitting the style of the city.

Celebrating a wedding amid the hustle and bustle of this great metropolis inspires sophisticated occasions that draw on the city's great historical past.

ANCIENT ROMAN WEDDINGS

Patrician weddings in ancient Rome were celebrated with the ceremony of the *confarreatio*. The night before the wedding, the bride would make an offering of all her childhood possessions at her family altar and would present her *bulla* (an amulet worn since birth) to her father. The next morning, she would be dressed in saffron-colored robes and a red-orange veil. The colors of her wedding costume symbolized fire and were believed to protect her from evil spirits. Her outfit would be completed by a woolen sash, tied around her waist by her mother, which could only be removed by her future husband. The ceremony would be officiated by the *flamen dialis* (a high priest) and the *pontifex maximus* (the ancient Roman equivalent of the pope) in front of ten witnesses, who symbolized the ten original Roman tribes. A simple exchange of vows between bride and groom—*"Ubi gaius ibi gaia"* ("You are husband, I am wife") and the joining of their hands completed the union. After the vows, the bride and groom would share a slice of farro cake, a symbolic offering prepared by the vestal virgins. After the wedding feast, a torchlit procession would lead the bride and groom to their new home. Along the way, onlookers would shower the bridegroom's path with nuts, believed to promote a fertile union. When they reached their new home, the groom would carry his bride over the threshold, which was anointed with sacred oils and covered with greenery.

CEREMONY AND RECEPTION LOCATIONS

Palazzo Ferrajoli

In the heart of the Eternal City, not far from the posh Via Condotti and the changing of the guard at Piazza Venezia, Palazzo Ferrajoli is an elegant residence with a mesmerizing view of Piazza Colonna. This grand mansion dates back to 1548, and over the years it has been a home to cardinals, chancellors, and marquises.

The tall windows of the palace's five salons overlook Piazza Colonna, a wide plaza off the busy Via del Corso. The curious column rising in the center of the piazza was found on nearby Montecitorio in 1709, having originally been erected by the Roman senate in 174 C.E. as a tribute to Emperor Marcus Aurelius Antoninus. Its one hundred feet of sculpted bas-reliefs are dramatically lit at night, creating an enchanting ambience that is best experienced from inside Palazzo Ferrajoli.

Receptions at Ferrajoli are celebrated with the highest level of decorum and savoir faire, beginning with an aperitif served in the warm and inviting drawing room. An eighteenth-century piano is played for the guests, while candlelight plays across gilt-framed mirrors, crystal chandeliers, and the ancient tomes lining the shelves of the inviting adjoining library.

As the party wanders in to dinner, an impressive view opens before them through five massive doorways that link the five adjoining salons. The rooms are filled with priceless artworks and antiques, many documenting Piazza Colonna and its obelisk. The first *sala,* with its golden-ecru color scheme, has a nostalgic painting of Piazza Colonna from 1900, offering a portal into the palace's past. The ceiling's large crossbeams are completely hand-painted with shells and scrolls. Along the top of the walls, frescoes depict melancholy scenes of ships sailing past temple ruins, a popular theme for eighteenth-century artists following the archeological discoveries at Pompeii and Herculaneum. The room's fifteen-foot-tall doors, delicately painted in celadon and gold, open to reveal a balcony that overlooks the square.

The palace's five adjoining halls offer the possibility of choosing just one of the rooms to host an intimate sit-down dinner or of using the entire floor for an elegant cocktail reception. The palace has an exclusive atmosphere suited for particularly refined receptions and is an especially cozy location for winter weddings.

You may select your own catering. Reception capacity ranges from 50 to 120 guests. PALAZZO FERRAJOLI, Piazza Colonna 355, 00187 Roma , tel. +39 06 692 00497, email info@palazzoferrajoli.it, www.palazzoferrajoli.it. Walking directions: follow Via del Corso to Piazza Colonna. The palazzo is at the south end of the piazza. Cost: EE to EEE.

Palazzo Brancaccio

Built in the late 1800s for a Neapolitan prince and a New York socialite, Palazzo Brancaccio's design and architecture epitomize the ostentation of late Renaissance Revival style. One of the last of the Roman princely palaces to be built in Italy, the neoclassical palace was designed by the architect Luca Carimini, then decorated in French Renaissance style by Francesco Gaj, a close family friend of the Brancaccios.

Today, private walls and gates enclose Palazzo Brancaccio, creating a protected setting with no trace of the city's frenetic pace. In the park, the Roman Revival Casina del Laghetto (lake cottage) greets you with its ornate shape nestled among the garden palms. The casina originally floated above the Brancaccio's own man-made lake, which filled the area that today holds gardens and a circular fountain. The interior is rose pink, with white bas-relief stuccos shaped into cherubs, festoons, lutes, and garlands decorating the wall panels and twenty-foot-tall doors. The chapel-like space is covered on one side by a glass cupola and on the other with a brilliant fresco of angels in flight, creating a lively setting for an indoor ceremony.

The palace entrance is through a crimson-brocaded hallway, where crystal chandeliers illuminate cornices decorated with gilt acanthus leaves. The ballrooms, where Princess Brancaccio once entertained the king of Savoy, have elaborate gilded plaster ceilings, cornices with bouquets of flowers, trompe l'oeil rosettes, and heavy valences draped in silk and velvet.

Larger parties of up to five hundred guests can be held in the theatrical Salone di Gala, whose elaborate forty-foot ceiling and violet-and-gold theme would seem equally at home in a grand opera house. On the ceiling, golden rosettes alternate with reclining muses and giant cartouches. Immense floor-to-ceiling arched windows are topped by valences with ornamental moldings. The Sala degli Angeli, an oval room with a pale blue cupola and rococo putti (cherubs), is a perfect room for smaller receptions.

Palazzo Brancaccio is managed by Rome Party, a catering and party-planning company. In their offices above the palace, they can show you countless varieties of table settings, place cards, and ideas for unique menus including a wide range of specialties like *vellutata principessa* (princess bisque), *cuore di vitello alla Rossini* (Rossini-style veal fillet), belle époque ravioli, and risotto with partridge slices.

PALAZZO BRANCACCIO, Largo Brancaccio 82A, 00184 Roma, tel. +39 06 487 3177, fax +39 06 487 3181, email palazzobrancaccio@ palazzobrancaccio.com, www.palazzobrancaccio.com. Walking directions from the Colosseum: climb the Colle Oppio along Via N. Salvi. Turn right on Via Terme di Tito, and right again on Viale del Monte Oppio. The palace is at the end of Viale del Monte Oppio. Cost: EE.

Villa Giovanelli Fogaccia

Set in its own wooded park in the Roman countryside, just five minutes west of St. Peter's, the Villa Giovanelli Fogaccia is a tiny country palace with an inimitable spirit. Built in 1929 as the ancestral home for

Count Piero Fogaccia, the villa was constructed of the finest materials in the spirit of earlier Roman patrician mansions. Part *casale* (farm estate), part *palazzetta*, Villa Giovanelli Fogaccia's architecture is a delightful combination of Italian and European historical elements. Its setting and the rough-hewn stone façade are characteristic of Roman farmhouses. The villa's symmetrical plan with two lateral towers gives the impression of a medieval castle's ramparts, while its elegant windows and portals follow a Renaissance theme. Finally, its tile roof, ceramic pavements, and gilded wood chandeliers evoke the earthiness of the Spanish hacienda.

Impressive attention was given to the details that complete the villa's interior decorations. In the cool white entrance space, colored floor tiles form the Fogaccia family heraldic shield. The barrel-vaulted ceilings, clean white walls, and arched niches are an elegant backdrop for a classical trio that can greet reception guests as they arrive. A travertine staircase with mahogany pillars leads upstairs to the three ballrooms and terrace, where parties and receptions are hosted.

The largest hall, the Salone delle Feste, has room for 130 guests to dine at tables illuminated by the room's grand chandeliers and gilt sconces. The sienna-colored hall is decorated with a large gilded shield and mirrors, nacre door frames, and intricately painted floor tiles. Large windows overlook the terrace that wraps around the villa (a perfect spot for toasting), which is reached through the fifteen-foot-tall doors that open to one side of the room.

The smaller Sala da Pranzo, the family's original dining room, has salmon-colored walls and heavy wood ceilings. A cycle of frescoes depicting religious scenes circles the room. Spanish Colonial chandeliers and a carved stone fireplace complete the elegant decor. The Sala da Pranzo is a warm setting for sit-down dinners for eighty guests; across the landing, the small celadon-colored Sala Verde can seat thirty for dinner or provide a setting for after-dinner cocktails.

The romantic garden surrounding the summer residence is filled with the heady smell of lemon and orange blossoms and can be used for large outdoor receptions. Nearly hidden by exotic palms and shady pine trees, a small pond is crossed by two wooden bridges—a romantic place to hold a wedding ceremony or give a wedding toast.

The villa is situated in the quiet outskirts of Rome, between Boccea and Aurelia, in an area with many protected parks. The villa has in-house catering and ample parking.

VILLA GIOVANELLI FOGACCIA, Via Nazareth 35, 00166 Roma , tel. +39 06 624 7121, fax +39 06 624 7121, email info@villagiovanelli.it, www.villa giovanelli.it. Driving directions: take the A1 (Roma-Milano) highway and exit at Roma Nord. From the Grande Raccordo Anulare (G.R.A. ring road), exit at Via di Boccea (exit 2). Continue toward Città Vaticano. Turn right on Via Nazareth. Cost: EE.

Castello Odescalchi di Bracciano

One of Italy's largest and best-preserved medieval castles, Castello Odescalchi di Bracciano, sits high atop a hill overlooking Lake Bracciano. Here, just thirty minutes from Rome, you can host a castle wedding in one of the grandest examples of feudal architecture in Italy. Odescalchi boasts more than fifteen halls, its own church, a stocked medieval armory, a secret garden, five turrets, an interior courtyard with two levels of arched loggias, a granary, and an original library complete with ancient tomes. During the day, the castle is a popular museum filled with impressive period pieces; for events, guests are entertained alongside the museum's collections.

Wedding dinners are often held in the Hall of Caesars, where banquets have been hosted for over four hundred years. The hall is lined with busts of the twelve Caesars and with fifteenth-century frescoes by the papal court painter Antoniazzo Romano. The Hall of Arms holds the castle's impressive collection of medieval weaponry. Displays of knights in armor stand guard, while others sit holding tilting lances atop mounts clad in horse armor. From the loggia, a path around the castle connects the five circular turrets, once patrolled by castle henchmen, now an excellent vantage point for taking in the surrounding lake view.

Religious ceremonies can be held in the delicate fifteenth-century church just outside the walls. Dedicated to Santo Stefano, it has a simple façade and barrel-vaulted interiors. Outdoor ceremonies can be held in the secret garden, dominated by two ancient Lebanese cedars. The garden is constructed on the roof of a subterranean section of the castle, where secret passageways provided a quick getaway to the lake. From the garden there are breathtaking views over Lake Brancaccio.

The castle can organize authentic period entertainment, including dramatizations of enthralling battles between gladiators and warriors, dueling knights in costume, exhibitions of falconry, and fireworks displays. The castle is easily reached from Rome and is near two small picturesque lakeside medieval towns, Trevignano and Anguillara.

Guided visits to the castle museum are available March through September; check the website for schedules. Reception capacity ranges from thirty to twelve hundred.

CASTELLO ODESCALCHI DI BRACCIANO, Piazza Mazzini 14, 00062 Bracciano (RM), tel. +39 06 998 02379, fax +39 06 998 02380, email castello@ odescalchi.it, www.odescalchi.it. Driving directions from Florence: take the A1 (Firenze-Roma) highway and exit at Magliano Sabina. Continue ten kilometers to Civita Castellana, then eleven kilometers to Nepi. After Nepi, take the Via Cassia toward Roma, and exit at Settevene. Follow the signs another eleven kilometers to Trevignano, then continue on to Bracciano. Driving directions from northern Rome: take the Grande Raccordo Anulare (G.R.A. ring road) and exit at Cassia Veientana (Cassia-bis), continuing toward Viterbo. Follow the road for fifteen kilometers to Cesano. After Cesano, continue first toward Osteria Nuova, then follow the signs to Bracciano. Cost: EE to EEE.

CIVIL CEREMONIES

Piazza del Campidoglio

Just behind Victor Emmanuel's white marble "Wedding Cake" memorial rises the Capitoline Hill, the seat of power of the Roman Republic for over two millennia. Cherished as a sacred place in antiquity, the site was used as a religious and political center first by the Etruscans and the Sabines; later, the Romans placed a gold-filled temple dedicated to Jupiter atop this hill.

The Campidoglio's Renaissance piazza follows the ingenious plan Michelangelo created in 1536. The plaza was created to serve as a stage for the triumphal entrances of returning emperors, kings, and popes. A twelve-point interlaced star paves the space that leads to the Palazzo Senatorio, which has housed the Roman senate since the twelfth century. Two lateral staircases sweep up the front of the building, bringing bride, groom, and witnesses directly to the main floor. Like many Roman rituals (such as espresso drinking), the ceremonies are brisk, usually taking no more than fifteen minutes, and are conducted in the red-brocaded hall reserved for weddings. After the ceremony, do as the Romans do and wander into the Forum for a photo shoot among the ruins.

For civil ceremonies in Rome, first contact the marriage office: Ufficio Matrimoni, Via Petroselli 50, 00186 Roma, tel. +39 06 671 03066, www.comune.roma.it/info_cittadino/schede/an_ma_03.htm.

PALAZZO SENATORIO, Piazza del Campidoglio, 00186 Roma. Walking directions from Piazza Venezia: walk along Via del Teatro di Marcello, following the signs to Campidoglio. Piazza del Campidoglio is reached by a large staircase that rises from Via del Teatro di Marcello. Cost: E to EE.

Complesso di Vignola Mattei

Civil ceremonies can also be celebrated at the Complesso di Vignola Mattei, across the street from another landmark from antiquity, the Terme di Caracalla. Both are located on the Celian Hill, a neighborhood that has been protected since the turn of the century because of its wealth of archeological artifacts. The area presents a quiet contrast to the bustle of the rest of the ancient city, with tree-filled parks that lead to views across the Appia Antica. The Caracalla thermal baths (217 C.E.) were built in antiquity's most fashionable district for wealthy Romans. Today, large lawns and shade trees are interspersed among the remarkably well-preserved walls and intricate mosaics, creating an impressive setting for wedding photos.

COMPLESSO DI VIGNOLA MATTEI, Via di Valle delle Camene 2, 00184 Roma. Walking directions from Terme di Caracalla: begin directly in front of the Terme in Piazzale Numa Pompilio. The Complesso di Vignola Mattei lies directly across the piazza on Via di Valle delle Camene. Cost: E to EE.

CATHOLIC CHURCHES: ROME AND THE VATICAN CITY

Città Vaticano: San Pietro Cappella del Coro

Devout Catholic weddings may be celebrated in St. Peter's Chapel of the Choir, one of eleven grand chapels in the Vatican's prodigious basilica. St. Peter's represents a pinnacle of religious expression through art and architecture, with masterworks by the greatest of Italy's artists and architects, such as Bramante, Michelangelo, Bernini, and Raphael. The Vatican is a sovereign state governed by the pope, and legal requirements for weddings at the Holy See vary slightly from those in Italy in that the religious paperwork supersedes civil requirements. The American Catholic Church of Rome, at Chiesa Santa Susanna, can help facilitate the arrangements, which include extensive religious interviews with the couple. Because weddings here are celebrated in strictest accordance with the church's wishes, it is not recommended for those who have been previously married.

> For Catholic weddings at St. Peter's Basilica at the Vatican or Santa Susanna Church in Rome, contact:
>
> THE PAULIST FATHERS, Via Antonio Salandra 6, Int. 10, 00187 Roma, tel. +39 06 488 2748, fax +39 06 474 0236, www.santasusanna.org.
>
> SAN PIETRO CAPPELLA DEL CORO, 00120 Città del Vaticano, www.vatican.va. Walking directions from Ottaviano metro station: turn left on Via Ottaviano and walk three blocks to Piazza del Risorgimento. Cross the piazza and continue on Via di Porta Angelica to the Vatican.

San Bartolomeo all'Isola

According to the historian Livy, the island in the middle of the Tiber was formed when bountiful wheat harvests were tossed into the river by the expelled Tarquins, who hoped to spite the conquering Romans. In the tenth century, the church of San Bartolomeo was built atop the ruins of a temple dedicated to Aesculapius (the Roman god of medicine). Red granite columns, believed to be relics from the ancient temple, divide the church's richly decorated nave and aisles. The Romanesque bell tower dates from 1118; the baroque façade was added in the seventeenth century. The church can be reached by crossing the oldest of the Tiber's bridges, the Ponte Fabricio, first constructed in 62 B.C.E.

> San Bartolomeo all'Isola, Isola Tiberina 22, 00186 Roma, tel. +39 06 687 7973. Walking directions from Piazza Venezia: follow Via del Teatro di Marcello to Piazza Monte Savello and then to the river. Cross the Ponte Fabricio to Isola Tiberina. Ceremony capacity: Eighty.

Sant'Andrea al Quirinale

Bernini, the great architect of the Roman baroque period, considered Sant'Andrea al Quirinale his only perfect work. Reportedly, Bernini asked to be paid for this luminous masterpiece only with bread baked in the Jesuits' ovens. Completed in 1671, Sant'Andrea al Quirinale sits on the Quirinal, the highest of Rome's seven hills. Surmounted by a Greek Revival pediment held up by two giant Corinthian columns, a semicircular staircase marks the entranceway through the pearly marble façade. The rich interior is almost entirely lined with red-and-white-veined Sicilian jasper and ornamented with gilt stuccowork. Rising high above the apse is a golden oval cupola; inspired by the Pantheon, the oval was Bernini's ingenious architectural solution to a space too narrow for a circular dome. Four chapels circle the outside of the ellipse, and archways frame the church's precious paintings. After the ceremony you can stroll two blocks to another masterpiece of Roman baroque style, the Fontana di Trevi.

> Sant'Andrea al Quirinale, Via del Quirinale 29, 00187 Roma, tel. +39 06 474 4801. Walking directions from Barberini metro station: cross Piazza Barberini and follow Via delle Quatro Fontane to the left. After two blocks, turn right at Via del Quirnale. Continue two blocks to Sant'Andrea al Quirinale. Ceremony capacity: Eighty.

Santa Maria in Cosmedin (Bocca della Verità)

Built over an ancient temple dedicated to Ceres, today Santa Maria in Cosmedin is best known for the mysterious marble face that resides under its portico. According to legend, a person who places his or her

hand inside the mouth of the Bocca della Verità (Mouth of Truth) must tell the truth or risk a bite. Actually, scholars now believe the face is a depiction of the god Faunus, whose attributes were fertility and prophesy—both fitting wishes for a wedding blessing. Inside, the church nave is divided from the aisles by twelve ancient marble columns, and the pavements are richly patterned with colored marble. Across the street, the wonderfully preserved round Temple of Hercules and the rectangular Temple of Portunus leave no doubt that you are in the Eternal City.

SANTA MARIA IN COSMEDIN (Bocca della Verità), Foro Traiano 80, 00187 Roma, tel. +39 06 679 8013. Walking directions from Piazza Venezia: follow Via del Teatro di Marcello to Piazza Bocca della Verità. Ceremony capacity: Eighty.

Santa Sabina

On the splendid Aventine Hill, in the area called the Grande Aventino, Santa Sabina is one of the most fascinating remaining Paleo-Christian churches. The church was built in 425 C.E., on the spot believed to have been the location of Saint Sabina's house. Sabina was a Roman noblewoman martyred by Hadrian after converting to Christianity. The church is entered through a covered porch and massive cedar doors carved with scenes from the Bible, including one of the earliest known depictions of the Crucifixion. The nave is lined with twenty-four recycled Roman Corinthian capitals. The church's luminous arched windows are intricately paned with opalescent selenite crystal rather than glass. The cloister circles a quiet garden with alternating single and double columns. Its central well is the perfect place to make a wish for your future together.

SANTA SABINA, Piazza Pietro d'Illiria 15, 00153 Roma, tel. +39 06 574 3573. Walking directions from the Circo Massimo metro station: Follow Via del Circo Massimo toward the river. Turn left at Piazzale Ugo la Malfa and follow the Via di Santa Sabina to the church. Ceremony capacity: 150.

Practical Information

GETTING THERE

By air: Rome is served by two major airports Leonardo da Vinci—Fiumicino (airport code FCO) and Roma Ciampino (airport code CIA). A new website covers schedules and tourist information for both airports at Aeroporti di Roma, www.adr.it.

By car: The A1 highway connects Rome with Florence in the north and Naples to the south. In Rome, the GRA (Grande Raccordo Anulare) ring road circles the city.

By train: Regular rail service connects Rome with all major cities in Italy. Rome's central railway station is Rome Termini (www.romatermini.it). Schedules and information are available on the official site for Italy's state railway, www.fs-on-line.com.

Within the city: Rome has a wide network of public transportation options, from buses to trams to the metro. The public transportation authority publishes maps and schedules, available at www.atac.roma.it.

WHEN TO GO

The months of May and June, and the period between September through early November are considered high season in Rome. During the Ferragosto holiday in August, most natives head for the beaches, leaving much of the city strangely deserted.

HELPFUL ADDRESSES

Official Tourist Information Offices and Websites

APT—Azienda di Promozione Turistica (Tourist Promotion Agency)

IAT—Ufficio Informazione e di Accoglienza Turistica (Tourist Information and Assistance Office)

A.P.T. CENTRO VISITATORI DI ROMA, Via Parigi 5, 00185 Roma, tel. +39 06 360 04399, fax tel. +39 06 491 9316.

A.P.T. VIA PARIGI 11, 00185 Roma, tel. +39 06 488 991, fax +39 06 481 9316, email editoria@apt-roma.it, www.romaturismo.com.

A.P.T. STAZIONE TERMINI, Piazza dei Cinquecento, tel. +39 06 487 1270 or 06 482 4078.

I.A.T. Via Sistina 9, 00100 Roma, tel. +39 06 474 4104, fax +39 06 482 3837.

Tourism Websites

SCALA REALE is a Rome-based group of scholars, architects, and historians who offer customized walking tours through Rome: www.scalareale.org.

ROMA PREVIEW is a city guide to events and happenings in Rome: www.romapreview.it.

CHAPTER 7

SOUTHERN ITALY AND THE ISLANDS

Secluded Escapes

AMALFI COAST

Few parts of Italy have a closer association with an Italian *luna di miele* (honeymoon) than the *Costiera Amalfitana,* the Amalfi Coast. Sorrento's peninsula, just south of Naples and Pompeii, separates the Gulf of Naples from the Gulf of Salerno. On its southern side, the Amalfi Coast is filled with striking landscapes and some of Italy's bluest seas. Beginning at the tip, which points toward the isle of Capri, a procession of seaside villages clings to steep cliff sides including such world-famous enclaves as Positano, Amalfi, and Ravello.

Couples who honeymoon along the Amalfi Coast often find themselves so taken with the experience that they return year after year to celebrate their anniversaries. Perhaps it's because of this that the historic hotels along the coast are notoriously difficult to reserve, unless you plan your trip well in advance. Some of the most intriguing places to stay include hotels housed in villas that were originally built by Amalfi's wealthiest merchant families. The earliest examples were built in the twelfth and thirteenth centuries in a fascinating blend of Mediterranean and Arabian styles. Their majolica domes, airy courtyards, and Moorish arches give way to lush Mediterranean gardens, filled with scents and a profusion of color.

From the coast, you can venture by boat to the mythic Galli islands or to ever-popular Capri. You can climb along the cliffs, following secluded paths between the lemon groves, or, if you're feeling adventurous, you can brave the rugged *sentiero degli dei* (the gods' path). Either way, your reward is the sublime views of sea and horizon the area is famous for, with jagged cliffs, turquoise seas, and luminous skies. Alternatively, spend your days lazing in the sunshine on your private balcony above the sea, or venture out to the bougainvillea-laden gardens of the Villas Rufolo and Cimbrone.

Although the area can be filled with throngs of tourists, most of the villages empty out in the evenings when the day-trippers return to Naples. At night, you'll share the view with the locals and a few other fortunate individuals who have found paradise along the sea.

Accommodations in Amalfi Coast Cliffside Villas

MAIORI

Casa Raffaele Conforti

A nineteenth-century agricultural magnate, Raffaele Conforti, built Casa Raffaele Conforti in the center of charming Maiori. He used his fortune to create this sumptuous palace, hiring the era's most talented painters to decorate its walls with elaborate allegorical frescos and rococo flourishes. Today, the second story is a boutique hotel with just eight guest rooms. The rooms are still decorated with the furnishings Conforti commissioned in the late 1880s, a mix of ornate baroque mirrors, sculptures, and Empire-style settees. As in many noble residences along the coast, the ceilings are high and the floors are tiled with hand-painted majolica from the kilns at Vietri. Each of the individually named rooms is unique, with decorations that follow a theme. The Camera delle Muse (Muse's room) is frescoed with feminine angels; the Camera Turca (Turkish room) has dancing Arabian odalisques painted on its walls. The Filomena Reale suite has celestial blue walls, elegant antiques, and a large bathroom with a hydromassage tub. In the morning, breakfast is served in the house's original dining room under a frescoed ceiling covered with allegorical paintings and surrounded by elaborate sculpted moldings.

Maiori is a charming village just a few kilometers from Amalfi. The filmmaker Roberto Rossellini staged at least five of his neorealist films in Maiori, using the villagers as cast and crew. Maiori has its own small beach, and from the town there are pretty walking paths connecting it to Minori and Ravello.

CASA RAFFAELE CONFORTI, Via Casa Mannini 10, 84010 Maiori (SA), tel. +39 089 853 547, fax +39 089 852 048, email info@casaraffaeleconforti.it, www.casaraffaeleconforti.it. Driving directions from Naples: t ake highway A3 to Salerno. Exit at Vietri S. Mare and connect to state highway S163. Follow the signs for Amalfi-Maiori. Eight rooms; doubles from E to EE.

POSITANO

Palazzo Murat

At the very center of lower Positano, Palazzo Murat is a Neapolitan baroque palace that was once a residence belonging to the king of Naples. After his marriage to Caroline Bonaparte, Gioacchino Murat was appointed king of Naples by Napoleon in 1808. Like many person-alities of the era, Murat was a flamboyant character and a daring caval-ryman who enjoyed all the trappings of the noble class. For his Positano palace, one of many landed possessions he held, no expense was spared to make it worthy of his title and position.

One peek into the palace's lush courtyard and you'll know you've chosen the right base for your coastal stay. The Murat's multilevel gardens boast some of Positano's most dramatic, draping bougainvillea, which seems to spill over every possible wall and arch. The five rooms in the palace's original wing have eighteenth-century details like soaring ceilings, frescos, and tall doors that open onto views of Amalfi. The rest of the rooms, in a newly built section of the hotel, have a newer, though no less elegant, Mediterranean look.

One of the delights of staying at Palazzo Murat is dining in the hotel's garden restaurant, al Palazzo. Tables are set amid lush Mediterranean

flora, and a view of Santa Maria Assunta's Moorish majolica dome floats above in the night sky. The courtyard is also used for morning breakfasts and, occasionally, evening chamber music performances.

PALAZZO MURAT, Via dei Mulini 23, 84017 Positano (SA), tel. +39 089 875 177, fax +39 089 811 419, email info@palazzomurat.it, www.palazzo murat.it. Thirty rooms; doubles from EE to EEE.

La Sirenuse

In all the glamour and glitz of modern-day Positano, it's easy to overlook its rich historical and mythological past. The Galli Islands just across the water from Positano are one of the legendary settings from Homer's *Odyssey*. As the story goes, after braving winds and enduring the fickle temperaments of the gods, Ulysses passed this way as he continued his voyage south. Having been warned of the dangers that lay before him, Ulysses had himself lashed to the mast of his ship and had his crew's ears filled with wax to prevent them from hearing the bewitching songs of the sirens that inhabited the Galli islands.

Across the water from the Galli, La Sirenuse (named for those alluring sirens) has beckoned travelers since the hotel first opened in 1951. The eighteenth-century palazzo has always been owned by the same Neapolitan noble family, the Marchesi Sersale. At first, the family offered just eight lovely patrician rooms in their private palace to guests, but over the years this enchanting hotel has grown to offer sixty-three delightful guest rooms.

The palace's facade is eye-catching, with its red ochre walls and sparkling white baroque window frames. Inside, the bright airy rooms are elegantly appointed. The family's antiques and heirlooms adorn the museum-like interiors. Each of the suites is uniquely decorated with large canvases by old masters; in some of the bathrooms you can soak in the tub while enjoying the seascape through huge arched windows. Best of all, the suites have private balconies for enjoying breakfast with a view of the sea.

The hotel's romantic La Sponda restaurant has a vaulted ceiling across which bougainvillea vines have been trained into a lush green lattice. Every table is illuminated by candlelight, and the green polished ceramic floors glisten. In the summer, the dining area is extended to include the pool's terrace, surrounded by a Mediterranean garden, marble columns, and the unforgettable view.

The hotel offers guests daily shuttled trips aboard their private wooden cabin cruiser out to the Galli islands. There, you can get a first-hand view of the sirens' mythological home and swim in some of the area's most beautiful waters.

Contrary to the patrician look of the rest of hotel, Gae Aulenti's design for its recently opened Aveda Concept spa is sleek, sophisticated, and decidedly modern. If you have any stress left after settling into your home-away-from-home in Positano, you can schedule a massage, facial, or steam bath, or work out in the spa's fitness center.

La Sirenuse is enormously popular; rooms are usually booked well in advance. The hotel is just a short walk from the center of town, although once you're here you'll never want to leave.

LA SIRENUSE, Via C. Colombo 30, 84017 Positano (SA), tel. +39 089 875 066, fax +39 089 811 798, email info@sirenuse.it, www.sirenuse.it. Sixty-three rooms; doubles from EE to EEEEE.

RAVELLO

Palazzo Sasso

Like Ravello's magical Villa Rufolo, Palazzo Sasso was built in the twelfth century in a mix of Moorish and Romanesque styles. As you step into its central lobby, where Corinthian columns and lancet arches surround a central atrium space flooded with light, you could imagine yourself stepping into an emir's North African palace.

In the fifties, Palazzo Sasso became a luxury hotel and one of the area's most popular getaways, attracting celebrity couples like Ingrid Bergman and Roberto Rossellini. In the seventies, the hotel fell into a period of decline, then was finally rescued from oblivion by mogul Richard Branson. Today, it is richly restored and a posh vacation spot a thousand feet above the Bay of Salerno.

The palace sits on a terraced perch in the center of Ravello. The lower level in front of the hotel has a broad esplanade that leads to its sparkling pool. The gardens are full of exotic plants, profuse colors, and Mediterranean perfumes. The roof is a spectacular spot to watch the sunset over the bay, either from the sun terrace or from one of the hotel's secluded hot tubs. Inside the palace, polished marble halls lead to the elegant guest rooms. The hotel's most luxurious room is the Belvedere Suite, which has its own spacious private terrace for outdoor dining. All of the guest rooms are individually furnished with eighteenth- and nineteenth-century antiques and most have sea views.

The hotel's highly rated Rossellinis restaurant offers an elegant spot for dinner (see page 320). You can also start your evenings at the Caffè dell'Arte bar, where you can sip cocktails to live piano music.

PALAZZO SASSO, Via San Giovanni del Toro 28, 84010 Ravello (SA), tel. +39 089 818 181, fax +39 089 858 900, email info@palazzosasso.com, www.palazzosasso.com. Driving directions from Naples: Take the A3 highway south to Salerno. Exit at Angri. Follow the signs Costiera Amalfitana-Valico di Chiunzi-Ravello. Forty-three rooms; doubles from EE to EEEEE.

Palumbo

This Moorish-Gothic palace high above Ravello began its life as twelfth-century Palazzo Confalone, an Episcopal palace that hosted visiting clergy. The palace was greatly expanded over the centuries, and many elements date to the seventeenth century. An unpredictable maze of corridors and passageways meanders through the palace's spaces, with imported Greek and Roman columns, seventeenth-century majolica floors, and other ornaments creating an intoxicating blend of exotic styles. The lobby court is a Moorish riot of columns and Gothic arches flooded by sunlight from a light well much like those of North African palaces.

During the Victorian era, owners Pasquale Palumbo and his society wife, Elisabeth Von Wartburg, opened the first Hotel Palumbo. Elizabeth had been born into a well-connected family whose circle included Richard Wagner. Wagner visited the Palumbos' and after declaring that he had found his "Klingsor's magic garden," was inspired to pen his opera Parsifal. Since those early days, Palumbo has always been a popular spot for an international list of celebrities. The hotel was a favorite haunt for filmmaker Federico Fellini and his wife Giulietta Masina as well as for Italy's most beloved comedian, Toto.

Each guest room is individually named and features a mix of Gothic arches, inset niches, barrel vaults, and passageways that reveal the palace's eclectic construction. Like the rest of the palace, they are furnished with the owners' hand-selected collection of antiques, with pieces that date to the seventeenth and eighteenth centuries. Two particularly charming rooms are the Scale suite, which has an intimate sitting area and luminous vaults, and the Persiana suite, which has a view over the garden and a luxurious bathroom.

Lush Mediterranean gardens surround the palace in a profusion of vines and pergolas. The garden's seventeenth-century colonnade frames sweeping vistas of Ravello's crystalline sea and sapphire sky.

The dining room of the hotel's Confalone restaurant (page 319), one of the palace's most opulent halls, has a ceiling elaborately frescoed in royal blue, sienna, ochre, and burnt-umber hues. You can spend magical evenings dining here after returning from a visit to the family's Episcopio winery, where guests are invited to taste their Rosso di Ravello wine, first blended by Pasquale Palumbo in 1875.

HOTEL PALUMBO, Via San Giovanni del Toro 16, 84010 Ravello (SA), tel. +39 089 857 244, fax +39 089 858 133, email reception@hotelpalumbo.it, www.hotel-palumbo.it. Driving directions from Naples: Take the A3 highway south to Salerno. Exit at Angri. Follow the signs Costiera Amalfitana-Valico di Chiunzi-Ravello. Eleven rooms; doubles from EEEEE.

Villa Cimbrone

Villa Cimbrone is famous for being Greta Garbo's refuge from stardom when she ran away from Hollywood with her *amore,* conductor Leopold Stokowski. In those days, this hideaway, fifteen hundred feet above the bay of Salerno, was a private residence whose romantic gardens had been laid out by an English expatriate, Lord Grimthorpe, in the early 1900s. The garden he designed is full of an eccentric combination of time periods. Its monuments include imported battlements, Greek temples, Roman ruins, and medieval cloisters all surrounded by rambling English style gardens.

A dramatic pergola-covered walk, shaded by violet-blooming wisteria vines, leads to the bust-lined Belvedere of the Infinity, world famous for its view over the Gulf of Salerno. You'll instinctively try to find the exact spot on the horizon at which the blue of the sky meets the intensity of the sapphire sea. Tucked away in other corners of the garden are eighteenth-century marble statues, hidden grottoes, rose beds, and a Gothic crypt.

The gardens are open to the public until sunset, but the exclusive hotel, set in Garbo's villa hideaway, is hidden behind private gates. You'll share this idyll with just twenty other guests, and in the quiet solitude of the villa and its gardens you can capture the same romantic spirit that drew D. H. Lawrence and Virginia Woolf to sojourn here.

The villa's guest rooms have been renovated to include modern comforts, while original details like frescoed ceilings and stone fireplaces have been carefully preserved. Tall windows let in views of the sea or the pretty park. Each room has polished Vietri tiled floors and a mix of antique furnishings like dressing tables, plush chaise lounges, and elegant armoires. Guests share the villa's patrician common rooms, which feature an elegant mix of artifacts and comfortable chairs for reading and relaxing.

Thanks to a recent renovation, the hotel has a restaurant where guests can dine under the somber Gothic arches of the medieval crypt, previously an exclusive spot for weddings and special events. The hotel continues to organize wedding banquets, and elegant dinners are served either under the shady arches of the crypt or in the villa's verdant gardens. If you plan your wedding here, you can start your reception with a sunset toast on the Belvedere of Infinity and end with wedding cake served under the cloisters.

The hotel is a ten-minute walk from the center of Ravello.

VILLA CIMBRONE, Via Santa Chiara 26, 84010 Ravello (SA), tel. +39 089 857 459, fax +39 089 857 777, www.villacimbrone.it. Driving directions from Naples: take the A3 highway south to Salerno. Exit at Angri. Follow the signs Costiera Amalfitana-Valico di Chiunzi-Ravello. Thirteen rooms; doubles from EEE to EEEE.

Tables for Two along the Amalfi Coast

AMALFI

La Caravella

La Caravella is an elegant spot in the center of Amalfi's historic marina. The owners have transformed an ancient boathouse into a refined establishment that was one of southern Italy's first restaurants to receive a Michelin star. Specialties include pâté made from shellfish and pistachios, braised octopus with lentils, fettuccine with baby calamari, flying squid (*totani*) filled with zucchini and tomato, and pezzogna fish with lemon velouté. If you're not in the mood for fish, there are also dishes like veal scaloppine. For dessert, choices include lemon soufflé, profiteroles, and chocolate pear cake.

LA CARAVELLA, Via Matteo Camera 12, 84011 Amalfi (SA), tel. and fax +39 089 871 029, www.ristorantelacaravella.it. Driving directions from Naples: take highway A3 to Salerno. Exit at Vietri S. Mare and connect to state highway S163. Follow the signs for Amalfi. Closed on Tuesdays and for the month of November. Fifty seats; reservations recommended. Cost EEE.

Da Gemma

In the summer, reserve a seat on Da Gemma's front terrace with a view of Amalfi's cathedral. Since 1872, the restaurant has been known for its excellent fish dishes, which include *zuppa di pesce* (fish stew), *alici all'amalfitana dorate con mozzarella* (anchovies "Amalfi style": filled with mozzarella, battered, and fried), and fresh fish of the day served either grilled, steamed, or in *acqua pazza* (crazy water). The cellar is furnished with the best regional wines and some very good national wines.

DA GEMMA, Via Fra' Gerardo Sasso 9, 84011 Amalfi (SA), tel. +39 089 871 345. Closed on Wednesdays, and for holidays from January 15 to February 15. Forty seats; reservations recommended. Cost: EEE.

POSITANO

Chez Black

Right on the beach, Chez Black is an ever-popular spot in Positano. Seafood is central to the menu, and this is a good spot to taste fresh fish carpaccio, pasta tossed with scorpion fish and shallots, and baked gilthead bream while you watch the Positano scene. Desserts include white almond cake and a refreshing lemon granita.

CHEZ BLACK, Via del Brigantino 19, 84017 Positano (SA), tel. +39 089 875 036. Closed January 7 to February 15. One hundred eighty seats; reservations recommended. Cost: E.

Da Adolfo

If you arrive in Positano with your own boat, Da Adolfo is an ideal spot for you. The easiest way to access this seafront locale is by boat. To arrive you can either take the restaurant's own launch, which shuttles diners from Positano's beach between 11 A.M. and 1 P.M., or climb down the long stairway that descends from Via Nazionale. Da Adolfo's characteristic dishes are antipasti di mare with vegetables, *polpette di melanzane* (eggplant dumplings), spaghetti garnished with mussels or clams, fresh grilled fish, and *fior di latte* cheese melted on a lemon leaf. Homemade tarts and the house's own *limoncello* are the perfect finish.

DA ADOLFO, Spiaggetta di Laurito, 84017 Positano (SA), tel. +39 089 875 022. Open for lunch only. Closed from October to May. Sixty seats; reservations recommended. No credit cards. Cost: E.

Il Capitano

From Il Capitano's panoramic terrace you can enjoy the view that Positano is famous for. This refined spot is a family-run restaurant, with Mamma in the kitchen and Papa minding the cellar selection. The seasonal menu includes regional favorites like spaghetti with anchovies and green peppers and tomatoes from Furore, lobster ravioli, and fettuccine with red mullet. As a bonus, both the *grissini* (breadsticks) and the bread are made on the premises. To finish, try the *delizia al limone* (lemon pie) or the apple strawberry cake.

IL CAPITANO, Via Pasitea 119, 84017 Positano (SA), tel. +39 089 811 352, fax +39 089 811 251. Closed on Thursdays from December 26 to June 15; open every day in the summer. Closed for holidays from November through Christmas. Seventy seats. Cost: EE.

La Cambusa

La Cambusa was opened in 1968 by two young partners whose simple goal was to offer excellent fresh fish dishes. Not much has changed since those days, and the restaurant, located right on the central square, still espouses the founders' original philosophy. First courses like penne tossed with shrimp and arugula or spaghetti with mussels, are typical of the fare served at La Cambusa. The catch of the day is on display so you can choose your own fish and its method of preparation. La Cambusa also features an interesting selection of local cheeses, like *caciottine di pecora* (a soft ewe's-milk cheese) and *latticini* (fresh milk cheeses).

LA CAMBUSA, Piazza Amerigo Vespucci 4, 84017 Positano (SA), tel. +39 089 875 432. Ninety seats. Cost: EE.

RAVELLO

Confalone at the Hotel Palumbo

Whether under a sumptuously painted ceiling with baroque flourishes or on the garden terrace surrounded by the scent of roses and lemon blossoms, the Confalone restaurant at Hotel Palumbo is one of the most elegant spots for sharing a meal in Ravello. The ancient palace that houses the hotel and restaurant has been declared a national monument, and one peek inside immediately reveals why this treasure above the sea merits the status.

Chef Antonio Sorrentino has created a menu of elegant dishes. Start with a refreshing lobster salad made with local artichokes and beets, or with fresh anchovies with shavings of *bottarga* (dried tuna roe). Light

primi include ravioli filled with sheep's-milk ricotta and served with asparagus, or risotto seasoned with fresh herbs and scampi. Main courses include quail glazed with honey, or sea bass baked with olives and capers. The hotel's original proprietors began blending their Episcopio wine in the late 1800s; now it's included on the list of carefully selected wines offered to guests.

CONFALONE AT THE HOTEL PALUMBO, Via San Giovanni del Toro 16, 84010 Ravello (SA), tel. +39 089 857 244, fax +39 089 858 133, www. hotel-palumbo.it. Closed from January 6 to March 15. Thirty-six seats; reservations recommended. Cost: EEEE.

Rossellinis

Rossellinis is part of the Palazzo Sasso hotel, situated in an enchanting panoramic position in Ravello. From the restaurant's marvelous terrace, one thousand feet above the sea, the view stretches into the infinite. Chef Antonio Genovese is renowned for his cuisine and proposes a creative selection of dishes flavored with the region's key ingredients. Start with anchovies filled with mozzarella and fried in lemon leaves, or a pigeon salad with fava beans and arugula served with potato rosemary focaccia. For a second course, choose between sea bass risotto with clams and peas in a lemon-thyme-basil sauce, or hand-cut chili spaghetti with zucchini, shrimp, and red Tropea onion. Main courses include grilled red mullet with caponata and tomato vinaigrette, beef fillet in a marrow-pancetta crust, and sweetbreads and mozzarella in a pistachio, pine nut, and almond butter. Elegant desserts prepared by the restaurant's pastry chef include chocolate soufflé with licorice ice cream.

ROSSELLINIS, Via San Giovanni del Toro 28, 84010 Ravello (SA), tel. +39 089 818 181, fax +39 089 858 900, email info@palazzosasso.com, www.palazzosasso.com. Open for dinner only. Closed from January 5 to February 28. Seventy-five seats; reservations recommended. Cost: EEEEE.

SORRENTO

O' Parrucchiano

O' Parrucchiano is one of Sorrento's historic locales, open since 1868. The restaurant, in the heart of old Sorrento, is set in its own garden; from the covered terrace, tables look upon laden lemon trees. Inside the old stone building are many charming details, like amphorae set in niches, exposed brick arches, lush ferns, and dramatic iron chandeliers. The cuisine is a mixture of traditional dishes and new favorites. Specialties include the restaurant's own cannelloni, made following a recipe that first debuted here in 1870, classic *zuppa di cozze* (mussel soup), and calamari *in casseruola*. Fresh fish is prepared *al forno* (roasted), *ai ferri* (grilled), *al sale* (in salt), or *all'acqua pazza*. Finish your meal with one of their house-made cordials flavored with roses, basil, fennel, or myrtle.

RISTORANTE LA FAVORITA O' PARRUCHIANO, Corso Italia 71, 80067 Sorrento (NA), tel. and fax +39 081 878 1321, email info@parrucchiano.it, www.parrucchiano.it. Closed on Wednesdays and from November to March. Three hundred seats; reservations recommended. Cost: E.

Il Buco

Reached via a characteristic *vicolo* (narrow street), Il Buco is located in one of Sorrento's oldest buildings. The dining room is both rustic and elegant, with terra-cotta sculpted accents, white walls, and barrel-vaulted ceilings. In the summer, outdoor tables are set along the ramp in front that leads to the port. Seafood is central to the menu, with dishes like baby calamari tossed with potatoes and lobster saffron risotto, but there are also offerings for meat lovers, like roasted chicken stuffed with leek and porcini mushrooms in rosemary oil or roasted lamb with an herb crust. There is a carefully selected wine list.

IL BUCO, Via il Rampa Marina Piccola 5, 80067 Sorrento (NA), tel. +39 081 878 2354, www.ilbucoristorante.it. Closed on Wednesdays, and for vaction from January 15 to February 15. Fifty seats; reservations recommended. Cost: EE.

Watching the Sunset

AMALFI COAST

A Sunset Cruise—Amalfi Coast

You can catch breathtaking sunsets from almost any point along the Amalfi Coast. With an icy *limoncello* in hand, find a spot on a terrace and watch as the sun dips into the horizon. Or, plan a romantic sunset cruise: by boat, you can venture out to the Galli Islands or travel to Capri just as the sun is setting. Finish your evening with a dinner for two at one of Capri's hot spots.

AMALFI MARINE organizes cruises along the shoreline and to the islands of Galli and Capri. The company also has a variety of motorboats and personal watercraft for rent. Amalfi Marine, Via Lungomare dei Cavalieri, Pontile Il Faro, Amalfi, fax +39 089 872207, info@amalfimarine.com, www.amalfimarine.com.

AMALFI SAILS organizes themed excursions like "Capri by Night" or trips that follow the ancient pirate routes along the coast. Should you want to sail on your own, note that the company rents forty-foot sailboats and cruisers of various sizes. Amalfi Sails, Spiaggia del Porto, Amalfi, fax +39 089 852911, info@malfisails.it, www.amalfisails.it.

For those who are looking for the luxury of chauffeured boat service (and who have the resources to pay for it) TAXI DEL MARE offers a twenty-four-hour taxi service between any two points along the coast. www.taxidelmare.it.

Picnic Spots

AMALFI COAST

Summit of Monte Solaro—Anacapri

From the center of Anacapri on the island of Capri, a single-passenger chair lift departs for the nineteen hundred-foot summit of Monte Solaro, the island's highest point. The mountain is covered with flower-carpeted meadows and has a breathtaking view of the Faraglione islands, just off the coast of Capri.

The lift was built in 1952 and renovated in 1998. The trip to the summit takes twelve minutes. The chairlift station is just a short walk from Piazza Vittoria.

SEGGIOVIA MONTE SOLARO Via Caposcuro 10, 80071 Anacapri (NA), tel.+39 081 837 1428.

Romantic Excursions

AMALFI COAST

Abbazia di Santa Maria de Olearia—Maiori

Hidden in a cliffside grotto on the Amalfi Coast, the Abbey of Santa Maria de Olearia was founded by religious hermits in 973. The settlement began simply, with a few buildings and an olive press. As the monastical following grew, three chapels were built in succession, one on top of the other. The founding monks came from the eastern Mediterranean, and the overall style and impression of the architecture and art is Greco-Italian. The oldest and lowest has frescoes that date to the early Middle Ages, among the oldest in the Campania district. On the second level, the middle chapel is also frescoed, and its arched windows and courtyard have views of the sea. The most recently built chapel, on the third level, has a fresco cycle depicting the life of Saint Nicolo of Nera.

Visits to the Abbey are by appointment; reservations can be made by contacting the Maiori City Hall via email. The ABBEY OF S. MARIA DE OLEARIA, email comunemaiori@ecostieramalfitana.it, www.ecostieramalfitana.it/comunedimaiori/gboleari.htm. The abbey can be reached by car from state highway 163 or by hiking along the footpath from Maiori. The path follows a gentle incline, and it takes a little over two hours to reach the summit.

Chamber Music in the Gardens of Villa Rufolo—Ravello

Villa Rufolo was built on the Amalfi Coast in the thirteenth century by a wealthy merchant family who had made their fortune through trade with Northern Africa and the East. Their villa above the sea reflects Arab and Byzantine details they might have seen in their travels. In the nineteenth century, the villa was acquired by the Scotsman Neville Reid, who restored the property and arranged the beautiful gardens that now surround it.

Villa Rufolo's idyllic gardens are the setting for a romantic chamber music festival, held each year. Visiting maestros, soloists, and orchestras come from all over Europe and beyond to perform under the stars in this magical location. During the first week of July, the Wagner music festival is held, an annual commemoration of his 1880 visit.

The events are managed by the Ravello Concert Society, who maintain a helpful website with schedules and ticket sales online. See www.rcs.amalficoast.it or contact them at tel. +39 089 858 149. VILLA RUFOLO'S gardens and enchanting Moorish cloisters are open for visits from 9 A.M. to 6 P.M. daily, tel. +39 089 857 657.

Practical Information—Amalfi Coast

GETTING THERE

By air: The closest airport to the villages along the Amalfi Coast is Naples Capodichino (airport code NAP).

By car: Amalfi's picturesque seaside highways are extremely narrow and often congested with tour buses and other traffic. In the villages, parking is limited. Along the coast there is ample public transportation, so if you are not planning lots of inland excursions you might forgo renting a car.

By train: Italy's state managed rail line connects Rome to Naples and to Salerno. Schedules and information are available on the official site for Italy's state railway at www.fs-on-line.com. Additionally, Circumvesuviana has lines that run from Naples to Sorrento and to Baiano. Schedules and information are available at www.vesuviana.it.

By boat: Alilauro (www.alilauro.it) ferries link Naples, Sorrento, Ischia, and Capri. Cooperativa Sant'Andrea (www.coopsantandrea.it) has boat service to Alerno, Minori, Maiori, Amalfi, Positano, Capri, and Sorrento.

By bus: SITA buses link most of the coastal towns. See www.sita-on-line.it for information.

WHEN TO GO

The climate on the Amalfi Coast is temperate year round. High season begins in early April and continues through October. Many of the popular hotels and resorts are reserved a year in advance, so if you are planning a honeymoon along the coast, book as early as you can.

HELPFUL ADDRESSES

Official Tourist Information Offices and Websites

AACST Azienda Autonoma di Cura Soggiorno e Turismo—Autonomous Agency for Hospitality and Tourism

AMALFI: A.A.C.S.T. Corso delle Repubbliche Marinare 27, tel. +39 089 871 107.

Maiori: A.A.C.S.T. Corso Reginna 73, tel. +39 089 877 452, fax +39 089 853 672.

Positano: A.A.C.S.T. Via del Saracino 4, tel. +39 089 875 067, fax +39 089 875 760.

Ravello: A.A.C.S.T. Piazza Duomo 10, tel. +39 089 857 096, fax +39 089 857 977.

Municipal Websites

Comune di Amalfi: www.comune.amalfi.sa.it, available in English. Information on Amalfi's historic regatta.

Tourism Websites

Positano Online: www.positanonline.it, available in English. History, activities, and a photo tour of Positano.

Costa di Amalfi: www.costadiamalfi.it, available in English. Information on accommodations, restaurants, gastronomy, and activities along the coast.

PUGLIA

At the southernmost tip of Italy (so southern, in fact, that you are almost in Greece), in the *tacco,* or heel of the boot, lies the region of Apulia, or Puglia as it is called today. The peninsula, enclosed by the Adriatic Sea and the Gulf of Taranto, features some of the most stunning coastline in all of Italy. Along the Adriatic, hidden grottoes and sun-bleached rock formations rise from crystalline waters. Inland, mortarless stone walls, dating from feudal times, separate endless groves of gnarled olive trees from rocky pastures inhabited only by grazing goats and sheep. Amidst the olive groves are the *masserie* or fortified farmhouses, whose walls once housed both landlord and laborer. Greek and Arab influences are evident in their angular whitewashed walls, which create a brilliant contrast against the azure sky and the intense green palms and lush bougainvillea found throughout the region. A characteristic feature of many *masserie* is an enclosed citrus garden, the *agrumento*, originally conceived as a place where the perfume of orange blossoms could revive weary travelers.

Whether isolated by a vast terrain or rooted on rocky sea cliffs, the *masserie* represent the ancient topology of the region's agricultural heritage. Today, more than two thousand remain throughout the region, having survived years of Saracen invasions and pillaging. The heel of Italy's boot has long been the landing stage for invasions of the peninsula, and this fact seems to have determined the self-contained nature of the *masseria's* architecture. Typically, solid walls enclose a central courtyard surrounded by buildings for quartering livestock, living quarters for landowners and workers, the ever-present *frantoio* for olive pressing, a *caseificio* for cheese making, and finally the family chapel. Many of the masserie have been rescued and transformed into luxury hotels, *agriturismi,* and estates for celebrating special occasions.

Puglia's combination of sea, landscape, history, and warm Mediterranean hospitality offers an idyllic setting for a romantic escape or a secluded wedding. For excursions beyond the walls of the masserie, there are the mysterious *trulli* of Alberobello (tiny limestone houses with mortarless conical tops) and the baroque cities of Lecce, Martina Franca, and Otranto to discover. For food lovers, Puglia is not only the largest producer of olive oil in Italy—with no less than fifty varieties of olives—but it also has plenty of DOC wines. Excursions to *cantine* to taste the region's wines and to *frantoii* to sample the area's prized olive oils are a fun way to meet the locals and discover new scents and tastes. You'll also get to taste freshly made pastas like orecchiette and *cavatelli*, and ultrafresh cheeses like *burrata* and ricotta, served with the wild herbs and vegetables that are prized in Puglia.

Accommodations in Puglia's Masserie

MONOPOLI

Il Melograno

Along the Adriatic coast, a chain of watch towers and fortified agricultural hamlets were built by the Knights of Malta in an era when pirate incursions and Saracen invasions were commonplace. Today, what was once Masseria Torricella has been carefully restored and transformed into the luxury hotel Il Melograno.

As with many of the restored *masserie* in Puglia, it was a singular passion that restored this sixteenth-century farm into a hotel worthy of inclusion in the Relais & Châteaux hotel group. The owner, Camillo Guerra, an antique and art dealer, has filled the hotel with precious treasures collected from all over Europe. The elegant rooms and suites are filled with oriental carpets and centuries-old chests and art, all seamlessly integrated with every modern amenity you would expect from a hotel of this caliber.

The individual buildings that house the accommodations surround a giant court, paved in heavy stone, that once would have been the center for the workings of the farm. The stark white space is punctuated by greenery-filled amphorae, olive and pine trees, and splashes of Mediterranean blue and yellow. At the head of the court, the oldest part of the *masseria* hosts the reception area, the comfortable bar (housed in the farm's former stables), and the hotel's elegant restaurant. Two massive olive trees, each almost one thousand years old, flank the dining room, and are lit like living museum pieces. Here you can enjoy traditional Apulian cuisine, carefully prepared and elegantly served.

In summer, sun worshippers have the option of enjoying the pool on the hotel grounds or venturing (in the hotel's private shuttle service) to Il Melograno's exclusive seaside beach on the Adriatic, located on the grounds of an ancient *pescheria*, a fishery dating to the time of the Bourbon occupation. The beach resort, La Pescheria, has three spring-fed swimming pools and restaurant, a sundeck that seems to float above the Adriatic, and direct access to the sea.

For food lovers, Diane Seed, author of *The Top One Hundred Pasta Sauces* and other books on cooking and eating Italian-style, hosts a cooking school at the hotel during the summer months, where students can learn the secret to making orecchiette by hand.

Il Melograno is just sixty kilometers from Bari's airport, and close to the ancient ruins of Egnazia, the Castellana caves, and Alberobello's acres of *trulli*.

IL MELOGRANO, Contrada Torricella 345, 70043 Monopoli (BA), tel. +39 080 690 9030, fax +39 080 747 908, email melograno@melograno.com, www.melograno.com. Driving directions: from Bari, take highway SS16 and exit at Monopoli. Follow indications for Alberobello, and after three hundred meters turn right at the sign for Il Melograno. Thirty-seven rooms; doubles from EE to EEEEE.

OSTUNI

Masseria Il Frantoio

Unless you already live in the country, at one time you have probably fantasized about permanently escaping the confines of the city to a secluded farm where you could have your own vineyard, raise horses, or simply grow tomatoes. Armando Balestrazzi and Rosalba Ciannamea are two people who have made their dream come true. Il Frantoio, the farmhouse they've restored and turned into a lively *agriturismo,* is a magical place surrounded by the complements of a real farm (horses, chickens, and—in the eclectic style that is a key ingredient of the place—peacocks and lovebirds), as well as the scents and flavors of a Mediterranean garden oasis. The farm occupies 178 acres of hundred-year-old olive groves in the Ostuni countryside. Here life moves at a slow pace, following the gentle rhythms of those long lazy summer days we once enjoyed as children.

The *masseria's* eighteenth-century manor house has been lovingly restored and filled with a very personal collection of antiques and heirlooms. Eight guest rooms are available in a variety of sizes, each named after a flower from the garden, like *Mughetti* (daisies), *Narcisi* (narcissus), and *Glicine* (wisteria). Each room has its own individual personality, making you feel as if you're staying at a friend's country house. The Victorian-Italian country furnishings include cast iron beds, old majolica, antique photographs, and embroidered linens. Guests share the house's living room and library (filled with Armando's precious collection of books), an elegant dining room, and comfortable kitchen where you can enjoy a glass of wine in front of the cozy hearth.

The white stone courtyard directly in front of the house has tables where guests can sit and enjoy the scents from the garden. Cascading wisteria and bougainvillea surround the space. At the end of the courtyard, the *agrumento* opens from an archway, its orange trees perfuming the air.

In summer, dinner is served in this courtyard, with tables dramatically candlelit and a starry sky overhead. The proprietress is legendary for her cooking, and ten-course meals are a common occurrence. The cooking is based on the flavors of Puglia—meats from the pasture, fresh cheese (made that day), greens, aromatic herbs, and handmade pastas like *cavatelli* and orecchiette. To accompany the meals, indigenous wines like Negro Amaro and Primitivo are served. At the end of the meal, home-made *rosolii di casa* (cordials) are offered as a digestif—but be forewarned, the strongest, *foglie di olive* (olive leaves), is fifty proof.

The owners' eclectic collections exceed the confines of the house, extending to two old horse carriages, used for children's hayrides, and Armando's vintage Fiat cars, which he uses to take guests on tours of the farm property.

The old state road that leads to the farm wanders through cypresses and pines, with miles of stone walls that edge the olive groves. The location is the perfect departure point to tour the Itria Valley, the *trulli* of the Murgia, and the grottoes at Castellana.

MASSERIA IL FRANTOIO, SS. 16 km 874, 72017 Ostuni (BR), tel. +39 0831 330 276, email armando@trecolline.it, www.trecolline.it. Driving directions: from Bari, take highway SS16 toward Brindisi. Take the exit for Ostini and continue to mile marker 874, where you will soon see a sign for the farm. Eight rooms; doubles from E.

FASANO

Masseria Marzalossa

As you pass through the iron gate to the seventeenth-century Masseria Marzalossa, you'll be struck by the cultivated beauty of the farm's landscape and the great care that has been directed at its preservation and cultivation. The property's olive trees, some over eight hundred years old, embody the character of this land, having borne witness to the arrival of the ancient Greeks, Saracens, Normans, and more. Owners Mario and Maria Teresa Guarini have exceptional taste and have carefully equipped the *masseria* with charming furnishings and antiques. The rooms and suites have been carved out of old sections of the masseria; although completely renovated and equipped with modern amenities, they feel absolutely true to the spirit of the old farm, with exposed masonry, cross-vaulted ceilings, dark wood beams, and stone floors. Guest rooms are furnished with delicately scrolled wrought-iron bed frames, framed oil paintings, oriental carpets, and bathrooms with both marble and modern fixtures. A few of the suites have working fireplaces, and the double rooms open onto their own private gardens. In spring and summer, lovely iron tables are set in the vaulted stone court for breakfasting outdoors. The court leads to the swimming pool, enclosed by walls and circled by stone columns, lemon trees, and cascading bougainvillea. Entering the space, you feel as if you have walked back in time onto the grounds of a Pompeian villa. From the pool, an intoxicating scent of orange blossoms draws you to the *agrumento*, a large walled garden filled with specimen orange trees. When we visited, a large "honeymoon" suite in the oldest part of the *masseria* was being prepared to receive guests directly over the orange garden, so guests can fall asleep as their perfume drifts up through the windows. Guests who elect to eat lunch and dinner at the *masseria* are treated to a selection of carefully prepared traditional dishes, prepared from the farm's own organic ingredients. If you choose to venture from this Shangri-la, you can rent one of the farm's bicycles or use their boat for coastal excursions.

Masseria Marzalossa is forty-five minutes from Bari's airport, and close to Alberobello, whitewashed Ostuni, and the quaint baroque city of Martina Franca.

MASSERIA MARZALOSSA, Contrada Pezze Vicine 65, 72015 Fasano (BR), tel. and fax +39 080 441 3780, email masseriamarzalossa@marzalossa.it, www.marzalossa.it. Closed November through February. Driving directions: from Bari SS16 toward Brindisi, exit at Fasano. Connect to SS379 toward Ostuni; when you reach Fasano, continue toward Pezze di Greco. After two kilometers (across from the Consorzio di Fasano), turn right at the indication for the Masseria, then immediately left. Continue to follow the yellow signs for Masseria Marzalossa until you reach the gate. Eight rooms; doubles from EE to EEE.

PEZZE DI GRECO

Masseria Salamina

Built over the sixteenth and seventeenth centuries, Masseria Salamina is a massive fortified farmhouse edged with classic castle-like battlements. Once upon a time, it was completely encircled by defensive walls, built as another measure of protection from marauders. These days the walls have vanished; instead, you reach the *masseria* by a gravel road flanked by groves of gnarled olive trees and fields seasonally carpeted with Queen Anne's lace and bright yellow mustard. A singular palm stands guard in front of the rose-colored manor house, whose central lookout tower once kept watch over the Adriatic coast just a few miles away. The manor house is the central construction in the complex of buildings, which have been renovated to include seven guest rooms and eight apartments, each with its own independent entry. Staying here is like being part of a tiny farm hamlet, where cats roam and laze in the sun, and the family dog will gladly nudge you for some attention. The *masseria* is primarily an *agriturismo,* making it well suited for longer holiday stays, as well as a great place for families traveling to Puglia. Apartments are equipped with kitchens, so you can shop at the local *caseificio* (cheese maker's shop), and *macellaio* (butcher's) and feast on your own version of Apulian cuisine. The rooms on the second floor of the *masseria* have shutters that open to reveal views across the countryside—all the way to the sea. A broad balustraded terrace wraps around both levels of the guest accommodations, with tables and chairs for sitting outside and enjoying the view. The comfortable rooms are furnished in modern Italian resort style. The *masseria* offers half and full board rates, so you can enjoy their home-style cooking in the cozy restaurant on the ground floor of the *masseria.* It's close to the Adriatic for beach visits, but you can also hang out at the farm where, upon request, they will organize courses in cooking Apulian specialties, or decoupage and painting.

MASSERIA SALAMINA, 72010 Pezze di Greco (BR), tel. +39 080 489 7307, fax +39 080 489 8582, email salamina@mailbox.media.it, www.masseriasalamina.it. Driving directions: rom Bari, take highway SS16 and exit at Pezze di Greco. Just as you reach the entrance to the town, turn right just before the indication for the *centro abitato*. Seven rooms and eight apartments; doubles from E.

SAVELLETRI

Masseria San Domenico

Arriving at Masseria San Domenico, you get the feeling that you could be somewhere in North Africa, with the palms and massive white stone architecture recalling Tunis or Casablanca, but the bustle of the marketplace is absent; instead, all is quiet. Quickly you'll remember that you are in Italy, standing in the shade of one of the oldest feudal fortifications in this part of the territory. The knights of Malta erected San Domenico's watchtowers in the fourteenth century to ward off invasions by the Turks and to maintain a key stronghold here. The estate is surrounded by 150 acres of ancient olive trees. The Adriatic sea is only a few kilometers away—so close, in fact, that you can hear the waves breaking as you relax in the shade and seclusion of the *masseria*.

Masseria San Domenico has been completely refashioned into a luxury hotel, with an adjoining spa facility regarded as one of Italy's finest. This is the perfect place to honeymoon if you are looking for a secluded escape where you can spend leisurely days lingering by one of the hotel's pools and only worry about what time you should start your spa treatments. The spa at San Domenico specializes in thalassotherapy, a type of spa regimen using seawater and sea products for a variety of health treatments. The spa at San Domenico purifies water from the nearby Adriatic for seawater treatments that range from water jet massages to marine body scrubs. The seawater in Puglia is naturally rich in potassium, magnesium, iodine, and saline, all believed to rest and rejuvenate the skin and circulation.

The luxury guest rooms and suites are airy and bright and filled with Italian provincial furnishings. The decor follows the refinement of the rest of the complex, with smooth marble floors, rough-hewn stone sconces, rococo iron light fixtures, and rich wood antique furniture. The spacious bathrooms have every modern amenity, with deep jacuzzi tubs, marble tile, and plush terrycloth robes and slippers. The hotel's restaurant, San Domenico, is set in a section of the farm that dates to the 1700s. The romantic dining room is crowned by church-like stone cross vaults that rise high overhead. Tables are comfortably spaced for intimate dining, and the massive seven-foot stone hearth warms the room during the cooler months. Live piano music drifts in from the bar and beautiful examples of Apulian pottery decorate the walls. In warm weather, iron tables are set in the courtyard and around the pool, where you can continue to soak up the sunshine.

More vigorous activities can include eighteen holes of golf at the hotel's course, and or a game of tennis at the courts on the premises. There is also a private beach, and for guests who are interested the hotel will arrange skeet shooting, horseback riding, and scuba diving.

MASSERIA SAN DOMENICO, 72010 Savelletri di Fasano (BR), tel. +39 080 482 7769, fax +39 080 482 7978, email info@masseriasandomenico.com, www.imasseria.com. Closed January and February. Driving directions: from Bari, highway SS16 toward Brindisi, exit Savelletri. Follow the coast road SS379 toward Torre Canne, after two kilometers you will see the entrance to the *masseria*. Thirty-five rooms; doubles from EE to EEEEE.

Tables for Two in Puglia

ALBEROBELLO

L'Aratro

Alberobello's *trulli*, recognized as a world heritage site by UNESCO, create one of the most unique landscapes in Italy. The town has become quite a tourist attraction, but the *trulli* are still worth seeing and the surrounding countryside provides beautiful landscape for touring.

In the most characteristic section of Alberobello, where the road climbs through the *trulli*, L'Aratro is a quaint restaurant with red-and-white-checkered tablecloths and a classic menu of local specialties. Dishes include *fave e cicorie* (sautéed fava beans and chicory), *cavatellucci mare* (large orecchiette with seafood), and steak and sausages cooked over an open fire.

L'Aratro, Via Monte San Michele 25/29, 70011 Alberobello (BA), tel. +39 080 432 2789. Driving directions: from Bari, take highway SS16 and exit at Monopoli. Follow indications for Alberobello. Cost: E.

L'Olmo Bello

L'Olmo Bello gets its name from the two gigantic elms that once were used in Alberobello for posting proclamations and dispatches. In the summer the restaurant offers enchanting outdoor dining under a gazebo that looks out over cherry and olive trees. Specialties from Puglia include *orecchiette con cime di rape* (pasta with turnip greens), *purè di fava con cicorielle* (fava puree with chicory), *patate e riso con cozze* (rice and potatoes with mussels), *coda di rospo steccata con acciughe* (monkfish "larded" with anchovies), and *trippa soffocata* (braised tripe).

L'Olmo Bello, Via Indipendenza 33, 70011 Alberobello (BA), tel. +39 080 432 3607, fax +39 080 432 3607. Closed Tuesdays, and for the month of November. Driving directions: from Bari, take highway SS16 and exit at Monopoli. Follow indications for Alberobello. Cost: E.

Il Poeta Contadino

One of our favorite meals while traveling in Puglia was at the Poeta Contadino. The restaurant has won high praise through the years, especially for its wine cellar; the wine list is so vast that it is in a bound volume. The charming restaurant is set in an old building used as a stable in the 1700s. Lofty cross-vaulted ceilings rise high overhead, and limestone floors are under foot. The restaurant has an extremely formal atmosphere, with waiters in black jackets and service to match. Recipes take their cues from regional cuisine like the *involtino di melanzane con pescatrice* (eggplant rolled with monkfish) and the Apulian staple, *burrata,* a fresh mozzarella-like cheese, served with a terrine of wild chicory and fresh tomato. We also enjoyed fresh orecchiette with local *funghi cardoncelli* (king oyster mushrooms) and sausage, and the *piatto di buon ricordo* (souvenir dish), sea bass alla Leonardo, exquisitely prepared in fresh tomato and olive oil. For dessert, a trio of delights included a ricotta-filled *cannolo* pastry, a pear poached in red wine, and a gelato of Primitivo wine.

IL POETA CONTADINO, Via Indipendenza 21, 70011 Alberobello (BA), tel. +39 080 432 1917, email ilpoetacontadino@tiscalinet.it, www. ilpoetacontadino.it. Driving directions: from Bari, take highway SS16 and exit at Monopoli. Follow indications for Alberobello. Closed Mondays from October to June, and for holidays January 7 to 31. Sixty-nine seats; reservations esstential. Cost: EEE.

BARLETTA

Antica Cucina

Barletta lies on the coast fifty-five kilometers northwest of Bari. In July the city hosts the Disfida di Barletta, a *palio* (horse race) that began over five hundred years ago (see page 343).

In an old *frantoio,* the Antica Cucina has a large, welcoming dining room. The seasonal menu includes dishes like *zucchine e sugo di riccio* (zucchini with sea urchins), *rustico con composta di peperoni e melanzane* (pastry with peppers and eggplant), *zuppa di grano e cicerchie* (grain soup with dry grass peas), and *orecchiette alle rape con favette e cicorie* (orecchiette with turnip greens, fava beans, and chicory). For dessert, enjoy a mousse made with *fichi di India* (prickly pears), or fresh ricotta cake. The wine list includes good local wines as well as national "cru" vintages.

ANTICA CUCINA, Via Milano 73, 70051 Barletta (BA), fax +39 0883 521 718. Driving directions: from Bari, take highway A14 and exit at Barletta. Closed Mondays, and for the month of July. Seventy seats; reservations recommended. Cost: E35.

CAROVIGNO

Già Sotto l'Arco

Carovigno is a little town twenty-eight kilometers from Brindisi, at the eastern edge of the Murgia, the high plateau southwest of Bari. An ancient legend says that the city was built atop the ruins of a Messapi settlement called Carbina. The city still retains much of its medieval aspect, with seven fortresses in the surroundings. Just outside the city, the Santuario della Madonna del Belvedere, built in the 1500s, is frescoed in Byzantine style.

Situated in an old palazzo in the center of the city and managed by a husband and wife team, Già Sotto l'Arco has a beautifully appointed dining room and serves well-presented dishes like monkfish *in guazzetto* (prepared in white wine, parsley, garlic, and tomato), *straccetti* (pasta "rags") dressed with salt cod and garbanzo beans, wild mushrooms in pastry, risotto with squash blossoms and truffles, rabbit with porcini mushrooms, lamb in herbs, and, for dessert, *fichi mandorlati* (figs dried and filled with an almond, then baked), and *panna cotta al caffè.* A great selection of wines from all over Italy is available to accompany your meal.

GIÀ SOTTO L'ARCO, Corso Vittorio Emanuele 71, 72012 Carovigno (BR), tel. +39 0831 996 286. Driving directions: from Brindisi, take state highway 379 and exit at Carovigno. Closed Mondays. Forty seats; reservations essential. Cost: E.

CEGLIE MESSAPICA

Al Fornello da Ricci

Ceglie Messapica rises above the plain at the southeastern edge of the Murgia. Surrounded by olive groves and vineyards, the town has documented origins as far back as 473 B.C.E. In the surrounding landscape you can look for the *specchie*, mysterious mortarless constructions dating to the Iron Age, which may have either marked ancient property divisions or served as lookout points.

Al Fornello da Ricci is set in the hilly countryside just one kilometer from medieval Ceglie Messapica. Up a narrow drive you'll find the restaurant, housed in a restored farmhouse. It is regarded as one of the region's best, and although the cuisine follows the traditions of the region, the cooking is fresh, creative, and unique. It is probably due to this combination that they have been awarded a Michelin star, and Antonella Ricci, the chef, has been inducted into the Jeunes Restaurateurs of Europe. To best experience what they have to offer, have Sunday lunch in the warm rustic dining rooms and let the able wait staff be your guide for a menu *degustazione*. If you prefer to choose for yourself, the day's menu will be described to you aloud by the maitre d'. Antipasti include *capocavallo*, a locally cured meat similar to coppa; deep fried quail eggs with a truffled puree; and a puree of wild greens topped by a creamy cheese—presented in a *tazza* (tea cup). Delicious pastas include homemade ricotta-filled gnocchi with puree of fava beans and basil, shaved local truffle, and a fried squash petal. For a second course, try a *grigliata mista* of delicate, well-spiced sausage, pancetta wrapped in *rotolini* filled with various offal, lamb, or pork rib chops.

AL FORNELLO DA RICCI, Contrada Montevicoli 71, 72013 Ceglie Messapica (BR), tel. +39 0831 377 104. Closed Monday evenings, Tuesdays, and for holidays from February 1 to 15, and for the month of September. Driving directions: from Bari, take highway S16 to Ostuni, then follow signs for Ceglie Messapica. Contrade Montevicoli is just southwest of Ceglie Messapica; look for indications for the Grotte Montevicoli, then indications for the restaurant. Seventy seats; reservations recommended. Cost: EE.

MARTINA FRANCA

Ciacco

Martina Franca is one of the region's most appealing towns, filled with baroque stone architecture and narrow pedestrian-only alleyways.

Right in the heart of Martina Franca, Ciacco is a charming three-story restaurant housed in a characteristic eighteenth-century building. The interior has been carefully restored, and the original architectural details are beautifully preserved. In the white-on-white dining room, rustic elements like polished stone, dark woods, wrought iron, and copper create an elegant contrast. Tables are arranged near the fireplace. Flavors drawn from the traditional dishes of Martina Franca form the foundations of the seasonal menu and include *polpette fritte* (fried meatballs) and pastas like orecchiette and *cavatelli* in traditional sauces.

CIACCO, Via Conte Ugolino 14, 74015 Martina Franca (TA), tel. +39 080 480 0472, email info@ristoranteciacco.it, www.ristoranteciacco.it. Driving directions: from Bari, take highway S16 and exit at Fasano. Follow the signs for Fasano, then continue to Martina Franca. Closed Mondays. Cost: E.

OSTUNI

Porta Nova

Ostuni is a striking whitewashed city, thirty-five kilometers northwest of Brindisi. The town hosts two summer festivals that perpetuate the ancient traditions of its people. On August 15 is *vecchi tempi* (old times), when traditional costumes, jobs, and music are displayed along the streets of the old town. On August 26 and 27 is the traditional *cavalcata* (cavalcade), a parade dedicated to the patron saint of the town, with horses and riders dressed in red and white ribbons.

Porta Nova restaurant is situated at one of Ostuni's old Roman gates, in the actual rampart wall that surrounds the ancient village. A covered terrace faces the panorama of a valley of olive groves and the Adriatic coastline. The simply decorated dining rooms have characteristic terra-cotta floors and whitewashed vaulted ceilings. The menu changes daily, and you are likely to be asked what you would like before being told what is available. When we dined there, our delicious lunch began with a parade of antipasti courses so extensive that a side table was brought in to hold all the dishes. Some of the highlights: tender stewed octopus, fried artichoke hearts, orzo salad with *frutti di mare*, creamed onions, prawns with garbanzo beans, fried ricotta with saffron velouté, and house-cured salmon with fresh fennel.

PORTA NOVA, Via Gaspare Petrarolo 38, 72017 Ostuni (BR), tel. +39 0831 338 983, www.ristoranteportanova.it. Driving directions: from Bari, take highway S16 to Ostuni. Closed Wednesdays. Cost: E.

Osteria del Tempo Perso

In the center of Ostuni and not far from the cathedral, Osteria del Tempo Perso is in a rustic building that in the sixteenth century housed the communal ovens. Traditional Apulian cooking is served in two contrasting dining rooms: the first, all white and museum-like; the second in an old grotto carved into the rock. On the walls are objects from country life, old farm implements, and horseshoes. Taste excellent country-style dishes like *purea di fave e cicorielle selvatiche* (puree of fava beans and wild chicory), *cardi stufati con crostini di pane* (cardoons—an artichoke relative—layered with crostini), *ricottina di capra su pesto di rucola* (goat's-milk ricotta with arugula), and *cosciotto di capretto al forno* (oven-roasted leg of goat).

OSTERIA DEL TEMPO PERSO, Via G.T. Vitale 47, 72017 Ostuni (BR), tel. +39 0831 303 320, email info@osteriadeltempoperso.com, www. osteriadeltempoperso.com. Driving directions: from Bari, take highway S16 to Ostuni. Closed Mondays. One hundred seats; reservations recommended. Cost: E.

POLIGNANO A MARE

Grotta Palazzese

Polignano a Mare lies thirty-eight kilometers south of Bari on the Adriatic coast. A windswept, whitewashed cityscape recalls Polignano's origins as a Greek settlement in antiquity. The town is famous for its cliff line, where houses cling to rocky perches above natural sea grottoes. Some of the caves are deep enough to extend under the center of town. The largest and most famous caves in Polignano are the Grotta Stalattitica, the Grotta della Foca, and the Grotta Palazzese.

Having a meal at Grotta Palazzese must be one of the world's most unusual dining experiences. The restaurant's summer dining room is set inside the most famous of Polignano's sea caves. Perched above breaking waves, it offers a breathtaking view of the sea. The natural grotto has been used as a giant outdoor dining room since the 1700s, when it hosted grand banquets and feasts for visiting nobility. Today the grotto is annexed to Hotel Ristorante Grotta Palazzese, a small, elegant hotel situated above the restaurant. The restaurant's menu highlights Mediterranean specialties and dishes based on fish, lobster, and shellfish.

GROTTA PALAZZESE, Via Narciso 59, 70044 Polignano a Mare (BA), tel. +39 080 424 0677, fax +39 080 424 0767, email grottapalazzese@grotta palazzese.it, www.grottapalazzese.it. Driving directions: from Bari, take highway S16 and exit at Polignano a Mare. Cost: EE.

Da Tuccino

Da Tuccino has one of the most beautiful sea terraces in all of Italy, with a view of the clear waters off Polignano. The restaurant offers classic Apulian cuisine, with an emphasis on locally caught fish and shellfish. The owner, Pasquale Centrone (the son of the restaurant's namesake, Tuccino) welcomes guests with warm hospitality and enjoys offering a menu crafted from whatever was freshest at the morning's fish-market. Look for dishes like *zuppa Santa Caterina* made with mussels, clams, and fresh herbs, or *orecchiette al nero di seppie* made with clams, prawns, and squash blossoms. Conveniently, reservations can be made through the restaurant's website.

DA TUCCINO, Via S. Caterina 69/F, 70044 Polignano a Mare (BA), tel. +39 080 424 1560, fax +39 080 425 1023, email info@tuccino.it, www.tuccino.it. Driving directions: from Bari, take highway S16 and exit at Polignano a Mare. Closed Mondays, and for holidays December 16 to February 15. Seats: ninety. Cost: EE.

TRANI

Torrente Antico

Trani, founded in Roman times on the coast forty-two kilometers northwest of Bari, was an important commercial center for the Byzantines and the Normans. Along the waterfront, parts of the old walls were used in 1823 to build the shady gardens of the Villa Comunale, an excellent spot for an afternoon *passeggiata.*

Torrent Antico is among Puglia's best restaurants, with an intimate, welcoming atmosphere in which you can taste cooking based on ancient traditions. Excellent regional dishes are prepared with creative touches, like *linguine alle code di scampi* (fresh pasta with scampi tails), *sformatino di melanzane e gamberi* (terrine of eggplant and prawns), *scampi flambati al tartufo* (scampi flambéed with truffles), *filetto di rombo in crosta di patate* (turbot in potato crust), and excellent meat-based main courses. The wine cellar is also noteworthy.

TORRENTE ANTICO, Via Edoardo Fusco 3, 70059 Trani (BA), tel. +39 088 348 7911. Driving directions: from Bari, take highway S16 north to Trani. Closed Sunday evenings and Mondays, and for the month of July. Thirty-five seats; reservations recommended. Cost: EE.

Romantic Lore and Local Festivals

PUGLIA

The Legend of the "Right of First Night"

Throughout Italy the legend of *jus primae noctis,* or the "right of first night," is retold in various incarnations. The story always follows a similar vein—an abusive overlord or prince used his power to demand to share the wedding bed with his peasants' brides. In Grottaglie, a city near Taranto known for its majolica, the story goes that one such abusive *signorotto* continually humiliated the people of his village, until one young groom-to-be swore that he would put an end to this dishonor before the prince could have his future bride. The young man's plan was to lie in wait for the prince, dressed in his bride's wedding clothes. Unfortunately, having forgotten to shave off his beard and moustache, he was discovered and killed before he could exact revenge on the tyrannical prince. The ceramicists of Grottaglie commemorate the legend through elaborately decorated majolica bottles in the forms of the young bridegrooms, each with matching clothes. The groom is represented with his moustache and sword, and the bride is represented with her breasts exposed. Traditionally the bottles were used to hold gifts of homemade *rosolii* (cordials).

DOMENICO CARETTA MAIOLICHE in Via Crispi 20, Grottaglie (TA), tel. 099 866 1725, sells the *pupe* (dolls) in various sizes, each a small *capolavoro* (masterpiece) of baroque majolica.

Lantern Festival—Calimera

The traditional Festa di San Luigi e dei Lampioni (celebration of lanterns in honor of San Luigi) has been held since Byzantine times on the summer solstice, June 21, in the village of Calimera (south of Lecce). For the celebration, the villagers fashion figural lanterns in many shapes and sizes—up to twenty feet tall—from humble materials (reeds, twine, paste, tissue paper). On the evening of the solstice, the streets are magically illuminated with the lanterns and there is traditional singing and dancing.

The Rock of San Vito—Calimera

On the day of *Pasquetta* (Easter Monday), a tiny chapel dedicated to San Vito is opened for an unusual celebration. In the center of the church's nave is a boulder with a large hole carved through it, the surviving relic of an ancient pagan ritual. Villagers believe that if you can successfully crawl through the rock on this day you will be assured of good health and fertility in the coming year.

Disfida di Barletta

On February 13, 1503, in a neutral field between Andria and Corato, a knightly joust took place to defend Italian honor after an imprisoned French captain had questioned Italian valor at a banquet dinner. The Italians' victory became a symbol of hope for Italian reunification at a time when much of the peninsula was under foreign occupation.

Every year in Barletta, during the month of February and again in July, the battle is reenacted with thirteen costumed Italian riders and thirteen riders who play the part of the French. Teams fight with swords on and off horseback, until the last man is left standing. After the victory, there is feasting and celebration throughout the city.

Danza delle Spade—Torrepaduli

A ritualistic sword dance, the Danza delle Spade is an intricate miming of a bloody duel, with dancers using their forefinger to represent a knife. During the festival of San Rocco on August 15, villagers in Torrepadule, near Lecce, perform a frenetic dance to the incessant rhythms of a *pizzica tarantata* played on tambourines. This ancient ritual is said to date to the Turkish occupation of Puglia.

Il Corteo Storico di Federico II e Torneo dei Rioni—Oria

In Oria, at the start of August each year, a tournament is held that dates to the days of Emperor Frederic II, also known as Barbarossa (Red Beard). According to legend, Frederic II, in anticipation of the arrival of his future bride, Isabella di Brienne, proclaimed a tournament in her honor between the four ancient quarters (*rioni*) of Oria. The modern reenactment of this tournament was reborn in 1967 and today includes over five hundred costumed participants who recreate Frederic's *corte storico* (historic court). There are processions in medieval costume and feats of arms on horseback; teams from the different districts of the town compete with one another in games and contests.

The Tarantella

At some point during almost every Italian wedding, the sounds of the traditional tarantella are played. Legend has it that the dance originated between the fifteenth and seventeenth centuries when there was an epidemic of tarantism in Taranto. Its victims, always women, were thought to have been bit by the poisonous tarantula spider. After the supposed bite, they would fall into a trance that could only be cured by frenzied dancing to the rhythmic playing of mandolins, guitars, and tambourines. Today the spiders no longer cause trances, but the tarantella is still danced at just about every Italian wedding.

Romantic Excursions

PUGLIA

Cellar Visits and Wine Tasting in Puglia

Puglia's winemakers were once associated with mass production and inexpensive export wine, but in recent years there has been a push toward careful cultivation and producing wines of quality. It has become one of the most exciting winemaking regions, with each passing year bringing better vintages. Gioia del Colle, Castel del Monte, and Salento are just a few of the areas producing great wines these days. Cellar visits can be scheduled at the following wine estates, and all offer direct wine sales on the premises. As in other regions in Italy, wineries in Puglia are open by appointment and a few charge for tastings.

Wine Estates in Puglia

RIVERA'S highly rated wines come from 136 acres of vineyards in the Castel del Monte region. Noteworthy wines include Il Falcone, made with uva di troia and montepulciano grapes. Rivera, Contrada Rivera, SS 98 km 19,800, Andria (BA), tel. +39 0883 569 501, fax +39 0883 569 575, www.rivera.it, email info@rivera.it. Driving directions: from Andria, take state road SS98 toward Canosa until you reach the crossroads for Montegrosso; after two hundred meters you will see signs for the cantina. Tastings are by appointment only.

The AZIENDA AGRICOLA SANTA LUCIA estate was founded in 1628 and has been producing wine continuously ever since. The estate's vineyards include fifty acres planted with uva di troia, negro amaro, and bombino nero grapes. Azienda Agricola Santa Lucia, Strada Comunale San Vittore 1, Corato (BA), tel +39 080 872 116, fax +39 081 764 3760, www.vinisantalucia.com, email info@vinisantalucia.com. Driving directions: from the A16, exit at Trani and continue toward Bari. After passing the bridge, continue seven kilometers to the SS98, continuing toward Foggia. After one kilometer, turn right, following signs to the Azienda. Tastings are by appointment only.

AZIENDA VINICOLA TORREVENTO lies at the foot of Castel del Monte, along a road that runs through acres of vineyards. The estate's cellars are housed in a

Benedictine monastery established in 1600. Azienda Vinicola Torrevento, SS170 km 28,000, Corato (BA), tel. +39 080 898 0923, fax +39 080 898 0944, www.torrevento.it, email info@torrevento.it. Driving directions: from Bari, take highway SS98 toward Foggia; after Rivo di Puglia, follow the signs for Minervino, Spinazzola Castel del Monte. After ten kilometers along the SS170, the cantina is on the right.

BARSENTO produces a crisp rosé wine, called Magilda, from malvasia nera grapes, and their Casaboli wine is made with 100 percent primitivo. Azienda Vinicola Barsento, Strada provinciale per Martina Franca, Contrada San Giacomo, Noci (BA), tel. +39 080 497 9657, fax +39 080 497 6126, www.cantinebarsento.it, email info@cantinebarsento.it. Driving directions: from the A14 highway, exit at Gioia del Colle, and continue to Noci. In Noci, follow the signs from Piazza Garibaldi to the estate.

Weddings in Puglia

Puglia offers unique locations for weddings in settings unlike those in any other Italian region. They include the rustic storybook *trulli*, the solid country *masserie*, and southern castles. You can stage your very own fairytale with a backdrop of Alberobello's *trulli* or, if a more patrician event is what you are looking for, plan your wedding in one of Puglia's gorgeous palaces with their baroque chapels and pergolas set in Mediterranean gardens.

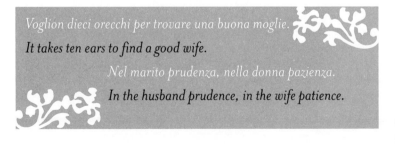

Voglion dieci orecchi per trovare una buona moglie.
It takes ten ears to find a good wife.

Nel marito prudenza, nella donna pazienza.
In the husband prudence, in the wife patience.

CEREMONY AND RECEPTION LOCATIONS

Selva Club Monacelle

Selva di Fasano is at the edge of the *zona dei trulli,* one of the prettiest landscapes in Puglia. The Selva Club Monacelle is a charming hamlet of thirty linked *trulli,* which were once part of a monastery dating to 1600. The old stone buildings have been restored to offer hospitality for overnight stays and ample space for wedding receptions. Each *trullo,* with its characteristic conical roof, is completely individual. Seven rooms have been individually decorated with antiques and named after Puglia's indigenous flowers: Camelia, Agrifoglio (holly), Gardenia, Azalea, Veronica, Ginestra (broom), and Callisto (bottlebrush). The restaurant on the premises can prepare an authentic Apulian wedding banquet.

SELVA CLUB MONACELLE, 72010 Selva di Fasano (BR), tel. +39 080 930 9942, fax +39 080 930 7291, email info@selvaclubmonacelle.it, www. selvaclubmonacelle.it. Seven rooms; doubles from E.

Tenuta Donna Lavinia

Sheltered by stone walls and groves of olive trees, Tenuta Donna Lavinia, a beautifully restored farmhouse, is used exclusively for events and celebrations. Weddings, communions, anniversaries, and parties are celebrated in the carefully restored farm buildings and gardens, which are landscaped with palms and flowers. In the center of the courtyard, the giant wood gears and stone wheels of the original olive-pressing centrifuge are now a dramatically lit sculpture. The baronial manor house—the old *frantoio*—can host up to 250 guests.

TENUTA DONNA LAVINIA, Vicinale Farucci, S.S.. 378, 70059 Trani (BA), tel. +39 0883 508 925, fax +39 0883 583 932, email contatti@tenutadonna lavinia.it, www.tenutadonnalavinia.it. Driving directions: from Bari, take highway S16 to Trani.

Castello Dentice di Frasso

San Vito dei Normanni is one of Puglia's most charming small towns, with a central piazza filled with chatting locals and hints of historic architecture. The town was constructed around the Castello Dentice di Frasso, one of the oldest castles in the province. Today, the castle has been carefully restored into an elegant structure where receptions can be held for up to 150 guests.

A Gothic arched *portone* (front gate), with massive double doors, opens into the castle courtyard. The ground level of the castle keep houses the family chapel, which was San Vito's first parochial church. Above the entranceway to the church, a heraldic seal carries the Dentice family motto *Noli me tangere* ("Let no one touch me"; a reference from the Bible) above a dentex fish.

The complex, once circled by a working moat, was restored during the last century at the request of Prince Luigi Dentice di Frasso. The castle has thirty rooms and halls, filled with antiques and heirlooms.

Two ground-floor halls, decorated with ceramic tiles from Vietri and frescoes on the ceilings, still carry the aspects of their former functions in the castle. *Fumer,* the smoking room, was created for court gentlemen to retire to after dinner to discuss politics over a cigar, while *delle Dame,* the women's hall, was used by the ladies for socializing. The gentlemen's hall features bookcases, mounted antlers, and leather chairs, while the ladies' hall has red velvet settees and china cabinets. Leading upstairs there is a *loggiato,* an arched, ivy-laden staircase that leads to a cross-vault covered loggia. In the castle courtyard, receptions for up to two hundred guests can be held under the stars.

CASTELLO DENTICE DI FRASSO, Via Crispi 6, 72019 San Vito dei Normanni (BR), tel. and fax +39 0831 951 459, email info@castellodenticedifrasso.it, www.castellodenticedifrasso.it. Driving directions: from Bari, take highway SS16 and exit at San Vito dei Normanni. Doubles from EE.

Castello Monaci

This massive, fortified castle, with its vine-covered watchtowers, dates to the fourteenth century. Records, still conserved in the castle library, suggest that the name *Castello Monaci* (monk's castle) derives from a group of monks from Cisternino, who came here after splitting from a congregation at Cluny. Once a place of refuge for those seeking protection and meditation for Christian pilgrims, now Castello Monaci is used exclusively for parties and receptions.

The castle is set in a verdant park filled with pines and palms. For receptions, umbrella tables can be set in front of the facade's battlements for guests to enjoy an aperitif. Inside the castle is filled with vast halls, which can accommodate small or large wedding parties. The Great Hall, paved with terra-cotta and topped by towering ceilings with heavy wood beams, is one of the most elegant spots for an indoor reception. Other halls have massive stone fireplaces and cross-vaulted ceilings. There is also a pool, and an enclosed courtyard filled with vines and palms, with a dramatic staircase perfect for staging photos.

To add to the romance, a room is available for the bride and groom to spend their first night together in the quiet of their very own castle.

CASTELLO MONACI, Contrada Castello Monaci, 73015 Salice Salentino (LE), tel. +39 0831 666 071, fax +39 0831 665 804, www.castellomonaci.com. Driving directions: From Brindisi, take highway SS7 to Mesagne, connect to the SS605 and continue to Salice Salentino. Follow the road that leads to Manduria; the castle is between Guagnano and San Pancrazio.

Practical Information—Puglia

GETTING THERE

By air: Two major airports have daily flights that connect Puglia to other major Italian cities. Bari Palese (airport code BRI) has connections from both of Milan's airports and airports in Verona, Venice, Torino, and Rome. Brindisi Casale (airport code BDS) has connecting flights from Rome and Milan. Schedules and flight information are available at www.seap-puglia.it.

By car: Highway A14 connects Foggia, Bari, and Taranto. Highway A16 connects Naples to Bari.

By train: Most cities in Puglia are connected by rail lines managed by the Ferrovie Sud Est or FSE. Schedules and station information are available through their website at www.ditutto.it/fse/.

When to Go

Puglia has a typically Mediterranean climate with mild winters and warm dry summers. The area is particularly beautiful to visit beginning in late April when much of the countryside is green and in full bloom. High season runs from late June through the end of August, when visitors arrive to take advantage of the peninsula's beaches.

Helpful Addresses

Official Tourist Information Offices and Websites

APT—Azienda di Promozione Turistica (Tourist Promotion Agency)

IAT—Ufficio Informazione e di Accoglienza Turistica (Tourist Information and Hospitality Office)

ALBEROBELLO: I.A.T. Piazza Ferdinando IV, tel. +39 080 432 5171.

BARI: I.A.T. Piazza Moro 32/A, tel. +39 080 5242361, fax +39 080 524 2329, email aptbari@pugliaturismo.com.

BRINDISI: A.P.T. Via C. Colombo 88, tel. +39 0831 562 126, email aptbrindisi@pugliaturismo.com.

FASANO: I.A.T. Piazza Ciaia 10, tel. +39 080 441 3086.

MARTINA FRANCA: I.A.T. Piazza Roma 37, tel. +39 080 480 5702, email martinafranca@pugliaturismo.com.

OSTUNI: I.A.T. Corso Mazzini 6, tel. +39 0831 301 268.

TARANTO: I.A.T. Corso Umberto 113, tel. +39 099 453 2392, email apttaranto@pugliaturismo.com.

Tourism Websites

PUGLIA TURISMO: www.pugliaturismo.com, available in English. Links to the five regional APT tourist sites (Azienda di Promozione Turistica), information on events, and Puglia's castles.

ITINERAWEB—LA PUGLIA IN RETE: www.itineraweb.com, available in English. Information and descriptions of traditional events, street markets schedules, concerts, itineraries, and gastronomy.

SICILY, SARDINIA, AND THE AEOLIAN ISLANDS

Italy's island destinations are rich in natural beauty and distinctive cultures. The two largest offshore islands, Sicily and Sardinia, offer a unique blend of Mediterranean architecture, language, and cuisine. And for those who long to find a remote getaway with Italian flavor there are the tiny Lipari Islands, just off Sicily's north coast.

Straddling the waters that separate Italy from North Africa, Sicily is a fiery combination of landscape and culture. Sicily's monuments, from the Greek temples in Agrigento to Palermo's Moorish shrines, are a testament to the many conquerors who have arrived on its shores. An inimitable

spirit is displayed in the island's many religious festivals, which are carried out with plenty of Sicilian drama and fervor.

Sardinia, to the west of the peninsula, possesses some of the Mediterranean's most alluring coastline with crystal clear water, secluded coves, and pristine beaches. The island's interior is wild and arid with desert-like summer temperatures and mysterious prehistoric ruins. On the island's eastern coast, the Costa Esmeralda has been a favored destination of Europe's rich and famous since it was first developed in the sixties.

Off Sicily's northeastern coast, the Lipari Islands are a beautiful volcanic archipelago. Sometimes referred to as the Aeolian Islands, they consist of seven rugged islands—Alicudi, Filicudi, Lipari, Panarea, Salina, Stromboli, and Vulcano—formed by active volcanos millions of years ago. The islands are characterized by deep caverns, steep cliffs, and sapphire blue waters, heated in some spots by underwater lava flows. Apart from a recent outburst in 2002, the island's volcanic activity is usually limited to an occasional plume of smoke, and one of the main tourist attractions is excursions to the craters.

Accommodations on the islands range from lavish palaces built during the reign of the Kingdom of the Two Sicilies to beach resorts that rival St. Tropez for glitz and glamour. Romantics can go in search of Sardinian wedding rings, attend one of Sicily's flower-filled festivals, or simply bask in the sun.

Accommodations in Sicilian Baroque Palaces

CATANIA

Palazzo Biscari

After a devastating earthquake in 1693 razed most of Catania's medieval buildings, the town's leaders began an ambitious reconstruction project. The rebuilding of Catania coincided with the peak of the baroque movement in Italy, and today Catania's major monuments are among the most noteworthy examples of the style's expression.

One of the grandest examples is the Palazzo Biscari, commissioned by Ignazio III, the Prince Paternò Biscari, in the eighteenth century. The palace took over a century to complete and involved many architects and artisans in its construction. One of its most striking features is a seaside facade completely covered with sculpted figures. Along the surface, winged *putti* carry fruit baskets, flit near robed goddesses, and busy themselves with festooning the window ledges with garlands. This riot of phantasmagorical imagery was intended to impress visitors as they arrived from the sea. Inside the palace, the halls are paved with polished majolica floors, and the lavishly decorated ceilings look like butterfly wings.

The palace's most impressive room (of the more than six hundred) is the *salone*, designed for grand galas. Shaped like an elongated oval, it is crowned by an elaborately painted ceiling depicting mythological figures at play among the clouds. The decoration almost succeeds in disguising the musician's gallery, where the orchestra would be secreted for parties.

The palace is still owned by the original prince's descendants, and its rooms are often used for spectacular balls and events. The family also rents out a single sumptuous apartment where, for a night, you too can live like Sicilian royalty.

PALAZZO BISCARI, Via Museo Biscari 10-16, 95131 Catania (CT), tel. + 39 095 715 2508, fax +39 095 321 818, email info@palazzobiscari.com, www.palazzobiscari.com. Driving directions from Taormina: take the S114 south and exit at Catania. Driving directions from Siracusa: take the S114 north and exit at Catania. One apartment, doubles from EEEEE.

Accommodations in Island Getaways

SARDEGNA—PORTO CERVO

Cala di Volpe

The Costa Esmeralda along Sardinia's northern coast boasts miles of emerald waters and fine sand beaches. Since its development in the sixties, it has drawn glitterati from all over Europe. Film stars, royals, and wealthy business magnates arrive in luxury yachts from Monaco and St. Tropez to frolic along this exclusive stretch of coastline.

Since it first opened in the sixties, the Cala di Volpe in Porto Cervo has been a mecca for luxury travelers. The hotel was designed by architect Jacques Couelle to resemble an old fishing village, and its appearance takes cues from ancient Sardinian architecture. The hotel is a rambling collection of towers, archways, and terraces with an irregular roofline immersed in the natural landscape of rosemary bushes and rockroses.

The hotel's interiors have a timeless sixties appeal, with primary colors punctuating whitewashed spaces. Guest rooms are spread throughout the hotel-village, all with panoramic views. Each room is individually decorated with an eclectic mix of luxury furnishings and artworks.

The hotel features five-star luxury amenities and services. You can swim in the Olympic-size swimming pool or relax on your own private deck chair while your every whim is catered to. The hotel has multiple restaurants (including a piano bar you may recognize from the James Bond movie *The Spy Who Loved Me*), tennis courts, and its own putting green.

CALA DEL VOLPE, Località Cala del Volpe, 07020 Porto Cervo (SS), Costa Esmeralda, Sardegna, tel. +39 0789 976 111, fax +39 0789 976 617, www.starwood.com. Driving directions from Olbia: take the S125 to Porto Cervo. One hundred twenty-three rooms; doubles from EEEE to EEEEE.

SARDEGNA—ALGHERO

Villa Las Tronas

Along Sardinia's northwest coast, the city of Alghero was occupied by Spain in the fourteenth century and still bears traces of its Catalan roots today. Settlers from Catalan left their mark on the city by filling it with Aragonese palaces and Spanish-Gothic churches. The city has a rich texture of Spanish, Italian, and Sardinian cultural influences, making it one of the most interesting places to visit on the island.

On its own secluded peninsula at the edges of town, the Villa Las Tronas was once a summer residence for Italian royalty. The castle-like villa was passionately restored by its current owners, who have filled it with their own personal collection of precious antiques. The result is a patrician style hotel with the feeling of a private residence. It sits on its own rocky point, surrounded on three sides by crystalline seas. The side away from the sea is filled with large gardens, making the hotel a quiet oasis.

Guest rooms have breathtaking sea views or views of the park; some even have their own private balconies. The rooms have elegant antique bed frames, white walls, and cool tile floors, and the renovated bathrooms are spacious, with modern fixtures. For relaxing, the hotel has a comfortable bar and restaurant with sea views. At the farthest reach of the point, the villa's seawater pool beckons, but you also have the option of swimming in Alghero's pristine bay, where you will find some of Europe's best snorkeling and scuba diving. The hotel offers bicycles for excursions and equipment for fishing the coastal waters.

VILLA LAS TRONAS, Lungomare Valencia 1, 07041 Alghero (SS), tel. +39 079 981 818, fax +39 079 981 044, www.hotelvillalastronas.it. Driving directions from Alghero Airport: following signs to Alghero "centro." When you reach Alghero, continue following indications for the center and the port. At the traffic lights, turn left on to Via Lido. Just past the harbor, bear to the left, keeping the gas station on your left, then stay to the right of the first and second stone towers. This road will bring you into Piazza Sulis. Drive through the piazza and then bear right, following signs for Bosa. As you turn the corner, you will see the hotel ahead of you. Twenty-nine rooms; doubles from EE to EEEE.

SARDEGNA—PULA, CAGLIARI

Is Morus

Immersed in its own pine woods by the seaside, the Is Morus hotel is a secluded spot just southwest of Cagliari, with sixteen villas sheltered in a seventeen-acre park. All are a short stroll from the hotel's private beaches, where you can relax under the shade of a thatched umbrella or swim in the sapphire-blue Mediterranean. Throughout the park there are shady paths and secluded spots to sit with a good book or to have a quiet conversation. The hotel's style is Mediterranean, with whitewashed walls, red tiled roofs, and a lush landscape filled with draping bougainvillea and tiled fountains. The accommodations are spaced throughout the property to give guests the utmost privacy during their stay. Guest rooms are furnished with antiques, beds with wrought-iron frames, and cool tiled floors. From the rooms, large doors open to covered terraces filled with comfortable bamboo settees with loose cotton cushions. You can enjoy classic regional seafood dishes in the hotel's own open-air restaurant with a view of the sea.

Is Morus Relais, Località Santa Margherita di Pula, SS195 km 37,400, 09010 Pula (CA) Sardegna, tel. +39 070 921 171, fax +39 070 921 596, www.ismorus.it. Driving directions: from Cagliari, take state highway S195 to Pula. Closed from November to April. Eighty-five rooms; doubles from EE to EEEEE.

ISOLE EOLIE

Hotel Raya

On Panarea, the smallest of the Aeolian Islands islands, is the secluded Hotel Raya. The trip from the Sicilian coast takes two hours; once you arrive, you'll feel completely insulated from the stress of city life. The hotel resembles a small cliffside village in stark white and terra-cotta, a sharp contrast against the bright blue of the skyline. The rooms look out at tiny uninhabited islets near the shore and Stromboli's smoking stack across the water.

The hotel was founded as an escape from civilization for a well-traveled Italian couple in the 1960s. Over time, it has grown into one of the most fashionable getaways for those seeking nothing but perfect views, sun-drenched spaces, and crystal clear water for swimming, snorkeling, and diving.

Each room has its own terrace and all are furnished in a modern minimalist style with crisp white linens and a spare use of dark hardwood accents. When you aren't in the water, stretch out and relax on a lounge chair on one of the bougainvillea-covered terrace. The hotel has a romantic lantern-lit terrace restaurant; you can also wander down into the charming village of Panarea to one of the local trattorias.

HOTEL RAYA, Via San Pietro, 98050 Panarea (ME), Isole Eolie, tel. +39 090 983 013, email info@hotelraya.it, www.hotelraya.it. SNAV hydrofoils for the Isole Eolie depart from Palermo, Milazzo, and Messina. For schedules, see www.snavali.com. Thirty rooms; doubles from EE to EEEE.

Tables for Two in Sicilia

CATANIA

Cantine del Cugno Mezzano

The phantasmagorical baroque decorations of Palazzo Biscari are among the crowning achievements of the style's expression on Sicily. Ignazio Paternò, the prince of Biscari, wanted his palace to be heavily embellished so that anyone arriving by sea could admire its magnificence. Today the palace is available for special events and has a sumptuous independent apartment to rent (see page 352).

The Cantine del Cugno Mezzano, named after a baron who once lived in the palace, is located on the palace's ground floor in what were once the prince's stables. The restaurant and wine bar feature seasonal dishes paired with an excellent wine selection. In warm weather, you can plan a candlelit dinner in the small palace courtyard and dine on well-prepared dishes like spicy octopus stewed with cinnamon or risotto with almonds and goat cheese.

CANTINE DEL CUGNO MEZZANO (Palazzo Biscari), Via Museo Biscari 8, 94124 Catania (CT), tel. +39 095 715 8710 fax +39 095 715 8710, www.cugnomezzano.it. Driving directions from Taormina: take the S114 south and exit at Catania. Driving directions from Siracusa: take the S114 north and exit at Catania. Closed on Sundays and Mondays at lunch and for holidays from August 10 to 28. Between May 15 and October 15, the restaurant is open only in the evenings. Cost: E.

Osteria i Tre Bicchieri

Chef Carmine Iaquinangelo and his team of able chefs bring a high level of artistry to the seasonal menu at this highly rated Catania establishment. The dining room, with its soft lighting and patrician furnishings, is a romantic spot to share a candlelit dinner for two. The cellar features over one thousand international labels, and an amiable sommelier is always on hand to assist you in matching wines to your selections. After dinner, cigar aficionados can relax in a comfortable leather chair in the smoking room.

The restaurant also has a casual *enoteca* (wine bar) where you can sample small plates and taste wines from the restaurant's cellar. The bar also has an extensive selection of spirits and hosts live jazz on Thursday evenings.

OSTERIA I TRE BICCHIERI, Via San Giuseppe al Duomo 31, 94124 Catania (CT), tel. +39 095 715 3540, fax +39 095 250 0712, www.osteriaitre bicchieri.it. Driving directions from Taormina: take the S114 south and exit at Catania. Driving directions from Siracusa: take the S114 north and exit at Catania. Closed on Sundays, on Mondays at lunch, and for holidays in August. Fifty seats; reservations recommended. Cost: EEE.

La Siciliana

La Siciliana is a family restaurant that first opened in 1968. Set in a nineteenth-century villa, the restaurant's appearance is that of a rustic country bungalow in an oasis under the palms. The atmosphere is warm and inviting, and the food is a simple, straightforward selection of Sicilian dishes. This is a great place to try local favorites like *neonata* (tiny "newly born" fish) served either in a gratin or as a light *frittelle* (fritter) or *ripiddu nivicatu*—a risotto made with cuttlefish ink and fresh ricotta cheese. The menu also includes hearty meat dishes like *stinco di maiale* (roast pork shank). The desserts are all fresh and made in-house. La Siciliana is a member of the Ristoranti di Buon Ricordo, so if you sample their specialty, *calamari ripieni alla griglia* (grilled stuffed calamari), you'll receive a commemorative plate.

LA SICILIANA, Viale Marco Polo 52/a, 95126 Catania (CT), tel. +39 095 376 400, fax +39 095 722 1300. www.lasiciliana.it. Driving directions from Taormina: take the S114 south and exit at Catania. Driving directions from Siracusa: take the S114 north and exit at Catania. Closed Sunday evenings and Mondays, and for holidays the month of January. Ninety seats; reservations recommended. Cost: EE.

MILAZZO

Piccolo Casale

In the heart of the city of Milazzo, in a historic palace that was once the residence of General Zirilli (a personality from the era of Garibaldi), the Piccolo Casale is a warm and welcoming spot to share a dinner for two. A simple and elegant ambience is created with white tablecloths, vaulted ceilings, terra-cotta tile, and iron chandeliers. There is also an outdoor terrace for warm-weather dining. You can start with swordfish marinated in fine herbs or tuna in mint with eggplant, then try a fresh pasta dish like linguine with prawns, artichokes, and asparagus. Main courses include a selection of fresh fish or meat dishes like beef fillet in rosemary and roasted leg of lamb. The desserts follow Sicilian traditions, highlighting ingredients like almonds, citrus, and fresh ricotta. There is an excellent choice of Sicilian wines and many labels from the peninsula.

PICCOLO CASALE, Via R. d'Amico 12, 98057 Milazzo (ME), tel. +39 090 922 4479, email piccolocasale@tiscalinet.it. Driving directions from Messina: take the S113 west and exit at Milazzo. Sixty seats; reservations recommended. Cost: EE.

MODICA

Fattoria delle Torri

Modica is one of the picturesque cities near Ragusa whose center was almost entirely rebuilt in baroque style after the earthquake of 1693. The city is divided into Modica Alta (Upper), where buildings scale the city's hillside, and Modica Bassa (Lower), spread across the valley below.

This highly rated restaurant, directed by chef Giuseppe Barone, is set in a diminutive eighteenth-century palazzo in Modica Bassa. Its two elegant dining rooms have airy vaulted ceilings and tables carefully laid with fine crystal and porcelain. The innovative cuisine includes combinations like risotto with pigeon and dates or ravioli made with snails and summer truffles. The wine list is a well-researched collection of some of the finest Sicilian labels, as well as excellent wines from Tuscany and Piedmont.

> Fattoria delle Torri, Vico Napolitano 14, 97015 Modica (RG), tel. +39 0923 751 286. Driving directions from Ragusa: take the S115 highway south and exit at Modica. Closed on Mondays and the first week in July. Forty-five seats; reservations recommended. Cost: EE.

RAGUSA IBLA

Locanda Don Serafino

Set in what were once the stables of a noble palace, Locanda Don Serafino is elegant and refined. The renovated dining room makes use of the old palace's architectural elements with exposed masonry, white vaulted ceilings, and illuminated niches creating an old-world ambience. The menu is centered around fresh fish brought in each day from Donnalucata on the southern coast. Starters include fresh tuna in balsamic, and fried fish with pistachios. Pastas include linguine with swordfish, eggplant, and baby fennel, or *tagliolini* with lamb ragout. For a main course, try sea bream with potatoes and Salina capers or the specialty of the house: *zuppa di pesce* (fish stew). The wine list includes four hundred prestigious labels and an excellent selection of dessert wines.

> Locanda Don Serafino, Via Orfanotrofio 39, 97100 Ragusa Ibla (RG), tel. +39 0932 248 778, www.locandadonserafino.it. Driving directions: the S115 highway arrives from the east and west into Ragusa. Once in town, follow indications for Ragusa Ibla (Old Ragusa). Closed on Tuesdays. Ninety seats; reservations recommended. Cost: E.

Duomo

Among the baroque palaces of Ragusa Ibla, La Rocca of Santippolito, near the Duomo, stands out as one of the more beautiful. Its facade is decorated with eight balconies, each uniquely embellished with baroque motifs ranging from cherubs to musical instruments. Between balconies decorated with mandolins and flute players is the Duomo restaurant.

Chef Ciccio Sultano proposes a menu of creative dishes like foie gras marinated in Pantelleria passito and served with prickly pears in an Inzolia wine reduction, black spaghetti with shellfish sauce and red pepper mousse, veal medallions filled with caciocavallo cheese, or venison cutlets with Savoy cabbage and *lardo di Colonnata* (cured pork fatback). Desserts include ricotta tart with candied yellow squash and coffee ganache, or the chef's own take on the classic ricotta-filled cannoli. The wine list is well researched, with an emphasis on rare dessert wines.

DUOMO, Via Capitano Bocchieri 31, 97100 Ragusa Ibla (RG), tel. +39 0932 651 265. Driving directions: the S115 highway arrives from the east and west into Ragusa. Once in town, follow indications for Ragusa Ibla (Old Ragusa). Closed on Mondays. Fifty seats; reservations essential. Cost: EE.

TAORMINA

Casa Grugno

The Grugno family arrived in Taormina from Spain during the era of Frederick II (1198-1250). The restaurant that bears their name, Casa Grugno, is situated in one of the medieval city's Gothic-Catalan residences. The beautifully appointed dining room features dramatic Gothic vaults, high-backed chairs, and candlelit tables. The cooking style espoused by Casa Grugno marries tradition with innovation. Chef Andreas Zangerl, an Austrian by birth, proposes a menu he describes as a fusion of light Mediterranean flavors. Pastas are all made on the premises, and breads are fashioned from a variety of hand-milled flours. Dishes include fresh raw fish appetizers and opulent main courses like a fillet of beef glazed in Nero d'Avola wine and served with foie gras. The international wine list is ample and includes many of Italy's best wines as well as a wide selection of spirits.

Casa Grugno, Via Santa Maria dei Greci, 98039 Taormina (ME), tel. +39 0942 212 08, www.casagrugno.it. Driving directions from Messina: take highway A18 south and exit at Taormina. Closed on Wednesdays, and for vacation the month of February. Thirty-six seats; reservations essential. Cost: EEE.

SIRACUSA

Jonico 'a Rutta' e Ciauli

This restaurant, in an early twentieth-century seaside villa, has a warm summer terrace overlooking the water. The atmosphere is warm and welcoming, and the service is friendly. The cooking is classically Sicilian, highlighting fresh seafood. You can try favorites like stewed octopus, gilthead bream in orange sauce, and grouper with tomato, onions, and almonds. Desserts include traditional Sicilian cannoli and sweets made from almonds. The cantina has a selection of Sicilian wines as well as carefully chosen grappas.

JONICO 'A RUTTA' E CIAULI, Riviera d'Ionisio il Grande 194, Quartiere Acradina, 96100 Siracusa (SR), tel. +39 0931 655 40. Closed on Tuesdays, and for holidays on Christmas, New Year's, and Easter, and during the month of August. One hundred eighty seats; reservations recommended. Cost: EE.

Watching the Sunset

SICILIA

Sunset from Mt. Etna's Summit

Mount Etna is a living symbol of everything Sicily stands for: fiery, dramatic, and strangely beautiful. The ancient Greeks dubbed the mountain "Vulcan's Forge," and thousands of years later it is still smoking and burning, with glowing lava flows and steaming crevices. As long as you visit during a time when Etna's volcanic activity is quiet, you can catch some of the mountain's drama, along with a sunset, from one of her summits. There are many ways to approach a climb of the mountain. The park authority suggests itineraries for a variety of levels, from casual walks to hikes for serious enthusiasts. A seventy-mile railway, which departs from Catania, circles the mountain and offers a relaxing alternative to braving the primordial trails across the lava flow.

Parco dell'Etna, the official website for the national park, offers ideas for multiday itineraries for exploring Etna. You can also contact the park authority for weather conditions and volcanic activity levels. The Parco dell'Etna visitor's center is located in Fornazzo, on the eastern side of the mountain. www.parks.it/parco.etna/.

The official website for the Circumetnae railroad (www.circumetnea.it) posts rates, timetables, and photos of views from the electric train.

Romantic Lore and Local Festivals
SICILIA

Festa delle Milizie (Militia Festival)—Scicli

A medieval battle fought between Christians and Muslims in 1091 is reenacted each year at the end of May in the main square of Scicli, fourteen miles south of Ragusa. The centerpiece of the festival is a full-scale baroque statue depicting the Madonna as a warrior on horseback. She is paraded through the streets atop a mound of fresh roses, and the streets are filled with figural lights shaped like baroque chandeliers and candelabras.

Costumed participants dress as both sides of the historic battle: Saracens in scarves and scimitars and Normans in chain mail and sabers. The *Festa delle Milizie* commemorates the victory of Christian troops led by King Ruggero over Saracen soldiers led by the Emir Belkar. According to legend, the apparition of a Madonna warrior on horseback ensured victory for the Christians. The festivities include a reenactment of the battle, a horse race, and processions through the streets of Scicli. For more information, contact the Comune di Scicli, Via F. Mormino Penna 2, 97018 Scicli (RG), tel. +39 0932 839 111, email comune.scicli@tiscali.it.

Inforiata (The Flowering)—Noto

Noto is one of Sicily's most baroque towns. After the earthquake of 1693, the entire city was rebuilt with the local honey-colored tufa stone. Each year in late May, the streets are paved with flower-petal carpets for the festival of the *Infiorata*. Thousands of multicolored petals are used to create religious, mythological, and social artworks. Local artists work through the night to lay the floral paintings, which stretch through some of Noto's prettiest baroque streets. For more information, see www.infioratadinoto.it.

Candlemas Festival of Saint Agatha—Catania

One of Sicily's most baroque festivals is the early February celebration in Catania of Candlemas. Held in conjunction with the feast of Saint Agatha, the city's patron saint, it draws thousands of devotees from all over Sicily. Elaborately decorated *candelore* (blessed Candlemas candelabras) and a silver bedecked Madonna are carried in processions through the city streets. The eleven *candelore* represent the city's ancient guilds and date back to the Swabian reign of Sicily. Fishmongers, vintners, floriculturists, grocers, butchers, and bakers are among those represented. Each *candelore* is decorated with images of the saints, griffins, flowers, and rococo flourishes.

The festival has been celebrated for five centuries and includes three days of cult devotion, folklore, and traditional displays in the streets. The first day, February 3, begins with solemn processions and ends with fireworks displays in the Piazza Duomo. On February 4 and 5, effigies of Saint Agatha are carried throughout the city's districts. For more information, contact Catania's tourist office: APT, Via Cimarosa 10, 95124 Catania, tel. +39 095 730 6211.

Palio dei Normanni (Palio of the Normans)—Piazza Armerina

This annual historic festival in Piazza Armerina commemorates the eleventh-century Norman conquest of Sicily. The Palio dei Normanni (Palio of the Normans) is played in honor of the city's patron, the Madonna of the Victories. Teams participate in a contest of skill for a sacred banner, which was presented to Conte Ruggero d'Altavilla by the pope in 1060. The banner became the victory sign for the count's successful liberation of Sicily from Saracen domination. The festival commemorates the various phases of the count's arrival in the ancient city. The first day, a historic procession commemorates the arrival of the Norman troops and the ceremonial offering of the keys to the city to Conte Ruggero. The next day the Palio, or Quintana, is played, a contest between four teams of five riders in period costumes who represent the ancient divisions of old Plutia (Piazza Armerina). The festival is held each year on August 13 and 14. For more information, see www.piazza-armerina.it.

SARDEGNA

Matrimonio Selargino—Selargino Wedding

Each year in the middle of September, the community of Selargino, ten kilometers northeast of Cagliari on Sardinia, revives ancient traditions with the Matrimonio Selargino (Selargino Wedding). An elaborate wedding is staged in the town, with an elaborately costumed bride and groom and a processional of *traccas* (decorated carts) through the streets as musicians play *launeddas* (traditional reed flutes).

The wedding rite begins with a ceremonial blessing of the couple by their parents, who sprinkle their heads with corn and salt while wishing them prosperity and high moral standards. Then the couple and their entourage make a procession to the church courtyard. Along the way, village women holding plates of corn and salt recite blessings and give the couple more wishes and advice. After the couple has passed, the women drop the plates onto the pavement, breaking them to guarantee a fertile union for the betrothed. At the church, the wedding, in Sardinian dialect, is celebrated before a costumed crowd. The bride and groom are bound to one another with a *sa cadena* (silver chain), a symbol of the everlasting bonds of matrimony. The couple leaves the church to applause, their mothers give them one last blessing: *"Potzàis bivi medas annus con saludi e trigu"* (live long in good health and prosperity), and the banquet (called *su combidu*) begins, with dancing into the night. For additional information, contact Cagliari's provincial tourist office: EPT - Ente Provinciale per il Turismo, email ept.cagliari@regione.sardegna.it.

Picnic Spots

SICILIA

Palermo's Gardens

Palermo, on Sicily's north coast, has three beautiful Mediterranean gardens where you can have a quiet picnic in the midst of this busy city. The Giardino Inglese, reached from Via Libertà, is filled with rare examples of tropical and subtropical plants and is divided into large greenery-filled areas by wide promenades.

The Garibaldi Garden (Giardino Garibaldi), named for Italy's Risorgimento hero, is found in Piazza Marina in the historic center. Among the park's magnificent examples of *Ficus magnolioides* you will find busts of Garibaldi's generals (Rosolino Pilo, Giovanni Corrao, Raffaele De Benedetto, and Luigi Tukori).

Along the waterfront and just next to the botanical gardens, Villa Giulia's gardens are planted in neoclassical Italianate style with geometric ornamental arrangements. Palermo's first public garden, it was designed by Nicolò Palma in 1777. The villa and garden are named after Giulia Guevara, the wife of Palermo's Spanish viceroy at the time the garden was built. Fountains and statuary fill the garden, and paths intersect at a central fountain, where a cherub plays with timepieces representing the solar system's celestial phases.

Il Giardino Ibleo—Ragusa Ibla

At the edge of old Ragusa in Sicily, the Giardino Ibleo is a pretty park with a palm-lined *viale* and hedged gardens. Built in 1858 for local nobles, it has a dramatic promenade that overlooks the Valle dell'Irminio. Throughout the park are quiet marble benches where you can sit and enjoy a picnic for two. Afterward, you can visit the park's surrounding monuments: the baroque churches of San Vincenzo Ferreri, San Giacomo, and dei Cappuccini.

Romantic Excursions

SICILIA

Il Fango di Vulcano—Vulcan's Mud Baths

The ancients believed that the island of Vulcano was home to Vulcan, the god of fire, who guarded the entrance to Hades. A visit to the island's Laghetto di Fanghi (mud baths) might convince you that those ancient ideas had some merit. The thermal springs that warm the mud emit a pungent, otherworldly aroma, and in some places the heat can reach a scalding boil. Despite this, tourists have come here for years to seek out the mud's therapeutic properties, which are claimed to heal a variety of ailments. After braving the sulfur-colored mud, visitors rinse off in the nearby bubbling sea water, which is heated by underwater lava flows.

Vulcano is ten minutes by boat from Lipari, the largest of the Aeolian Islands. Hydrofoils also connect the island with the Sicilian mainland. The SNAV hydrofoil service links Milazzo, Messina, and Palermo with the Aeolian Islands. For schedules, see their website at www.snavali.com or call +39 081 761 2348.

SARDEGNA

La Fede Sarda—Sardinian Wedding Rings

Sardinian goldsmiths are renowned for their fine, filigreed decorations in which golden threads are intertwined like lace. Much of the traditional jewelry they produce relates back to ancient talismans worn to promote fertility or to ward away the *malocchio* (evil eye). The most famous of the traditional pieces is the Fede Sarda, the traditional Sardinian wedding band, made from intense yellow gold. The rings are fashioned in various filigreed configurations and are covered with tiny pinpoint golden beads arranged like grape bunches. You will find talented goldsmiths all over the island, especially in Alghero near Sassari, Quartu Sant'Elena outside Cagliari, and Dorgali in the province of Nuoro.

LOREDANA MANDAS, Via Sicilia 3, Cagliari (Ca), makes traditional jewelry using gold filigree, pearls, and semiprecious stones.

Aniello De Filippis via Roma 41/43, Alghero (SS), fashions jewels that incorporate local coral, an art form famous in Alghero.

At Pietro Angelo Fiorino you will find traditionally styled jewelry in gold and silver with semiprecious stones and seed pearls. Pietro Angelo Fiorino via Principe di Piemonte 8/10, Sassari (SS), tel. +39 079 234 687, www.ilfiorino.it.

Creazioni Antonello, Via Malta 13, 08100 Nuoro, tel. +39 0784 390 08, offers handmade rings, earrings, and necklaces fashioned with traditional methods.

The jewelry at goldsmith Paola Asquer seems to be inspired by ancient Phoenician relics. Paola Asquer, Via Sidney Sonnino 30, 09125 Cagliari, tel. +39 070 663 563.

Weddings in Sicily

Sicilian baroque palaces, built for seventeenth- and eighteenth-century princes and nobility, have their own distinctive style. They are characterized by imaginative, dramatic sculpted figures in high relief, varied textures in stone and marble, and palatial scale.

The devastating earthquake of 1683, which razed the medieval centers of many of Sicily's eastern cities, ironically paved the way for the expression of the baroque style in Sicily. The cities of Siracusa, Noto, Modica, and Ragusa were all rebuilt in the baroque style, while in and around

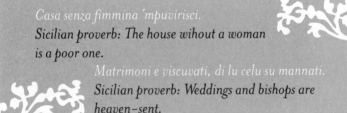

Casa senza fimmina 'mpuvirisci.
Sicilian proverb: The house wihout a woman is a poor one.

Matrimoni e viscuvati, di lu celu su mannati.
Sicilian proverb: Weddings and bishops are heaven-sent.

Palermo an increasingly wealthy upper class remodeled their existing palaces in the new style.

Sicilian baroque palaces drip with drama and decoration, designed as they were to impress and entertain illustrious visitors. Teams of skilled artisans were used to inlay marble floors, sculpt relief panels and statuary, gild frames and doorways, weave silk for brocades, and fresco and paint. The palaces were designed to accommodate the lifestyles of Sicily's aristocratic class, with grand ballrooms for hosting parties and hidden galleries for chamber musicians.

Today, many of the palaces remain in the hands of the original noble families who first commissioned them. For those planning weddings in Sicily, they offer an opulent setting for large events.

CEREMONY AND RECEPTION LOCATIONS

Palazzo Butera

Palermo's Butera palace began its life as a humble block of tenement houses. In 1692, the massive group of buildings was acquired by the Branciforte dukes, who transformed them into one of the city's grandest palaces. In the early eighteenth century, the palace passed to the princes of Butera, who transformed the existing residence into a fanciful baroque palace. The princes brought in decorators and designers from all over Italy to fill the palace rooms with sculpted marble figures, delicate intaglio, and dramatically painted frescos.

Today, the well-preserved baroque palace is often used as a venue for fashion shows or as a film set—*The Godfather III* was filmed in part of the palace. The balance of the time, grand galas and wedding receptions are hosted inside its elegant halls.

For modern events at the palace, guests arrive at the regal entrance along Via Butera. They are greeted by the *androne*, an elegant covered reception hall, where carriages once delivered guests into the palace. Invitees, now as then, enter the palace and climb the polished red marble staircase to the main floor. The first of the palace's princely halls to greet visitors is the Galleria. Fifteen French doors line one side of the room, each grand doorway surmounted with heraldic paintings that illustrate former feudal holdings of the Branciforte dukes; the rest of the room is decorated with large ancestral portraits. The doors open onto the palace's most spectacular feature: a green-and-white paved terrace that spans the entire length of the palace, with a view of Palermo's sea promenade. Parties for as many as seven hundred guests are often held here.

After passing through the gallery, visitors reach a succession of halls, each named for its decor and decorated with finely carved fireplaces and richly brocaded walls. Following the baroque theme, allegorical frescoes feature gods and goddesses, such as Apollo and Diana the huntress. The largest of the halls, Sala Dorata (gilded hall) and the Salone Rossa (red room), have always been used for the palace's richest parties and entertainments. The gilded walls of the Dorata are complemented by sconces and crystal chandeliers, while the Salone Rossa has frescoes that depict the Four Seasons.

PALAZZO BUTERA, Via Butera 8/18, 90133 Palermo (PA), tel. +39 091 611 0162, email palazzobutera@libero.it, www.palazzobutera.com. Reception capacity ranges from seventy-two to seven hundred guests. Cost: EE to EEE.

Villa Chiaramonte Bordonaro

North of Palermo's city center, at the foot of Mount Pellegrino, the Parco della Favorita was created as a hunting ground for King Ferdinand, for his entertainment during his exile in Sicily. His monumental villa at the center of the park drew the attention of the best of Sicilian society; they followed suit by building their own summer palaces in close proximity to the King's estate. Today, the immense royal park they created extends to almost one thousand acres, and it is still a natural setting in Palermo, filled with a mixture of typical Mediterranean trees including olives, carob, figs, palms, and cypress.

The king's villa and estate are still owned by his descendents, the barons of Chiaramonte Bordonaro. The king's former residence, Villa Bordonaro, is a monumental four-story home with richly decorated interiors. Just as in the days of Ferdinand's court, the villa continues to be used for palatial-style events. Its regal halls are embellished with gilded stuccos, Murano chandeliers, and dramatic staircases that provide an elegant backdrop for banquets and receptions.

The surrounding gardens, whose paths are shaded by blooming horse chestnut trees and citrus trees that perfume the air, are also used for outdoor receptions. Guests can stroll along the garden's romantic walks, lined with hawthorn hedges, statuary, and columns in neoclassical style, before they dine on Sicilian specialties under the stars. The enormous spaces of this former king's palace, both inside and out, are perfectly suited for large events.

VILLA CHIARAMONTE BORDONARO, Via delle Croci 7, 90139 Palermo (PA), tel. +39 091 328 505, email info@villabordonaro.it, www.villabordonaro.it. Sites for ceremonies and receptions include multiple halls that can accommodate up to four hundred guests, an outdoor terrace with room for two hundred, and a large courtyard with a central fountain with a capacity of over one thousand guests. Catering is managed on the premises. Reception capacity ranges from one hundred to one thousand guests. Cost: EE to EEE.

Palazzo Beneventano del Bosco

Palazzo Beneventano del Bosco is a monumental baroque palace in the heart of historic Syracuse. The palace was aquired by Baron Guglielmo Bosco in 1775. The baron's first move, after purchasing what was then a crumbling sixteenth-century palace, was to hire an acclaimed architect, Luciano Ali, to turn the former fortress into a sumptuous palace. When it was completed, the baron received such distingished guests as Admiral Horatio Nelson in 1798, and Ferdinand II, the king of the two Sicilies, in 1806.

The palace is one of Syracuse's landmark buildings; apart from hosting special events in its Grande Salone, it also hosts a musuem filled with rare maps and etchings. Its rooms are filled with baroque decorations that include frescos by the Palermo artist Ermenegildo Martorana and imported Venetian glass chandeliers and mirrors. The palace's central staircase is one of its most dramatic architectural features, with ramps lined with massive marble columns that rise to painted ceilings. The central courtyard is uniquely paved in round black and white stones, executed to look like a giant oriental carpet.

The palace shares Piazza Duomo with some of the most important landmarks in Syracuse: the duomo with its unique portals and statuary, and Syracuse's city hall.

PALAZZO BENEVENTANO DEL BOSCO, Piazza Duomo 23, 96100 Siracusa (SR), tel. +39 0931 464 079, fax +39 0931 464 079, email info@beneventanodelbosco.it, www.beneventanodelbosco.it.

Practical Information—Sicily

GETTING THERE

By air: Sicily has two major airports, Palermo—Falcone e Borsellino (airport code PMO) and Catania Fontanarossa (airport code CTA).

By car: Cars can be rented at both airports and in most major cities.

By train: Express rail service connects Milan and Rome with Palermo, Syracuse, and Catania. In Calabria, the rail cars are loaded onto a ferry and taken across the strait to Messina. Schedules and information are available on the official site for Italy's state railway at www.fs-on-line.com.

By boat: Hydrofoil and ferry service is available from Naples to Palermo. Tirrenia (www.gruppotirrenia.it) offers overnight car ferry service year round and from April to October, SNAV (www.snavali.com) operates daily hydrofoils and catamarans. Both services link Sicily's coastal cities with the Aeolian Islands, Ustica, and Pantelleria. Information about ferries can be found at www.traghetti.com.

WHEN TO GO

The best times of year to visit Sicily are in spring (April to May) and autumn (October to November). During these seasons, the scenery is beautiful, and the temperatures are warm and mild. Summer months are hot and dry, and high season begins in June and continues through August.

Official Tourist Information Offices and Websites

APT—Azienda di Promozione Turistica (Tourist Promotion Agency)

IAT—Ufficio Informazione e di Accoglienza Turistica (Tourist Information and Hospitality Office)

CATANIA: A.P.T. Via Cimarosa 10, tel. +39 095 730 6233, fax +39 095 730 622, email info@apt.catania.it, www.apt.catania.it.

MESSINA: A.P.T. Via Calabria Isolato 301 bis, tel. +39 090 640 22, fax +39 090 641 1047.

PALERMO: A.P.T. Villa Igiea - Salita Belmonte, tel. +39 091 540425, fax +39 091 637 5400, email info@aapit.pa.it, www.aapit.pa.it.

PALERMO: I.A.T. Stazione centrale FS, tel. +39 091 616 5914.

RAGUSA: A.P.T. Via Cap. Bocchieri 33 Palazzolo Rocca, tel. +39 0932 621 421, fax +39 0932 654 823, email info@ragusaturismo.com, www.ragusaturismo.com.

SIRACUSA: A.P.T. Via Maestranza 33, tel. +39 0931 652 01, fax +39 0931 464 255, email info@apt-siracusa.it, www.apt-siracusa.it.

Siracusa: I.A.T. Via Sebastiano 45, tel. +39 0931 677 10.

Practical Information—Sardinia

GETTING THERE

By air: Sardinia has three major airports. In the northwest part of the island connections are available to Alghero Fertilia (airport code AHO). In the south, connections are available to Cagliari-Elmas (airport code CAG), and on the eastern side of the islands flights are available to and from Olbia-Costa Smeralda (airport code OLB).

By car: Cars can be rented at the airports and in most major cities.

By train: Rail service connects Cagliari with Sardinia's major cities. Schedules and information are available on the official site for Italy's state railway at www.fs-on-line.com. The Trenino Verde (Green Line) is a tiny historic rail line that travels through much of Sardinia's most scenic country. For information see www.treninoverde.com.

By boat: Hydrofoil and ferry service is available from Genova, Civitavecchia, and Naples to Arbatax, Cagliari, and Olbia. Tirrenia (www.gruppotirrenia.it) offers overnight car ferry service year round. Information about ferries can be found at www.traghetti.com.

WHEN TO GO

Sardinia is one of the most popular summer destinations for vacationing Italians. Spring is a pleasant time to visit the island's archeological sites as during the summer months temperatures can reach 104°F. High season begins in June and continues through August.

HELPFUL ADDRESSES
Official Tourist Information Offices and Websites

IAT—Ufficio Informazione e di Accoglienza Turistica (Tourist Information and Hospitality Office)

A.A.S.T.—Azienda Autonoma di Soggiorno e Turismo (Autonomous Agency for Travel and Tourism)

CAGLIARI: I.A.T. Piazza Matteotti 9, tel. +39 070669255, fax +39 070664923.

ALGHERO: A.A.S.T. Piazza Porta Terra 9, tel. +39 079 979 054, fax +39 079 974 881.

OLBIA: A.A.S.T. Via Catello Piro 1, tel. +39 0789 214 53, fax +39 0789 222 21.

ARZACHENA—COSTA SMERALDA I.A.T. tel. +39 0789 214 53

Tourism Websites

SARDEGNA WEB: www.sardegnaweb.it, available in English, has information on the culture, gastronomy, and archeology of Sardegna.

PRACTICAL GUIDE TO PLANNING A WEDDING IN ITALY

Making Your Italian Wedding Legal

The first step to planning a wedding in Italy is to decide what type of ceremony you want: civil, religious, or ceremonial. Although many different kinds of wedding ceremonies are held in Italy, only two types of weddings are legally recognized: Catholic ceremonies performed in a church, and civil ceremonies performed in a city hall or city-sanctioned location. Non-Catholic religious ceremonies are not legally binding in Italy, so if you are planning a religious ceremony other than a Catholic one you will need to plan a civil ceremony as well. The simplest way to make sure your wedding will be legal at home is to have a civil ceremony in your local city hall in the United States, but then you will forego all the fun and adventure of the Italian bureaucratic system.

Civil ceremonies are performed either by the *ufficiale di stato civile* (civil registrar), the *sindaco* (mayor), or one of his assistants. Ceremonies are performed in Italian and usually last from fifteen to thirty minutes, and the officiant wears a tricolor sash in the colors of the Italian flag. The process for making a marriage legally binding in Italy involves specific bureaucratic steps that must be followed in sequence and within a prescribed time frame. First, the bride and groom must make a declaration that there is no impediment to the marriage. Second, a declaration of the intention to marry must be made in the city where the marriage will take place. Third, if either person is an Italian citizen or has resident status in Italy, banns (a public notice of the ceremony) must be posted in the town hall (this allows the townspeople to contest a pending marriage). Finally, the wedding can take place, either ten days after the banns have been posted, or when banns are not required, anytime after the sworn declarations are obtained. A translator must be present, and all documents must be translated into Italian.

If both of you are Catholic, church weddings in Italy's historic churches or an English service in Vatican City can be organized with the assistance of your parish priest. For Catholic weddings in Italy, you will need the name of the Italian parish priest in the town or church where the ceremony will be held. Have your priest make inquiries for you. Weddings at the Vatican can be organized by contacting Santa Susanna, the American Catholic church of Rome. Catholic weddings in Italy or the Vatican follow the rules of the Roman Catholic church: baptismal and confirmation certificates, and pre-cana instruction are required. Pre-cana marriage preparation usually includes sessions with a priest regarding the Catholic teachings on the sacrament of marriage. The churches mentioned in this book are popular locations for weddings, so it is a good idea to plan well enough ahead to make sure your preferred location is available.

In the largest cities there are wonderful non-Catholic religious centers like the synagogues of Venice and the Anglican, Episcopalian, and Greek Orthodox churches of Florence and Rome. Weddings held in these locations are considered ceremonial and are legally valid only when they are preceded or followed by a civil ceremony.

The villas, castles, and palaces in this guide also have wonderful gardens, country vistas, or interior halls that are lovely spots to stage a ceremony. Blessings held in these locations will need to be combined with a civil ceremony to be legally binding.

Generally, legally performed marriages in Italy will also be legally binding in the United States. To be certain of the validity and the requirements in your state, you should contact your state's attorney general. Make sure you are provided with copies of all the final paperwork before you leave Italy, as they will be important to validate your wedding in the United States.

Italian wedding planners can be extremely helpful and valuable in simplifying the legal process. For the most part, their rates for assistance are quite reasonable, and they can be well worth the investment. They can assist with the translation of all documents and scheduling all the appointments needed with city offices in Italy.

NINE TO TWELVE MONTHS BEFORE YOUR WEDDING

Reserve the site(s) for your ceremony and reception.

Make sure both you and your spouse-to-be have valid passports.

SIX MONTHS BEFORE YOUR WEDDING

Obtain copies of both of your birth certificates, and in the case of a prior marriage, any appropriate death or divorce certificates, and have them certified with Hague certifications. (Public records issued outside of Italy and intended for use in Italy must have a Hague certification, also referred to as an apostille seal. This form, affixed to the public record by the secretary of state, is an internationally recognized notary seal that confirms that the document has been issued in accordance with the Hague treaty. In most states, apostilles can be obtained by sending documents to the state's office of the secretary of state. When obtaining any required birth, death, or divorce documents, ask the issuing office for instructions and fees for obtaining an apostille, or contact your state's office of the secretary of state.)

Make a declaration of "no impediment" (atto notorio) to an Italian consular officer: (If you live in a state where there is an Italian consular office, you should complete this step before you leave the United States; otherwise, see instructions on page 380 for how to do this in Italy.) Make an appointment with your local Italian consulate to make a declaration, sworn to by four witnesses before an Italian consular officer, stating that according to the laws to which you and your fiancé are subject, there is no obstacle to either of you marrying. This document verifies that both parties are of a legal age and are legally free to marry. This document, along with your birth certificates and any necessary death or divorce certificates, will be translated into Italian and certified by the Italian consular officer.

ONCE YOU ARRIVE IN ITALY

Make a declaration of "no impediment" (*atto notorio*) in Italy: If you have not completed the *atto notario* in the United States, you will need to make an appointment to appear with two witnesses before the town clerk in the *ufficio atti notori* (notary's office) of the *pretura civile* (lower-court house). Knowledge of Italian will be helpful when you call this office. Prior to the appointment, two types of stamps must be purchased and brought to the appointment so that they can be attached to the *atto notorio*: a *marche per atti giudiziari* (administrative stamp) and a *marche madre-figlia*. Stamps can be purchased at a *tabaccaio* (tobacco shop). When you call the *pretura* to make your appointment, inquire as to the correct denominations for the stamps.

Make a declaration to an American consular officer (*nulla osta*): You will need to make another declaration, called a *nulla osta,* in front of an American consular officer stating that there are no obstacles to your marriage as defined under American laws. The *ufficio legalizzazioni* (legalization office) at the provincial *prefettura* (prefecture) must then authenticate the notarized signature of the consul, affixed to this document. A *marca da boll* (administrative fee stamp) may be required in some regions. Stamps can be purchased in a *tabaccaio* and presented to the clerk at the *ufficio legalizzazioni* for each document to be authenticated. This process shouldn't take more than an hour and can be done on a weekday morning once you arrive in Italy.

Make a declaration to the civil registrar (*ufficiale di stato civile*): Four days before your wedding date, you must appear in the civil registrar's office to make a declaration of your intention to marry. All documents should be presented at this time.

Post banns (*pubblicazioni*): If one of the parties is Italian or if the U.S. citizen is a resident of Italy, it is necessary for banns, or marriage announcements, to be posted at the local *comune* (city hall) for two consecutive Sundays before the marriage occurs. However, if neither party to the marriage is Italian and neither is residing in Italy, banns are usually waived by the *ufficiale di stato civile.*

Ceremony: Assuming no objections to the banns, the couple may be married in a civil or religious ceremony on the fourth day following the second Sunday on which the banns are posted (or any time after banns have been waived). The presence of a translator at the ceremony is required by law if neither party speaks Italian.

After the ceremony, the parish priest or civil servant presiding over the ceremony will send the license to the county registrar, where it will be entered into the public record, making the marriage official.

If you plan to have the marriage recognized in the United States, the marriage certificate should be taken to the *prefettura* at the *ufficio legalizzazioni* (the same office that authenticated the *nulla osta*) to request the placement of an apostille on the certificate. You will need to contact your state's registrar or vital records office to find the appropriate information about your state's requirements for registering a marriage abroad.

Special circumstances: If any of the following conditions apply to either the bride or groom, additional documents are necessary.

ADDITIONAL DOCUMENTS IF ONE OF THE PARTIES IS ITALIAN OR RESIDES IN ITALY

- **Banns of marriage (*pubblicazioni*):** Obtained from the *ufficio di stato civile.*

- **Certificate of event of publication (*certificato di avvenuta pubblicazione*):** Issued by the city registrar after the time period for posting banns is finished. This certificate has a duration of 180 days and must be given to the *ufficiale di stato civile* to enter the marriage date into the public record.

ADDITIONAL DOCUMENTS FOR THOSE WITH PRIOR MARRIAGES

- **Death certificate of prior spouse (*copia integrale dell'atto di morte del coniuge*):** Required for widows/widowers.

- **Copy of previous marriage certificate (*copia integrale dell'atto di matrimonio precedente*):** Requested from the appropriate court or officials that commuted the divorce.

- **Pronouncement of divorce (*sentenza di divorzio*):** Required for anyone who has been divorced or has previously been married, if a period of three hundred days has not passed from the time that the divorce was pronounced. Issued by the papal chancery or by the court who has commuted the divorce.

ADDITIONAL DOCUMENTS WHEN GROOM IS AN ITALIAN CITIZEN

- **Photocopy of military dismissal (*fotocopia del congedo militare*):** This is required only when the groom is Italian.

ADDITIONAL DOCUMENTS FOR MINORS

- **Authorization for minors (*autorizzazione del tribunale dei minori*):** If one or both of the American citizens are under the age of eighteen they will need a sworn statement of consent to the marriage made by their parents or legal guardian. In this case there will be a three-month waiting period before the wedding can take place.

DOCUMENTS FOR CATHOLIC WEDDINGS *(In Chiesa)*

Beyond the documents necessary for the civil ceremony, the following are required for Catholic weddings in Italy and the Vatican City:

- **Certificate of baptism (*certificato di battesimo*):** Obtained from the parish priest of the parish in which one was confirmed. Valid baptisms are recognized from the following churches and ecclesiastic communities: Orthodox, Methodist, Baptist, Lutheran, and Anglican, and in general all baptisms administered in the name of the Holy Trinity.

- **Certificate of confirmation (*certificato di cresima*):** If the date of the confirmation is noted on the baptism certificate, this additional certificate is not required.

- **Certificate of ecclesiastical free state (*certificato di stato libero ecclesiastico*):** The sworn testimony of "worthy persons of faith" (your parish priest) who can confirm that the bride and groom are free to marry.

- **Certificate of attendance to the course of preparation to the wedding (*attestato di frequenza ai corsi di preparazione al matrimonio*):** Pre-cana instruction is carried out in accordance with the customs of each individual parish.

- **Religious banns (*pubblicazioni religiose*):** After the collection of the documents and a discussion with the parish priest regarding the intentions of the spouses and the acceptance of the requirements of the religious wedding, banns are posted for eight days within the parishes of the two spouses and within the parish in which they will be married.

- **Certificate of the event of publication (*certificato di avvenuta pubblicazione*):** Issued by the parish priest once the term of the posting of the banns has expired.

- **State of documents (*stato dei documenti*):** The parish priest who has carried out the matrimonial preliminary investigation will give license to the other parish priest by transmitting the summary certificate of necessary documents and the *nulla osta* (nonimpediment) received from the municipality.

Catering (*Ricevimenti*)

After you have selected a location for your Italian wedding, ask the venue manager for a list of caterers who have experience with that particular location. Once you engage a caterer they will send you a *preventivo:* a proposal that will outline the services offered with each related cost.

Italian catering quotations are almost always inclusive of chairs, tables, flatware, crystal, and linens. Most caterers in Italy do not itemize these costs separately on the service quote. Usually, a per-head price will include all the service items, a cocktail service, a five- to seven-course meal, the wine, all other beverages, and the cake. An open bar (after dinner) is usually itemized separately.

Tipping for catering services is not expected. If you want to offer a gratuity to the service staff, it is at your discretion. Prices for services in Italy carry a value added tax (VAT) of approximately 20 percent. Foreign citizens (non-European Community) may be eligible to recover some of this tax when they exit Italy; for more information, see the U.S. Embassy in Italy's website at www.usembassy.it/cons/acs/iva.htm.

Wedding dinners are usually seated, with round tables of eight or ten, but some caterers will offer table settings *all'imperiale,* a single, extra-long "imperial" table that can be dramatically decorated with candelabras and floral arrangements down the center. Rome Party, at Palazzo Brancaccio in Rome, can set a party for thirty at a single gigantic round table. Waiters dress either in tuxedo jackets, which Italians refer to as *lo smoking,* or in a style called *alla francese:* long aprons and vests. As part of their service, caterers often provide printed menus, personalized with your names and your wedding date.

LIGURIA

Capurro Ricevimenti

Via Pratolongo, 6/r

16131 Genova (GE)

Tel. +39 010 377 3514

Website: www.capurroricevimenti.it

Email: info@capurroricevimenti.it

GEMI Piccoli Grandi Eventi

Via Palestro, 29, int. 3

16121 Genova (GE)

Tel. +39 010 837 6006

Fax +39 010 837 6006

Website: www.gemi-eventi.com

Le Tre Civette

Via Nino Franchi, 4

16147 Genova (GE)

Tel. +39 010 374 2456

Fax +39 010 307 3014

Website: www.trecivette.it

Email: info@trecivette.it

Maestro di Casa
Via Arrigo Boito, 8
20121 Milano (MI)
Tel. +39 02 720 23181
Fax +39 02 876 201
Website: www.maestrodicasa.it
Email: info@maestrodicasa.it

VENETO

Chef Party SRL
Via Toniolo, 2
37136 Verona (VR)
Tel. +39 045 582 900
Fax +39 045 582 999
Website: www.chefparty.it
Email: chefparty@netbusiness.it

Cose Belle di Luciana & Romolo Maistrello S.R.L.
Via Euganea, 71
35037 Treponti Di Teolo (PD)
Tel. +39 049 990 0236
Fax +39 049 990 2660
Website: www.cosebelle.it

Do Forni
San Marco, 468
30124 Venezia (VE)
Tel. +39 041 523 0663
Fax +39 041528 8132
Website: www.doforni.it

Harry's Bar
San Marco, 1323
30124 Venezia (VE)
Tel. +39 041 528 5777
Fax +39 041 520 8822
Website: www.cipriani.com

Marchioro Outside Catering
Via Roma
35010 Vigonza (PD)
Tel. +39 049 809 5057
Fax +39 049 809 5586

Maria Franchi Consulente d'Eventi
Via Toto Speri, 28
25010 S. Zeno Naviglio (BS)
Tel./Fax +39 030 266 393
Website: www.questionedistile.it
Email: info@questionedistile.it

Rosa Salva S.R.L.
Ponte Ferai, 951
San Marco
30124 Venezia (VE)
Tel. +39 041 521 0544
Fax +39 041 520 0771
Website: www.rosasalva.it
Email: info@rosasalva.it

Scapin Buffet
Via A. Diaz, 20
37121 Verona (VR)
Tel. +39 045 801 2755
Website: www.scapin-buffet.it

TUSCANY

CS Catering Service
Piazza Badia a Ripoli, 1/R
50126 Firenze (FI)
Tel./Fax. +39 055 653 2022
Website: www.csricevimenti.it

Ciabatti Ricevimenti
Vicolo Ridi, 5/7/9r
50126 Ponte a Ema (FI)
Tel. +39 055 645 738
Fax +39 055 641 838
Website: www.ciabattiricevimenti.it
Email: ciabattiricevimenti@tin.it

Convivium
Viale Europa, 4/6
50126 Firenze (FI)
Tel. +39 055 681 1757
Fax +39 055 681 1766
Website: www.conviviumfirenze.it
Email: convivium@dada.it

Guidi Lenci
Via G. Marconi, 68R
50131 Firenze (FI)
Tel. +39 055 578 077
Fax +39 055 580 489
Website: www.guidilenci.com
Email: mail@guidilenci.com

ROME

Ganimede Catering
Via Nazionale, 243
00184 Roma (RM)
Tel./Fax +39 06 487 0341
Website: www.ganimedecatering.it
Email: ganimedecatering.ganimed@tin.it

Vecchia Roma Banqueting
Via Ovidio, 20
00192 Roma (RM)
Tel. +39 06 688 09540
Website: www.vecchiaroma.it

Favors (Bomboniere)

In Italy the traditional favor given to wedding guests is called the *bomboniera*. The name comes from eighteenth-century France, where it was the custom to exchange *bonbons*: gifts of packaged sweets. For the wealthy, sweets were presented in elaborate works of art in gold, crystal, and enamelware. For the gentry, small cloth bags were used to hold sugar candies. In fifteenth-century Italy, brides, grooms, and their families exchanged sweets in tiny silver boxes to celebrate the occasion of an engagement. In the following century, a tradition of presenting a *coppa amatoria* ("courting cup") to the bride before a wedding became the fashion for Italian grooms. These small plates, fashioned by master artisans working in majolica, were elaborately decorated with a portrait of the betrothed, or family crests and seals. After a gift of fruit or sweetmeats was presented to the bride, the *coppa* would become an everlasting token of the groom's love.

Today in Italy, traditional wedding favors (presented to the wedding guests) have evolved to include an incredible variety of materials and presentations. Typically, each *bomboniera* will contain an odd number of sugared almonds (commonly five) symbolizing health, wealth, happiness, fertility, and a long life. The sugared almond itself represents the union of bitter and sweet in life and marriage.

In most Italian towns, the local *pasticceria* ("pastry shop") will offer the service of packaging custom *bomboniere*. Sugar almonds are the traditional candy, but there are also regional specialties like the *confetti di Pistoia*, almond-filled hard candies that resemble tiny bombs; *cannellini*, cinnamon-flavored candies that resemble their namesake bean; *anelli d'amore*, interlocking rings of sugar-covered chocolate; and realistic marzipan fruits in the shape of cherries, pears, and apples. Two companies, Confettificio Pareggi and Confetti Pelino, fashion sugared almonds into miniature bouquets of calla lilies, daisies, or dogwood blossoms.

If you are interested in something more elaborate, shops specializing in *bomboniere* containers offer a staggering assortment of porcelain, Murano glass, sterling silver, terra-cotta, and crystal. Tokens range from tiny boxes, candy dishes, and baskets to vases, frames, and whimsical figurines. In Italy it is traditional for elaborate *bomboniere* to be sent to the guests after the wedding celebration, rather than being presented to them at the wedding.

Loreti

Piazza di Spagna, 9
00186 Rome (RM)
Tel. +39 06 699 23654
Website: www.loretionline.com
Email: info@loretionline.com

Loreti has been producing wedding favors since 1852. Customers have included the Italian royal family and Pope Pius IX, who personally placed his orders for sugared almonds with the company's founder, Gioacchino Loreti.

Astuni

Via E. Fermi, 17
36028 Rossano Veneto (VI)
Tel. +39 0424 843 67
Fax +39 0424 848 214
Website: www.astuni.it

Astuni manufactures a wide range of *bomboniere* that can be personalized for brides and grooms. Crystal vases hand decorated with platinum filigree, Murano glass frames, sterling silver and leather frames, and porcelain candy dishes are just a few of the many objects to choose from.

Car Bomboniere

Website: www.carbomboniere.it

For thirty-five years, Car Bomboniere has been manufacturing gift boxes and accessories in porcelain, resin, crystal, and silver. For a list of stores that carry their products, see their website.

Confetteria Orefice

Via Fratelli Rossi, 10B
80144 Napoli (NA)
Tel. +39 081 738 2550

Confetteria Orefice has been manufacturing candies in Naples since 1900. Only the highest-quality almonds are selected for their candies, and they take pride in preparing their confections with the greatest care. While they employ traditional methods of Neapolitan candy making, one new invention of theirs has achieved enormous popularity. *Fede intrecciate personalizzate* are interlocking candy rings, covered with white sugar, then individually hand painted with the wedding date and the bride and groom's names. Almost too pretty to eat, they make a one-of-a-kind wedding favor. Available at fine pastry shops and candy stores throughout Italy.

Confetti Pelino
Via Stazione Introdacqua, 55
67039 Sulmona (AQ)
Tel. +39 0864 210 047
Fax +39 0864 552 03
Website: www.pelino.it

In 1783, the Pelino family began manufacturing *confetti* ("confections") following a simple recipe that has remained unchanged since then. Fifty workers produce sweets on machines following a secret four-day process that will never be completely industrialized. The company manufactures packaged chocolates, sugar almonds, dragées, and "bouquets" of almonds fashioned into daisies and roses in compositions of colored tulle and cellophane. Available at fine pastry shops and candy stores throughout Italy; store listings are available on their website.

Florists (Addobi Floreali)

LIGURIA
Amanda Casassa Addobbi Per Matrimoni
Via Villa Berrone, 15
16014 Campomorone (GE)
Tel. +39 010 726 1383

VENETO

Carollo Fiori S.R.L.
Via Canova, 54/A
36030 Centrale Di Zugliano (VI)
Tel. +39 0445 364 889
Website: www.carollofiori.it
Email: carollofiori@tin.it

Luca Zaggia
Via Umberto I, 74
35122 Padova (PD)
Tel. +39 049 875 1226
Fax +39 049 875 4565
Website: www.fioreria-zaggia.it
Email: luca.zaggia@libero.it

TUSCANY

Eurofiori
Via G. D'Annunzio, 98
Firenze (FI)
Tel. +39 055 609 642
Website: www.eurofiori.it

Floralia
Via Masaccio, 204/A
50132 Firenze (FI)
Tel. +39 055 577 487

Florandia
Via Galliano, 142 a/b
50144 Firenze
Tel. +39 055 331 329
Fax +39 055 321 7898
Website: http://web.tiscali.it/florandia
Email: florandia@tiscalinet.it

Romano Fiori
Via Tomacelli, 20
00186 Roma
Tel. +39 06 687 6145

Tulipani Bianchi
Via dei Bergamaschi, 59
Roma
Tel. +39 06 678 5449

Invitations (Participazioni)

Pineider
Florence: Piazza Signoria, 13/R
Tel. +39 055 284 655
Florence: Via Tornabuoni, 76/R
Tel. +39 055 211 605
Rome: Via dei Due Macelli, 68
Tel. +39 06 679 5884
Rome: Via della Fontanella Borghese, 22
Tel. +39 06 687 869
Genoa: Via Roma, 48/r
Tel. +39 010 595 8371
Website: www.pineider.com

In 1774, Franceso Pineider opened his first stationery shop in the heart of Florence. His visiting cards, personalized with flowery initials and family crests, became de riguer among the Florentine noble class. Today, the firm continues to hand design its stationery, invitations, business cards, menus, and announcements with the same level of attention its founder brought to the art of printing. The unmistakable Pineider style—classic, timeless, and elegant—is perfect for announcing your Italian wedding.

Grafica Acquaviva

Via Pestalozzi, 10

20143 Milano

Tel. +39 02 891 20859

Fax +39 02 891 50023

Website: www.graficacquaviva.it

E-mail: info@graficacquaviva.it

Grafica Acquaviva produces high-quality announcements in classic and original styles, offering estimates and purchases on their website. Printed pieces can be personalized with an image of your choice and closed with a wax seal stamped with the bride and groom's initials. Printing techniques vary from traditional offset to raised enameled type and embossed looks. Grafica Acquaviva's designs harken back to the days when letter writing was a noble art.

Legatoria Piazzesi

Campiello della Feltrina

San Marco 2511

Tel. +39 041 522 1202

The art of paper making in Venice is almost lost today, but thankfully, Legatoria Piazzesi still prints its papers with ancient wood blocks following the Venetian tradition. Hand blocked, marbleized, stenciled, and accented with dyes, their papers make an impressive backdrop for thank-you notes and wedding invitations.

Amalfi nelle Stampe Antiche di Luigi D'Antuono

Piazza Duomo, 10

84011 Amalfi (SA)

Website: www.cartadiamalfi.it

Email: cartadiamalfi@tiscalinet.it

The tradition of paper making in Amalfi dates back to the eighth century, when Arab traders passed the craft on to the region's artisans. The hand-made cotton paper produced in Amalfi has been treasured and sought after for centuries; in fact, many ecclesiastical archives are full of ancient documents written on paper with the Amalfi watermark. *La carta di Amalfi* continues to be used today by dukes and princes to announce their own weddings and celebrations.

Nardecchia Books and Prints
Piazza Navona, 25
00186 Roma
Tel. +39 06 686 9318

If you are planning a wedding at one of Italy's historic monuments—like the Campidoglio in Rome, or Florence's Palazzo Vecchio—a pre-1900s etching could be the perfect image for your wedding invitation. Before the advent of photography, romantic travelers purchased collections of etchings as souvenirs (*ricordi*) of treasured vacations. But how to find the exact image you're looking for? Simply go to Nardecchia. This lovely shop in the Piazza Navona is packed with printed treasures, and the owners are more than happy to help you find even the most obscure items.

Marriage Offices (Uffici Matrimoni)

MILAN

Ufficio Anagrafe
Via Larga, 12
20122 Milano, Italia
Tel. (+39) 02 884 62132
Mon-Fri 8:30 A.M.-noon, 2:30-3:30 P.M.

VENICE

Ca' Farsetti
San Marco 4136
30124 Venezia, Italia
Tel. (+39) 04 1274 8833
Fax (+39) 04 1274 8475

GENOA

Ufficio Matrimoni
Corso Torino, 11
16121 Genova, Italia
Tel. (+39) 010 557 6866
Fax (+39) 010 541 720

FLORENCE

Ufficio Stato Civile
Palazzo Vecchio, Piazza Signoria
50100 Firenze, Italia
Tel. (+39) 055 276 8518
Fax (+39) 055 261 6715
Wed, Thurs, Sat 8:30 A.M.-1 P.M.

ROME

Ufficio Anagrafe
Via Petroselli, 50
00195 Roma, Italia
Tel. (+39) 06 671 03066

NAPLES

Ufficio Matrimoni
Piazza Municipio, Palazzo San Giacomo
80100 Napoli, Italia
Tel. (+39) 081 551 0364

Photographers (Fotografi)

Working with a photographer in Italy is much the same as in the United States. They will offer "packages" with varied numbers of prints, proofs, and albums for each price level. You can ask about purchasing the rights to the negatives of your wedding pictures, which will save you from calling Italy every time you want a reprint. Many Italian photographers offer a beautifully made wedding album as part of the package.

LIGURIA

Studio Fotografico Claudio Beduschi
Via Dagnino, 11
16156 Genova Pegli (GE)
Tel. +39 03 296 278850
Email: bedoimage@hotmail.com

Luca Raina Progetti Fotografici
Viale S. Marco, 14
Venezia Mestre (VE)
Tel. +39 0348 726 9249
Website: www.weddinginitaly.biz
Email: info@weddinginitaly.biz

Mauro Ranzato
35028 Piove di Sacco (PD)
Tel. +39 049 584 0437
Website: www.mauroranzato.it

TUSCANY

Bibi Fotografo
Piazza Gramsci, 7
58022 Follonica (GR)
Tel./fax +39 05 664 0354
Website: www.fotobibi.it

Carlo Carletti
Viale Marconi, 111
53036 Poggibonsi (SI)
Tel. +39 0577 937 260
Website: www.weddingphotos.it

Francesco Dini
Via Roma, 11
50026 San Casciano Val di Pesa (FI)
Tel. +39 055 822 8194
Email: francescodini1@libero.it

Carlo Giorgi
Websites: www.carlogiorgi.com and www.tuscanphoto.com
Email: cgiorgi@dada.it

Gianni Ugolini Fotografia
Via Ripoli, 60
50126 Firenze (FI)
Tel. +39 055 681 3264
Fax +39 0 55 683 259
Website: www.gianniugolini.it
Email: info@gianniugolini.it

LAZIO

Stefano Musa
Via dei Corazzieri, 64
00143 Roma (RM)
Tel./fax +39 06 591 0612
Website: www.stefanomusa.it

Photopoint 3000
Via delle Sorgenti, 28
00046 Grottaferrata (RM)
Tel./fax +39 06 943 16078
Website: www.photopoint3000.com

Studio Fotografico Inimmagine
Vinicio Ferri
Via S. Spirito, SNC
00062 Bracciano (RM)
Tel. +39 06 998 8165
Email: vinicio.ferri@tiscalinet.it

Maurizio Vittori
Viale Carnaro, 30/A
00141 Roma (RM)
Tel./fax +39 06 818 9507
Website: www.mauriziovittori.it

Wedding Consultants

As you plan your wedding in Italy, you will discover a plethora of websites that offer coordination services online. While there are many wonderful wedding planners in Italy, there are an equal number of firms that specialize in travel services rather than wedding planning and prefer to sell packages rather than individualized services. When selecting a wedding planner for your Italian wedding, beware of anyone who claims to be the *only* one who can perform a particular type of service, and ask for references. Happy brides and grooms love to talk about their successful weddings, so any reputable planner should be able to offer you terrific references.

Wedding planners and coordinators can be very helpful, especially with regard to the legal documents required for civil ceremonies and in making appointments with the city offices in Italy. Services offered include translation of documents and ceremonies, reservations of the wedding venue, management of the caterer and menu presentation, photography and videography services, flower arrangements and bouquets, and musicians for ceremonies and receptions. Some planners can help find and coordinate accommodations for you and your guests. Typically, wedding planners mark up all services about 10 percent, and they request deposits be paid in advance. Quotes should always be presented in writing and agreed upon before you arrive in Italy.

LIGURIA

Omnia Service
Vico del Pozzo, 2/1
16035 Rapallo (GE)

Tel./fax +39 0185 567 34
Website: www.omniaeventi.com
Email: omniaservice@libero.it

Omnia Service can help you organize your wedding in one of Liguria's splendid villas, abbeys, or historic monuments. Cristina König and Luciana Sudano began their event-planning firm in 1992, with a mission to provide the highest level of service for weddings and conferences. They will organize every detail including personalized menus with typical Ligurian dishes, flower arrangements, music, elegant place cards, and for weddings at San Fruttuoso, they'll even arrange shuttle service by boat.

VENETO

Venice Weddings
Website: www.venice-weddings.com

Venice weddings can assist you with civil ceremonies, Jewish Orthodox blessings, and Protestant wedding ceremonies in the city of Venice. They also will also assist with invitations, transportation, music, and accommodations.

TUSCANY

Happening Ricevimenti
Via Dianella, 48
Vinci (FI)
Tel. +39 0571 508 166
Fax +39 0571 904 615
Website: www.happening.it
Email: Info@happening.it

While they specialize in planning weddings in Tuscany, the friendly staff at Happening can also help you plan an event in Rome, Venice, the Amalfi Coast, or Portofino. Founders Veronica Billeri and Maria Fulvia Conforti have impeccable taste and an eye for those extra Italian details that make a wedding in Italy truly unforgettable. Assisted by their able staff, Morena Gori and Laura Benedet, they can even help you plan a wedding at the ultra-private Villa Dianella Fucini in Vinci. The villa was once a Medici residence, but after careful restorations by Veronica's family, today it is a superb place for gala events or a relaxing holiday in the heart of Tuscany.

LAZIO

Gabriella LoJacano

Tel./fax +39 06 439 0678
Mobile +39 348 517 4184
Website: www.wedding-in-rome.com
Email: gabriellalocano@tin.it

Gabriella LoJacano is regarded as a logistical wonder, expert at smoothing Italian red tape. While she would probably recommend planning as far in advance as you can, she has successfully planned weddings in a matter of weeks. Gabriella can help you make your dolce vita experience complete, with a vintage Ferrari that will sweep you away to your own photo shoot in front of the Colosseum.

CAMPANIA

Amalfi Life

In the U.S. contact: Laurie Howell
41 Schermerhorn Street, Suite 128
Brooklyn, New York, 11201
Tel. 718-797-9300
Fax 718-243-1547
In Italy contact: Giocondo Cavaliere
Via Corte, 1
84011 Amalfi (SA) Tel. +39 089 813 028
Fax +39 089 874 194
Website: www.amalfilife.com

Amalfi Life tailors weddings to each individual couple's tastes and needs. Whether you'd like a quiet civil ceremony at Amalfi's historic Duomo, an intimate family wedding at your own clifftop villa, or a protestant ceremony overlooking the sea, Laurie Howell and Giocondo Cavaliere can arrange all the details for you. Giocondo Cavaliere hails from a long line of *amalfitani* and his infectious passion for his native land will inject your wedding event with southern Italian charm and hospitality. Stateside, Laurie Howell bridges the divide between Italy and the United States with her broad industry knowledge and her understanding of American tastes and sensibilities.

ARCHITECTURAL GLOSSARY

abbey   A monastery or convent that serves location for the religious seclusion of monks or nuns.

allée   A passage, road, or path bordered on either side by trees or hedges.

amphitheater   A circular or oval edifice with a central arena surrounded by rows of seats, which progressively recede as they rise up and away from the arena.

antependium   A decorative hanging for the front of an altar, or pulpit.

apse   The projected section of a building that forms a semicircular termination in plan with a domed or vaulted ceiling. In a church, the apse is the recess at the east section in which the choir and altar are placed.

arabesque   In decorative arts, a term that refers to applied arts that follow stylized motifs taken from fantastical plants and creatures. In garden design, a complexly groomed topiary garden.

architectonic motif   An element in a decorative design that takes its cues from architectural elements such as columns, portals, or pediments.

armory   A place where arms and weapons are stored.

balustrade   A row of small columns or pilasters joined by a rail and serving as a fence or enclosure for altars, balconies, staircases, terraces, and tops of buildings.

banquette   In castles, a platform lining a trench or parapet high enough to enable defenders to fire over the crest of the parapet.

baroque   A style of art and architecture popular in Europe from the sixteenth to eighteenth centuries characterized by dramatic curving forms and heavy ornamentation.

barrel vault A semi-cylindrical-arched ceiling supported by parallel walls.

bas-relief A mode of sculpturing in which the figures are fairly flat against the surface.

bastion In castle fortifications, a huge mass of rock, earth, or brick standing out from the angles of a fortified wall to create a defensive stronghold.

capital The top part of a pillar or column.

casework Architectural millwork or cabinetry built directly into a room or space.

castle keep The central fortification in a castle, usually a tower or a strongly fortified building that provides a final defensive position. The keep is often the tallest fortification in a castle, with a commanding view of all the surroundings.

cartouche A structure or figure, often in the shape of an oval shield or oblong scroll, used as an architectural or graphic ornament.

chiaroscuro The arrangement of light and dark elements in a decorative work of art.

cloister A covered walk with an open colonnade on one side, often circling an inner courtyard. Cloister is also the area of an abbey or monastery to which the nuns or monks are restricted.

coffer In architecture, a decorative sunken panel in a ceiling, dome, soffit, or vault.

colonnade A series of columns placed at regular intervals.

corbel An architectural support or stone protrusion that projects from a wall and is used to support structures such as machicolations.

cornice A horizontal molded projection that crowns or completes a building or wall.

crenellation Battlements atop a parapet with alternating notched intervals called merlons, allowing the defenders to fire at the enemy from behind the protection of the merlons.

cross vault In a vaulted ceiling, ribs which travel from the floor across the ceiling arch and down to the opposite side forming a cross pattern.

crypt   An underground vault or chamber, especially one beneath a church, that is used as a burial place.

edgework   Decoration applied to the top or edge of a wall or ceiling.

embroidery   In garden design, hedges or plantings that follow a design inspired by embroidery patterns.

esplanade   A flat, open stretch of grass or pavement, especially one designed as a promenade.

façade   The face of a building, especially the principal face.

fresco   The art of painting directly onto fresh, white plaster with pigments dissolved in water.

Ghibelline crenellation   Notched battlements in which the merlon is topped with an inverted swallowtail or chevron shape.

Gothic   An architectural style prevalent in western Europe from the twelfth through the fifteenth century characterized by pointed arches, rib vaulting, and flying buttresses.

Gothic revival   An architectural and decorative style popular during the late nineteenth century, which romanticized the design elements of the medieval period.

granary   A building used for storing grain.

griffon   A fabulous beast with the head and wings of an eagle and the body of a lion.

grotto   A small cave or cavern.

Guelph crenellation   Notched battlements in which the merlon is topped by a v-shaped notch.

Ionic   An order of classical Greek architecture characterized by fluted columns set on bases with two scrolled volutes in the capitals.

labyrinth   In gardens, an intricate maze of interconnecting hedges.

lancet window   A slender window crowned with a sharply pointed arch.

Liberty-style   A term used in Italy to describe the art nouveau style in architecture and decorative arts.

loggia   An open-sided, roofed gallery or arcade along the front or side of a building often behind a colonnade.

Longobardo style   A term sometimes used to describe Italian architecture dating to the Longobard (long beard), or Lombard, occupation of Italy during the sixth and seventh centuries.

lunette A crescent-shaped or circular space, usually over a door or
window, that may contain another window, sculpture, or a mural.

machicolation A projecting gallery at the top of a castle wall, supported
by a row of corbelled arches and having an opening in the floor
through which stones and boiling liquids could be dropped on
attackers.

Mannerism An artistic style of the late-sixteenth century characterized
by a distortion of elements such as scale and perspective.

manor The main house on a landed estate.

merlon The solid portion of a crenellated wall that rises up between
two open spaces.

molding An embellishment in a strip form, made of wood or other
material, that is used to decorate or finish a surface, such as a wall or
the surface of a door or window.

mullion A slender vertical strip that divides the panes of a window.

muse A source of inspiration, usually a woman or female figure.

nacre Mother-of-pearl. A hard pearly substance taken from the inside
of a mollusk shell.

neoclassical A style characterized by the revival of classical elements
and order, symmetry, and simplicity of style.

neo-Gothic A building designed following the elements of the Gothic
revival of the nineteenth century.

orientalized To give an oriental character or style to a design or
artwork.

parapet The walkway directly behind the crenellations of a castle, or
the fighting platform at the top of a castle tower.

parterre An ornamental garden having flowerbeds, paths, and low-cut
hedges arranged to form a pattern, and often incorporating decorative
elements such as topiary and statuary.

patinated Having acquired or being covered with a patina, or color that
has been acquired by age.

pediment A wide, triangular gable surmounting the facade of a
building.

pergola An arbor or passageway of columns supporting a roof or
trelliswork on which climbing plants are trained to grow.

piazza   A public square.

piazzetta   A tiny public square.

polychrome   Decorated with or having many or various colors.

portal   A large and imposing doorway, entrance, or gate.

portcullis   A grating of iron or wooden bars lowered to block the passage into a castle.

portico   A porch or walkway with a roof supported by columns, often leading to the entrance to a building.

presbytery   The section of a church reserved for the clergy.

putto, putti   A cherub, or winged child.

rampart   A fortification consisting of a broad embankment, often surmounted by a parapet.

relief   The projection of forms or figures from a flat background.

Renaissance   The humanist revival of classical art, literature, and learning that originated in Italy in the fourteenth century.

rococo   A style of art and architecture originating in eighteenth century France characterized by elaborate ornamentation with a profusion of scrolls, foliage, and animal forms.

Romanesque   A style of European architecture prevalent in the eleventh and twelfth centuries containing elements from Roman and Byzantine design and characterized by thick walls, barrel vaults, and simple ornamentation.

sawtooth   Having a jagged or zigzag pattern resembling the edge of a saw.

scrollwork   Embellishment with a scroll motif.

siren   From Greek mythology, one of a group of sea nymphs who lured sailors to their destruction with their singing.

stuccowork   Ornamental details or molding made from plaster.

swallow-tail   A shape that resembles the deeply forked tail of a swallow.

terrazzo   A flooring material of marble or stone chips set in mortar and when dried the surface is ground and polished.

topiary   The grooming of live shrubs into decorative shapes.

travertine   A soft quarried stone indigenous to Italy and used for the interior and exterior decoration of buildings.

trefoil   A three-lobed, cloverleaf type pattern.

triptych   A work containing three painted or decorated panels hinged together.

triumphal arch   An arch erected to commemorate victory in battle.

trompe l'oeil   In French, literally "to fool the eye." Paintings or decorative works that are created to give the illusion of reality.

turret   A small tower or tower-shaped projection on a castle.

valance   An ornamental drapery hung from the top edge of a window, bed, or canopy.

wainscot, wainscoting   Decorative wood paneling used to decorate the lower part of a wall.

watchtower   An observation tower from which a guard can keep watch for approaching enemies.

BIBLIOGRAPHY

Aligheri, Dante. *The Divine Comedy.* Translated by Lawrence White. New York: Pantheon Books, 1948.

Anderson, Burton. *Wines of Italy.* London: Octopus Publishing Group, 1999.

Bardwell, Sandra, Stefano Cavedoni et al. *Walking in Italy.* Victoria, Australia: Lonely Planet Publications, 2003.

Barker, Graeme and Tom Rasmussen. *The Etruscans.* Oxford: Blackwell Publishers, 2000.

Belford, Ros, Susie Boulton, Christopher Catling et al. *Eyewitness Travel Guides: Italy.* New York: DK Publishing, 1997.

Blanchard, Paul. *Blue Guide: Northern Italy.* New York: W.W. Norton & Company, 2001.

Blunt, Anthony. *Sicilian Baroque.* London, England: Weidenfeld and Nicolson, 1968.

Boni, Ada. *Italian Regional Cooking.* New York: Bonanza, 1969.

Boulton, Susie, Christopher Catling et al. *Eyewitness Travel Guides: Venice.* New York: DK Publishing, 1995.

Bozzo, Colette Dufour. *Villa Durazzo in Santa Margherita Ligure.* Milan, Italy: Skira Editore, 1997.

Calvi, Fabio and Silvana Ghigino. *Villa Pallavicini: Parco Romantico di Pegli.* Genoa, Italy: Sagep Libri & Comunicazione S.R.L., 1997.

Carcopino, Jerome. *Daily Life in Ancient Rome: The People and the City at the Height of the Empire.* Edited by Henry T. Rowell. New Haven, Conn.: Yale University Press, 1940.

Casson, Lionel. *The Horizon Book of Daily Life in Ancient Rome.* New York: Simon & Schuster, 1975.

Cernilli, Daniele, Gigi Piumatti et al. *Italian Wines 2003.* Rome, Italy: Gambero Rosso ñ Slow Food Editore, 2003.

Dal Lago, Adalberto. *Villas and Palaces of Europe.* London: Cassell, 1988.

Ercoli, Olivia, Ros Belford et al. *Eyewitness Travel Guides: Rome.* New York: DK Publishing, 1999.

Facaros, Dana and Michael Pauls. *Cadogan Guides: Tuscany, Umbria, and the Marches.* London: Cadogan Books, 1990.

Fantelli, Pier Luigi. *Il Castello del Catajo e i suoi Giardini.* Battaglia Terme, Italy: La Galiverna Editrice, 2000.

Firpo, Marina. *Palazzo Tursi - Municipio.* Genoa, Italy: Sagep Libri & Comunicazione S.R.L., 1997.

Floreale, Monica, ed. *Trattoria Italia.* New York: Rizzoli, 1999.

Hare, Augustus J. C. *Walks in Rome.* London: Hazel, Watson, & Viney, 1893.

Holmes, George, ed. *The Oxford History of Italy.* New York: Oxford University Press, 1997.

Kahn, Robert, ed. *City Secrets Rome.* New York: The Little Bookroom, 1999.

Mariani, John. *The Dictionary of Italian Food and Drink.* New York: Broadway Books, 1998.

Michelin staff. *The Green Guide: Italy.* Michelin Travel Publications, 2000.

Morton, H.V. *A Traveller in Rome.* London: Methuen & Co., 1959.

Russell, Vivian. *Edith Wharton's Italian Gardens.* London, England: Bulfinch Press, 1997.

Tonini, Domingo, Giorgio Rossini et al. *Ville nel Genovesato.* Genova, Italy: Sagep Libri & Comunicazione SRL, 1999.

Wharton, Edith. *Italian Backgrounds.* Hopewell, NJ: The Ecco Press, 1998.

Wharton, Edith. *Italian Villas and Their Gardens.* New York, NY: Da Capo Press, 1988.

Yriarte, Charles. *Florence: Its History, The Medici, The Humanists, Letters, Arts.* Philadelphia, Penn.: The International Press, 1897.

Zorzi, Alvise. *Venetian Palaces.* New York: Rizzoli, 1989.

ONLINE SOURCES

Church of Santa Susanna. *Weddings in Rome.* www.santasusanna.org/weddingsRome/weddingsRome.html, 2001.

Giusti, Giuseppe. *Dizionario dei Proverbi Italiani.* www.utas.edu.au/docs/flonta/DPbooks/GIUSTI/GIUSTI.html, 1996.

Grandi Giardini. *The Abbey of San Gerolamo della Cervara, Villa Arvedi.* www.grandigiardini.it, 2000.

Thayer, William P. *A Gazetteer of Italy.* www.ukans.edu/history/index/europe/ancient_rome/E/Gazetteer/Places/Europe/Italy/home.html, 1998.

U.S. Department of State. *Marriage of American Citizens in Italy.* http://travel.state.gov/italy_marriage.html, 1998.

U.S. Diplomatic Mission to Italy. *Marriage of American Citizens in Italy.* www.usembassy.it/florence/cons/acs/marriage.htm, 2001.

ACKNOWLEDGMENTS

I would like to thank the following people for assisting with this work and allowing Robin Resch and I to photograph their locations: the entire Famiglia Arvedi for their kind hospitality, Katharina Trauttmansdorff and Count Umberto Emo Capodilista at La Montecchia, the gracious Mariella Bolognesi Scalabrin at Villa Pisani, Giovanna della Francesca at Castello del Catajo, Clara Cortesi at Villa Maiano, Manuela Pazzaglia at Castello di Vincigliata, Signore Fucini and the warm staff at Castello di Gargonza, the staff at Fattoria di Titignano, Signora Papa at Palazzo Ferrajoli, and the staff of Palazzo Brancaccio.

Additionally, the following people contributed stories, history, and general information: Patrizia Cignatta and the staff at Villa Durazzo Centurione, Gianenrico Mapelli and his talented staff at La Cervara, Dottore Clavio Romani at the Comune di Genova, Luciana Sudano at Omnia Service, Alessandra Mura at Villa Foscarini Rossi, Francesa di Thiene at Castello di Thiene, the staff at Castello di Bevilacqua, the Jewish Community of Venice, Pierangela Fontana at Ca' Zanardi, Ca' Zenobio, Simone Coppi at Castello il Palagio, Stefania at Castello di Montegufoni, Angelika Mattes at Villa Artimino, Lucia Casini and Claudio Baggiani at Palazzo Borghese, Tiziana Antonini at Orto degli Angeli, Gianna at La Casella, Famiglia Costanzi at Abbazia San Pietro in Valle, Sanda Pandza at Castello Odescalchi, Ginevra Giovanelli at Villa Giovanelli Fogaccia, Armando Balestrazzi at Il Frantoio, Gioele Romanelli at Hotel Flora, the entire staff at Happening Ricevimenti, and historian Vicenzo Labella for his insights on ancient Roman weddings.

Thanks to my agent, Elizabeth Pomada. Thanks also to Kirsty Melville and Carrie Rodrigues at Ten Speed Press for their vision and enthusiasm for Italian weddings and romantic holidays. Thanks to all the friends and family who attended my own Italian wedding, to Jana Little for her editorial assistance, to recipe advisers and taste testers Jake and Jerilyn Hesse, to Joan Uhler who provided garden tutorials, to Pamela Dunham for enthusiastic support, to Robin Resch for her friendship and delightful photographs, to my parents for sending me on my very first trip to Italy, and to my husband, David, for his unending patience, editorial support, and fabulous recipes, and for being my inspiration.

Photo Credits

The author is grateful to acknowledge the following photographers and individuals for permission to reproduce their photographs:

R. Avolio/Trovafoto: page 310.

Claudio Beduschi/Trovafoto: pages ii, 2, 34, 43, and 376.

Stephen Chappell/Istock Photo: page 285.

Corels: pages 75, 76, and 77.

G. Crupi/Trovafoto: page 335.

P. Gasparini/Trovafoto: page 86.

Graficamente/Trovafoto: pages 316, 315, and 320.

Happening: page 227.

Istock Photo: page 255

Stefan Junger/Istock Photo: page 222.

S. Massolo/Trovafoto: pages 12, 19, and 39.

Dave Miss/Istock Photo: page 351.

FPG International/Antony Nagelmann: page 113.

F. Natali/Trovafoto: page 110.

Tobias Ott/IstockPhoto: page 70

Robin Resch: pages 91, 123, 131, 146, 149, 166, 211, 232, 237, 264, 276, 286, and 304.

S. Santioli/Trovafoto: pages 161 and 197.

Villa di Maiano: page 209.

INDEX